Library Acquisition Policies and Procedures

Library Acquisition Policies and Procedures

Edited by Elizabeth Futas

A Neal-Schuman Professional Book

 ORYX PRESS

Operation Oryx, started more than 10 years ago at the Phoenix Zoo to save the rare white antelope—believed to have inspired the unicorn of mythology—has apparently succeeded.

An original herd of nine, put together through Operation Oryx by five world organizations, now numbers 34 in Phoenix with another 22 farmed out to the San Diego Wild Game Farm.

The operation was launched in 1962 when it became evident that the animals were facing extinction in their native habitat of the Arabian peninsula.

Copyright © 1977 by The Oryx Press
3930 E. Camelback Road
Phoenix, AZ 85018

Printed and Bound in the United States of America

Library of Congress Cataloging in Publication Data

Main entry under title:

Library acquisition policies and procedures.

   "A Neal-Schuman professional book."
   Bibliography: p.
   Includes index.
   1. Acquisitions (Libraries).   2. Libraries, University and college—United States. 3. Public libraries—United States.   I. Futas, Elizabeth.
Z689.L49   025.2   77-7275
ISBN 0-912700-02-5

289452

For my mother, Eleanore R. Futas

Contents

Preface

Library Acquisition Policies and Procedures is designed to aid librarians, library school students and publishers to understand some of the factors which underlie and influence library materials selection. In addition, considering the current strong emphasis on collection and resource development, it is intended as an aid to librarians presently grappling with the development—or redevelopment—of policies.

Materials for this book were selected from responses to a letter mailed during July 1976 to 3,600 academic and public libraries in the United States and Canada. Over 500 replies to this letter and 300 selection policies were received. A number of the libraries that answered had no formal written selection policy; the majority were either writing them or contemplating doing so in the near future. Many seemed genuinely interested in what other libraries had written. Twelve public library and 14 academic library policies have been reprinted in full with only minimal editing on the part of the publisher in the interest of standardization.

Policies were selected for their representativeness in several categories: size, geographic representation and content. Also, 56 partial selections from policies representing 18 public and 38 academic libraries have been reprinted to bring further depth, variation and comprehensiveness to this collection. These partial selections represent the elements which most policies have in common.

Since most policies seem to indicate a more or less ideal state of affairs rather than day-to-day reality, a follow-up questionnaire was sent to all 500 libraries who replied to the original letter. The results of this survey are discussed in depth in the "Introduction."

A literature search of the past seven years was made to determine what else has been written in the field of acquisitions.

It is hoped that all three of these elements will aid in both the understanding and the development of selection policy and practice.

A perusal of the policies received reveal that there is no one definition of selection or one type of selection policy which is appropriate for all libraries. In some libraries the policy statement is a theoretical document which stresses the intellectual reasoning used to select material for inclusion in the collection. For others it is a practical explanation of fiscal, community and space limitations which control the purchasing of items. Most of the 300 policies received fall somewhere in between. Those documents which are used as public relations tools become immediately obvious by their format. Equally evident are those policies which are mainly in-house documents,

As a whole, this collection is intended to represent a cross-section of the current thinking that governs librarians in both public and academic libraries with respect to selection and acquisition functions. They suggest the subjectivity as well as the objectivity of collection development, the constraints that must be dealt with, the philosophy and judgments behind selection and the practices that underlie the entire acquisitions process. The intention is to offer readers a view of the different levels of decisions, judgments and limitations which go into the process of selection as it is currently being practiced in public and academic libraries. The editor and publishers have used their best efforts in this compilation and have no legal responsibility for any omissions or errors.

Acknowledgements

I wish to extend my appreciation to all the libraries who so generously allowed their selection statements to be reprinted in full or in part. I also wish to thank those libraries who answered the questionnaire survey that was sent out.

Special thanks are due to Patricia Glass Schuman, Carolynn Weiner, Victor Camlek and Joy Simon, without whose assistance this work would never have been completed.

Elizabeth Futas
March 15, 1977

Introduction

Selection is the process of choosing. It is an ongoing process which takes place within a specific context. Goals and objectives are developed, parameters and boundaries are established, and all types of constraints are recognized. The ability to take into account this phenomenal number of variables is what differentiates the human race from lower-order life forms. Sometimes selections are made without knowing why, or without a conscious effort to select correct choices. These seemingly unconsious selections reveal patterns which are noticeable and distinct.

The process of selection in libraries occurs in many areas, from choice of location, to building design and staff, to hours of service and arrangement of the collection. Sometimes choices have been made long before the current staff appeared on the scene. One of the most important ongoing processes of selection with which many librarians are deeply involved is in the area of materials. What monographs, serials, media, microforms, realia and the like should be bought for the collection? Choices are made daily and almost all librarians select material at some time in their careers. For some, selection of materials *is* their career.

How *do* librarians select materials? On what basis do they choose? As in any process of selection, all variables affect the judgments that are made. Efforts to document procedures dealing with the variables of selection have led to an increasing number of written materials selection statements. As the *Intellectual Freedom Manual* states in its chapter on essential preparations:

Why is written policy stressed? First, it encourages stability and continuity in the library's operations. Library staff members may come and go but the procedures manual, kept up-to-date, of course, will help assure smooth transitions when organization or staff changes occur. Secondly, ambiguity and confusion are far less likely to result if a library's procedures are set down in writing.

Additional and convincing reasons for maintaining written procedures can be outlined:

1. They show everyone that the library is running a businesslike operation.

2. They inform everyone about the library's intent, goals and aspirations and circumvent ambiguity, confusion and trouble.

3. They give credence to library actions; people respect what is in writing even though they may not agree with every jot and tittle in the library's procedures manual.

4. They are impersonal; they make whimsical administration difficult.

5. They give the public a means to evaluate library performance; publicly pronounced policy statements prove that the library is willing to be held accountable for its decisions.

6. *They contribute to the library's efficiency; many routine decisions can be incorporated into written procedures.*

7. *They help disarm crackpot critics; the accusations of local cranks seldom prevail when the library's operations are based on clearcut and timely written procedures that reflect thorough research, sound judgment and careful planning.*[1]

In the 1950s, it became difficult for people to protect themselves from accusations of un-American activities. Censorship played an important role in library selections. Librarians sometimes acted as self-censors and kept controversial material off the shelves simply by not purchasing them, or by secreting the offensive items away from the eyes of patrons. Materials selection statements written during the fifties and early sixties reflect the concerns the library profession felt in regard to the concepts of intellectual freedom, freedom to read and censorship. Materials selection statements written in the late sixties and early seventies reflect another area of concern: social responsibilities. These are concerns that the profession feels toward racial and sexual stereotyping of materials as well as representation of ethnic and other minority points of view. Recently another trend is evident: a concern with diminishing budgets, burgeoning information resources and shrinking facilities. The need for a written policy statement has never been greater than it is right now.

While the majority of librarians realize this need, writing policies seems to be a difficult process for most. Two problems emerge frequently in letters from libraries. The first is lack of time; the second is bewilderment as to *how* to write policy. Most libraries still do not have written selection statements. Writing a useful document is not easy; writing a document which must be open for public inspection will never be easy. Careful thought, preparation and wording is essential. Involvement by the entire staff, professional and support personnel, and input from the entire user population is a requirement. It is also essential that input from the entire community, those who use the library and those who do not use it, be solicited if the document is to achieve its goals. As Leroy Merritt points out: "The writing of a selection policy, if it is done seriously and deliberately, should produce other benefits besides the end product of a useful and workable policy statement. Among these is the intellectual stimulation afforded the staff in the process of thinking through an *a priori* statement of precisely what is to be in the library. Another is the public relations value of drawing the whole community into observing and participating in the process."[2] The need for a written selection policy and the benefits of the process of writing one are obvious.

What goes into developing and writing a materials selection policy? In order to write a selection statement, librarians must know *who* they serve. What kind of people live in the community? Who are the people who use the library and who are those who do not use it? In a public library setting this kind of analysis would include ethnic and economic background, age, gender, and religious and political affiliations. Local government and the business community should be analyzed as well. In an academic library the same type of analysis may be done on the faculty, students and administrators. Such analysis should consider departments, subjects, courses, curricula and the community in which the college is located.

A second analysis often consists of examining current practice with respect to building, staff and collection. The latter is an inventory with an eye to gaps that exist, the strengths that have developed over the years and the ongoing commitments that have been made. It is essential that this examination be objective, since with new budgetary constraints many libraries now face commitments that may have to be curtailed or dropped completely. There are obligations to patrons and other commitments made to co-operatives, networks and consortia which have been formed to supply the needs of a larger community.

The third analysis stage is the recognition of constraints. These include financial and space constraints, as well as unbreakable commitments to network, cooperation and consortia contracts. A library may have to continue buying in a particular area, regardless of need, in order to honor cooperative agreements. In this third stage, practical policy statements are also considered. Nine areas are most often mentioned in policy statements: introduction, philosophy and goals, objectives, selection, problem areas, special formats, methods of collection which do not require financial outlay, intellectual freedom and weeding.

Most policies begin with introductory statements which set the tone for the entire selection document. These usually state theoretical or practical purposes of the policy. Short or lengthy, the beginning explains the way the policy was written and the reason for its publication or distribution. Wording among policies is often similar. Descriptions of the community served are often included, as is a definition of selection. There are usually two types of policies: those which are mainly for the library staff (Rolling Prairie Libraries, St. Albans Free Library); and those which are frequently directed to the community served by the library (Baltimore County Public Library, Kansas City Kansas Community Junior College Library). Many policies describe their community in glowing terms, but a few (North Country Library System, St. Louis Public Library) are more objective and realistic.

In philosophy and goals statements, libraries either mention ideals of a theoretical nature or continue to set the tone of the introduction, which may be more or less practical. Policies that have no introductory statement often use philosophy and goals paragraphs to set tone and justify writing the policy. Goals statements usually reflect the ideas and ideals of the parent body (Roanoke-Chowan Technical Institute Library, Northeastern Illinois University Library). Academic libraries often start their policies with philosophy and goals statements rather than a community analysis or statement of objectives. Even in the most theoretical document, statements of objectives present the libraries' practical ideals: the translation of theoretical statements set forth in introductory, philosophy and goals paragraphs. Conditions of acquiring materials, limitations, constraints, scope of collection and purposes of the collection *vis-à-vis* the community served are stated (Fresno County Public Library, South Georgia College Library).

The heart of every policy is its selection statement. The library informs its patrons: *who* does the selection (College of the Desert Library, Tri-County Technical College Library, Rensselaer Public Library, Ontario City Library); *how* it is done (Muscatine Community College Library, Western Maryland College Library, Vigo County Public Library, Seattle Public Library); and *what* is done (Clermont General & Technical College Library, Yavapai College Library, Free Library of Philadelphia, Hamilton Public Library). Within the selection statement items such as budgetary limitations (North Carolina Central University Library, Rockingham Community College Library), selection aids (Malone College Library, Blue Mountain Community College Library, Camden County Free Library), levels of selection within subject departments served by the library (University of California at Los Angeles Library, Public Library of Cincinnati and Hamilton County) and factors affecting the purchase of materials (University of Wyoming Library, Hartwick College Library) are frequently mentioned. Public libraries also deal with the additional factor of differing ages among their clientele (young adult—Baltimore County Public Library; children—Hamilton Public Library). The guidelines and criteria used to select materials are sometimes stated and sometimes only implied. When reading selection statements it is important to keep in mind that they often represent the ideal—what librarians would like to see happening, e.g., faculty selecting, two reviews for each book selected. They may not accurately convey the reality of the situation. These sections are often used as public relations tools and as such may reflect what librarians think their patrons want to hear. Even though the reality differs from the ideal, the latter may be exactly what the policy should say.

Since policies are not often updated, rarely are statements of absolutes written. Flexibility is necessary if the policy is to serve for any length of time.

Selection aids often change (The *Weekly Record* spins off from *Publishers Weekly*, new selection aids like *Reference Services Review* are published, etc.), communities change and budgets and financial limitations vary from year to year. A policy can become dated in a comparatively short period of time. Most of the policies reprinted in this volume were written after 1970 and many represent the new, tighter money problems of the middle to late '70s.

Within selection policies, librarians use examples of areas which have caused specific problems. The most frequently mentioned are duplication and multiple copies of materials (Grand View College Library, Catonsville Community College Library, Wayne County Public Library), replacement of lost materials (Yavapai College Library), binding of books (Library of the College of St. Catherine, University of Miami in Ohio Library) and textbooks used for courses (Hartwick College Library, Public Library of Cincinnati and Hamilton County).

Book selection policies in general are fast being replaced by material selection policies. With the new emphasis on nontraditional sources of information, librarians must contend with many formats other than books. These range from other print media, e.g., newspapers and periodicals (Lynchburg College Library, Appalachian State University Library, Public Library of Cincinnati and Hamilton County) and pamphlet or ephemera collections (Library of the College of St. Catherine, Ontario City Library) to nonprint formats (Ricks College Library, Baker Junior College of Business Library, Free Library of Philadelphia). The selection policy seems a good place to inform patrons of the availability of new media. Some policies deal with newer forms of the more traditional material, e.g., microforms (Appalachian State University Library). Selection responsibilities, guidelines, criteria, acquisitions and handling may be entirely different from those for the more standard forms of information, or libraries may ignore the differences in formats and attempt to treat everything as if it were a book.

Due to the information explosion, the large number of items published and increasingly stringent budgets, librarians are finding it difficult to buy all that they need. In answer to this problem, nonmonetary methods of acquiring material have received greater publicity and are being mentioned in most policies. The oldest method of acquiring material without paying is accepting gifts. Community members donate materials to public and academic libraries in such great quantity and with so little application of critical judgment that it has become necessary to include gift statements in selection policies (New Hampshire Vocational Technical College Library, Virginia Beach Public Library Department). Another method used mainly by academic libraries in the past, but apparently increasing in use by public libraries, is interlibrary loan (St. Albans Free Library). This is an excellent method of acquiring material on a temporary basis for patrons. As the resources of the larger libraries are being taxed by the incredible number of requests for interlibrary loans, a system of charges has been developed. To get around these and similar finance charges, networks and consortia have formed (Suomi College Library, McNeese State University Library, Mansfield Public Library, Free Library of Philadelphia) to make large numbers of materials available to member libraries free of charge for reciprocal services. Cooperatives seem to be the wave of the future and are often dealt with in newer policies.

To guard against problems of censorship, libraries often include the concept of intellectual freedom and confidentiality—the cornerstones of modern librarianship—in their selection policies. Sometimes libraries append the *Library Bill of Rights,* intellectual freedom documents and freedom to read statements as developed and supported by the American Library Association. (These documents are reproduced in the appendices to this book.) Frequently libraries supplement these with their own policy statements (Skyline College Library, South Georgia College Library, Malone College Library, Virginia Beach Public Library Department, Orillia Public Library).

Every library faces the problem of disposing of material. No library has enough space or money to keep everything it once bought. To make room for new material and newer formats and equipment, older superseded material and seldom or never used items must be discarded. Some libraries feel it necessary to discuss the weeding and de-acquisition problem in depth (Roanoke-Chowan Technical Institute Library, Camden County Free Library).

The policies in this volume exemplify successful planning and execution of written statements. Yet the majority of libraries do not have written selection policies. Why? Answers from letters are indicative:

"Because we are so small we have never found it necessary to follow structured policies and procedures."

"We regret to report that our library does not have a written acquisitions policy or procedure. It is something that we feel we should do but never make the time to do it."

"After much discussion over a period of years, the faculty and library bibliographers, in concert, tore up whatever written acquisitions policy was available."

"We have no written policies regarding book acquisitions—would that we did! We buy almost everything the faculty requests, and attempts to get this into a budgetary framework have been futile. I realize as well as you do that this is not the way to run a library, but am having a hard time convincing the faculty of this."

"Our library has never operated under a written acquisitions policy nor are most other policies a matter of written record. A variety of memos are in existence and do cover various situations that have arisen in the past. However, I am not in possession of these memos."

"Our library does not have a written policy for book purchasing, or for periodical subscriptions. The general rule in effect is to buy wisely, which is rarely observed."

"This state's Library Commission does not, at this time, have a written acquisitions policy. There is a rumor that there was a policy at some point during the Commission's history, but no copies seem to have survived."

These comments underline the dearth of existing written policy statements, but there is a feeling within the profession that such policies should be written down.

Among the many reasons libraries offer for not having policies, none seems entirely adequate. The need to keep policies up-to-date was frequently mentioned in letters during the compilation of this book.

"Our procedures vary with the needs of the times. Our present involvement with OCLC has changed many of them."

"Our policies and procedures have been drastically changed during this budget crisis year and our manual is badly in need of updating. We are likewise awaiting the arrival of a new director in November."

"Since we are currently under a new administration we are somewhat uncertain of the institution's future programs and directions; therefore priorities are difficult to establish, for example the emphasis of printed material versus nonprint."

"Our procedures in the acquisitions area are in flux due to plans to move to an on-line computerized acquisitions system with the Washington Library Network."

Many librarians responding offered great detail about their procedure, even when written policies did not exist.

"Materials selection is the function of approximately 60 people, and the major problem is to persuade them to act cooperatively and coherently. Obviously, if 20 locations are going to order copies of one title it is better to do so all at the same time, to facilitate placing the order, receiving the volumes, cataloging and processing the material. Our major effort is in this direction. Usually such orders drift in to us at the rate of one or more over something like eight months."

"When considering costly items for purchase, we consider the potential availability of these items through our participation in the Southwest Academic Library Consortium. This is of course a two-way street in that we may purchase some materials in our specific subject interest because of our consortium participation, and we may continue the subscription to a highly specialized but expensive periodical because of our responsibility to cover certain subjects within the consortium."

"For many years almost the sole means of selection of books has been the initiation of orders by teaching faculty members. Departmental limits to the total amount ordered in each discipline have been determined by an allocation formula consisting of factors which take into account each discipline's number of students, number of faculty, average cost of serials and books, relative age of the discipline as a reflection of publishing history, and size of graduate program."

"We have always operated on a kind of traditional understanding. It has always been understood that the library purchased whatever a faculty member considered to be necessary materials for a given course; in short, if a faculty member orders it, and we have the funds, we do our best to get it. It has been further understood and practiced that the librarians had a special knowledge of the collection and that any librarian could and should order books to 'fill in' and 'balance' and 'strengthen' the collection."

A number of librarians seemed to unburden themselves. They also managed to offer enormous details regarding budgets and the *real* way in which materials are selected. In some cases it seemed that "off-the-cuff" statements were truer reflections of selection reality than the carefully worded policies to which they were attached:

"The budget in the library is dependent upon the financial condition of the university. At no time have we received less than 5% of the tuition dollar. Our purchasing is separated into two areas: books and periodicals; our budget is divided in the same manner. Our budget for this year is $200,000 for books and $105,000 for periodicals. We are currently working on a clearer delineation of serials and annuals which may result in a considerable budgetary alteration."

"The Library Committee for several years has recommended that strict allocations in the book fund not be made to divisions and that Choice Reviews on Cards *be continued as the basic buying guide, with the library staff making the initial selections and their recommendations being sent to the divisions for their approval and priority. A professional librarian oversees the book collection for each division, fills in gaps in the collection, checks bibliographies, etc., makes recommendations to division chairmen on important publications, reprints, etc. Former allocations are used as a rough guide."*

Survey

After carefully examining the policies submitted, reading letters from acquisitions librarians and making a literature search, a questionnaire was developed to clarify a variety of topics. What was sought was a clear statement of actual practice, and not an ideal or abstract philosophy. The analysis is anonymous as confidentiality was promised.

Over 450 questionnaires were sent; 246 useable ones were returned by the deadline date. Of the respondents, 175 were academic librarians and 71 were public librarians. They represent libraries greatly divergent in size and geographic location. In certain cases, particular questions were not answered and when this was thought to be significant it is mentioned. In other cases, even with the most careful preparation of the questionnaire, a few librarians' interpretations of what certain questions were asking differed from the great majority of answers and had to be thrown out. A picture does emerge of what is actually going on in libraries. This sometimes belies the policy statements and sometimes backs up more strongly what is being stated in the policies. The original letters sent to libraries requesting their policies also asked for participation in a follow-up questionnaire survey. The majority answering were affirmative, but they only represent about 20 percent of the original number contacted. Some answers may shed light on the reason for this showing:

"We would be willing to answer your follow-up questionnaire if it doesn't take more than two or three days."

"We would be unwilling to participate in your follow-up questionnaire without having seen it and its length."

"I doubt a follow-up questionnaire will be helpful to you."

"I would be unable to participate in your follow-up questionnaire due to staffing shortages."

"Let me assure you that I would be glad to participate in your questionnaire survey, but I hope you get your homework done and don't ask for information which is available in print. I am constantly getting questionnaires asking for information which the enquirer could easily find in any public library."

As a result of answers like the above, the questionnaire sent was only one page in length. Only 12 questions were asked and, hopefully, their answers cannot be found in any public library, but they could be answered by the respondents without too much time-consuming effort. Most libraries did respond very positively when asked to participate in the survey and many were even excited over the prospect and interested in the results.

Academic Libraries

Academic institutions returning the follow-up questionnaire varied from those with over $12,000,000 total budgets to those with under $10,000 total budgets.

For identification purposes the name of the library and its total budget were asked. Answers included materials budgets or total budgets encompassing everything from federal and state monies to grant funding. The majority of libraries qualified their answers by stating what this dollar amount indicated. Sometimes salaries, or maintenance, or state and federal funding, or capital budgets were excluded. Just as often these figures were included. Some gave last year's figures, some estimated next year's budget, some rounded off the figures and some did not. Although a picture does emerge of the average size of the library which answered, it is difficult to say with any accuracy what is really being shown. All the figures are interesting but it would be unwise to draw too fine a conclusion about them from such a small sampling.

MATRIX I
Total Academic Library Budget*

TOTAL MATERIALS BUDGET	1 million & over	$500,000–$999,000	$100,000–$499,000	$50,000–$99,000	Below $50,000
1 million & over	6				
$500,000–$999,000	9	2			
$100,000–$499,000	7	15	9		
$90,000–$99,000		1	3		
$80,000–$89,000		1	5		
$70,000–$79,000		2	7		
$60,000–$69,000		1	7	1	
$50,000–$59,000		1	5		
$40,000–$49,000			10		
$30,000–$39,000			3	3	
$20,000–$29,000			6	8	1
$10,000–$19,000			4	5	2
0–$9,999				2	2

*Only those libraries which provided total library budget and total materials budgets are included.

The median library budget, falling in the exact middle of the range with as many libraries having budgets larger as smaller, had a total library budget of $198,000. Only 19 libraries had budgets over $1,000,000 while 38 had budgets under $100,000. The majority had budgets between $100,000 and $999,000. Within this figure, most were between $100,000 and $499,000, and the majority of these fall between $100,000 and $199,000.

Question One: *What is your materials budget (please give break-down if available by type, e.g., monographs, periodicals, standing orders, media, microforms, etc.)?*

Some academic libraries gave only one total figure, some did not respond, others repeated their total library budgets. The majority (130) filled in a figure. Comparing this number to the total library budget, we were able to ascertain the percentage of the total budget that particular libraries spent on materials.

There was a high of 95% of the total library budget spent on materials and a low of 3.9%. No explanations were offered for either of these extremes. It is possible that grant money not counted in the regular library budget was spent on materials, thus skewing the percentages. The 3.9% figure may represent only monograph expenditures. It may be more realistic to examine those academic libraries which represent the middle range. Only 14 libraries stated that their materials budget represented over 50% of their total library budget. Eleven said that their materials budget represents less than 15% of their total library budget. Some 105 libraries responding show that their materials budget is between 15% and 50% of their total library budget. There is no correlation between the size of these libraries and percentages allocated for materials. A breakdown of total materials budgets follows:

	High %	Low %	Average %	Total # of Questionnaires Counted
Monographs	99.9	11.6	31–74	133 (13 below 30%; 15 above 75%)
Periodicals	83.9	.1	16–44	134 (16 below 15%; 17 above 45%)
Standing orders	49	1.2	6–24	38 (1 below 5%; 2 above 25%)
Media	57.1	.1	1–24	65 (5 below 1%; 5 above 25%)
Microforms	29.1	.09	1–14	47 (1 below 1%; 2 above 15%)

The average figures for the two most frequently mentioned categories— monographs and periodicals—are broken down even further:

Monographs	Periodicals
19 fell between 30–39%	42 fell between 20–29%
18 fell between 40–49%	34 fell between 30–39%
27 fell between 50–59%	14 fell between 40–49%
0? fell between 00 00??	

Academic libraries still seem to be buying more monographs than any other item, but fewer than before. Less than 50% of their materials budgets are being spent on monographs. From the comments that were attached to these budget figures, it appears that many academic institutions still have separately funded media centers which may further skew the data regarding how much is spent on media. For microform purchases, funding may not be by format but may be included in monograph and periodical figures. The figures do indicate that academic libraries favor print over nonprint material and are still book oriented. Even when media is purchased 'they do not represent a large or even substantial portion of the materials budget.

Question Two: *Who primarily initiates requests for purchase of monographs?*
A simple count shows overwhelmingly that faculty are prime initiators, but few libraries checked only *one* initiator (see Chart 1, page xxii):

- 34 checked only faculty, 104 listed faculty plus others;
- 6 listed students;
- 69 listed director of library (several of these indicated that the director is also the acquisitions librarian);
- 27 listed subject bibliographers;
- 51 listed acquisitions librarians;
- 6 listed branch librarians.

Others mentioned include the coordinator of public services, reference librarians, collection development officer and college administration. Seventy-seven libraries checked more than one primary initiator. In small college libraries, the director is often also the acquisitions librarian. It seems that he or she may delegate many responsibilities, but the acquiring of material remains the director's perquisite until the administration of the library itself becomes a full time position. There were 30 libraries who did not mention faculty as selectors at all. A comparison of the response to this question with library budgets appears to reveal a trend toward professional librarians as primary initiators as the size of the library increases. Edelman and Tatum note that the responsibility of professional librarians for selection has a certain backing in the history of academic libraries:

An important factor in the shaping of the collections was the almost complete control by the university faculties of book selection and the allocation of book budgets. Because of the varying specialized interests of faculty members, it has always proved difficult to balance a program of buying in support of immediate curricular needs with systematic long-range development of the collections of research tools. Immediate needs have tended to receive the lion's share of the attention in those institutions with large numbers of students. Faculty involvement in library affairs has assumed an endless variety of formats, but by 1910 most institutions were governed by a library board, which exercised control over the book budget. The available funds were usually allocated to academic departments, and members of the departments were responsible for making purchasing suggestions. The librarian's role was to approve and place the orders, or, at best, to encourage or discourage faculty members.

Only at the largest institutions, notably Harvard and Yale, was the library staff seriously involved in the selection process, and there is little doubt that this participation contributed substantially to the successful collection development programs at those universities. [3]

It would appear that historically, as libraries became larger in size and importance, faculty played an increasingly smaller role in choosing material for the collection. A trend of this nature can be slightly discerned from the questionnaires, in the policies themselves, and at an even greater level in professional literature. As a trend it is seeping down to libraries in smaller colleges and has been raised in the literature by such writers as Gration and Young:

. . . it appears that the major tasks of university bibliographers are related to selection, with only occasional attention to reference work or formal instruction. In contrast, the college reference bibliographer devotes approximately equal commitment to reference and selection duties, and increases accessibility by placement in the reference or public services department. The reference-bibliographer possesses more specialized subject competencies than the generalist college reference librarian and a broader subject area mandate than some university bibliographers. [4]

Question Three: *Are budget allocations made primarily by type, subject, faculty department, branch library, or other?*

The overwhelming number of libraries chose format (monograph, periodical, etc.) in answer to the question. Of the 165 libraries who answered, 38 picked more than one method. All of these included "type" as one of the choices. One hundred and four libraries allocate budgets by format; 73 allocate by faculty department; 29 allocate by subject area. Although seven stated that they allocate by branch library, the assumption was that in an academic setting this refers to large departmental libraries, perhaps medical or law libraries, and would fall under faculty or subject divisions. Ten smaller libraries said no division of any sort was made.

Question Four: *Do you automatically purchase the selections of any of the following: acquisitions librarians, faculty, subject bibliographers, director of the library, student, branch librarian or other?*

CHART I
Primary Initiators of Requests in Academic Libraries

	Total number who selected	Number of those selecting one choice only
Acquisitions Librarian	51	4
Faculty	93	18
Subject Bibliographers	22	1
Director of the Library	72	10
Student	16	1
Branch Librarian	12	—
Collection Development Officer	3	2
Other	4	4
None	43	43

Again, many indicate that more than óne person's selections are automatically purchased, although 43 indicate that no purchase was automatic. Only 18 automatically purchase faculty selections, 10 those of the director of the library, 4 the acquisitions librarian, and one automatically purchases student requests. There is a trend toward not purchasing any request automatically; this may be an answer to budget constraints.

Question Five: *Are there financial limitations on the purchase of single books?*
The results indicate that there is no fixed amount limitation. One hundred forty-nine state that there were no limitations; only 24 actually indicate figures. These ranged from $16–$20 to $5,000. The majority who give dollar amounts usually indicate that $50 for a single item is the point where items requested were questioned. One library comments that single books of $500 are sent to the Dean of Faculty for approval, reporting that in all cases when this was done, the Dean had not refused the purchase.

Question Six: *Of those purchases which require approval, whose approval is necessary?*
No choices were given to this question, only a blank space, but most libraries who answered used the choices that had been given in questions two and four.

CHART II
Purchasing Approval in Academic Libraries

Whose Approval Necessary	Number of Respondents
Director of the Library	83
College Administrator	19
Faculty	26
Acquisitions Librarian	21
Subject Bibliographer	19
Collection Development Officer and/or Committee	14
Other	8
No Answer	28

As was predictable from previously answered questions, 83 require the library director's approval, 26 require faculty approval (in most cases this represented the heads of the various departments approving of their own faculty's selection), 21 require the acquisitions librarian's approval and 19 the subject librarian's approval. Of the other answers which were written in, the most interesting appeared to be the college administrator. Nineteen replied that these were the final authority in their colleges. In all, 32 had no answers.

Question Seven: *Are most of your selections made from reviewing media, publishers' brochures, LC slips or proof sheets, "Weekly Record," advertisements or other? Please specify.*

Respondents were asked to rank these in order of importance to their selection procedure. Many chose to ignore the rankings and just checked what they used. In all, 345 answers of all ranks were given to the five items mentioned.

	No Rank	First Choice	Second Choice	Third Choice	Fourth Choice	Fifth Choice
Reviewing media	67	61	13	3	0	0
Publishers' brochures	32	10	43	16	2	0
LC slips or sheets	3	0	3	3	1	1
"Weekly Record"	10	4	4	5	3	0
Advertisements	18	6	6	25	5	1

Of the 164 libraries who answered this question, 144 picked reviewing media either without ranking or of first, second or third importance. That the use of reviewing media as the overwhelming selection method is borne out by the selection policies examined. The surprising feature of the responses to this question is the number of libraries relying on publishers' brochures and advertisements for selection. One hundred and three picked brochures as a major procedure with the majority (43) ranking these in second place. The third top choice was advertisements, sixty-one using these at some point in the process. One librarian in an outlying area explained that he uses publishers' brochures and advertisements because they come by plane while journals come by boat or train. Most libraries do not encounter quite the same problem, but speed is essential in the selection process and reviews often come out too slowly. Twenty libraries wrote that faculty are part of the selection process; nine added approval plans. While our responses definitely indicate that publishers' brochures are the second favorite method of selecting materials, and advertisements third, no library readily admits this in their written policy statement.

Question Eight: *Please list the major selection tools used by your library in order of preference.*

In all, 136 libraries picked *Choice,* with the majority (103) picking it first. *Library Journal* (96), *Publishers Weekly* (40), *Booklist* (39), *New York Times Book Review* (37) and professional journals (43) were mentioned. Among 71 additional items mentioned are all kinds of materials ranging from *RQ, Magazines for Libraries, NUC, BNB, PTLA, ARBA, Booklist* and the *Baker List.* Sixty-five libraries mentioned publishers' brochures or advertisements of some sort (see Chart III).

Question Nine: *Are the majority of your purchases ordered through jobbers or direct from publishers?*

One hundred and sixty-five said jobbers and 25 said they order direct from the publishers. Only eleven libraries checked *only* direct to publishers.

CHART III
Ranking of Selection Aids in Academic Libraries

	No Rank	#1	#2	#3	#4	#5
Choice	2	105	9	10	8	2
Library Journal	2	13	53	21	4	3
Publishers Weekly	1	5	10	11	9	4
Booklist	0	1	14	9	10	5
New York Times Book Review	0	1	7	14	7	8
Professional Journals	0	3	10	14	8	8
Publishers' Brochures	1	5	8	5	7	6
Publishers' Catalogs	1	3	0	4	4	7
Approval Plans	0	5	1	1	0	0
Books for College Libraries	0	6	7	1	7	1
Books in Print	0	7	3	2	4	1

Almost all these libraries were very small. Most respondents noted that they use a jobber for most purchases, but that there are always some materials which must be bought directly from the publisher. In only one case did a library say it uses a jobber exclusively and never orders directly from publishers.

Question Ten: *Are there limitations on the purchase of any of the following materials: paperbacks, multiple or duplicate copies, textbooks, microforms, or media? Please explain what sort of limitations exist.*

Of the 175 respondents, 39 did not have limitations. Fifty-four libraries mention some kind of limitation on paperback books; most have a distinct preference for hardcover. One hundred and two specified some limitation on duplicate and multiple copies. Limitations are based on a formula, such as how many students in a class, or on a flat number policy of buying anywhere from 25 copies to never buying more than one. Ninety-nine libraries have limitations concerning textbooks, 41 rarely purchase them and 20 never purchase them. The limitations concerning microforms (14) and media (29) are fewer in number and media limitations are explained by comments that the college has a separately funded department which buys all media materials and equipment. Comments also reveal that librarians still think the binding and paper of paperback books are of inferior quality. (It seems hard to justify this answer when many hardcover bindings are poor, as is the paper, while some publishers are putting out very high quality paperbacks.)

CHART IV
Limitations of Materials in Academic Libraries
(by Format)

	Paperback	Multiple Copies	Microform	A-V	Textbooks	Other	None
Unspecified	18	37	4	5	25	4	39
	Not available hardcover 17	2 copies 2	Rarely purchased 8	Formal limitation 3	Never 20		
	Prefer hardcover 12	3 copies 7	Prefer fiche 1	Rarely 7	Rarely purchased 41		
	If a quality paperback 3	5 copies 6	No 1	None 12	One-copy 3		
	Never 2	6 copies 1		Prefer print 2			
	If at least $3.00 cheaper 2	10 copies 2					
		25 copies 1					
		Rare 33					
		Never 11					
		Formula from reserves per student 2					

Question Eleven: *If you have a selection policy statement, how often is it reviewed?*

Many said that the question was not applicable (38) and others (52) indicated they had no policy. Of those that do have policy statements, many rarely (17) or never (2) review them, or never have yet (16) reviewed them. For those that do review them (47), they are reviewed anywhere from constantly (2) to every decade (1), but the majority (24) review them on an annual basis.

Question Twelve: *Who wrote or is writing your selection policy?*

Fifty-eight libraries answered indicating that they had no written policy. Of the 117 who have written policies, a number said that they were currently being written by the director, the collection development officer, the acquisitions librarian or a committee of some or all of the professional staff.

The answers to these twelve questions indicate that selection policy statements do not reflect the reality of the procedure used by most acquisitions departments. Libraries use their selection policies to present an ideal state; that this state does not yet exist is evident from the answers to the questionnaires. There are discrepancies between the policy statement and the answers to questions in this survey. For instance the indication by many policies that faculty do most of the selecting is not confirmed by the survey.

Public Libraries

There were 71 useable questionnaires filled out by public libraries. The range in size and geographical location is similar to that of the academic library respondents, as is their answer to the total budget question. Again this may account for some of the extremes that appear in the first analysis. When reaching conclusions about the type of public library responding, these extremes must be disregarded. The public libraries who answered do tend to be large. This may be due to the fact that the original letter was sent to libraries with materials budgets over $10,000, as these were thought the most likely to have written selection policies.

Sixty libraries furnished enough detail on total library and materials budget to reach some type of profile. The highest total library budget was $16,000,000 and the lowest was $28,000. The majority of the answers came from libraries with total budgets of between $100,000 and $499,000. Materials budgets range from a high of $2,189,595 to a low of $5,150.

The percentage figures for the relationship of materials budget to total budget are more revealing, ranging from a high of 97.2% to a low of 2.8%. Disregarding the extremes at both ends of the spectrum (seven libraries had percentages over 25%, five fell below 10%), the overwhelming number of libraries spend between 11% and 24% of their budgets on materials. Further breaking this down, it can be seen that 23 public libraries spend between 11% and 14% of their total library budgets on materials, while 19 spend between 15% and 19% on materials. Only eight public libraries spend between 20% and 24% of their budgets on materials.

Question One: *What is your materials budget (please give breakdown if available by type, e.g., monographs, periodicals, standing orders, media, microforms, etc.)?*

Not all libraries who supplied materials budget figures broke these down into all of the categories mentioned. There were 54 libraries who gave figures for monographs. One public library spends 92.5% of its budget on monographs, while another indicates that 25% of its total materials budget is for the purchase of monographs. The majority of the libraries responding spend 60%–89% of their total materials budget on monographs. This represents 49 of the 54 who answered.

Of the 51 public libraries who broke down their materials budgets into periodicals, the highest percentage of a total materials budget spent on

MATRIX II
Total Public Library Budgets*

TOTAL PUBLIC LIBRARY MATERIALS BUDGET	1 million & over	$500,000–$999,000–	$100,000–$499,000	$50,000–$99,000	Below $50,000
1 million & over	5				
$500,000–$999,000	6				
$400,000–$499,000	3				
$300,000–$399,000	5				
$200,000–$299,000	1				
$100,000–$199,000	7	6	1		
$50,000–$99,000		4	4		
$40,000–$49,000			4		
$30,000–$39,000			3		
$20,000–$29,000			6		
$10,000–$19,000				3	
$1–$9,999				1	1

Only those libraries which provided total library budget and total materials budget are included.

periodicals is 75%, while one library indicated that only 1.3% is spent on periodicals. The majority of those responding spend 6%–24% of their materials budget on periodicals; this represents 44 public libraries. Only 13 libraries break down materials budgets by the number of standing orders.

Forty-four public libraries responded with figures on how much of their materials budget they spend on media. The highest figure given is 23.5% while the lowest indicates that 0.2% of the total materials budget is spent on media. The majority of public libraries answering this question spend between 4% and 14% of their total materials budget on purchasing media for their libraries. This represents 37 of the responding libraries. Only 14 libraries answered breaking down the microform budgets.

The most significant result of this question is the wide difference between how academic and public libraries apportion their materials budgets. College and university libraries spend much more on periodicals and standing orders, while public libraries seem to have accepted more readily the challenge of the newer media and technology.

Question Two: *Who primarily initiates requests for purchase of monographs: acquisitions librarian, subject bibliographer, director of the library, patron, branch librarian, other (please specify)?*

Due to the multiple choices provided, there were 107 answers. The majority of these indicated that orders are initiated by subject bibli-

ographers, professional staff or the director of the library. A number state
that branch librarians are the primary purchasers, 21 name subject bibliographers, 17 indicate the professional staff, but do not specify who, and 11
name the acquisitions librarian. Only 6 said that patrons were part of the
selection process, which puts public libraries in a completely different mode
than academic libraries, whose answers to this question indicate that the
faculty and other nonlibrarians are often among the primary initiators of
requests. It appears that in the public library the librarian tends to be *the*
professional.

Question Three: *Are budget allocations primarily made by type, subject, faculty
department, branch library or other?*

The larger the library's budget, the more likely it was to check more than
one way of allocating its budgets. Smaller public libraries often checked only
one method, usually by type of material.

CHART V
Primary Initiator of Requests
in Public Libraries

Professional Staff (not specific)	17
Subject Bibliographers	21
Acquisitions Librarian	11
Director of the Library	16
Patrons	6
Branch Librarians	13
Selection or Review Librarian or Committee	8
Division heads	5
Adult, Young Adult & Children's Librarian	5
Purchase few or no monographs	3
Other	2

There were 95 responses to this question from 71 public libraries.
Thirty-six indicate that their budgets are allocated by type, 23 by subject of
materials, 18 by branch. Only five libraries said they allocate by age level.
Although this seems low, it was not one of the choices offered on the
questionnaire and had to be added by the respondents. It may have been
overlooked by some. In five instances, departments received the budget
allocations, which in a public library situation might indicate subject departments. If this is true, then allocation by some sort of subject would run a very
close second to allocating by type of material. An interesting comment came
from one of the largest libraries in the survey, which spends over $1,000,000
per year but said it has no formal budget allocation method.

Question Four: *Do you automatically purchase the selections of any of the following: acquisitions librarian, subject bibliographer, director of the library, branch librarian, patron?*

CHART VI
Budget Allocations in Public Libraries

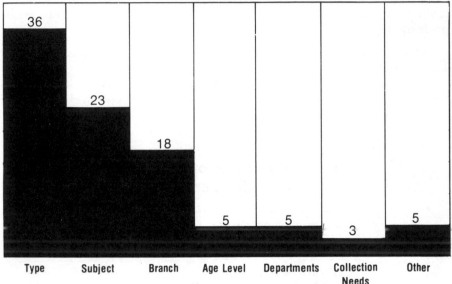

Type	Subject	Branch	Age Level	Departments	Collection Needs	Other
36	23	18	5	5	3	5

In all there were 93 answers to this question from the seventy-one public libraries answering the survey. Twenty-three state that no purchase is automatic. It appears that the larger the library budget, the less likely it is that *anything* is bought automatically. This matches the results obtained from academic libraries.

Question Five: *Are there financial limitations on the purchase of single books?*
Similarly to the academic library response, the overwhelming number of public libraries indicated that no financial limitations were imposed. This response was received from 65 of the libraries. Only six libraries indicated any dollar amount and this figure ranged from $50.00 to $150.00.

Question Six: *Of those purchases which require approval, whose is necessary?*
Seventeen public libraries had no answer for this question, indicating perhaps that no approval was necessary for any of the selectors. Only the director of the library received any significant response; 26 libraries state that their director's approval is necessary for purchase. As indicated by the responses to Question Four, this takes into account a number of public libraries with only one librarian and some two-librarian libraries where the director and the acquisitions librarian are one and the same. Among the 68 answers, 35 different individuals are named. These range from the children's librarian to the coordinator of materials management.

CHART VII
Automatic Purchase of Materials in Public Libraries

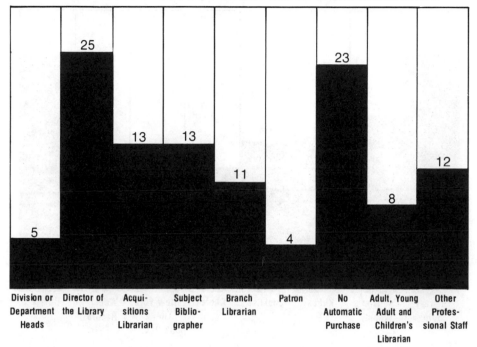

Division or Department Heads	Director of the Library	Acqui- sitions Librarian	Subject Biblio- grapher	Branch Librarian	Patron	No Automatic Purchase	Adult, Young Adult and Children's Librarian	Other Profes- sional Staff
5	25	13	13	11		4	23	8	12

Question Seven: *Are most of your selections made from reviewing media, publishers' brochures, LC proof slips or sheets, "Weekly Record," advertisements, other (please specify)? Please indicate the order of importance.*

From the 71 public libraries responding, there were 145 answers.

	No Rank	First Choice	Second Choice	Third Choice	Fourth Choice	Fifth Choice
Reviewing media	12	55	2	0	1	0
Publishers' brochures	9	1	18	4	3	1
LC proof slips	2	1	0	0	0	0
"Weekly Record"	4	0	3	4	4	0
Advertisements	6	0	2	9	1	3

The ranked choices indicate that publishers' brochures and adver-tisements are becoming more important in the selection of materials; the reason again appears to be that the reviewing media is not fast enough.

Question Eight: *Please list the major selection tools used by your library (in order of importance).*

All of the public libraries in the survey answered this question and there were 66 different sources mentioned.

CHART VIII
Major Selection Aids in Public Libraries

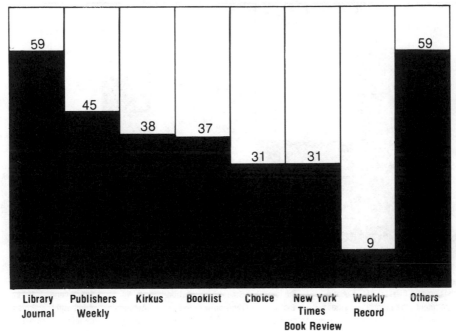

Library Journal	Publishers Weekly	Kirkus	Booklist	Choice	New York Times Book Review	Weekly Record	Others
59	45	38	37	31	31	9	59

The most frequently mentioned were *Library Journal, Publishers Weekly, Kirkus, Booklist, Choice, The New York Times Book Review Section,* and "Weekly Record." In addition to these sources, many of the public libraries also mention their local newspapers, e.g. *The Chicago Tribune, The North Carolina Observer.* It is interesting to see the *New York Times Book Review* ranked so highly, especially since not all of the libraries which mentioned it are on the East Coast.

Question Nine: *Are the majority of your materials ordered through jobbers or direct from publishers?*

Most libraries indicate that they use jobbers to purchase materials. Sixty-five of the libraries responded in this manner while only five indicated that they use publishers at all. Nine public libraries state that they go directly to the publisher to order materials; five of these use jobbers as well. Four of the libraries say they use a systems or network arrangement.

Question Ten: *Are there limitations on the purchase of any of the following material: textbooks, multiple copies, paperbacks, media, microforms? If so, please specify what kind of limitations exist.*

Libraries indicating limitations of textbooks state that they buy them if part of an adult education program or if they are the only available source of material for a field. Most mentioned an unwillingness, much like that of the academic libraries, to buy textbooks which were used in their school systems.

CHART IX
Limitations on Materials in Public Libraries
(by Format)

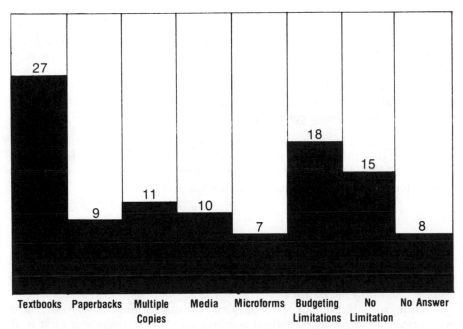

Textbooks	Paperbacks	Multiple Copies	Media	Microforms	Budgeting Limitations	No Limitation	No Answer
27	9	11	10	7	18	15	8

Few public libraries indicate any limitation on the purchase of paper-backs. Fifty-four academic libraries did cite limitations of this form, while only nine public libraries did so. It appears that public libraries use more paperbacks, although they may not add them to their collections but have separate areas in the library to shelve them.

Libraries indicating limitations on the number of copies of any one item commented that they use a formula of one additional copy for each five or six reserves placed on a book. Some libraries say they rent multiple copies of books in heavy demand instead of buying them. Some absolute limitations exist, usually amounting to many more copies than any academic library would buy (10 or more).

Only ten libraries indicate limits on the purchase of audio-visual mate-rial, mostly by format, with only one library mentioning that they never purchase any AV material.

Limitations on microforms exist in seven public libraries who answered the survey, with two indicating that they buy only their local newspaper or archives of the town in this format.

Eighteen public libraries state that budgetary considerations are the only limitations on buying any material. This seems to call into question the answers received for item number five, which asked for specific financial limitations. Only five public libraries indicated that there were any.

In addition, fifteen public libraries state that they had no limitations on any of the forms mentioned and eight libraries did not answer this question at all.

Question Eleven: *If you have a written selection policy, how often is it reviewed?*
Thirteen public libraries have no policy and 11 did not answer this question, which probably means that they have no policy. Thus, a large percentage of those answering the questionnaire still have no written policy. Of the 47 who do have policies, there is no clear cut answer to how often they are reviewed. As with the response from academic libraries, the review process is taking place anywhere from never to constantly, with the majority centered around annual revision.

Question Twelve: *Who wrote or is writing the policy?*
Almost one-third of the public libraries had no answer to this question. The rest all had differing answers that ranged from "now being written by committee," to "written by the director over ten years ago."

The academic and public library questionnaire survey answers, although certainly not conclusive of any trends, do provide some interesting commentary on what happens in the practical world of library acquisitions.
Aside from the policies, the letters and the questionnaires sent out, there is a certain feeling one gets when reading all of these together. First is an absolute commitment on the part of the profession to a written selection policy. Even those libraries which do not have such documents stress in their letters the need they feel; most are anxious to begin working on one. There is evidence that times are getting worse financially and that these written documents will be needed for support against budgetary encroachments. The days of the sixties, with government support and ever increasing budgets, not only are over but will never return. Some libraries are distressed at this, while others view the situation as a challenge and are applying their resources and ingenuity to figuring out ways to maintain services and standards developed in better times. We begin to question as a profession the manipulation of outsiders from the publishing world, the community, governing bodies, faculties and administration. The best that can be said of times like these is that perhaps we can finally prove to others, as well as to ourselves, what it really means to be a professional librarian: to take charge of our own profession and begin to demand that we be treated with respect; to have our concern become the concerns of our patrons. We may begin to take stands on the rising prices of materials, the proliferation of "junk" publications, interference by others in matters of collection development, and the administration of our own professional lives and the libraries in which we work. With the new management tools of programming being taught to novice library science students, the zero-based budgeting with which the nation will now be faced, and the lack of room to make costly mistakes we used to take in our stride, the time has come for professional librarians to take charge of the library: To prove that we can move ahead

into the 21st century and deal with skill and assurance with all the technology. We can accept nothing blindly, and we cannot afford to be pressured into buying useless items or useless sources that we do not need. Selection may not yet be a science, but it is an art that must be developed.

REFERENCES

1. American Library Association. Office for Intellectual Freedom. *Intellectual Freedom Manual,* Part IV, "Before the censor comes: essential preparation." (Chicago: ALA, 1974), pp. 3–4.
2. LeRoy Charles Merritt. *Book Selection and Intellectual Freedom.* (New York: H. W. Wilson Company, 1970), p. 26.
3. Hendrik Edelman and G. Marvin Tatum, Jr. "The development of collections in American university libraries." *College and Research Libraries,* vol. 37, no. 3 (May, 1976), p. 226.
4. Selby U. Gration and Arthur P. Young. "Reference-Bibliographers in the college library." *College and Research Libraries,* vol. 35, no. 1 (January, 1974), p. 28.

Libraries Whose Policies are Reprinted in Full

Akron-Summit County Public Library, Akron, OH 44326. *Materials Selection Policy*

Crandall Public Library, Glen Falls, NY 12801. *How Crandall Chooses, Selection Policies for Adult Library Materials*

Dickinson College Library, Carlisle, PA 17013. *Acquisitions Policy*

East Texas State University, James G. Gee Library, Commerce, TX 75428. *Library Acquisitions*

Edwin A. Bemis Public Library, Littleton, CO 80120. *Materials Selection Policy*

Evanston Public Library, Evanston, IL 60201. *Library Materials Selection*

Gettysburg College Library, Gettysburg, PA 17325. *Collections Policy Statement*

Holy Names College Library, Oakland, CA 94619. *Library Acquisitions Policy*

Houston Community College Learning Resources Center, Houston, TX 77007. *Materials Selection Policy*

Iowa State University Library, Ames, IA 50011. *Acquisitions Policy*

Kingsport Public Library, Kingsport, TN 37660. *Book Selection Policy*

Knoxville-Knox County Public Library, Knoxville, TN 37902. *Materials Selection Policy*

Montgomery County Community College Learning Resources Center, Blue Bell, PA 19422. *Acquisitions Policy*

Moorhead State University, Livingston Lord Library, Moorhead, MN 56560. *Policy for the Selection of Library Materials*

Northern Oklahoma College Learning Resources Center, Tonkawa, OK 74653. *Acquisitions Policy*

Orange County Public Library, Orange, CA 92668. *Materials Selection Policy*

Pikes Peak Regional Library District, Colorado Springs, CO 80901. *Book Selection and Retention Policy*

Portland State University Library, Portland, OR 97207. *Book Selection Policy*

San Antonio College Library, San Antonio, TX 78284. *Acquisitions Policy*

San Diego Public Library, San Diego, CA 92101. *Book Selection Policy*

Schenectady County Public Library, Schenectady, NY 12305. *Materials Selection Policy*

St. Louis Public Library, St. Louis, MO 63103. *Materials Selection Policy*

Suffolk University College Library, Boston, MA 02114. *Collection Development Policies and Operating Procedures*

Libraries Whose Policies are Partially Reprinted

Appalachian State University, Belk Library, Boone, NC 28608. *Library Acquisitions Policy*

Baker Junior College of Business Library, Flint, MI 48507. *Procedures Manual*

Baltimore County Public Library, Towson, MD 21204. *Materials Selection Policy Statement*

Blue Mountain Community College Library, Pendleton, OR 97801. *Procedures-Acquisitions*

Camden County Free Library, Voorhees, NJ 08043. *Book Selection Policy*

Catonsville Community College Learning Resources Center, Baltimore, MD 21228. *Materials Selection Policy*

Clatsop Community College Library, Astoria, OR 97130. *Acquisition Policy*

Clermont General and Technical College Library, Cincinnati, OH 45103. *Acquisitions Policy*

College of St. Catherine Library, St. Paul, MN 55105. *Materials Selection Policy*

College of the Desert Library, Palm Desert, CA 92260. *Library Materials Selection Policy*

College of the Virgin Islands, Ralph M. Paiewonsky Library, Saint Thomas, Virgin Islands 00801. *Acquisitions Policy*

Eastfield College Learning Resources Center, Mesquite, TX 75150. *Selection Policy Statement*

Emerson College, Abbot Memorial Library, Boston, MA 02116. *Collection Development Policy*

The Free Library of Philadelphia, Philadelphia, PA 19103. *Policies and Procedures*

Fresno County Public Library, Fresno, CA 93721. *Book Selection Policy*

Grand View College Library, Des Moines, IA 50316. *Acquisition Policy*

Hamilton Public Library, Hamilton, Ontario, Canada. *Statement on Book and Periodical Selection*

Hartwick College Library, Oneonta, NY 13820. *Hartwick College Faculty Library Manual*

Kalamazoo College Library, Kalamazoo, MI 49007. *Library Book Purchases Recommendations*

Kansas City Kansas Community Junior College Library, Kansas City, KS 66112. *Selection Policy*

Lynchburg College, Knight-Capron Library, Lynchburg, VA 24501. *Acquisitions Selection Policy*

Malone College, Cattell Library, Canton, OH 44709. *Materials Selection Policy*

Mansfield Public Library, Mansfield, OH 44902. *Materials Selection Policy*

McNeese State University, Frazer Memorial Library, Lake Charles, LA 70601. *Selection Policy*

Miami University-Middletown, Gardner-Harvey Library, Middletown, OH 45042. *Book Selection Policy*

Muscatine Community College Library, Muscatine, IA 52761. *Guidelines for the Development of the Library Collection*

New Hampshire Vocational Technical College Library, Nashua, NH 03060. *Acquisitions Policies*

North Carolina Central University, James E. Shepard Memorial Library, Durham, NC 27707. *Acquisitions*

North Country Library System, Watertown, NY 13601. *Book Selection Policy of the Service Center*

Northeastern Illinois University Library, Chicago, IL 60625

Ontario City Library, Ontario, CA 91764. *Materials Selection*

Oregon State University Library, Corvallis, OR 97331. *Acquisitions Program*

Orillia Public Library, Orillia, Ontario, Canada. *Policies Adopted by the Board*

The Public Library of Cincinnati and Hamilton County, Cincinnati, OH 45202. *Book Selection Policy*

Rensselaer Public Library, Rensselaer, IN 47978. *Contractual Libraries Book Selection Policy*

Ricks College Learning Resources Center, Rexburg, ID 83440. *Policy Statements*

Roanoke-Chowan Technical Institute Library, Ahoskie, NC 27910. *Procedures for Selection Policy*

Rockingham Community College Learning Resources Center, Wentworth, NC 27375. *Materials Policies*

Rolling Prairie Libraries, Decatur, IL 62522. *Materials Selection Policy*

Seattle Public Library, Seattle, WA 98104. *Materials Selection Policy Statement*

Skyline College Library, San Bruno, CA 94066. *Selection Policy*

Snead State Junior College Library, Boaz, AL 35957. *Acquisitions Procedures*

South Georgia College, William S. Smith Library, Douglas, GA 31533. *Policies and Procedures Manual*

St. Albans Free Library (Vermont Library Association), St. Albans, VT 05478

Suomi College Library, Hancock, MI 49930. *Materials Selection*

Texas State Technical Institute Library, Waco, TX 76705. *Book Selection Criteria–Suggested Guidelines*

Tri-County Technical College Library, Pendleton, SC 29670. *General Policy of Acquisitions*

University of California at Los Angeles Library, Los Angeles, CA 90024. *Collection Policy*

Bibliography

American Library Association. Office for Intellectual Freedom. *Intellectual Freedom Manual*. Chicago: American Library Association, 1974.

Boyer, Calvin J. and Nancy L. Eaton. *Book Selection Policies in American Libraries*. Austin, TX: Armadillo Press, 1971.

Buckeye, Nancy. "A plan for undergraduate participation in book selection." *Library Resources and Technical Services* Vol. 19, no. 2, Spring 1975, pp. 121–125.

Carter, Mary Duncan, Wallace John Bonk, and Rose Mary Magrill. *Building Library Collections*. 4th edition. Metuchen, NJ: The Scarecrow Press, Inc., 1974.

De Gennaro, Richard. "Escalating journal prices: time to fight back." *American Libraries* Vol. 8, no. 2, February, 1977, pp. 69–74.

Deller, A. Michael. "Your book/media selection policy: a public relations opportunity." *Michigan Librarian* Vol. 39, no. 2, Summer 1973, p. 5.

Dessauer, John P. "Library acquisitions: a look into the future." *Publishers Weekly* Vol. 207, no. 24, June 16, 1975, pp. 55–68.

Douglas, J. W. H. T. "Selection principles: a beginner's guide." *New Library World* Vol. 74, no. 882, December 1973, pp. 274–275.

Edelman, Hendrik and G. Marvin Tatum, Jr. "The development of collections in American university libraries." *College & Research Libraries* Vol. 37, no. 3, May 1976, pp. 222–245.

Gration, Selby U. and Arthur P. Young. "Reference-Bibliographers in the college library." *College & Research Libraries* Vol. 35, no. 1, January 1974, pp. 28–34.

Katz, Bill. *Magazine Selection: How to Build a Community-Oriented Collection*. NY: R. R. Bowker Company, 1971.

Lunati, Rinaldo. *Book Selection: Principles and Procedures*. Metuchen, NJ: The Scarecrow Press, Inc., 1975.

Melcher, Daniel. *Melcher on Acquisition*. Chicago: American Library Association, 1971.

Merritt, LeRoy Charles. *Book Selection and Intellectual Freedom*. NY: H. W. Wilson Company, 1970.

Serebnick, Judith. "The 1973 court rulings on obscenity: have they made a difference?" *Wilson Library Bulletin* Vol. 50, no. 4, December 1975, pp. 304–310.

Spiller, David. *Book Selection: An Introduction to Principles and Practice*. London: Clive Bingley, 1971.

Vosper, Robert. "A century abroad." *College & Research Libraries* Vol. 37, no. 6, November 1976, pp. 514–530.

PART

I

PUBLIC LIBRARY POLICIES

Webster Parish Library (LA)
Schenectady County Public Library (NY)
Kingsport Public Library (TN)
San Diego Public Library (CA)
Pikes Peak Regional Library District (CO)
Evanston Public Library (IL)
Edwin A. Bemis Public Library (CO)
Orange County Public Library (CA)
Crandall Library (NY)
St. Louis Public Library (MO)
Knoxville-Knox County Public Library (TN)
Akron-Summit County Public Library (OH)

Webster Parish Library

POLICIES AND OBJECTIVES

The purpose of this policy on book selection is to guide in the selection of materials and to inform the public about the principles upon which selections are made. This statement was approved and adopted on July 28, 1972, by the Webster Parish Library Board, which assumes full responsibility for all legal actions which may result from the implementation of any policies stated herein.

LIBRARY AIMS

The aim of the Webster Parish Library is service to all people. This encompasses individuals and groups of every age, education, philosophy, occupation, economic level, ethnic origin and human condition. Fulfilling the educational, informational and recreational needs of these people is the Webster Parish Library's broad purpose. More specifically, it helps people to keep up with change in all areas, educate themselves continually, become better members of their families and communities, become socially and politically aware, be more capable in their occupations, develop their creative abilities and spiritual capacities, appreciate and enjoy literature and art, contribute to the overall expanse of knowledge, and stimulate their own personal and social well-being. All printed and nonprinted materials are selected by this library in accordance with these basic objectives.

RESPONSIBILITY FOR MATERIALS SELECTION

This library board adopts as part of its policy the following paragraphs from the *Library Bill of Rights*:

1. As a responsibility of library service, books and other library materials should be chosen for values of interest, information and enlightenment of all people of the community. In no case should library materials be excluded because of the race or nationality or the social, political, or religious views of the authors.

Webster Parish Library, Minden, LA 71055

2. Libraries should provide books and other materials presenting all points of view concerning the problems and issues of our times; no library materials should be proscribed or removed from libraries because of partisan or doctrinal disapproval.[1]

Final responsibility for selection of books and library materials is and shall be vested in the librarian. However, the librarian may delegate, to such members of the staff as are qualified by reason of training, the authority to interpret and guide the application of the policy in making day-to-day selections. Unusual problems will be referred to the librarian for resolution. Any books and library materials so selected shall be held to be selected by the board.

CRITERIA FOR SELECTION

Certain factors influence the selection of library materials. Among these are:

1. The author's reputation and significance as a writer;
2. The importance of subject matter to the collection;
3. Availability of material in the system, in other libraries or in print;
4. Timeliness or permanence of the book;
5. Authoritativeness;
6. Inclusion in standard bibliographies or indexes;
7. Price;
8. Format, including possibility of rebinding, as well as type and legibility.

SCOPE OF THE COLLECTION

The library recognizes its obligations to provide reference and research materials for the direct answering of specific questions and for continuing research. It also recognizes the purposes and resources of other libraries in the community and shall not needlessly duplicate functions and materials.

The library acquires textbooks and other curriculum-related materials when such materials serve the general public.

The library acknowledges a particular interest in local and state history; therefore, it will seek to acquire state and municipal public documents, and it will take a broad view of works by and about Louisiana authors as well as general works relating to the State of Louisiana, whether or not such materials meet the standards of selection in other respects. However, the library is not under any obligation to add to its collections everything about Louisiana or produced by authors, printers, or publishers with Louisiana connections if it does not seem to be in the public interest to do so.

GIFTS

Unconditional gifts, donations, and contributions to the library may be accepted by the librarian on behalf of the Library Board of Control. No gifts or donations conditionally made shall be accepted without the approval of the Library Board of Control.

WEBSTER PARISH LIBRARY
521 EAST & WEST STREET
MINDEN, LOUISIANA 71055

CITIZEN'S REQUEST FOR RECONSIDERATION OF LIBRARY MATERIAL

Author: _____

Title: _____

Publisher (if known): _____

Request initiated by: _____

Address: _____

City: _____ State _____ Zip _____ Telephone _____

Complainant represents:

_____ Himself

_____ (Name of Organization) _____

_____ (Identify other group) _____

1. To what in the material do you object? (Please be specific; cite pages.)
   _____

2. For what age group would you recommend this material?_____

3. Is there anything good about the material?_____

4. Did you read the entire material? ____ What parts?_____
   _____

5. Are you aware of the judgment of this material by literary critics?_____

6. What do you believe is the theme of this material?_____
   _____

7. In its place, what material of equal literary quality would you recommend that
   would convey as valuable a picture and perspective of the subject treated?
   _____

Signature of Complainant:

_____

Generally, collections of books will not be accepted with restrictions which necessitate special housing, or which prevent integration of the gift into the general library collection.

The same standards of selection will govern the acceptance of gifts as govern purchase by the library. If material is useful but not needed, it may be disposed of at the discretion of the librarian.

MAINTAINING THE COLLECTION

Systematic withdrawal of materials no longer useful is necessary in order to maintain relevant resources. The same criteria will be used in weeding materials from the collection as are used in their acquisition. The decision to withdraw library material shall be based on the physical condition, use of the material as determined by last date of loan or by number of loans in the last five years, and age of the material as a misinformation factor, especially in the area of the sciences. Library staff members are to be thoroughly instructed with regard to the necessity for discarding books and library materials.

CENSORSHIP

The selection of library books and materials is predicated on the library patron's right to read and, similarly, his freedom from censorship by others. Many books are controversial and any given item may offend some persons. Selections for this library will not, however, be made on the basis of anticipated approval or disapproval, but solely on the merits of the material in relation to the building of the collection and to serving the interests of the readers. This Library holds censorship to be a purely individual matter and declares that—while anyone is free to reject for himself books and other materials of which he does not approve—he cannot exercise this right of censorship to restrict the freedom of others.

With respect to the use of library materials by children, the decision as to what a minor may read is the responsibility of his parent or guardian. Selection will not be inhibited by the possibility that books may inadvertently come into the possession of minors.[2]

REFERENCES

[1]American Library Association. *Library Bill of Rights* (adopted June 18, 1948; amended February 2, 1961, and June 27, 1967, by the ALA Council).
[2]Policy includes American Library Association *Resolution on Challenged Materials* [adopted July 22, 1974 by the ALA Council].

Schenectady County Public Library

PURPOSE

The materials selection policy of the Schenectady County Public Library has been compiled with the intent of clarifying for the librarians and the public the criteria used in materials selection as well as the responsibility for it.*

The Schenectady County Public Library is a community institution, dedicated to serving interested individuals and groups and to working actively to introduce library materials to as many people as possible.

The library acquires, organizes and encourages the use of materials in various media which:

- Help people to know more about themselves and their world;
- Supplement formal study and encourage informal self-education;
- Stimulate thoughtful participation in the affairs of the community, the country and the world by giving access to a variety of opinions on matters of current interest;
- Support the educational, civic and cultural activities within the community;
- Aid in learning and improving job-related skills;
- Assist the individual to grow intellectually and spiritually and to enjoy life more fully;
- Meet the changing informational needs and interests of the entire community.

Free and convenient access to the world of ideas, to information and to the creative experience is of vital importance to every citizen today. Therefore, the Schenectady County Public Library incorporates as part of this policy the *Library Bill of Rights,* adopted by the Council of the American Library Association, June 27, 1967, and the *Freedom to Read Statement,* prepared by the Westchester Conference of the American Library Association

*Policy includes American Library Association *Library Bill of Rights* and "Request for Reconsideration of Library Materials" as appendices.

Schenectady County Public Library, Schenectady, NY 12305

and the American Book Publisher's Council, May 2 and 3, 1953. The former states: *As a responsibility of library service, books and other reading matter selected should be chosen for values of interest, information and enlightenment of all the people of the community. In no case should any book be excluded because of the race or nationality or the political or religious views of the writer. There should be the fullest practicable provision of material presenting all points of view concerning the problems and issues of our times–international, national and local; and books or other reading material of sound factual authority should not be proscribed or removed from library shelves because of partisan or doctrinal disapproval.*

Materials acquired include source materials, original documents, and thoughtful interpretations of the past and present. Contemporary materials of current interest and possible future significance and materials which entertain and enhance the individual's enjoyment of life will be sought. Experimental and ephemeral materials and those representing various sides of controversial subjects will be purchased to keep abreast of and to anticipate fluctuations in community concern. In a world in which change is so rapid and pervasive, the library's obligation extends beyond meeting present conditions. The library must also strive to anticipate future needs of the community.

COMMUNITY RESOURCES AS A FACTOR IN SELECTION

Educational Institutions

Consideration of the large, well-established collection at Union College influences the extent of the library's purchases in such fields as science and engineering.

Materials are purchased in response to the needs of area community colleges as they assemble and strengthen their own collections.

The public library provides supplemental enrichment materials for students, whether their demands are curriculum-oriented or derived from personal needs. However, extensive duplication to fulfill mass assignments is not feasible.

Special Libraries

The public library cannot duplicate specialized collections such as those maintained by the General Electric Company.

The Schenectady County Historical Society

The Society remains the prime repository for genealogical records and pictures, and for original documents relating to local history. Access to these is readily available.

DEFINITIONS

The words "book," "library materials," or other synonyms as they may occur in the policy have the widest possible meaning; hence, it is implicit in this policy that every form of permanent record is to be included, whether printed or in manuscript; bound or unbound; photographed or otherwise reproduced. Also included are audio records on tapes, discs or otherwise, and films and pictures in the form of photographs, paintings, drawings, etchings, etc.

"Selection" refers to the decision that must be made either to add a given book to the collection or to retain one already in the collection. It does not refer to reader guidance.

RESPONSIBILITY FOR BOOK SELECTION

To fit the interests and needs of specific neighborhoods, the collections of each branch and the extension division are selected from materials acquired by the central library. The comprehensive collection at the central library is available for reference and for subject depth. In addition, the central library is being developed as a strong reference center to serve the four-county area of the Mohawk Valley Library Association.

Final responsibility for book selection lies with the Director. However, the Director will delegate to the staff members authority to interpret and guide the application of the policy in making day-to-day selections. Unusual problems will be referred to the Director for resolution.

SELECTION FOR ADULTS

The aim of the library is to provide the mature, adult public with the materials needed for general reading, reference and recreation.

Selection is a critical and interpretive process involving a general knowledge of a subject and its important literature, a familiarity with the materials in the collection, an awareness of the bibliographies of the subject, and a recognition of the needs of the community. Along with an examination of current production, continual consideration is given to book reviews, authoritative discussions of the literature of the subject, pertinent bibliographical publications, publishers' advertising media, and requests of library patrons.

The library does not promulgate particular beliefs or views; nor is the selection of any given material equivalent to endorsement of the author's views. The library tries to provide materials representing all approaches to public issues of a controversial nature. The library is aware that one or more persons may take issue with the selection of any specific item, and welcomes any expression of opinion by patrons. However, the library does not undertake the task of pleasing all patrons by the elimination of items purchased after due deliberation under guidance of the policies expressed herein. To provide a resource where the free individual may examine many points of view and make his own decisions is one of the essential purposes of the library.

SELECTION FOR YOUNG ADULTS

The ultimate aim of library work with young adults is to contribute to the development of well-rounded citizens with an understanding of themselves and others at home and abroad. Since readers vary widely in ability and background, the books selected for them will, of necessity, vary in content and reading difficulty. In general, these books are selected for readers in the sixth through ninth grades. All titles are, however, purchased in the hope they will lead to continued reading on as high a level as possible for each reader.

Adult books which are related to young adult needs and interests are purchased for the young adult collection, as well as books specifically written for a young adult audience.

Since the young adult collection is primarily general and recreational in scope, no separate reference collection is maintained. Young adults are expected to use the adult reference and informational services.

SELECTION FOR CHILDREN

The public library's objective in selecting materials for children is to make available a well-balanced collection that satisfies informational, recreational and cultural needs from early childhood through seventh grade.

All Children's Department staff members share in the selection of materials for children. The Coordinator of Work with Children is responsible to the Director for the final inclusion of all materials used with children.

Books considered for purchase are reviewed by one or more children's librarians, who take into consideration these basic criteria: accuracy, literary and artistic quality; quality of content (including suitability of subject matter and appropriateness of vocabulary to the reader's age); the contribution of the book to the total collection; and quality of format.

Materials for children are selected with the realization that literature for children is an integral part of all literature. It is judged by the same standards which apply to adult materials, and it is equally related to social and political conditions. Books reflecting deliberately discriminatory attitudes or open political bias are not purchased.

Fiction is provided for a wide range of interests and reading abilities, including picture books, easy-to-read books and stories for children through the seventh grade. Fiction for children must reveal life with integrity and reflect sound human values. Well-written books of imaginative fiction and those which authentically portray a period, incident or way of life are selected despite the occasional use of an unacceptable word or illustration, provided the total impact of the book meets other basic criteria.

A few abridged adult classics are purchased if they meet the standards of good writing without weakening the original, but abridged versions of children's classics are not purchased.

Nonfiction must be accurate, informative and current and is selected in as wide a range of reading levels and interests as possible. Textbooks are added to the collection to provide information on subjects only when there is little or no material available in any other form. Books on human physical development are carefully selected based on scientific accuracy and dignity of presentation. Works of specific religious teaching or practice are not purchased.

Both fiction and nonfiction in series are evaluated by individual title.

A limited number of books in a variety of foreign languages are purchased, as are examples of books published abroad. The library does not provide an extensive collection in any one language or at all reading levels.

Paperback and large-type editions of books, pamphlets, periodicals, maps, phono-records and picture sets are purchased where needed, according to basic selection criteria.

The reference collection includes major encyclopedias and informational titles appropriate to the needs and interests of children and of adults who work with them, as well as reference copies of all juvenile New York State and Schenectady materials.

A small Schenectady Collection, or Area Collection, is available in the central Children's Room; it includes material written about the Schenectady area or written by area authors.

Several other special reference collections are maintained through gifts and purchases. At the present time there is an Illustrator Collection, a Newbery Medal Award Collection, a Caldecott Medal Award Collection, and a collection of books published in other countries. Occasionally a small memorial collection of gift books (composed of titles fitting into one or more of the above collections) is set aside with an appropriate sign designating the memorial gift.

Considerable duplication of titles is provided within the children's collection to meet demand. Frequently, copies of material in the young adult and adult collections are duplicated.

A request by patrons or staff members for library purchase of a title not in the collection will be honored by order, careful review and selection or rejection according to the basic criteria.

GENERAL POLICY

Bases for Exclusion

The library reserves the right to exclude books which it judges to have been written purely to appeal to a taste for sensationalism and/or pornography. However, a serious work which illuminates some problem or aspect of life will not be excluded because its language or subject matter may be offensive to some readers.

Books on controversial issues and current problems which are inflammatory, sensational, or prejudiced are not generally purchased. Works by national or world figures, even if prejudiced or violent, may be acquired because they have influenced thinking either in our own times or in the past.

Controversial Works

The library recognizes that many books are controversial and that any item may offend some patrons. Selections will not be made on the basis of any anticipated approval or disapproval, but solely on the merits of the work in relation to building the collections and to serving the interests of readers.

If any title in the collection is critized or questioned by individuals, organizations or librarians, the form "Request for Reconsideration of Library Materials" (Form No. 124) may be filled out. Upon receipt of this request, a complete written re-evaluation will be made. If the re-evaluation substantiates the original decision to include the title, it will remain in the collection. If the criticism is considered valid, the title will be removed from the collection. The final decision rests with the Director. A letter of explanation will be sent as promptly as possible to the person or organization concerned.

Library materials will not be marked or identified to show approval or disapproval of the contents, and no cataloged book or other item will be placed on closed shelves, except for the express purpose of protecting it from injury or theft.

Responsibility for the reading of children rests with their parents and legal guardians. Selection will not be inhibited by the possibility that controversial books may come into the possession of children.

Duplication

The library attempts to duplicate classics and standard works in every field.

Current popular books are duplicated to meet demand by renting books through the McNaughton Plan, which allows the library to keep books while they are popular and return them when the demand has subsided.

The library accepts responsibility for the provision of supplementary materials for school and college students, but keeps duplication of such materials to a minimum. Since it is expected that school and college libraries will assume chief responsibility for the needs of their students, no attempt is made to meet demands for large class assignments. To do so would monopolize the services of the library to the detriment of their use by the general public.

Gifts and Memorials

The central library and its branches accept gifts with the understanding that they will not necessarily be added to the library's collection. The material will be judged by the same standards of selection as those applied to the purchase of new materials. If the materials are not suitable because of condition, out-dated knowledge or other factors, they will be referred to other institutions or discarded. The library does not appraise gifts.

The library frequently receives from an individual or an organization the gift of a book, a group of books, or a sum of money for the purchase of books in memory of a family member, friend or co-worker. Library selection standards apply in these cases. A memorial gift plate is placed in these books. The library does not set aside a special section or set of shelves for gift or memorial books, except in the case of a few memorial children's collections.

Replacement

While the library tries to have copies of all standard and important works, it does not attempt to replace each copy withdrawn because of loss, damage or wear.

Several factors are considered when an item is to be replaced:

1. The extent of the present library collection on the subject;
2. The obsolescence of older information because of new developments;
3. The historical value of the material;
4. The indexing or listing in a standard library tool;
5. The amount of public interest in the subject.

Books often go out of print rapidly, and many titles cannot be replaced through regular channels. Efforts are made to replace important out-of-print materials through second-hand dealers.

SUBJECT FIELDS

Business and Technology

The library has built up a strong collection in business and technology to serve the great number of professional and industrial workers in Schenectady County. Recent, reliable information on such matters as investments, consumer concerns, accounting, and management of small businesses is constantly in demand. Material on electronics at many levels of complexity is acquired to answer a community need. In the past, the library has built a collection of books on locomotives and railroads and will add to this, given continuing interest in the subject.

With the advent of more leisure time for most segments of the population, current information on creative arts and practical crafts (such as home maintenance) is of increasing importance. However, books on explosives (including those on model rocketry) are selected with caution; and no material on fireworks is bought, since amateur manufacture or display of these is contrary to New York State law.

Fiction

The library recognizes the importance of the novel as an educational tool, as a medium for recording and molding public opinion, and as an instrument for changing individual attitudes. The sound treatment of significant social and personal problems or of racial and religious questions through novels of wide reader appeal contributes much to the betterment of human relations. For this reason, a substantial number of novels of serious purpose are purchased. Due attention is paid to maintaining a basic collection in attractive editions of standard novels, the classics, and the semiclassics of world literature. Attention is given also to acquiring fiction useful in meeting the educational and recreational needs of an adult public of limited reading ability.

In selecting fiction, the library has set up no arbitrary single standard of literary quality. An attempt is made to satisfy a public varying greatly in education, interests, tastes and reading skill. Under these circumstances, fiction selection means choosing not only the most distinguished novels but also the most competent, pleasing and successful books in all categories of fiction writing. A title is considered in comparison with good work which has been done in the writer's specific field. The literary criteria applied in the case of an experimental novel, for example, will differ from those by which a detective story is chosen.

The author's purpose and his success in achieving it are the best guides in judging a novel at a time when ideas about structure and style are so varied and conflicting. In the past, plot and characterization have been considered essential to the novel; but in recent years, plot has been almost abandoned by many leading novelists. The major interests among writers of serious fiction today are character and ideas, although plot may be said to survive in the development of the leading character. To secure a favorable reception among large numbers of readers, a novel distinguished for characterization and style must also possess a well-constructed plot. Titles that combine these qualities are sought and duplicated heavily, although care is taken to include representative works of experimental novelists and examples of new trends.

Novels, even though widely advertised, are not purchased if they fail to measure up to the library's rather broad standards of literary quality. A book in which the plot is trite, the characters stereotyped, or the writing dull or trivial is not purchased.

The library's policy in acquiring fiction is to include that which is well-written and based on authentic human experience, and to exclude that which is weak, incompetent or sentimental, as well as solely sensational, morbid or erotic.

Law Materials

The library emphasizes the purchase of law materials written for the layman. Standard and popular works such as *Everyone's Legal Advisor* and *Law for the Family* are examples of the type of material acquired. Subject areas covered include history of law, legal rights, court procedure and jury duty. Works of a more technical nature, such as *McKinney's Consolidated Laws of New York* and the *United States Code* are acquired for the reference collection.

The library makes no attempt to acquire law materials for the professional use of lawyers. The purchase of such material is not within the scope of public library service. Material for the professional use of lawyers is available from special law libraries, such as the New York State Law Library.

Local History

The general policy of the library is to acquire one reference copy of all printed items relating to local history. The library also maintains a representative reference collection of the works, both fiction and nonfiction, of local authors. These materials are designated as the "Schenectady Collection." Duplicates of such material may be acquired for circulation.

Besides local newspapers, the library collects periodicals issued by local agencies.

The reference department maintains an extensive file of clippings from local newspapers. These news clippings, which are chosen for their reference value, date back to the mid 1940s. They include biographies of local people and information about local industries, events, associations, buildings and school systems.

Official publications of Schenectady city and county units are added, when available, to the Schenectady reference collection.

Medicine and Related Subjects

Authoritative, up-to-date material, comprehensible to the adult layman and to students at junior or senior high school level, is selected in the fields of health, medicine and psychiatry. In these areas, one must rely heavily on the professional or academic qualifications of the author and on the reputation of the publisher. Favorable reviews by those who are experts in the field are a basis for the decision to acquire. Increased consideration is given to the needs of adults who are entering or studying for promotion within such health-related occupations as medical and psychiatric social work, public health and special education. Such subjects as geriatrics, obstetrics, mental health, space and environmental medicine, drugs, personal health and hygiene, first aid, public health and sanitation, chronic diseases and therapeutic diets are covered. Textbooks in these fields are purchased only when they are the best source of the information needed by the layman.

For general readers and students, the library acquires a limited number of texts in basic sciences like bacteriology, anatomy, physiology and biochemistry, and a greater number in nutrition and nursing.

Textbooks and clinical case studies for students and practitioners in medicine, dentistry, surgery, osteopathy, chiropractic, naturopathy and optometry are not purchased.

In the area of sex instruction, the library has the responsibility to supply materials suitable for lay readers at varying levels of educational background and reading ability. The materials must also reflect the differing social and religious customs in the community. The needs of parents, teachers, clergymen, social workers, adolescents and those married or about to be are kept in mind. Clear, authoritative, contemporary and well-balanced treatment is sought. Highly technical work is outside the library's scope.

Increasing concern with the use of narcotics in our society dictates that the library acquire a variety of materials on the subject. Information is sought concerning the chemical nature of drugs, their physiological and psychological effects and recognized treatments of addiction. Material should be by qualified authors who present this evidence in unsensational fashion.

Reliable material, objective in presentation, avoiding a rabid or reformist tone, is required on such subjects as alcohol and its abuses, the effects of the use of tobacco, and food fads, including diets.

Religion

Religion is one of the deep concerns of man, and theology is one of the major intellectual disciplines. It is essential that the library have the standard works of the major world religions in either the original language or translations. These include the Judaeo-Christian writings, ancient, medieval and Reformation and modern; and the sacred books of other religions such as the *Koran* and *Mahabharata*. Authoritative, well-written books on agnosticism and the psychology, philosophy and history of religion are also represented. Standard versions of the Bible are included, as are reliable commentaries, concordances, histories and atlases. A number of long runs of periodicals of wide, scholarly usefulness and the most needed encyclopedias are provided.

The following are bought if they meet the criteria of objectivity, good taste, clear writing and scholarship; able and dispassionate presentations of comparative religion and of doctrine; books about the Bible; church histories; lives of Christ and Biblical characters; lives of saints and religious leaders; practical handbooks on religious education, missions, church administration, pastoral work; rituals and services for various occasions; collections of prayers; stories of hymns and hymnals; and books that offer inspiration. Since users of the library vary widely in educational background and reading ability, an effort is made to choose material to fit differing needs while avoiding both the very specialized and abstruse, and the immature, over-simplified and saccharine.

As an educational institution, the library recognizes an obligation to identify and eliminate sectarian propaganda material which tends to foster hatred or intolerant attitudes toward other groups.

TYPES OF MATERIALS

Audiovisual Materials—Phono-Records, Films, Slides, Transparencies, Filmstrips, Tapes

Of the above-mentioned materials, phono-records are the only type currently purchased by the library. 16mm films for children and adults are, however, available through the Mohawk Valley Library Association and other sources, such as the New York State Library.

A collection of 4,000 color slides on American art is available through the New York State Division of Library Development. A complete listing of those available is given in a book catalog, "Arts in the United States." This is located in the Schenectady County Public Library's central library reference section (call number R 709.73 P62). Additional slide sets on world art are available through interlibrary loan from the New York State Library.

Many types of phono-records for both children and adults are acquired by the Schenectady County Public Library. Collections of classical and folk music, jazz, musical comedies, film sound tracks and educational recordings (such as demonstrations of musical instruments) are maintained. Selection is based on composition, performer, recording quality, requests and use.

Non-musical recordings include drama, poetry and prose readings, speeches, documentaries of historical events, nature sounds, sound effects and teaching and practice records (e.g. language and business techniques). In the selection of poetry, drama and prose recordings, the importance of both authors and performers is considered. Emphasis is placed on classics and works of permanent literary interest rather than those of a more ephemeral nature. Foreign language records are purchased as funds permit, with the aim of including as many languages as possible. Purchase of non-musical recordings in non-literary fields is governed by the same general principles applied to the acquisition of other library materials, plus consideration of the value of sound in conveying the subject matter to the listener.

Foreign Language Books

The aim of the foreign language book collection is to provide a representative selection of classic and modern works. Since the collection is intended primarily for recreational reading, literary works are most commonly purchased. Emphasis is placed on the acquisition of works written in the more widely spoken European languages, such as French, German, Italian and Spanish. In addition, because of large local ethnic groups, the collection includes Polish, Czech, Russian, etc., literature in the original languages.

Pamphlets and Government Publications

Up-to-date material on many subjects can often be supplied more cheaply and quickly in pamphlet than in book form. For this reason, several sources are checked regularly for pamphlet material. These are the "Vertical File Index," the "United States Government Publications Monthly Catalog," the "Monthly Checklist of State Publications," and the "Checklist of Official Publications of the State of New York." Other selection lists are checked at intervals.

Pamphlets are ordered and processed for reference or for circulation. Judgment is exercised to exclude biased material where the sponsorship is not readily apparent. Pamphlets which are primarily advertising are not suitable. A special effort is made to select materials in the fields of vocations and travel. Pamphlets are chosen which supply valuable statistical data or other facts to help answer reference questions quickly.

Paperbacks

The library maintains a collection of paperback books which serves to supplement and extend the hardbound book collection. The collection capitalizes on the advantages of the paperback book form; it provides a wide range of subjects and titles at minimum expense. The aim in paperback selection is to provide popular material of general interest. Paperbacks may also be purchased for the following reasons:

1. The title is in heavy demand;
2. The title is out of print or otherwise unobtainable in sturdier format;
3. The title has never appeared in any other format;
4. The title in the hardbound format is expensive, and useful only occasionally; therefore, the paperback edition will answer the need.

Periodicals and Newspapers

Periodicals are of ever-increasing importance for students and others who need to be informed of current thought before such material is available in book form. Periodicals are valuable sources of recreational and how-to-do-it information as well as book selection information for the library's professional staff. Periodicals are acquired by subscription and gift, and those with future reference value are stored indefinitely.

An important factor in selection is where a periodical is indexed, or whether it is indexed at all. All periodicals indexed in "Readers' Guide to Periodical Literature" are acquired. Indexing in any of the other periodical indexes received by the library is the most important criterion for the addition of other periodicals. Serial publications originating in Schenectady County, or having to do with New York State or local history, are sought.

The library aims to have as complete a collection as possible of all newspapers ever published in Schenectady. These newspapers have been microfilmed. Back issues of two nationally known newspapers, the "New York Times" (since September 1851) and the "Christian Science Monitor" (since 1960), are kept on microfilm. At present the library does not attempt to provide newspapers from other major American cities or in other languages.

Pictures

The library maintains a collection of framed prints which range from modern to traditional in style. Additions to the collection are made as budget and space permit. The general criteria for selection apply here.

A file of pictures and photographs clipped from magazines and other ephemeral sources is maintained to supplement the picture material available in books.

Textbooks, Workbooks, Studyguides, etc.

The library attempts to keep the purchase of textbooks and workbooks to a minimum. Since a workbook is intended primarily for classroom or laboratory practice, little, if any, of this type of material is purchased. Textbooks, however, are useful to the general reader in search of introductory material as well as to the student engaged in formal study. It is with this usefulness to the general reader in mind that the library purchases limited textbook material.

Synopses, summaries and study outlines are rarely purchased. Those which are purchased, such as "Masterplots," are usually acquired for reference purposes. The library feels that its responsibility is to make available literary works in their entirety and that the quality of most "short-cut" items does not justify the expenditure of library funds on these materials.

Civil service and other examination manuals are supplied to meet the needs of those seeking help in occupational advancement. Duplicates of the most frequently consulted titles are acquired.

Kingsport Public Library

The book and printed materials selection policy of the library is designed to help carry out its stated objectives. The library selects and makes available books, periodicals, newspapers, maps, pamphlets and other nonbook sources in printed form, films, tapes and recordings. It is the function of the library to provide materials for all ages and groups which conform to the needs of the community without being restricted by them.

Books which aid the individual in the pursuit of education, information, research and the creative use of leisure time are selected. The library especially endeavors to make easily accessible to groups materials which contribute toward the betterment of community living and relationships and general cultural development.

Particular attention is given to the educational and informational objectives to the end that the library may serve as a dependable source for most of the people most of the time.

In considering the total needs of the community the library is mindful of the titles requested for students' supplementary reading insofar as the budget will permit.

No attempt is made to supply textbooks used in the area schools but a book is not necessarily excluded because it is a textbook.

Every library on a limited budget must of necessity employ a policy of selectivity in acquisition. Books may be limited on the basis of cost, demand and availability in other libraries. Books written in a sensational, inflammatory manner or tending to stir class or race hatred, and those offensive to good taste or contrary to moral or ethical standards, call for positive exclusion. However, honest works which present an honest picture of a problem or side of life are not necessarily excluded because of coarse language or frankness in certain passages.

Books recognized as classics are purchased.

The library does not attempt to promote any beliefs or points of view but recognizes its responsibility to provide materials presenting all points of view on public questions insofar as possible. This is based on the belief that people have the right and the duty to make their own decisions on vital questions of the day.

Kingsport Public Library, Kingsport, TN 37660

Materials chosen by these principles shall not be prescribed or removed from the shelves because of partisan or doctrinal disapproval by groups or individuals.

The public library serves many and varied groups of people. It cannot, to satisfy any one group, sacrifice the interests of others.

The importance of the novel as a medium for recording and molding public opinion and changing attitudes is recognized. The sound treatment of significant social and personal problems or of racial and religious questions through novels can contribute much to the betterment of human relations. Therefore, novels of serious purpose are purchased in preference to many titles of light fiction and adventure. Due attention is paid to maintaining a basic collection in attractive editions of standard novels, the classics and semiclassics of world literature and the works of great novelists of the past. Since an attempt is made to satisfy a public varying greatly in educational and social background and taste, competent, pleasing and successful novels in varied categories are also chosen.

Although no single standard of literary quality can be set up, it may be said that the library's policy is to acquire fiction which is written and based on authentic human experience and to exclude the weak, the cheap and sentimental writing as well as the intentionally sensational, morbid or erotic.

High standards of print, binding and format are regarded in all selections. However, selection should not be limited by format when usefulness is the deciding factor.

The purchase of duplicates is governed by demand.

Standard library aids are employed in the selection of all materials.

In order to keep the collection up-to-date a continuous process of "weeding" is carried out.

The major objective in library work with young people is to contribute to the development of well-rounded citizens of their own country and world. Therefore, it is the function of the library to introduce them to the resources of the entire library; to stimulate reading interest through trained guidance; to bridge the gap between the children's room and the adult department as well as between the school and the public library.

To this end adult titles are selected that are keyed to young people's needs and interests as well as books that will tend to open up new interests in cultural, economic and social fields. Titles written specifically for young people are included in the collection as well as those written specifically for children. Variations in background and reading ability are kept in mind, but purchases are made with the thought of directing their reading toward adult fields.

In providing materials for children it is the library's objective to guide their love of reading toward the enjoyment and appreciation of good books which in turn may help them to broaden their horizons and develop as individuals. In selecting books for children the library tries to anticipate and meet diverse skills and interests of readers of all ages from the beginner to the child ready for adult books, keeping in mind the wide variety of reading levels.

Format and version of text of standard and classic titles determine choice of edition when several exist, rather than price alone. A well-printed cheap edition with text close to the original is preferred to an expensive "deluxe" edition with inferior translation. Duplication of desirable titles is emphasized, rather than the addition of mediocre titles for the sake of something new.

Critical and appreciative discussions of children's literature for adults in helping guide a child toward the enjoyment of reading are provided.

San Diego Public Library

GENERAL POLICIES

It is the aim and responsibility of the public library to provide circulation and reference materials to meet the needs of citizens of all ages. Within the limitations of budget, space and availability of material, the library attempts to meet and anticipate the community's demands. Major emphases are placed on the promotion of knowledge, cultural and intercultural understanding and an informed citizenry. At the same time book selection must help to dissolve ignorance, intolerance and indifference.

Representative materials are selected and maintained for general information, education, occupational and industrial uses, and the enjoyment and enrichment of leisure time.

Initial responsibility for the selection of materials rests with the supervisors of the Central Library Sections who specialize in their assigned fields. Judgments of professional librarians plus the evaluations of qualified book reviewers in national magazines provide a balance of opinion and a basis for selection.

Final decision is based on the value of the material to the library and its public, regardless of the personal disposition of the librarians involved.

Books selected may include works of a recognized mentor within the limits of his specific field regardless of his moral or political reputation; works of current or potential historic significance regardless of political or social variance; books in fields that represent a principle or idea which has not been completely authenticated; certain books whose language or content might be restricted to mature readers. Whenever possible, both sides of a question are represented.

The library believes that though anyone may reject for himself books which he finds distasteful, he cannot exercise this right of censorship to restrict another citizen's choice in reading matter.

Fiction Book Selection with Use of City Funds

A good novel can inspire, contribute to understanding and provide pleasure or distraction. The broad range of fiction poses a special problem in book selection, and a serious attempt is made to supply titles representing the entire spectrum.

Using book reviews, pertinent bibliographical publications and the judgment of the librarians who read the material, titles are recommended for inclusion on the basis of content, style, intended audience, and whether the author successfully achieved his objective in his presentation.

Classics—titles having enduring interest and appeal, and judged to be great literary works—form an essential part of any fiction collection. These extend beyond works from American and British literature to translations of classics from worldwide cultures.

Good historical and regional fiction accurately and vividly evokes the period or place it depicts. The quality of material in this area varies considerably, and emphasis is placed on selecting the best available, keeping in mind the range of reading interest and reading skill of our readers. The same criteria are applied to western fiction.

Classical mystery and suspense fiction is supplemented by modern detectives, mysteries and espionage novels. Guidelines from studies of the subject are used in the selection of science fiction, with increasing attention being given to paperbacks, in which form more and more original titles are being published.

Psychological, experimental and general contemporary fiction is selected by the same standards as other fiction as far as possible. Books are judged on total effect rather than specific words, passages or scenes which in themselves are offensive. Whether the sensational is used to insure commercial success or is an honest and sincere portrayal of a view of life is one of the judgments to be made. Best sellers are evaluated on their individual merits following selection policies outlined.

After all these considerations, it is realistic to note that when a book, however disturbing, is written by a recognized author, published by a reputable publisher, and reviewed favorably and widely in national and international journals by competent reviewers, this library will not set itself up as censor by invoking single items of its book selection policy to keep this work out of the collection.

The above statements were adopted as Board of Library Commissioners policy by action of the Commission at its regular meeting of October 9, 1974.

Juvenile Book Selection with Use of City Funds

The aim of service to children in the public library is to provide books and materials to meet the diverse reading interests and needs of the child from infancy into junior high school. Books are chosen, and individually reviewed, to assure a well-rounded collection of good quality. The General Book Selection with Use of City Funds holds true for much of library service to children, with the following specialized aspects:

1. *Textbooks.* The library generally does not purchase materials ordinarily supplied by schools. The exception is in areas where material is only available in text form (currently, books on mathematics, grammar, handwriting).

2. *Series.* Books in series are considered on an individual basis, and are accepted or rejected accordingly.
3. *Abridged classics.* Abridged classics are seldom purchased, and then only those that meet the standards of good writing without weakening the original.

Children's books reflect the wide diversity of our times. Children and adults will find a great range of material, including situations, information, and problems once thought inappropriate for children. Here too the library believes that individuals may reject for themselves (or their children) books which they find distasteful, but cannot exercise the right of censorship on others.

The above statement on selection of children's books with City funds was adopted by the Board of Library Commissioners at its regular meeting of March 10, 1976.

GIFT BOOKS

Guidelines

This statement of policy was approved by the Board of Library Commissioners in November 1954.

It is the policy of the San Diego Public Library to encourage gifts of books, or gifts of money for the purchase of books, which will increase the value of its collections. Book funds have not kept pace with San Diego's tremendous growth, and it is recognized that sufficient city funds cannot be secured to bring library collections up to our community's needs. Financial gifts and gifts of private libraries are therefore needed and welcomed.

The library accepts gift books with the understanding that books which are useful to library collections will be retained, and other books disposed of in whatever manner the library deems best—by giving them to other libraries or other institutions, by exchanging them for other books of equal value which the library needs, or by selling them. It is important that donors understand this policy.

The library is inclined to discourage gifts with strings, since these often are so restrictive that they make it difficult for the library to reorganize its collections and services with changing times and changing needs, in order to make them as useful as possible to readers. However if a collection is of sufficient value, the library will promise to make it "Reference," thereby restricting its use to library reading rooms and not permitting borrowing for home reading.

The library cannot promise to keep any collection or group of books on a special shelf segregated from all other books in the library. The library necessarily reserves the right to interfile gifts with other collections on the same subject, so that all collections are organized and classified according to library standards for the best public service.

Individual volumes will be marked with bookplates identifying the donor and the collection. If a collection is of sufficient size and value, special distinctive bookplates will be printed.

The library cannot accept any gifts which the donor specifies must be kept in a particular room. The library necessarily reserves the right to place such books where they belong in relation to other books in the collection. Obviously books of reference value in the field of Californiana will probably be placed in the California Room, books on genealogy in the Genealogy Room. However, even in these fields duplicates might be shelved in the storage area or very rare volumes in the vault.

Due to the limited size of the Wangenheim Room and the fact that the donors of this fine literary and historical collection tied no strings whatever to their gift, but left it entirely to the discretion of the librarian to add to the collection or to withdraw books from it, no other gifts may be made to the room which are less liberal in their terms. Books which in the opinion of the librarian are in keeping with the general character and purpose of the room may be added, but no guarantee will be made to the donor that these books may not later be shifted to some other part of the library in order to better serve the public.

The Board of Library Commissioners, at its regular meeting of March 10, 1976, recommended the following policy on gift books to the City Manager and the recommendation was accepted and will be part of the library policy as it pertains to gift books:

From donated books, the Library will select for public use those which have general information interest, or which have educational value or which have leisure time enjoyment which are in reasonably good condition and which promise good circulation.

The statement was in response to citizen desire to have certain series of adult and children's books accepted as gifts only. Examples of the adult series are:

- Harlequin Romances and varieties of Harlequin editions such as Mills and Boon;
- Laser Books, Candlelight Books, Fawcett Crest, Signet Romances, Ace Gothics.

Examples of children's series are:

- Books issued by the Stratemeyer syndicate with publication dates of 1959 and later. Series titles are: Nancy Drew mysteries, Dana Girls mysteries, Bobbsey Twins, Hardy Boys, Tom Swift, Jr.;
- Series similar to the above: Cherry Ames Nurse stories, Happy Hollisters.

Books received by agencies and which are not in the series mentioned above or which are not part of series but which may be of similar quality to those mentioned are to be sent to the Principal Librarian of the appropriate Division for review. Those acceptable will be returned to the concerned agency for addition to the gift book collection. Your cooperation in notifying the Principal Librarians of new individual titles or series available will be appreciated.

Paperback gifts and hardbound issues of the series mentioned as well as others not meeting selection standards for purchased books will be processed for circulation by the receiving agency and will not be cataloged. No reserve requests will be taken or honored and there will be no interagency or interlibrary loan requests taken for these books. Donor acknowledgment will be made for these books as with other gifts. None of the above series are to be purchased from City funds. Books that are purchased and gift books meeting purchased book selection criteria are to receive priority for shelving space. It is not intended to replace books selected under purchase standards with the gift books in series mentioned above.

All other gifts which are selected on the basis of standards used for City funds purchase which are normally cataloged will continue to be cataloged.

Appraisals

1. The appraising of a gift to a library for tax purposes is the privilege of the donor. The library may make arrangements for and suggestions concerning appraisals.
2. The library should at all times protect the interests of its donors as best it can and should suggest the desirability of appraisals whenever such a suggestion would be in order.
3. To protect both its donors and itself, the library, as an interested party, should not appraise gifts made to it, except in those cases where only items of comparatively low monetary value are involved.
4. The acceptance of a gift which has been appraised by a third—and disinterested—party does not in any way imply an endorsement of the appraisal by the library.
5. The cost of the appraisal would ordinarily be borne by the donor.
6. The library should not appraise items for a private owner. It should limit its assistance to referring him to such sources as auction records and dealers' catalogues and to suggesting the names of appropriate commercial experts who might be consulted.
7. A librarian, if conscious that his or her competence as an expert may have to be proven in court, may properly act as an independent appraiser of library materials. The librarian should not in any way suggest that such an appraisal is endorsed by the library (such as by use of the library's letterhead).

Pikes Peak Regional Library District

SELECTION AS A MEANS OF CARRYING OUT LIBRARY OBJECTIVES

Formulation of book selection policies necessarily begins with the examination of the community, of the organization and the existing collections of the library system, and of the services which the library is expected to perform. Flexibility and constant awareness of the changing needs of the many different kinds of people the library serves are essential in book selection. The book selection policy is intended to implement the general objectives of a public library. The purpose of the selection process is to obtain expertly selected books and other materials to further the library program of giving information, reference assistance, and help to those engaged in educational pursuits, as well as to provide general reading.

CONSULTANTS

The library often uses the services of consultants and outside experts to aid in the evaluation of new books or books to be withdrawn. These consultants may serve as individuals or committees.

CRITERIA FOR BOOK SELECTION

In general the library's policy is to purchase the books which best satisfy the clientele of the library within budget limitations. The established criteria for all fields are:

1. Permanent or timely value;
2. Accurate information;
3. Authoritativeness;
4. Clear presentation and readability;
5. Social significance;
6. Presentation of both sides of controversial issues;
7. Balancing of special group interests with general demand;
8. Inclusion of books of doubtful value occasionally for their timeliness. These are discarded when they have served their purpose.

Pikes Peak Regional Library District, Colorado Springs, CO 80901

Also considered in purchase: (a) author's reputation and significance as a writer; (b) importance of subject matter to the collection; (c) scarcity of material on the subject; (d) appearance of title in special bibliographies or indexes; (e) reputation and standing of publisher; (f) price; (g) availability of material elsewhere in area.

GIFTS TO THE LIBRARY

The criteria for book selection will also apply in the acceptance of gifts and donations of books and materials to the library. The library is grateful for gifts. However, in accepting a gift the library reserves the privilege of deciding whether it should be added to its collection, and in most instances of deciding where the book will be added. A book may be: (1) a duplicate of an item of which the library already has a sufficient number; (2) out-dated—interesting but not of sufficient present reference or circulating value to the library, which must scrutinize every book with the idea of shelf space and processing costs in mind; (3) in poor physical condition.

The library makes every effort to dispose of all gift material which it cannot use to the very best advantage. If at all suitable, it is offered to other libraries or institutions as a gift or exchange. Books not so disposed of may be sold and the money used to buy new books. Once a gift is accepted by the library, it is clearly understood that it becomes the property of the library, to be used or disposed of in strict accordance with the policies of the Board of Trustees.

SELECTION BY TYPE OF MATERIAL

Adult Book Selection

Points considered in adult book selection are literary, educational, informational and recreational value; authority; effectiveness of presentation; qualities conducive to critical thought and understanding; and available funds. Titles are selected on the basis of the content of the book without regard to the personal history of the author.

Book Selection for Children

The basic policy of book selection for children is to buy the best new books and to replace and duplicate older titles which have proved their value. Selection covers all fields—books for recreational reading; inspirational books of lasting value; books of information covering a wide range of knowledge which will satisfy the child's natural curiosity and widen his interests. Titles are selected on the basis of the content of the book without regard to the personal history of the author.

Textbooks

The library does not purchase textbooks per se. The library purchases textbooks only if the book is of value because of its content, its need in the book collection and the permanent demand by the general public. The library is not responsible for buying a volume purely because it is a textbook for a class offered in the community.

Book Selection for School Services

The public library's books are selected to provide educational and informational services to the total community. The library cannot accept the responsibility of duplicating the same book in sufficient quantity to serve a total class. Rather, the library will try to fill these requests through the use of the resources on hand. Likewise, the library assumes no responsibility to provide the same information in different forms—books, periodicals, newspapers (clippings), encyclopedias. The cooperation of the local schools in student-teacher-library relations is earnestly sought.

Newspapers

The library purchases the following types of newspapers:

1. Significant local newspapers;
2. Representative newspapers from major centers in the U.S. This group is determined by such criteria as:

   • The reference value of the newspapers;
   • The reflection of regional opinion on local and national issues;
   • The stature of the newspaper in the national scene.

Periodicals

In general the selection policies for periodicals parallel those for books. The purpose of the selection process is to obtain periodicals which are important to the accomplishment of reference and research work in the various subject areas, as well as to provide general and popular reading. An attempt is made to subscribe only to periodicals indexed in the major subject periodical indexes.

Pamphlets

Pamphlet material consists of inexpensive, ephemeral and timely publications. These are simply processed and used to supplement the regular book collections. Pamphlets should be periodically re-evaluated and weeded. Selection is made by the Head of User Services or someone designated by the Head of User Services. Selection is based on the need for subject matter, the authority of the author or publisher, the timeliness of material, and the presentation of representative points of view or levels of interest often not published in book form.

Periodicals System

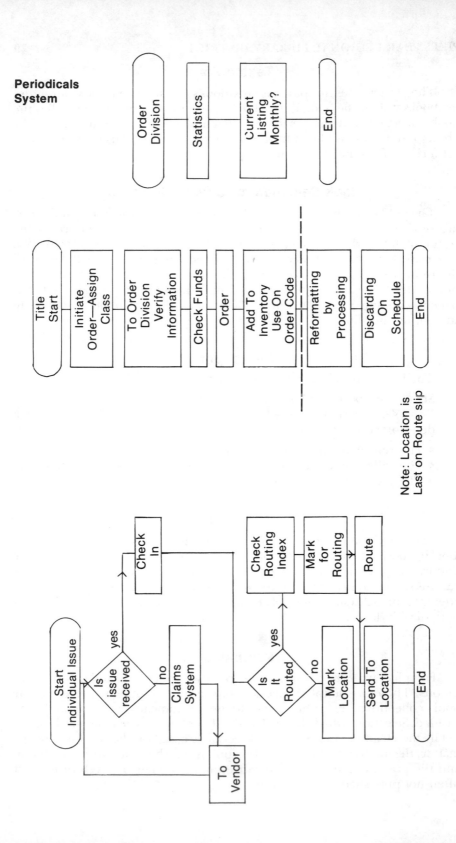

Note: Location is Last on Route slip

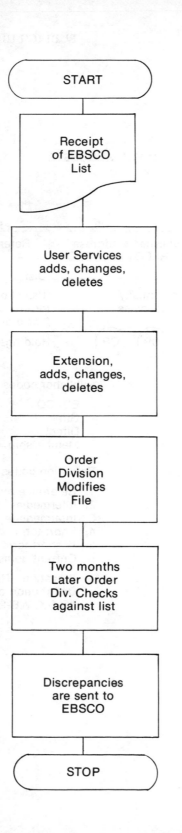

**Periodicals System
Annual Evaluation**

START

Receipt
of EBSCO
List

User Services
adds, changes,
deletes

Extension,
adds, changes,
deletes

Order
Division
Modifies
File

New orders are
added with anticipated
receipt date

Two months
Later Order
Div. Checks
against list

Discrepancies
are sent to
EBSCO

STOP

FORM FOR REQUESTS

_____ — _____   _____ Ret. x _____

       Title   Publisher & address   Retention code
                        for EBSCO put EBSCO

[_____]   /_____ /   (Dist_____ ( )_____)

Frequency   cost annually   (Use status codes
last issue rec.   not otherwise   for inventory
                                                      2 or more indicate.)

//_____//   (CR) (CR)   Holdings

      Extended cost

Periodical frequency code   Publisher codes

    AN = annually   EBSCO   = E
    BM = bimonthly   Gift   = G
    BW = biweekly   Direct   = D
    DA = daily   Membership = M
    DS = daily and Sunday
    IR = irregular   Retention codes
    MO = monthly
    QR = quarterly   1. Reference and research
    SA = semi-annually   2. Intermediate term
    SM = semi-monthly   3. Intermediate–short term
    SU = Sunday   4. Short term
    SW = semi-weekly   5. ½ short term
    TQ = tri-quarterly   6. Current items only
    WK = weekly
                                     (Location—Retention code—
Origin—EBSCO's code   Distribution code)
                                     (IS-1-X, WB-2-0)

SPECIAL PROBLEMS IN SELECTION

Controversial Items

The library asserts its right and duty to keep on its shelves a representative selection of books on all subjects of interest to its readers and not prohibited by law, including books on all sides of controversial questions. Books on any subject, if published by reputable and well-known publishers and sold without restriction in bookstores, are properly admitted to the library. The library has no right to emphasize one subject at the expense of another, or one side of a subject without regard to the other side. It must carry the important books on all sides and all subjects.

Labeling

The library will not indicate, through the use of labels or other devices, particular philosophies outlined in a book. To do so is to establish in a reader's mind a judgment before the reader has had the opportunity to examine the book personally.

Complaints of Patrons and Staff

Patrons and members of the library staff are free to suggest that certain materials be discarded. Forms are available from the User Services Librarian for this purpose. In cases where the patron or staff member feels materials are objectionable and should be discarded, a committee consisting of two library staff members, one board member, and two members of the Friends of the Library will read the book and make the decision. This will also be done if a patron or staff member thinks a book should be restricted. The complaining party will be notified of the decision.

Fiction

Fiction will be considered for purchase according to the same criteria as other library materials.

Religion

In the field of religion, the library's selection must be broad and tolerant. The selection of materials in this field must be consistently directed toward the choice of the best as regards authority, timeliness, and good literary quality. An impartial recognition of all religions, with an equal emphasis on all, is the selection goal.

Abridged Editions

The library does not purchase abridged editions of materials which are best read in their entirety. Books which are abridgments of scholarly works published by the author for popular consumption are purchased.

Book Selection Committee

The Book Selection Committee meets once a week. The Materials Selection Officer serves as chairman of the Committee. The Committee consists of:

1. Materials Selection Officer;
2. Head of User Services Department;
3. Head of Extension Department;
4. Heads of User Services Divisions;
5. Systems Librarian, ex-officio;
6. Others interested.

Duplication by Age Level

It is expected that duplication will occur in the public areas which provide service to the various age levels. Duplication of the same title between the Children's Library and the Adult Departments is permissible although kept to a minimum.

McNaughton Plan Books

The library strives to make available currently popular adult fiction and non-fiction as rapidly as possible. This is done by the rental of books from the McNaughton Company. These collections are supplemented monthly with newly published materials. As demand for the title decreases, the books are returned to the company. Bookmobiles and Branches, as well as Main, have McNaughton collections.

Book Disposal

Weeding the book collection and selection of books for discard is the responsibility of the Director, who may delegate responsibility to the Department Heads or Materials Selection Officer, and is determined on the basis of obsolete content or such poor physical condition of books that repair or rebinding is not feasible. Discarded books will not be given or sold to the public except in the case of a general book sale.

Binding and Repair of Books and Serials

It is the responsibility of departments to determine which books or serials are to be retained or discarded. Binding files and a record of all books at the bindery are kept by the Auxiliary Services.

Annual Budgets

Annually, the Director will establish budgets and objectives for the purchase of books, records and other materials.

SELECTION SYSTEM

This system documentation is designed to define processes, decision points, and responsibilities for the Materials Selection System.
It consists of:

1. System goals;
2. Keys to the system;
3. A flow chart of the process;
4. Samples of forms involved.

Goals

The system is initiated when a staff member or patron marks an order form or fills out an order request. For single orders, form on page 37 should be completed. It is acceptable to use publisher's lists, etc., when complete information is available. This information should include author, title, edition, publisher, publication date, list price, and if possible ISBN. The order should also show the division that the order originated in and shelf code. Special notes should be added.

The system terminates when an order is initiated.

The goals for the system are:

- Accountability related to division, department and library goals and objectives.
- Fiscal accountability.
- The direct responsibility for initiating requests to rest with departments and divisions.
- Greater involvement by Resource Specialists in the selection of materials and their shelf codes.
- Greater awareness for the Resource Specialists of materials available for selection and in the collection.
- For the materials selection process to follow the operating chain of command.

Keys

There are several keys which everyone must be cognizant of for the system to be effective.

The responsibility for initiating requests for the collection rests with the staff of the departments and divisions. If you do not request books they will not magically appear. The Materials Selection Officer will assume responsibility in specified assignments.

Requests for orders cannot stay on a desk for more than 24 hours. If a supervisor is absent the requests should go through unless other arrangements are made.

The process of approval of requests is to provide coordination rather than inhibiting orders.

Added orders must be marked as such. If a title is in the order file or in process file and the request is not marked "added order," they will be returned. If they are in the catalog they should be marked "added copies." If they are replacements they should be marked "replacements."

This system applies to all materials selected.

All persons involved should be aware of the objectives and policies of the system.

All decisions may have been made at the time the book is ordered. If so they should appear on the form. Initial location covers assignments to extension but are not a part of the call number.

Types are defined as:

Collection. Materials added to the permanent collection with an estimated useful life of over two years. They must be fully cataloged and permanently bound.

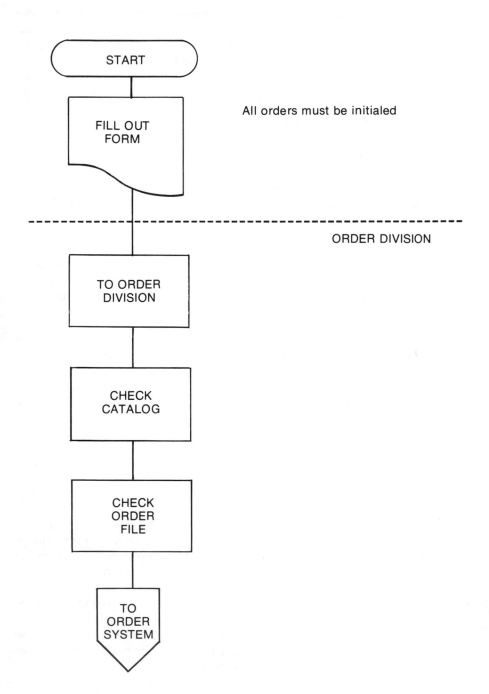

FORM

Request for order form.

*_____ / _____

            title   last name, first name, initial
                                             Author 1

/_____ — _____

      last name, first name, middle initial   publisher
                   Author 2

_____ (_____)   order: vendor

     date of publication   notes or series

_____, #ISBN   ?_____ ;_____

     list price   comments   dept., div., or program

=_____

   no. of copies

Source of review _____

_____

On back–

Possible comments

PR XXXXX   = Patron request (and patron's number, if patron wants to see after) receipt
SR XXXX   = Staff request and number
ME (name)   = Memorial book, name of donor
TE (vendor)   = Test by vendor
SO (vendor)   = Standing order by vendor
AC   = Added copy
AO   = Added order
RP   = Replacement (include number of book being replaced)

Popular materials.   Materials added to the collection with an estimated useful life of less than two years or immediate demand dictates an urgency to provide it. These items will not be fully cataloged and will receive no additional binding. These items may be transferred to Collection if appropriate to service needs.

The goals for the Popular Materials System are:

1. To provide an area where patrons may browse among new books.
2. To allow inclusion of materials for patron use which do not justify the cost of full processing.
3. To provide the mechanics for rapid processing of items which are in immediate demand.

The flow of the system is:

**Popular Materials
System**

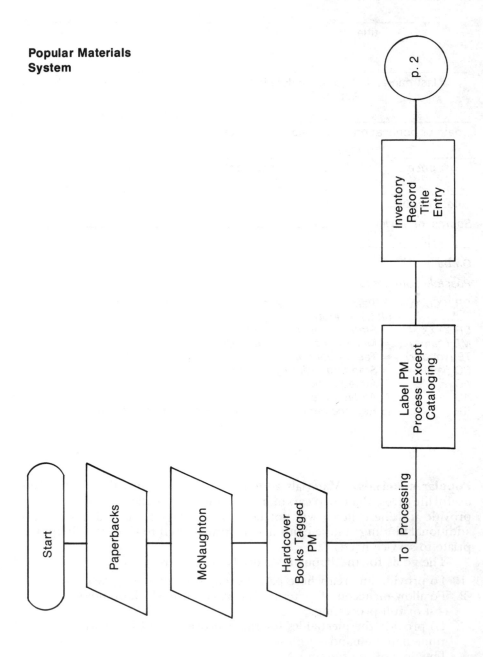

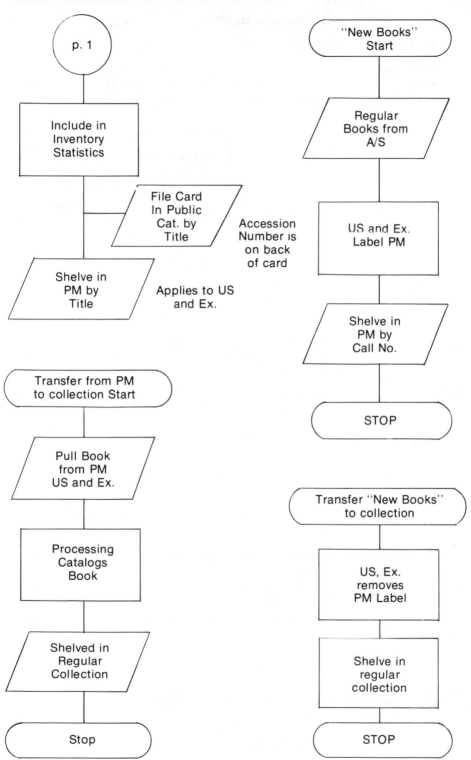

Selection—System

How materials arrive (channels):

- Preview;
- Gifts;
- Approval;

- Standing order (title);
- Standing order (publisher or vendor);
- Ordered (monograph, periodical).

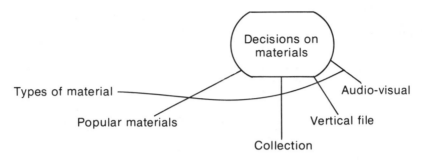

Definitions

Preview—unsolicited items which show up.
        Decision: 1. To keep;
                     2. Whether to get more copies;
                     3. Type of material;
                     4. Initial location.

Gifts—books donated to the library.
        Decision: 1. To keep;
                     2. Type;
                     3. Need for additional copies;
                     4. Initial location.

Approval—books sent by vendors to see if we want them.
        Decision: 1. To keep;
                     2. Type;
                     3. Need for additional copies;
                     4. Initial location.

Standing order (title)—books ordered on an annual basis.
        Decision: 1. Type;
                     2. Need for additional copies;
                     3. Initial location.

Standing order (publisher or vendor)—books ordered by category or publisher rather than by title.
        Decision: 1. Type;
                     2. Need for additional copies;
                     3. Initial location.

Ordered—books for which an order has been placed.
        Decision: 1. Type;
                     2. Need for additional copies;
                     3. Initial location.

Vertical file. Materials of an ephemeral nature which are checked in and sent to the department or division with no processing.

Audio-visual. Nonbook materials which are handled according to procedures established for each format.

Fall through routes. If not directed otherwise by the staff, the materials will follow these routes.

Previews. End up in the book sale unless otherwise directed.

Gifts. End up in the book sale unless otherwise directed.

Approval. Will be returned to the vendor unless otherwise directed.

Standing order (title). Will end up in Information Services circulating collection unless otherwise directed.

Standing order (publisher). Will end up in Information Services circulating collection unless otherwise directed.

There are two exceptions by format.

Paperbacks. Will end up in popular materials unless otherwise directed.

Pamphlets. Will end up in Information Services vertical file unless otherwise directed.

Materials defined as "collection" type may be further subdivided by shelf code. Refer to shelf code codification.

Evanston Public Library

POLICY STATEMENT ON THE SELECTION OF MATERIALS

Ideas are among mankind's most powerful forces and cherished heritages. Access to these ideas is essential to citizens concerned with their life, community and world. The Evanston Public Library Board of Directors subscribes to the basic belief that it is the role of the public library to provide full access to ideas, and establishes the following precepts for the selection and retention of materials for the library.

As the community source of information and recreation open to all, the Evanston Public Library collects and distributes printed and audio-visual materials which educate, enrich, entertain, and inform. It is the responsibility of the Evanston Public Library to provide, within its financial ability, a general collection of reliable materials which embrace broad areas of knowledge and interest—including both basic works of permanent value and timely materials on current issues. The selection of library resources is a prime activity within the library and is based on the needs and requests of patrons of all ages, races, and creeds, and of organizations with a wide variety of interests.

Four factors govern the selection of materials for the library:

1. Adherence to the *Library Bill of Rights* (American Library Association, 1961).
2. The needs of the individual and the community—those which are expressed and those which are basic and universal whether expressed or not.
3. The individual merit of each work.
4. The library: its existing collection, budget and services.

A singular obligation of the public library is to reflect within its collection differing points of view on controversial or debatable subjects. Materials will be judged on the basis of the content and style of the work as a whole, not by selected or random passages.

Initial decisions on the library materials to be selected for the library rest with the department heads in conference with the Acquisitions Librarian. The ultimate responsibility, however, for the selection of material, as for all library activities, rests with the Library Director, who operates within the framework of policies determined by the Library Board of Directors.

FACTORS AFFECTING MATERIALS SELECTION

The Community

Evanston is predominantly a city of homes, bounded on the south by the city of Chicago, on the west by the village of Skokie, on the north by the village of Wilmette, and on the east by Lake Michigan. Because it has no room for expansion except by the construction of more high-rise apartment buildings, its population is fairly stable in numbers. The population has increased from 79,283 to 80,010 in 1970.

This is also a city of schools, with its high school rated among the top ten in the nation in a recent survey (*Ladies Home Journal,* May 1968, p. 66), a junior college, a college of education, and a major university. As a result, many educators are numbered among its population. 27.2 per cent of its population are college graduates and 23.7 per cent work in professional fields.

Only 24.7 per cent of its inhabitants are under the age of 18, so it is predominantly a community of older people. The several fine retirement homes in the city house many senior citizens here. Another large segment of the population is black, numbering 10,688 out of the 1967 population figure 79,500. The 1970 elementary school enrollment figures show the black enrollment at 25% of the total. Evanston is a middle-class community, with incomes in a lower bracket than those of its neighboring suburbs. The median 1968 income is $12,200 as compared with a median of $17,900 for the entire North Shore. Evanston has the following institutions with libraries, most of which will give some service to Evanstonians or will cooperate with the Evanston Public Library: Evanston Historical Society, Northwestern University, National College of Education, Seabury Western Theological Seminary, Kendall College, Garrett Biblical Institute, and Woman's Christian Temperance Union.

The Library Structure

The Evanston Public Library serves both adults and children from the Main Library, branch libraries and a bookmobile, and cooperates with both public and parochial schools in service to children. The Main Library's public service units are the reference department, the art and music department, the film service, the children's room, and the reader's service and circulation department.

Development of the North Suburban Library System

Attached to this policy statement is the "Statement of Policy for the Selection of Library Materials," North Suburban Library System (Appendix II). The System, in providing support to the libraries in the area, will not replace the role or responsibility of the Evanston Public Library in serving its own clientele. The system will, however, assure the residents of Evanston that the majority of those titles beyond the scope or capability of the Evanston Public Library will be made available through a System service.

RESPONSIBILITIES FOR MATERIALS SELECTION

The Library Director

The ultimate responsibility for the selection of library materials, as for all library activities, rests with the Library Director, who operates within the framework of policies determined by the Library Board of Directors. This responsibility is shared in its execution by the various department heads of the library and members of the staff. The Library Director should be able to answer to the Board and the public for actual selections made by the staff and, therefore, has the right to reject or recommend any book contrary to the recommendations of the staff.

Department Heads

Recommendations of library materials to be selected for the reference department, the art and music department, the film and the adult services department are made by the department heads in the light of available budgets, within the framework of this materials selection policy, to the Acquisitions Librarian.

Branch Librarians and Bookmobile Librarian

The Branch Librarians are responsible for the selection, maintenance and weeding of the branch collections under the general supervision of the Adult Services Coordinator and the Children's Librarian. They recommend books for consideration and forward patrons' requests for book purchases to the Acquisitions Librarian.

Librarian in Charge of Children's Service

The Children's Librarian selects all the juvenile material for the main children's room collection and for the branches and bookmobile. The children's collection at each of these agencies is selected, maintained and weeded by the Children's Librarian with the assistance of the Branch Librarians.

Acquisitions Librarian

The Acquisitions Librarian selects adult books for purchase; selects from the gift books to be added; coordinates the selection which is done within the respective budgets by the heads of various departments; reconciles all these selections with the books received from the Booklist; and supervises the technical process involved in acquiring books and recordings.

SELECTION OF MATERIALS

Criteria of Evaluation

Involved in the choice of materials are the experience and knowledge of those selecting books and audio-visual materials, their knowledge of the community (its needs, demands and other library resources), the existing collection and the library budget. The overall value of the material is the chief criterion of selection. Material is judged on the basis of the work as a whole, not by a part taken out of context. No criteria are absolute or completely satisfactory and rarely will one think of specific principles during the actual procedure of selecting books.

READERS TO BE SERVED

Materials are purchased to meet the objectives of good library service to the whole spectrum of the community's population, adult and juvenile. Educational service to adults is a primary function. The library encourages the continuous learning process through the use of books and related materials, and provides recreational materials for leisure hours. The library recognizes the special needs of adults who are functionally illiterate or visually handicapped. School assignments for the elementary and secondary school student primarily are the responsibility of the school library. The public library will provide materials that satisfy the general informational, recreational and cultural needs of children and young adults.

GENERAL CRITERIA

1. Reputation and/or significance of the author, his skill, competence, and especially his purpose;
2. Content—its present and potential relevance to community needs, its importance as a document of the times, and its relationship to existing collections and other materials on the subject;
3. Treatment—its appropriateness and effectiveness of medium to content, its insight into human and social condition, and its suitability of subject and style for intended audience;
4. Suitability of physical form for library use;
5. Attention of critics, reviewers and the public (see Appendix I for "Aids to Selection").

SPECIFIC CRITERIA FOR EVALUATION OF WORKS OF IMAGINATION—FICTION, DRAMA, POETRY

1. Representation of important movement, genre, trend or national culture;
2. Vitality and originality;
3. Artistic presentation and experimentation;
4. Sustained interest;
5. Effective characterization;
6. Authenticity of historical or social setting.

SPECIFIC CRITERIA FOR EVALUATION OF WORKS OF INFORMATION AND OPINION

1. Authority;
2. Comprehensiveness and depth of treatment;
3. Objectivity;
4. Clarity, accuracy and logic of presentation;
5. Representation of challenging, though extreme or minority, point of view.

Application of Criteria in the Selection Process

WORKS OF IMAGINATION—FICTION, DRAMA, POETRY

Involved in the selection of imaginative literature is the existence of a variety of types, each with its own kind of excellence, and the need to satisfy readers of differing tastes, interests, purposes and reading levels. Some materials may be judged primarily in terms of artistic merit, scholarship or their value as human documents; others are selected to satisfy the recreational and entertainment needs of the community. The library has set up no arbitrary single standard of literary quality. In selecting novels and short stories its policy is to acquire fiction, whether amusing or serious, realistic or imaginative, which is well-written and based upon authentic human experience, and to exclude weak, incompetent, or sentimental writing, as well as that capitalizing on the sensationalism of the erotic, sadistic and morbid.

WORKS OF INFORMATION AND OPINION

In selecting nonfiction for general reading, readability and popular appeal, soundness of the author's attitude and approach, and quality of writing are to be considered. In the case of the more scholarly works, the library considers the lack of such material in the present collection, the authority and the reputation of the author, the inclusion of the book in indexes and bibliographies and, in some cases, the reputation of the publisher and the price. The library must balance its obligation to meet demand and to maintain tolerance with its obligation to exclude materials which are poorly prepared and are available from other sources at low cost.

There are certain categories of nonfiction material which have special implications for the Evanston Public Library. These categories and their implications follow:

Religious works.   The presence in Evanston of two seminaries with their specialized collections allows the Evanston Public Library to confine its religious selections to works of a more popular nature and in special demand by the public. However, the sacred and doctrinal works of major religions and denominations are selected together with basic concordances, commentaries, directories, dictionaries and encyclopedias. In the field of semi- or pseudoscientific and occult materials, some popular titles are provided.

Medical and health books.   The library recognizes its responsibility to supply authoritative, up-to-date, understandable material on health, hygiene, and common diseases. Medical and health books are selected with special care. In view of the increasing demands from the lay public, the library has amplified its original selection patterns to meet the needs of the many adults entering health-related occupations, and many already in them and studying for promotion. The library buys books in the areas of psychiatry, sex education, mental retardation, alcoholism, narcotics, public health, and other medical-social problems, but avoids clinical case histories and texts on diagnosis and treatment.

Foreign languages.   A limited number of books in foreign languages are bought, with the exception of French where a special fund from the French Club is available. Recent publications and some classics in the original language are provided for readers with general rather than specialized interests. Languages represented are those most popular: French, German, Spanish.

Art and music.   Books on art and music are selected on the basis of merit and appropriateness for the users of this library. All periods and phases of art and music are represented. In addition to the basic books, the collection provides specialized books and music scores which enrich the whole field of art and music. The original impetus for a separate Art and Music Department came from the memorial gift of Sadie Knowland Coe's music books and scores, with an endowment to maintain the collection, and from the gift of a book collection of the Evanston Art Center.

Science.   Science books of a general nature, aimed at informing the general reader, are collected. Books of a highly specialized nature are not purchased.

Law books.   The Evanston Public Library makes no effort to maintain a law collection. General works on the law, plus works on a specific law (i.e. Patman, Wagner) are collected but no attempt is made to collect specific law cases, state laws, or state Supreme Court cases.

Textbooks.   The library refrains from purchasing textbooks except textbooks such as principles of accounting, introductory works and annotated guides, when such books are the most reliable of the information available for the general reader.

Evanstoniana material.   Both books and ephemeral material are sought diligently for this collection, which is cataloged and shelved in closed stacks, with the location indicated on the catalog cards. Examples: Files of short-lived, defunct Evanston newspaper; *Our Indian Predecessors,* by Grover. Since the Evanston Historical Society has assembled and maintains a collection of books by Evanston authors, the library has not attempted to be inclusive in this field.

REFERENCE MATERIALS

Reference materials must be selected to satisfy the research and reference needs of adults with a variety of professions and interests, graduate and undergraduate students of local colleges and universities, and high school students. All materials must be accurate and authoritative, factual and informative. Yearbooks, business services and other serial publications are added regularly.

Books

Reference books should be evaluated by the following criteria: purpose
of the book and fulfillment of this purpose; authority (author's qualifications
and publisher's reputation); scope; timeliness; format (arrangement, indexing, organization and consistency); and suitability to the intended audience.

Pamphlets and Other Vertical File Materials

Pamphlets are selected on their value as supplementary material to the
book collection, usually on current subjects not yet published in hard-cover
format. The Vertical File includes a Travel File (current travel folders and
maps), a Play File (paper-bound copies of current New York productions,
plays to be produced in the metropolitan area, and duplicate copies of plays
in public demand), and a Modern Author's File (supplementary or current
material on modern and new authors). A separate Vertical File of reference
materials includes pamphlets particularly useful in answering reference
questions, City Council minutes, and reports and information about Evanston and Chicago government and activities. Chicago area and local newspapers are clipped for articles covering events, actions of city authorities,
and biographical information about local persons and organizations.

Periodicals

A well-balanced subject collection of periodicals is maintained as a current and in-depth supplement to the book collection. Selection is based
generally on the accessibility of a periodical's content through indexes, the
accuracy and objectivity of the editor and authors, and its contributions to
current thinking in the field covered as well as to the balanced viewpoint of
the collection. Microfilm copies of material will be purchased when this form
will serve better than the paper copy.

CHILDREN'S COLLECTION

In selecting books for children, the library's objective is to make available
a collection that satisfies the informational, recreational, and cultural reading needs and potentials of children from pre-school age to age twelve.
Books are included which meet the general demands of the majority of
children, along with books whose special qualities make them valuable to
children with special needs, talents, problems, or interests. Criteria for book
selection include literary and artistic worth, suitability of content and vocabulary to the age of the readers, and the contribution of the book to the
balance of the total collection.

Factors which determine the exclusion of certain books for children are:
1) lack of good taste or lack of sufficient literary merit; 2) inaccurate, unfair,
or unhealthy pictures of the subject; 3) insufficient need or value to the
balanced collection to justify expenditure.

Types of Literature in the Collection

Picture books.   Picture books which mainly are read aloud to pre-schoolers
and primary grade children are purchased in three categories: story books

concept books, and mood books. *Story books* should contain text with literary quality and well-executed imaginative pictures which complement the story. *Concept books* (books giving some understanding of colors, numbers, letters, etc.) should be imaginative and well-designed. *Mood books* should create a feeling for a time, place, or experience through a sensitive harmony of text and picture.

Textbooks and readers.   The library does not feel obligated to buy any of the basic texts used in the schools. Books on curriculum-related subjects are purchased when they meet the public library's criteria for book selection.

Although the library does not consider its function to advise the parent in how to assist the child in the mechanics of reading, basal readers are purchased as needed for pre-primer, first and second grades to help children in the process and practice of the reading skill.

Folk and fairy tale literature.   In the belief that this type of book frequently forms the basis of a child's literary heritage in addition to advancing an understanding of the world's people, the library considers it a responsibility to include titles which will provide as complete coverage of this area of literature as possible. Each new title in this classification is evaluated against previous titles of the same type, as well as in relation to its place in filling in gaps in the folk literature of the world. An effort is made to include a variety of editions, particularly when the compiler, translator, or illustrator is of sufficient distinction to add to the stature of the book.

Fiction.   Fiction will be selected for the pre-school to sixth grade reader. Outstanding junior high titles, some of which will be duplicated in the Young Adult collection, will be purchased sparingly. The thirteen- and fourteen-year-old junior high person can, therefore, use this specialized collection and for a broader and more sophisticated reading collection be guided to the Young Adult collection.

Classics.   Abridged adult classics are seldom purchased. Exceptions are made for those editions of titles long accepted as literary presentations, such as *Canterbury Tales, Don Quixote, Pilgrim's Progress,* or those meeting standards of good writing. Abridged versions of children's classics are not purchased. In the case of classic folk literature, editions for children are evaluated for literary merit before purchase.

Series.   Books in series are evaluated as individual titles and are added or rejected as they do or do not meet the basic quality standards for children's books.

Miscellaneous.   Books on certain aspects of guns, jujitsu, and hypnotism are not included in the children's collection, since a certain amount of maturity or adult supervision is necessary for use of such information.

Sex education.   Books on human physical development and sex are carefully selected as to accuracy, simplicity and dignity of presentation.

BRANCHES AND BOOKMOBILE

The selection of adult and children's books for the branches and the bookmobile will be governed by the characteristics of the community to be served and the goals of the particular branch. Branch collections follow the general book selection policy of the library. However, uniformity is not stressed at the expense of special community needs. Branch libraries may duplicate heavily certain titles indigenous to its area. Branch libraries contain the circulating materials adequate to supply most common needs, supplemented as necessary by more specialized materials borrowed from the main library. In branches where light fiction circulation is high, the fiction collection may be supplemented by a paperback collection. Nonfiction paperbacks are also used for specialized material where circulation will not require hard-bound volumes.

Branch collections include reference materials adequate to supply answers to the most commonly asked questions. Pamphlets are available to meet community requests.

Periodical selection, as book selection, is influenced by the character of the community served and the availability of space and funds.

Branch collections must necessarily be kept current and are weeded constantly for little used materials.

YOUNG ADULT COLLECTION

The Young Adult collection is a small, frequently changed collection of hard-cover and paperback books selected for their special interest to junior and senior high school students. The titles reflect current interests of young adults: i.e. black literature, science and space, and social problems.

All the titles selected for this collection meet the accepted standards of book selection for the library. Although some of the titles are purchased specifically for this collection, many titles are selected from the regular adult collection. A few titles are chosen for the slower reader who needs transitional books to bridge the gap between the juvenile and the adult departments.

Fiction has been purchased with several characteristics in mind. Are the characters credible? Is the dialogue stereotyped or contrived? What is the author's reputation and merit in previous works? Is the book relevant for today's youth?

AUDIO-VISUAL MATERIALS

Recordings

A balanced selection of quality recordings, including orchestral, choral, vocal, operatic, chamber and instrumental music, as well as folk music and jazz, musical comedy, prose, poetry, drama and documentary recordings, is provided. The selection of all recordings is based on the opinions of persons knowledgeable in the field or on the evaluations given by record reviewing services.

Films

The motion picture is one of the contemporary art forms and should be judged for its technique as well as its content. Film content, subject matter, and treatment are evaluated in relation to their validity, lasting value or timely importance, imagination and originality. Technical qualities connected with photography, sound track, color reproduction, or clarity of black and white prints are examined.

All films purchased for the library's collection are 16mm. Although the larger percentage of films purchased are sound, some classic comedians' silent films are included in the collection. Outstanding examples of the history and development of the motion picture, experimental techniques of film making, subjects of general adult and young adult interest, both cultural and practical, and productions which stimulate the creative imagination of children and offer them an aesthetic experience are included. Highly technical material and industrial training films for a specific technique as well as films useful primarily in the classroom are not purchased. Sponsored films which are more than advertisements of commercial products or propaganda for special interest groups are accepted. When poor condition or obsolescence indicates, films are withdrawn from the collection. Duplication of films is considered on the basis of popularity.

Slides

A collection of quality slides on many subjects is being developed. These slides, many of which have been given to the library, are selected for quality, interest and subject. A broad range of subjects which will appeal to young people and adults will be provided. If there is sufficient demand for the excellent commercial slides which are available, the library will enlarge the collection by purchasing them.

Framed Prints

Reproductions of paintings of recognized merit, suitably framed, are a part of the library collection.

Pictures

A file of pictures on all subjects is an important supplement to the library's book collection. Pictures are secured through purchase or gifts, or by clipping magazines.

GIFTS AND ENDOWMENTS

Gifts of books and other material are accepted by the library with the explicit understanding that they are not necessarily to be added to the collection, but that they may be disposed of by sale or transfer to appropriate institutions. When material of minor importance or dubious value is being considered as a gift, processing costs and shelf space are taken into account in making a decision. Selection of gift, memorial or endowment purchases involves the same search for excellence in content as applied in all areas. Special attention, however, is given to format and illustrations to enhance the significance of the presentation.

Memorial and Gift Funds

Funds for the purchase of memorial books or recordings are accepted with the responsibility for selection resting with the Acquisitions Librarian.

Attention is given to suggestions from the donor on any special field of interest that might be suitable.

Endowment Funds

Expenditures from some of the endowment funds are limited to books in the subject fields stipulated in the endowment.

Application of Criteria to Present Collection

DUPLICATION

Inherent in the selection process is the problem of evaluating demands and needs for duplication of materials. A sound, readable book in heavy demand should be duplicated if long use is anticipated. The library tries not to duplicate heavily at the expense of a first copy of important, less called-for material needed in the permanent collection.

While extensive duplication of trivial books, even those in great demand, is not considered desirable, the library gives serious consideration to multiplicity of reserves as a guide for duplication. The availability of paperbacks and leased duplicates often makes duplication possible at a nominal cost.

WEEDING

Selection of books for discarding is based on the following considerations:

1. Worn out through use;
2. Ephemeral material that is no longer timely;
3. Books no longer considered accurate or factual;
4. Combination of little use and questionable value;
5. Excess copies of a title no longer in demand.

Modification of this policy may be made if the Evanston Public Library is assigned a field of specialization as part of the cooperative effort of the North Suburban Library System. Some items which might be of value to other libraries are offered to them.

REPLACEMENT

It is the library's policy not to replace automatically all books withdrawn. Need for replacement is considered in relation to several factors: number of duplicate copies; existence of adequate coverage in the collection; and demand for specific title or subject.

Appendix I
Aids to Selection

Reputable book reviews and subject and trade bibliographies are, among other sources, tools for selection that the Evanston Public Library uses in identifying and evaluating material.

PERIODICALS

- The Booklist
- Choice
- Library Journal
- New Technical Books
- Publishers Weekly
- Saturday Review
- Chicago Sunday Tribune Book World
- Chicago Sun Times Book Week
- Chicago Daily News Panorama
- N.Y.T. Book Review
- New York Review of Books
- Science Books
- for identification: Forthcoming Books

BIBLIOGRAPHIES (a sampling)

- Public Library Catalog
- Standard Catalogs
- Reader's Adviser and Bookman's Manual
- American Historical Association's Guide to Historical Literature
- Books for College Libraries
- Catalog of Lamont Library (Harvard)
- Catalog of Julian Street Library (Princeton)

Appendix II
Statement of Policy for the Selection of Library Materials
North Suburban Library System

In the development of the collection of library materials, which is necessary to achieve the objectives stated in the Plan of Service of the North Suburban Library System, the System recognizes the following premises, has the following goal, and is guided by the following policies.

PREMISES

Library materials are defined as those materials of printed, photographic, electronic, or other form, which provide a basis for an educational or aesthetic experience, and which require the application of those techniques of acquisition, collection, preservation, and service appropriate to the public library.

In developing an acquisition program to meet the educational and aesthetic needs and interests of the constituents of the System and its members, the library materials owned by the member libraries and the library material owned by the System will be considered to constitute the total resource of the System.

In order to meet the objectives of the System, the development of the NSLS collection will be coordinated by the System staff.

The System assumes that the provision of library service adequate for the needs of today's citizens requires three levels of resource development:

1. *A basic collection at the local level.* This broad, general collection of library materials includes current popular fiction and nonfiction, basic reference material, and selected retrospective fiction and nonfiction sufficient to meet those special interests and needs demonstrated by the community. The materials should be held in sufficient subject and in sufficient quantity, including duplication of copies, to meet, in accordance with standards, the local community's requests for regularly used materials.

2. *A comprehensive supporting collection at the system level.* This collection, extensive both in quantity and in subject, complements the collections of its member libraries and includes in-depth reference materials beyond the normal scope of the basic collection at the local level. The collection is sufficiently inclusive of both book and nonbook materials so as to meet the needs of a large segment of the population and which according to standards are not the responsibility of the local library. It has materials in the latest and best editions for those with requirements for specific titles and also the major portion of authoritative materials with supporting bibliographies, periodicals and journals and other publications associated with a particular subject and which are required for independent research in that subject. The collection also contains materials of social significance that may not be held at the local level. Weeding of some obsolescent materials will take place at this level.

3. *Exhaustive collections at the state and national level.* These collections directed to a specific subject or group of related subjects endeavor so far as is reasonably possible to include everything on a subject, in all languages and in all formats. Materials at this level are expected to support historical research and provide a resource beyond the limits of the comprehensive supporting collection at the system level.

In developing the System's acquisitions program, the strength of the collections of member libraries will be ascertained, and the System will build on these strengths.

GOAL

The goal of the NSLS selection policy is to provide a broad collection of materials of contemporary significance and permanent value that will complement the collections of member libraries and will contribute to:

1. The objectives of the System as stated in the Plan of Service;
2. The advancement of knowledge;
3. The education and enlightenment of the constituents of the libraries served;
4. The availability and exchange of information;
5. The aesthetic and literary appreciation of the population served;
6. The individual objectives of the member libraries insofar as these objectives are consonant with those of the System.

POLICIES

General

Only library materials will be acquired which meet high standards of quality in content, expression, and form, or which, in special instances, are required to fulfill the goals and purposes of the System.

The selection of materials will be in accordance with the *Library Bill of Rights* and the *Freedom to Read* statement of the American Library Association.

Sponsored materials will be added only if they meet the same criteria as apply to materials purchased by the System.

The System staff will evaluate continually the needs of the System's community and will reflect this evaluation in the current selection and acquisition program.

Materials for acquisition by the System may be selected by members of the System's staff or by the System's designees.

Where it is found to be feasible and in the interest of the System, the System may contract with a member library or other institution for the selection, acquisition, and/or servicing of the System's library materials.

Books

The book collection shall be primarily adult, nonfiction material.

A special attempt shall be made to acquire books that are listed in standard library bibliographies and indexes.

Books will be purchased in single copies of a title, except in cases of proven, repeated demand, in which case duplicate copies may be purchased in an effort to provide prompt service to as many member libraries as possible.

The System may suggest that a member library acquire its own copy of an item which is repeatedly requested of the System.

Periodicals

Acquisitions will be in response to the needs of the member libraries.

Emphasis will be placed on acquisition of periodicals indexed in standard library indexes, and an attempt will be made to secure as complete holdings as appear to be useful to the fulfillment of the System's program.

Periodicals will be secured in a form that is easy to store, handle and circulate.

Insofar as periodical issues can be found in System collections and are readily available to member libraries, there will be no duplication of issues.

Other Nonbook Printed Materials

If it is necessary to provide material which has not yet been incorporated into more conventional printed sources and is in keeping with the avowed purpose of the System as a disseminator of information, such material should be added to the System collection.

Audio-Visual Materials

In keeping with the *Minimum Standards for Public Library Systems, 1966,* NSLS recognizes that audio-visual materials are an important part of the System's responsibility.

Selections of audio-visual material will follow the general policies and objectives outlined for books, with the exception that some materials will be selected to meet the demands of programming for children for public library programs.

Audio-visual materials will be selected for public library use and are not purchased for the classroom or for teacher training, which are responsibilities of the school.

In addition to the general criteria used as guides in selection of materials for the System, particular attention also will be paid to technical quality, technique, authenticity, effectiveness of presentation, and usefulness.

The content, subject matter, and treatment of films considered for purchase will be evaluated in relation to their lasting value, timeliness, imagination, and originality.

Other Sources of Information

As new forms are developed, they will be appraised by the System for possible use, and if their value appears appropriate and useful to the purposes of the System, the new forms will be incorporated in the selection activities of the System.

Gifts

Materials offered to the System as gifts must meet the System's selection standards and needs, before these materials will be added to the collection.

Gifts will be accepted with the understanding that the System has the right to dispose of the gifts in any way the System sees fit.

Withdrawal of Materials

The withdrawal of materials from the collection shall be the responsibility of the System's staff or the System's designee.

Materials will be withdrawn from the collection because of poor physical condition, obsolescence, or failure to contribute to the stated objectives of the System.

Suggestions will be welcomed from member libraries on materials that should be weeded from the collection of which they are custodians.

Discarded materials may be offered to member or other libraries, except that if the material presumably would be of use to the Illinois State Library or other research library, such material will be offered to that library before the material is discarded.

Revision

The Statement of Policy for the Selection of Library Materials for the North Suburban Library System will be under constant evaluation, and as the collection grows and situations demand, the Statement will be altered in accordance with the findings of the staff of the North Suburban Library System.

Edwin A. Bemis Public Library

COMMUNITY DESCRIPTION

The City of Littleton is a home rule city with a council-manager form of government. It is a suburban community located nine miles south of the City of Denver. Littleton is experiencing rapid growth within the city limits and in the areas adjacent to the city. It presently encompasses an area of 9.79 square miles and has an estimated population of 33,500 people.

The residents of Littleton are mostly white adults between the ages of 25 and 45. They have a median annual family income of $12,740. Only 3.2% of all families have an income below poverty level ($3,743).

Littleton's major industrial facilities fall into the light-industrial/research category. Among the most significant employers are Marathon Oil Company, Denver Research Center, Honeywell Test Instrument Division, Monaghan Division of Sandoz Wander Incorporated and the C. A. Norgren Company. Two other firms, outside of the city limits, also employ a number of Littleton residents. They are the Martin Marietta Company and the Johns Manville Company. Marathon Oil Company and the Martin Marietta Company both have well-developed special libraries with professional librarians to staff them. These facilities are available to area residents by special arrangement.

Judicial, health, welfare and educational services are provided to all areas, incorporated or unincorporated, at the county level. The Arapahoe County courthouse is a source of information concerning divorce records, deeds, recordings, and voter registration. Most records are available during business hours without prior arrangement. The courts division keeps records of judgments in civil, criminal and domestic cases. This division also has an extensive law library which is open to the public.

All of Littleton falls within Arapahoe County School District #6. 1970 census figures show that the average educational attainment for Littleton residents is 12.8 years of school. There are three high schools, four junior high schools and 17 elementary schools in the district. Each school has an instructional media center and at least one professional librarian on the staff. Curtis Media Center provides auxiliary services in the areas of technical processing and audio-visual materials.

The school district is also a member of the Southeast Metropolitan Board of Cooperative Services (SEMBCS). This board provides adult education, special education, vocational education and supplemental instructional media services to Cherry Creek, Englewood, Littleton, and Sheridan school districts.

Higher education is available through the Arapahoe Community College. The library of this facility is open for use by all residents of Arapahoe County. This institution also offers a varied adult education program.

Informal cultural and recreational opportunities are plentiful in the Littleton area. The South Suburban Metropolitan Recreation and Park District provides parks and recreation programs for the area of Arapahoe County west of Interstate Highway 25.

Centennial Race Course also offers entertainment. The Colorado Thoroughbred Breeders' Association, which has its headquarters at the race track, is a source of information concerning blood lines, racing results and course records. It also subscribes to a variety of specialized magazines. These materials are available for public use by prior arrangement.

The Littleton Area Historical Museum serves the city with collections of primary research materials, exhibits, and educational programs which focus on the Littleton area. The historical museum and Bemis library cooperate closely to provide services which complement rather than duplicate educational services.

The unincorporated area of Arapahoe County is provided with library services by the Arapahoe Regional Library District. This district contracts with the Edwin A. Bemis Public Library to provide supplemental services to county residents. In addition, wide area library service is provided by the Central Colorado Public Library System (CCPLS). This system is composed of 17 public libraries from Adams, Arapahoe, Boulder, Clear Creek, Denver, Douglas, Gilpin and Jefferson counties. Any individual who holds a valid library card from one of the member libraries can borrow from all other libraries in the system.

There are other cultural influences which exist in the Littleton area. The Littleton Fine Arts Guild is composed of a group of people dedicated to the advancement of art in the metropolitan Denver area. It sponsors regular juried shows in the library, banks, and area businesses. The most notable shows are the annual Spring Art Show and the Littleton Sidewalk Art Show.

And for those whose interest leans toward music there is the South Suburban Community Arts Symphony. It is a group of 85 players who donate their time to provide an opportunity for area residents to experience the pleasure of listening to fine music.

Littleton, then, is a distinctive community which provides many cultural, recreational and educational opportunities to its residents. This materials selection policy is designed to aid the library staff in serving such a community. As the nature of the community and the library collection change, this policy will be revised to reflect the changes.

RESPONSIBILITY FOR SELECTION

Final responsibility for selection rests with the Library Director, who operates within the framework of established policies and stated objectives.

The responsibility for the initial selection of materials is shared by each of the professional librarians on the staff, who meet for the purpose of book selection twice each month.

Suggestions from other staff members and library users are encouraged and seriously considered. In addition, at times, the library staff may consult with subject area specialists outside the institution to obtain advice about building certain technical fields.

INTELLECTUAL FREEDOM AND REQUESTS FOR RECONSIDERATION OF MATERIALS

In its selection of materials the library subscribes fully to the American Library Association's *Freedom to Read Statement,* the *Library Bill of Rights,* the *Intellectual Freedom Statement* and the *Statement on Labeling.*

All requests for reconsideration of materials will be handled in the following manner:

1. The staff member receiving the complaint will ask the patron to fill out the appropriate form.
2. When the completed form has been received, it will then be submitted to the Director.
3. The Director will ask the librarian in charge of the appropriate subject area to locate as many reviews of the title as possible.
4. The Director will also ask members of the book selection committee to review the title in question.
5. Time for discussion of the title will be scheduled on the agenda of the next book selection committee meeting.
6. After the discussion at the book selection committee meeting, the members will submit their recommendations to the Director in writing.
7. The Director will take all factors under advisement and come to a decision. This decision will be communicated to the complainant in writing.

OBJECTIVES AND GENERAL SELECTION CRITERIA

The Edwin A. Bemis Public Library seeks to select, organize, preserve, and make freely available those materials, print and nonprint, which will satisfy the informational, recreational, social and educational needs of the community which it serves.

Wherever possible, at least two favorable reviews from reputable sources will be required by the book selection committee before ordering a title. In addition, the following factors will be taken into account when selecting materials:

1. Expressed or anticipated interest in the subject within the community;
2. The contemporary significance and/or permanent value of the title to the collection;
3. The scope and depth of the existing subject collection;
4. The authority and literary standing of the author (No author's works

will be excluded from the collection solely because of her/his personal history, political affiliation, race, sex or cultural background);
5. The authority and reputation of the publisher or producer;
6. The technical excellence and durability of the format;
7. Availability of the same title or information elsewhere within the library system;
8. Appearance of the title in special bibliographies or indexes.

Selection by Clientele Served

ADULTS

Adult materials are those designed for patrons over 18 years of age or any patron with a minimum of an eighth grade reading level. The library will endeavor to provide a full range of materials for the adult user, including books, magazines, newspapers, pamphlets, records, cassettes, art and films.

SENIOR CITIZENS

Some materials which address themselves to the special needs or concerns of the citizen who is over 60 years of age will be added to the collection.

ADULT READERS OF LIMITED SKILL

To adequately serve readers whose reading and interest levels reflect less than an eighth grade reading level, high-interest, low-vocabulary materials may be added to the collection.

PHYSICALLY AND VISUALLY HANDICAPPED PATRONS

Equipment and materials specifically designed for the physically and/or visually handicapped patron will be obtained when there is a recognized demand in the community for them.

Talking books per se and Braille materials will not be selected. Patrons requesting this kind of material will be referred to the established services provided at the state level; however, a collection of large-print materials will be maintained.

CITY EMPLOYEES AND LOCAL OFFICIALS

The library will maintain a non-circulating collection of the published documents of the City of Littleton and other regional governmental organizations. Supporting documents and unpublished internal reports will be retained at the discretion of the book selection committee. Criteria to be considered for inclusion are: uniqueness, breadth of scope, and community interest in the subject matter. If additional copies of these materials are made available, they will be placed in the adult circulating collection. Requests from city employees concerning purchase of specialized materials will be considered when there is evidence of suitability for inclusion in the general collection.

YOUNG ADULTS

Young adult materials are those designated for people in the 12 to 18 year old age group. Although young adults have access to the entire library collection, special attention should be given to the selection of materials which reflect and serve the needs and interests of this large and unique segment of library patrons. Fads are a good example of an intense interest which is inherent in this group. Such interests are recognized as important and materials will be collected and purchased to satisfy these needs.

SCHOOL/PUBLIC LIBRARY RELATIONSHIPS

In recognition of the fact that school and public libraries serve many of the same patrons, the Edwin A. Bemis Public Library seeks to promote close cooperation and sharing of resources between institutions.

In general the school library should be considered as the primary resource for the student's assignments. The public library should provide materials for in-depth study, research and creative use of leisure time.

For ease in determining responsibility for selection the following definitions of terms may be used:

Textbooks. Books with basic course contents which require that the pupil read nearly all of the text. These should be provided entirely by the school.

Supplemental materials. Auxiliary reading materials designed to expand the basic course of study. These, too, should be provided by the school library.

Reference materials. General encyclopedias, almanacs, dictionaries, manuals, indexes and atlases are available in the school libraries. More specialized and technical reference materials are provided by the public library.

Materials for independent study. These materials differ from supplementary materials because they are assigned to individuals for study, book reports, and exploratory reading. Both the school and public libraries will be resources for these materials, but the school library will seek to build a collection which more accurately reflects the interests of the students and the content of the curriculum.

Books for recreational reading. This category is comprised of books which are not assigned by the school but which reflect the student's own highly individualized taste. These will be provided by the public library:

Textbooks	SCHOOL LIBRARY
Supplementary reading	
Reference reading	
Individual reading	
Research reading	
Recreational reading	PUBLIC LIBRARY

CHILDREN

There is a wide range of chronological and mental development in this age group, but the materials selected should cover the span of needs and interests from the preschool through the 12-year-old age group.

Policies by Format of Material

BOOKS

Hardbacks and paperbacks.   When there is a choice, hardback books are preferred to paperbacks. A title may be purchased in paperback. An uncataloged collection of donated paperbacks is maintained for the purpose of recreational reading. This collection is restricted to the following genres: mystery, science fiction, romance, adventure and westerns.

Textbooks are added to the collection when they are recognized as the best source of information on a subject or if they are intended to be used in the adult education program of the library.

Synopses and outlines.   Plot outlines, synopses and similar condensed materials may be purchased for reference purposes or, in certain cases, circulation.

SERIALS

Periodicals.   Periodicals are purchased or accepted as gifts for one or more of the following reasons:

1. To provide current information on topics which have not yet been covered in book form;
2. To supplement and enhance the total collection;
3. To provide an additional source of recreational reading;
4. For the use of the professional staff.

Accessibility of contents through indexes, cost of the subscription in relation to possible use, and availability of the title in nearby libraries are important special considerations in the acquisition of periodicals.

Newspapers.   To provide current news coverage, the library subscribes to a selection of the following types of newspapers:

1. Local newspapers;
2. Newspapers from other Colorado communities;
3. Newspapers from important cities in the United States;
4. Foreign newspapers, to a very limited extent.

Microfilm.   For economy of storage and for durability, microfilm will be purchased, if available, for back files of heavily used periodicals and newspapers.

PAMPHLETS

An active pamphlet file, organized by subject, is maintained to supplement the rest of the collection, particularly in areas of popular interest which are not covered extensively in books. Because this material is inexpensive or free, duplicates of useful pamphlets are often acquired at small cost. Since many pamphlets are issued for propaganda or advertising purposes, it is necessary that they be carefully examined before they are added to the collection. Advertising pamphlets which distort facts, include an excessive number of commercial messages, or contain misleading statements are not added to the collection. Propaganda pamphlets are expected to be one-sided, but those whose propagandist intent is clearly indicated by the name of the issuing agency are preferred to those whose sponsorship is not clearly identified. The aim in selection is to obtain a balance of viewpoints on controversial subjects. An attempt is made to avoid overloading the files with free publications of aggressive propaganda organizations to such an extent as to destroy the balance of viewpoint.

GOVERNMENT DOCUMENTS

The Edwin A. Bemis Public Library is a non-depository library and, therefore, selection must be made and orders placed for each government publication desired. Documents are selected according to the same general principles applied to other materials.

MAPS

The library maintains a representative collection of maps of all countries in atlas form. Free and inexpensive sheet maps, including street maps of major cities, are acquired to supplement those in books and atlases.

MANUSCRIPTS AND RARE BOOKS

No attempt will be made by this library to purchase or collect rare books, manuscripts, or archival materials. Patrons wishing to donate rare items of local interest will be referred to the Littleton Area Historical Museum. All other donations will be subject to the principles stated in the gift section policy.

SHEET MUSIC

The library does not maintain a collection of sheet music.

FILMS

Films are purchased according to the general criteria for selection, with special consideration given to technical quality. The collection is limited to Standard 8mm and Super 8mm size films in both black and white and color, silent and sound. The purpose of the library's film collection is to provide home entertainment and to illustrate the early history of film-making. The library does not buy "educational" films specifically designed for school curriculum purposes.

RECORDED SOUND

Records. The library maintains adult, young adult, and juvenile collections of musical and spoken records. The importance of the performer or composer and the quality of the recording are considered important factors in selection. Musical recordings constitute the bulk of the collection and will be selected from the classical, semiclassical, folk, musical comedy, opera and popular music fields. Several different recordings of the same work may be purchased in order to provide different interpretations.

Cassettes.   Emphasis is placed upon non-musical fields in the selection of cassette recordings. The subject matter should cover the topics of American, English and classical literature, children's literature, speeches, debates, present and past history, sociology and psychology. Musical cassettes may also be acquired when there is an expressed need for that distinct format. Cassettes will be selected using the same criteria applied to records. A non-circulating and a circulating copy will be purchased for each cassette title.

CIRCULATING ART COLLECTION

Art selected for purchase or accepted as gifts may be both framed pictures and sculpture. Both original works of art and reproductions may be chosen. Care will be used to select items of special interest to the Littleton community as well as to build and maintain a balanced collection with examples of as many periods, styles, media, and subjects as possible. The following general criteria will be taken into account in the selection of all items of this type:

1. Artistic merit of the original work of art.
2. Artistic reputation of the artist.
3. Importance of the artist historically, or in the contemporary or local scene.
4. The contribution the item will make toward a balanced collection.
5. The suitability of the item for general viewing; items obscene or pornographic in nature will be excluded.
6. The portability of the item; items of extraordinary size or weight will be excluded.

In addition to the above, the following criteria should be considered in the selection of these specific groups of art works:

Criteria for Children's Art Collection

1. A child should be able to carry her/his own selection.
2. Subjects of particular interest to children should be given priority.

Criteria for Two-Dimensional Works of Art

1. Original works of art:
   • The framing and mounting should be sturdy. Glass facing may be considered desirable when protection of the surface is warranted.
   • The medium should be durable; rough surfaces should be avoided to reduce possibility of damage due to careless handling.
2. Reproductions:
   • The quality of the reproduction should be good.
   • The frame and print should be durable; prints faced with glass or other easily broken material are not acceptable.

Criteria for Sculpture

1. The medium should be durable; the shape should not be easily distorted or broken by careless handling.
2. The shape should not be dangerous to a borrower who might handle the object carelessly; sharp edges and pointed pieces should be avoided.
3. The base or mounting should be tasteful.
4. Portability is an important consideration.

EQUIPMENT

Media equipment is purchased by the library for patron use and for library programming. Selection of media equipment is based on the following general criteria:

1. Quality of performance;
2. Ease of operation;
3. Durability and design, with emphasis on safety features;
4. Portability;
5. Ease of maintenance and repair;
6. Reputation of manufacturer;
7. Cost, in comparison with other models.

Policies by Subject of Material

ADULT FICTION

The fiction collection will include historical and regional novels, character studies, biographical novels, psychological novels, satire, fantasy, humor, romances, science fiction, mysteries, adventure stories, westerns and short stories. A basic collection of classics and semiclassics of world literature will also be maintained. Special criteria which must be considered in selection are:

- The quality of writing;
- The extent of public interest in a given title, author or genre;
- The originality of the work;
- The authenticity of the historical, regional or social setting.

Each novel will be judged on its individual merits. Ordinarily there will be no attempt at comprehensiveness in the library's holdings of an author's works. Characterization and language will be evaluated in relation to the work as a whole and will not be judged out of context. It is the library's policy to exclude fiction which is solely sensational in intent or erotic in theme.

CHILDREN'S FICTION

The standards stated in the policy for selection of adult fiction apply to the selection of children's fiction. In addition, other criteria apply:

- Life should be portrayed in a believable manner.
- Positive attitudes should be emphasized.
- Over-emphasis on violence and racial, sexual or religious prejudice is to be avoided.
- Books which fill an emotional need, or which serve as a stepping stone

to better reading, may be selected even though they may not be of the highest literary quality.

- Series titles will be purchased selectively.
- Illustrations should be clear, imaginative and artistic and should complement the text. In the case of juvenile easy titles, their purpose should be to provide enjoyment and to foster an interest in reading.

ADULT NONFICTION

Information should be accurate and clearly stated.

Currency of the information will be stressed where pertinent. Materials of historical importance to a subject field will also be selected.

The collection should include materials which reflect the fullest spectrum possible on controversial issues. Selection of a particular item does not indicate the library's endorsement of the author's point of view. Materials which appeal to sensationalism, or intend to incite hatred and intolerance, may be excluded.

CHILDREN'S NONFICTION

Illustrations, if any, should be clear and understandable and should complement the text.

REFERENCE

The reference collection is a non-circulating collection of materials designed to provide quick access to factual information within the entire range of human knowledge. The tools in the collection should supply as many reliable facts as possible with a minimum of duplication and overlap. Included in this area are dictionaries, encyclopedias, indexes, bibliographies, directories, price guides, almanacs, atlases, repair manuals and laws. As a general rule, only the latest edition of a reference tool will be shelved in the reference room. Older editions will be transferred to the circulating collection or discarded.

Titles which are not normally regarded as reference materials may be added to the reference collection when:

1. They are part of a special collection (i.e. genealogy).
2. They provide information in specific subject areas in which reference questions are received but not adequately answered in standard reference sources.
3. Cost of replacement precludes adding the title to the circulating collection.

Current catalogs from selected colleges and universities in the United States and a few foreign countries are ordered yearly for the reference collection. Special emphasis is placed upon Colorado colleges and those from surrounding states.

A collection of telephone directories is maintained in the reference room. It covers the following areas:

1. All cities in Colorado;

2. Highly populated and important cities in the United States, including most state capitals;
3. Foreign capitals to a very limited extent.

In selecting reference tools the following points deserve careful consideration:

1. The information should be clearly presented and arranged.
2. The book should have an adequate index.
3. Illustrations, charts and graphs should be easily understood and accurate.
4. The reference resources of area libraries should be considered, particularly when the title is expensive and highly specialized.

FOREIGN LANGUAGE MATERIALS

The library attempts to purchase a dictionary of each major language of the world. An effort is made to provide a sampling of standard literary works in each of the languages represented and also in English translations. The library also purchases materials necessary for self-instruction in the languages most widely studied by library patrons.

MEDICINE AND RELATED FIELDS

In the selection of books dealing with the subjects of folk medicine, health care and nutrition, special attention will be given to the author's credentials and the accuracy of information presented. Favorable evaluation by one or more reputable reviewers is also an important factor. Books purchased should be at levels suitable for laymen. Clinical texts on diagnosis or treatment will not be purchased.

NARCOTIC DRUGS

The library will provide educational materials on the physiological, sociological and psychological effects of narcotic drugs. Materials will be selected on the basis of scientific accuracy, objectivity and readability.

SEX

Adult. Every effort will be made to obtain only those materials which are balanced, authoritative and up-to-date. The object of such materials should be instruction rather than the stimulation of prurient interests. Whenever possible, materials in this area will be examined before purchase.

Children's. Books which explain the processes of human and animal reproduction and growth in a clear, informative way will be selected.

LAW

Selection in the field of law is generally limited to standard, popular works which are written for the layman. Appropriate subjects include jury duty, history of law, legal rights of citizens, and development of legal institutions. Emphasis will be placed upon law as practiced in the United States.

The library does not attempt to provide books of court cases except for a few standard collections of United States Supreme Court cases. Current editions and supplements of the *United States Code* and the *Colorado Revised Statutes* are purchased for the reference collection.

SEMI- AND PSEUDOSCIENTIFIC MATERIALS

Although all scientific theories are subject to challenge and re-examination, scientists have established standards by which to evaluate the credibility of new propositions. It is those ideas which have been affirmed by the scientific community which the library seeks to include in its collection. Because of popular interest or timeliness it is also necessary and desirable to consider the purchase of material in the borderline areas of science, medicine or social science. In these instances when the subject matter or treatment is not endorsed by reputable scientists, particular care should be taken to consider the following factors:

1. The author's reputation, academic position, and prior publications. In the case of a prominent person whose position makes her/his ideas of general interest, these factors are sometimes disregarded.
2. Unless there is a pressing need for a publication issued by a private press, only the publications of major trade publishers should be considered.
3. Particular emphasis should be placed upon locating at least one, and preferably two, favorable reviews of materials which fall into this category.

RELIGION

This collection will strive to reflect the religious interests of the community and will be aimed at popular appeal rather than scholarly or esoteric materials.

The library will attempt to choose materials which present the beliefs, religious practices, and rituals of the major world religions. The sacred writings of the major world religions such as the *Talmud,* the *Koran* and various translations of the *Bible* will be included in the collection. Materials which explain and interpret such sacred writings will also be selected.

Materials which examine a religion, practice or religious group critically may be purchased. Such materials should be factually accurate and designed to promote understanding rather than to malign or deride.

Other appropriate topics for selection include collections of prayers, lives of saints and religious leaders, guides to conduct of life, accounts of personal religious experiences, religious education, and pastoral and lay ministries.

GENEALOGY AND HERALDRY

Materials selected for the genealogy section will include general guides to genealogical research, compilations of records for general research, and other materials which have a broad reading public and long-term usefulness to the Littleton community.

Histories of specific, small geographic areas (i.e. Buck's County, Pennsylvania) and genealogies of individual families will not be collected. An exception will be made to this statement for materials which deal with Colorado state and local history.

Because of the context, arrangement, and cost of many items in this area, most of the collection will be restricted to the non-circulating collections of reference or Special Western History Collection materials.

SPECIAL WESTERN HISTORY COLLECTION (SWHC)

This non-circulating collection covers the following subject areas in depth:

1. The history, development and character of the American West—that is, the section of the United States lying west of the Mississippi River. Special emphasis will be placed upon the City of Littleton, the state of Colorado and those states contiguous to Colorado.
2. The history and culture of the Indians of the American West.

The collection should be comprised primarily of nonfiction materials. Highly specialized and ephemeral materials may be acquired. Fiction which makes a significant contribution to the study of Colorado history and culture may be selected. Materials may be acquired even if they do not meet the standards of selection in other respects; however, the library is under no obligation to add everything available on these subjects to the collection. Duplicates of SWHC materials which would complement the circulating collection will be acquired when available. Manuscripts and similar archival materials, paintings and museum objects are excluded; the collection and management of such materials is the province of the Littleton Area Historical Museum.

LOCAL AUTHORS

Materials written or produced by local authors must meet the general selection standards. None will be automatically added to the collection. Materials selected will be assigned to special collections only as their subject matter warrants.

PROFESSIONAL COLLECTION

The professional collection is a non-circulating collection of materials designed for the use of the library staff. For this reason the public will not have access to the collection through the public catalog.

The collection should cover all aspects of library science, with special emphasis on the management, policies, and practices of public libraries in the United States, especially as they relate to topics under consideration at Bemis Library. Duplicate copies of materials in this collection may be obtained for the circulating collection, when appropriate.

GUNS AND COMBAT TECHNIQUES

This section applies to materials dealing with the care, handling, repair and construction of guns and explosive devices and with combat techniques such as judo and karate. The value of these activities in recreation or self-defense should be stressed. Cautions in the use of equipment and techniques by laymen should be clearly stated in the material.

GIFTS

The library accepts gifts of materials with the understanding that only those materials which meet the selection standards applied to the purchase of all other library materials will be added to the collection. Unless the donor wishes them returned, all rejected materials will be discarded or distributed to agencies such as the county jail and hospitals.

Gift collections may be accepted only with the understanding that they may be integrated into the general collection.

Book plates will be placed in each book if requested by the donor.

The librarians are happy to provide suggestions of appropriate titles to groups or individuals who wish to donate new titles to the collection.

Gifts of art objects, paintings, etc. must be approved by the Art Selection Committee prior to acceptance by the institution.

WEEDING, BINDING, MENDING, DISCARDING, REPLACEMENT AND DUPLICATION

Weeding

Weeding is the systematic evaluation of the library's collection with an eye to the withdrawal of damaged or obsolete materials from the collection. This process is an integral part of collection development and maintenance.

In general, the same criteria apply to weeding as are used in the selection of new materials. Materials that fall into the following categories should be withdrawn:

1. Materials which contain outdated or inaccurate information;
2. Superseded editions;
3. Worn or badly marked items;
4. Duplicate copies of seldom used titles.

Binding, Mending, and Discarding of Books

Decisions must be made continuously on how to handle worn books—whether to mend, bind or withdraw them. Each decision is based on the actual condition of the book, the number of duplicate copies in the collection, the current validity of its contents, availability of the title for reorder, and the cost of mending versus the cost of replacement. In making such decisions, these guidelines should be followed:

1. Withdraw books under the guidelines outlined in the section entitled *Weeding.*
2. Assuming the title is still available, replacement is preferable to binding if costs are comparable. In cases where rebinding will not restore the

book to a condition suitable for normal use, the book should be replaced regardless of cost. Books which cannot be rebound due to overly narrow margins should also be replaced.

3. Binding is preferable to mending if a title is expected to have long-term usefulness and if an inordinate amount of mending is required.
4. Mending will be done only when need is detected early. In general, non-accessioned materials, such as pamphlets and paperbacks, which are in poor condition should be discarded.
5. In some special instances, an irreplaceable title of importance must be retained regardless of condition. Special handling will be given such a title.

Cataloged paperbound titles may be bound before circulation to withstand library use. Periodicals may be bound if the microfilm edition is not obtained or if volume of use justifies duplication. As a rule, non-circulating materials are not bound.

Mending and Withdrawal of Nonbook Materials

Damaged nonbook materials should be mended on the premises if at all possible. Materials which are beyond repair will have to be discarded. Such materials should be replaced (see the section entitled *Replacement*).

Replacement

Titles for which the last copy has been withdrawn are considered for replacement. The same criteria that apply in original selection will apply to replacement with particular attention given to the following:

1. The continued value of the particular title;
2. The demand for the specific title;
3. The extent of adequate coverage of the field in the existing collection;
4. The availability of newer or better material in the field.

Important out-of-print titles should be replaced in reprint editions, if available, or from second-hand dealers.

Duplication

Multiple copies of titles may be obtained when there is an expressed need. Duplication should be kept to a minimum but materials should be in sufficient supply to make the library a dependable source for most of the people most of the time.

Because of overlapping interests and reading abilities, titles will occasionally appear in more than one circulating collection (adult, young adult, or juvenile). Such duplication is determined by need and will be made at the discretion of the Book Selection Committee and the librarians in charge of these collections.

Duplication between circulating and non-circulating collections has been outlined elsewhere in this policy statement.

To satisfy temporary heavy demand for a particular title, paperback copies may be obtained and circulated, cataloged but unbound.

Orange County Public Library

INTRODUCTION

The Orange County Public Library serves a broad, suburban community comprised of unincorporated territory and municipalities whose residents represent all socio-economic and educational levels. The primary objective of the library is to provide and to organize significant library materials and to give skilled, personal guidance in their use toward helping people in their search for reliable information, greater understanding, and a creative pattern for living; within the context of library objectives, the County Library provides service to all individuals within its service area. Materials are selected and services are planned to satisfy residents both as individuals and as members of groups. The County Library is guided by a sense of responsibility both to the present and to the future in adding materials which will enrich the collection and maintain an overall balance.

The County Library's organization is based upon four levels of service: the Stations with small basic collections; Small Community Branches with broader basic collections; Large Community Branches with collections large enough to include some subject specialization; and Regional Branches with large, in-depth collections providing supportive assistance to the smaller branches within the region as well as direct service to the public. Additional services are given to and provided by the Santiago Library System.

The Santiago Library System is a cooperative effort in library service established through joint powers agreements. Its members are: Anaheim Public Library, Fullerton Public Library, Huntington Beach Public Library, Newport Beach Public Library, Orange County Public Library, Orange Public Library, Placentia Library District, Santa Ana Public Library, and Yorba Linda District Library. Funds of the cooperative system develop Regional Reference Centers and special services beyond the capabilities of any single member library.

MAJOR LIBRARY FUNCTIONS

To guide properly the materials selection for a library, the function of the institution itself must be defined. The major functions of the public

library are to select, to assemble, to make available, and to preserve informational, educational, and recreational books and related materials in organized collections; to provide opportunity and encouragement for children,
young people, and adults to educate themselves continuously; and to promote through stimulation and guidance an enlightened citizenship and
enriched personal life for all residing within the service area. Since the
Orange County Public Library is engaged in all of these activities in varying
degrees, each is surveyed below to show how it relates to our materials
selection.

Diffusion of Information and Preservation of Materials

In addition to an array of materials on all subjects, books for special, in-
depth reference are included in Regional Reference Collections. Bibliographic resources for businessmen and special interest groups, such as
genealogists, garden societies, etc., are included. As a county department,
the county library also has an obligation to assist other county departments
and the Reference Centers maintain an active collection of materials to aid
them. Because of our professional responsibility to be aware of new developments in the field of library service and to encourage interest in the profession, titles published in the field of library service should be purchased and
maintained in a special collection.

In recognition of its responsibility to build a California collection of
historical and local interest, the library will purchase one copy of all books
written by a local author. Additional copies purchased for the library system
will be selected on the basis of our general book selection policy. The library
also is charged with providing future generations with contemporary information. Our special concern is with Orange County information. Thus,
copies of books, documents, pamphlets, maps, etc., relating to Orange
County should be acquired.

Self-Education

In this county, there are many elementary, secondary, and higher education facilities each with its own library and, in addition, there are many
special libraries. Thus, while it has material on every subject and grade level,
the County Library makes no attempt to become curriculum oriented.
Consideration is given, however, to the needs of people engaged in self-
education programs and the County Library provides simple and introductory materials for those who wish to pursue independent study. Self-help
books on every level are provided to meet high community interest in self-
improvement; technical books, therefore, are slanted toward the general
reader rather than the specialist.

In serving as a supplementary source for student use, the County Library's function is to assist a wide variety of interests and a diversified
clientele. It does not provide multiple copies of individual books for student
assignments, nor can it extensively duplicate subject materials (either in
circulating or reference books) as a result of class assignment demands. The
County Library buys courses of study and textbooks adopted in the communities only if the subject material is not available in any other form. There are

many opportunities for residents in the County to be educated formally and there should be no need for the County Library to attempt to accept the responsibilities of a school library.

Enlightened Citizenship and Enriched Personal Life

The best method for a library to encourage an enlightened citizenship seems to be to provide the tools which encourage its growth. The County Library, therefore, attempts to provide basic information on all subjects and to present all sides of any question. Realizing that a democracy cannot operate in a vacuum, we do not avoid the controversial, but we try to present adequately all sides of an issue. However, we cannot purchase, nor should we be obligated to purchase, *all* books on every subject; we try to apply the normal selection criteria to books in each area and to select those most applicable to identified needs.

Because of the heavy commitments to academic and research materials on the part of other library facilities in the county, our patrons will turn readily to the County Library for recreational material. This is one area in which our specialization should be unique. All types of fiction for all types of readers should be provided. Best sellers are represented because of high reader demand. A book is valuable only in its relationship to its reader; thus, a light, poorly written novel may have the same effect on a given reader that a serious, classical work would have on another. Since people read books that suit their needs at a particular moment, a reader would not necessarily read the classic work even if light fiction titles were not available. Initially, we must reach each prospective borrower at his own level.

The recreational reader, however, is not a reader of fiction alone. Almost every conceivable subject—travel, sports, biography, hobbies—is touched upon by the person reading for no other reason than the enjoyment of reading. Therefore, most of the books in the collection are used by the recreational reader as well as those reading for other reasons.

While the library functions described above do overlap and their descriptions must of necessity be somewhat arbitrary, those enumerated serve to illuminate the direction in which the County Library should grow.

RESPONSIBILITY FOR SELECTION

The library materials budget of the Orange County Public Library is used to develop a balanced collection within the concept of the four levels of service. In accomplishing the above objective, it must be remembered that this is a public library system; the needs of the general reader rather than those of the specialist must be kept in mind in selecting materials even for the highest levels of service.

The ultimate responsibility for the selection of materials rests with the County Librarian operating within the framework of policies and objectives determined by the Board of Supervisors and the Statutes of the State of California. Responsibility for initial selection, however, has been delegated to the Collection Management Section of the Special Services Division of the Orange County Public Library. In Collection Management, an experienced group of librarians evaluate library materials within the context of the Materials Selection Policy and the limits of the library budget. These materials are made available for selection by the branches in response to community needs and interests within the total objective of the library system. Many staff members participate in the selection process; it is the responsibility of everyone working with the public to record patron requests so that they may be considered in selection. The County Library invites suggestions for purchase from patrons and may ask for specific advice from subject experts on the selection of materials.

SELECTION CRITERIA

The County Library recognizes its responsibility to have available a representative selection of materials on subjects of interest to its users. This responsibility includes having materials on the various sides of controversial questions. The County Library provides a resource where individuals can examine issues freely and formulate their own conclusions. The grossly sensational and the inflammatory are avoided, as are books exhibiting undue racial or religious prejudice and those containing undocumented charges of a libelous nature. The County Library seeks to present sound, factual data and honest expressions of opinion on all sides of controversial issues of public importance. This obligation arises not only from the need for balance and variety in the collection, but also from the obligation to uphold the traditional American doctrine of the freedom of speech and press, as guaranteed by the Constitution and supported by the American Library Association's *Library Bill of Rights.* In a democracy, it is essential that people have free access to ideas, even those of which a large majority of people disapprove. Wrong ideas can be combatted effectively only when they are understood. It must be emphasized that the library takes no sides on public issues; it does not endorse the opinions expressed in the materials held and, indeed, since materials often present diametrically opposing views, this would be impossible. Materials are selected without regard to whether they agree or disagree with the opinions of any or all members of the library staff on the merits of the question at issue. Once accepted, materials are not labeled or otherwise marked so as to prejudice a reader in advance as to its merits.

To build collections of merit and significance, materials must be measured by objective guidelines. All acquisitions, whether purchased or donated, are considered in terms of the following guidelines. Clearly, however, an item need not meet all of the criteria in order to be acceptable. Appraisal of library materials should take into account the degree of importance of each criterion as applied to the particular item under consideration.

Overall Purpose

One criterion is the presumed intent of the author and the sincerity of his purpose. This is a valid standard and, although only subjective judgments can be made concerning it, titles are selected on the basis of the context as a whole. The honesty and integrity of the author is closely scrutinized in all media. Reading tastes have changed in the direction of frankness; materials containing coarse language or certain subjects which may be objectionable to some people are included when it is judged that the author is sincere in what is being portrayed. While the Country Library recognizes its responsibility to protect the rights of mature, sophisticated users, it also realizes that some users may object; an attempt is made to balance the two viewpoints.

Reputation of the Author

In considering the reputation of the author, thought is given to determining whether or not that author's work is read and requested, even if a new title is not as well done as previous work. Some determination is also made of the need to have an author's complete work.

Timeliness

Books on issues of current interest are purchased if timeliness gives them relevance and importance. Illumination of the present or another era is an important consideration.

Permanent Value and Importance to the Collection

The comprehensiveness, clarity, accuracy, and logic of presentation are all considered in determining the permanent value and importance of material to the collection. In addition to competent and distinguished material, the library also acquires popular and experimental works having potential future value, for which immediate demand is small.

Popular Demand

Demand is a valid factor in book selection. To be of any value, best sellers must be chosen in time to meet mass demand. Usually these are selected as soon as they reach best seller lists.

Appearance in Book Selection Aids

Since it is impossible for the library staff to review personally the large number of books published, reviews found in professional, literary, specialized, and general periodicals are used as a beginning for selection in addition to the standard bibliographies, Winchell, *Public Library Catalog,* etc.

Reputation of Publisher and Material Format

The reputation of the publisher as a reliable producer is also considered in evaluation of materials. Specifically with books, the quality of paper, the press work, and the binding are all considered in evaluating the impression of the book.

MATERIALS IN FOREIGN LANGUAGES

The library's book collection includes materials in foreign languages emphasizing Spanish, German, French, and Italian with consideration given to population changes. Orange County Public Library also has accepted through the Santiago Library System a commitment for gathering materials in Danish, Icelandic, Norwegian, and Swedish; to fulfill this commitment, the County Library has agreed to add a minimum of five titles annually in each of these Nordic languages.

GIFTS

A gift for the library collection may consist of materials or of funds for the purchase of materials. While the County Library encourages unrestricted gifts of funds to permit their most flexible use to enrich the collection, funds are welcomed for the purchase of specific items consistent with the Materials Selection Policy as well as for the acquisition of materials recommended by the library staff.

Materials given to the Orange County Public Library are evaluated by the same standards as purchased material. It is explicitly understood that such factors as duplication, lack of community interest, processing costs, or inadequate housing may prevent the addition of gifts to the collection or their permanent retention and that, if the library cannot use them, it may dispose of the gifts in any appropriate manner.

SELECTION POLICIES BY TYPE OF MATERIAL

McNaughton Books

The library maintains a rental agreement with McNaughton Books, Inc., whereby current fiction and nonfiction titles are acquired on a temporary basis considerably in advance of the normal acquisition time. Books received through the McNaughton service conform to the Materials Selection Policy and usually are duplicates of current, popular titles either on hand or on order. Books not selected for inclusion in the permanent collection are not requested from McNaughton, although light fiction genre such as westerns, romances, or mysteries may be exceptions to this policy.

Paperbacks

The same standards for selection are applied to paperbacks as to other materials. The original copy of a book is usually bought in hard cover if available. However, paperbacks are bought and cataloged if there is no other edition available, if it is an original title appearing only in this form, or if it is a title which has only occasional or temporary interest.

Branch libraries purchase expendable paperbacks in accordance with these same standards. Expendable paperbacks essentially form a duplicate collection providing multiple copies of titles to meet temporary demands for best sellers as well as classic titles. Although popular reading genre such as westerns, romances, and mysteries may be widely purchased when appearing only in paperback format, the branch staff exercises sole initial evaluation and sole selection responsibility when purchasing paperback titles which are not represented in the catalog.

Phonodiscs and Audio-Cassettes

The County Library attempts to provide a balanced selection of phonodiscs and audio-cassettes. Classical music, opera, popular music, spoken
arts, and children's recordings are all included. Works of major composers
as well as the better known works of minor composers are purchased.
Attention is given also to acquiring recordings of outstanding performances,
important recording artists, and popular recording groups. Spoken recordings for adults and children are selected by the criteria applied to printed
material. Discs and tapes for self-instruction in languages and other subjects
are acquired as they become available. The technical quality of the recordings is also considered in selection.

Pamphlets

The selection of pamphlet file materials for a public library is based
upon the following objectives:

1. To accommodate nonbook items such as charts, pictures, maps, clippings, pamphlets and brochures that provide depth or currency for the
   study of a particular subject;
2. To present a variety of viewpoints on controversial issues and current
   problems, international, national and local, that may not be readily
   available in book form;
3. To supply brief coverage of topics such as how-to-do-it techniques,
   career guidance, travel information, and local history, where concise
   surveys or instructions are required;
4. To complement the book collection when seasonal demands such as
   school assignments or election campaigns place undue stress upon the
   book collection;
5. To reflect the varied community interest in a broader range at a nominal
   cost than the book budget would permit.

The same general principles that apply to other areas of selection apply
to the pamphlet collection. However, since much of this material will have
been obtained gratis, or at a nominal cost, from government agencies,
corporations, foundations and associations whose objectives are propaganda or advertising, it is important to strive for a balanced collection of
differing views, with items clearly identified as to the sponsoring agency.

Though it is well to recognize that total absence of bias is unattainable in
view of the origins of much of this material, it is essential that the materials be
screened for the purely sensational, inflammatory, or attack type of offering. Materials which obviously instigate prejudice, distort facts, over-empha-
size commercial messages, or contain false statements are to be avoided.

Periodicals

Periodical selection for a public library is based upon the following
objectives:

1. To provide in-depth research resources as related to indexes and other
   bibliographic tools;

2. To present all points of view concerning the problems and issues of our time, international, national and local;
3. To reflect the varied interests of the community;
4. To supplement the book collection's subject needs;
5. To provide current resources of the same scope and inclusiveness as books.

The principles upon which periodical selection is based are found in the *Public Library Service,* the A.L.A. *Standards of 1956,* and the *Library Bill of Rights.*

Since the library operates on a fixed annual budget and limited periodical funds, it must in its selection of periodicals as in its selection of books emphasize standard materials and services of first importance in the broad pattern of operation. The needs of the general reader must be first and foremost in the mind of the selector.

Because of their immediacy, periodicals usually represent new or extreme points of view not found in books. They are not necessarily rejected purely on the basis of their political, racial, or religious views or editorial policy, even though these may not be popular or widely accepted viewpoints within the community. As in book selection, a periodical is evaluated in its entirety rather than judged on the basis of objectionable material in a portion of the publication.

Government Documents

The library is a selective depository for United States Government and California State Documents, and is subject to governmental regulations governing depository collections. Selection of items to be received follows the same general principles as those for all other materials. Orange County and other local publications are of particular concern and are actively solicited from county, city and district agencies operating within the local area.

Duplicates and annual publications of particular significance are provided to branches as needed, on the basis of the general criteria.

DISCARDING

The library maintains an active discard policy based on the elimination of unnecessary items, outdated material, books no longer of interest or in demand, duplicates, and worn or mutilated copies. Frequency of circulation, community interest, and the availability of newer and more valid materials are of prime consideration. Fiction and nonfiction—excluding classics, local history, and materials on local industry—which were purchased to meet a demand that no longer exists are discarded.

CONTROVERSIAL MATERIAL

The library does not practice censorship. Patrons desiring reconsideration of any material should complete the "Request for Re-Evaluation of Materials in the Library." When a patron submits a written request for reconsideration, it will be considered by members of the library staff in light of the Materials Selection Policy and final determination will be made by the County Librarian.

OTHER MEDIA

Film Selection Policy

The Orange County Public Library currently has a collection of 8mm and 16mm films. Films have an immediacy and force of impact unlike that of other library materials. Films open people's minds to new ideas. At their best they bring out and encourage the most positive part of our humanness. The object in having this collection is several-fold:

1. To assist people in self-education;
2. To develop cultural appreciation, knowledge and understanding;
3. To provide pleasure and enjoyment to the viewer;
4. To interest nonusers in the library.

The library selects films which:

1. Show creativeness, originality, imagination and other qualities which mark this distinctive product;
2. Are timely and cover such cultural and social needs as are judged to be valuable to the community;
3. Are of educational, social, artistic, or entertainment value to all age groups;
4. Fill a need in the collection for a special subject area;
5. Are well-made technically in regards to narration, script, photography, sound, print, and color quality.

Framed Art Print Selection Policy

Color reproductions in the form of books or prints have brought the world of paintings to many who would never be able to own an original or visit a major museum. One may choose those reproductions which have a particular individual appeal and which will add to the patron's life an extra dimension of beauty and pleasure.

The Orange County Public Library's collection of framed art prints is intended to:

1. Further self-education;
2. Develop cultural appreciation, knowledge and understanding;
3. Provide pleasure and enjoyment for the borrower;
4. Interest nonusers in the library.

Crandall Library

OBJECTIVE

This statement proposes to define the standards of critical judgment and to describe the methods by which Crandall Library augments its collection of books and nonbook materials (such as periodicals, phonograph records and pamphlets).

The library seeks to serve a wide range of readers with diversified interests and intends that its collection will be sound, balanced and fair. Its patrons should find a collection carefully chosen for its intrinsic worth, its timeliness and its potential usefulness in the community.

SCOPE OF SERVICE

Crandall is the chartered library for Glens Falls, Queensbury and Moreau; and it is also the Central Reference Library of the Southern Adirondack Library System (commonly called SALS) for four counties: Warren, Washington, Saratoga and Hamilton. Since 1959, State funds provided a Central Book Aid (commonly called CBA) collection of more than 50,000 periodicals and serious and substantive books of adult nonfiction on microfilm; half of these titles were chosen by SALS and half by Crandall, with SALS determining the final choice. This ten-year State grant concluded in 1968, but provisions continued for the Central library to select 3,000 CBA titles annually. (1975—limited to $34,000 yearly.)

AUTHORITY

The Director of Crandall Library delegates to other professional members of the staff the duty of reading reviews and résumés, studying and scrutinizing the judgment of other libraries, and judging a suggested title in terms of present holdings and potential needs. The initial selection of material is the responsibility of the professional librarians so designated.

The director has the ultimate responsibility for such selection, within the framework of policies determined by the Board of Trustees.

CRITERIA

Material added to the collection must meet high standards of quality in content and expression. Factors to be considered in judging quality are: factual accuracy, effective expression, significance of subject, sincerity and integrity, and responsibility of opinion. The need for each item in relation to the rest of the collection and to the interests of the community also influences selection. Public demand is always considered, and books suggested for purchase by Crandall's patrons are given due consideration, and added if they meet the required standards of excellence and can be purchased within budget limitations.

SELECTION GUIDES

In choosing nonfiction on a controversial subject or a fiction title by an unknown author, several reviews are studied before the decision to purchase is made. The chief professional journals consulted are *Library Journal,* ALA *Booklist, Publishers Weekly* and *Virginia Kirkus Reviews.* Other critical reviews appearing in *Christian Science Monitor, Saturday Review, New York Times* daily and Sunday, as well as *Atlantic Monthly, Commentary, Commonweal* and *Christian Century,* are also considered. A monthly book review meeting at SALS headquarters is valuable in hearing oral reviews by professional librarians.

For detailed guidelines on special subjects, we consult the book selection policies published by the Enoch Pratt Library.

Adult Selection

In selecting books for adult readers, the overall value is the chief criterion. Works which present an honest picture of some problem or aspect of life are not excluded because of frank language, but books written to trade on sensationalism are not added knowingly. Freedom of speech and of the press are rights of our heritage guaranteed by the Constitution and defended by the courts. Crandall Library subscribes to the *Library Bill of Rights* of the American Library Association (*see* page 381), and to the *Freedom to Read Statement* endorsed by the ALA, American Book Publishers Council, American Booksellers Association, Book Manufacturers Institute and the National Education Association (*see* page 382). There has been some liberalizing of policies of selection in the fields of social, sexual and moral problems, reflecting increasing sophistication of the public at all levels. Crandall tries to draw the line at the point of greatest freedom combined with creative value, which is supported by at least a substantial minority of the community. Selection policies always keep in mind court decisions which have ruled that a book for adults should be judged in its entirety, not by passages taken out of context, and by its likely effect on a reasonably mature adult, not on a susceptible youngster.

Local Interests

A subject in which Crandall attempts full coverage is local history. Anything written about the local communities and much written about the adjacent counties is bought. Special local interests, such as paper and lumbering, antiques, music, art, ballet, horses and sports, are emphasized and represented in some depth in the selections.

Fiction

Crandall Library does not neglect or downgrade its fiction collection. Many novels are powerful and constructive. They present appealing portrayals of characters and life. They educate emotions, change points of view, help develop awareness, perception and sensibility.

Young People's Books

The ultimate aim of selection for young adults is to contribute to the development of well-rounded citizens with an understanding of themselves and others, at home and abroad. Some of the better teen-age novels are selected, as well as books on sports, careers and hobbies. Of greatest importance are books keyed to the young adult's needs and interests which tend to open new interests in cultural, economic, scientific and social fields.

CONTROVERSY

Crandall Library tries to provide material on all sides, as far as availability permits, of public questions on which there is a variety of opinion. Such books on controversial subjects or issues are selected which give evidence of a sincere desire to get at the facts, and which provide material for the patron to use in making his own decisions.

When a Book is Challenged

The library is opposed to the addition or withdrawal, at the request of any individual or group, of books which have been selected or excluded on the principles as outlined in the foregoing.

It is recognized, however, that the staff cannot read or even scan the approximately 7,000 books added yearly. Reliance must be placed on reviews and it is not always possible to read several reviews of all books. It is also true that not all reviewers are top quality. Thus, some books might be added unwittingly which might not meet all of the accepted standards of selection.

If a patron objects to a Crandall book, several professional staff members will read it; the reviews will be searched and reread and a decision made. The Director will be happy to discuss the pros and cons of the decision with the patron. If the patron is not satisfied, she/he may write a letter to the Board of Trustees stating the basic reasons for objecting to the decision, and the Trustees will then act upon the matter.

If a patron objects to a SALS book, the reasons should be stated in writing and the letter will be forwarded to the Director of the Southern Adirondack Library System.

Finally, it must always be remembered that since every book probably has something in it objectionable to somebody, there would be few books in the library if selectors tried to choose only books to which there might be no objections.

In a day such as ours, a library must choose to represent and recommend "all winds of doctrine," knowing that some will be repugnant and others disdained by many readers, but insisting on the right of the library to document the day and its mores. Crandall Library must also allow room on its shelves for the innovators, the experimenters, and authors of books that "stretch the mind." Some of the experimental writing of our day will undoubtedly become the classics of tomorrow.

POLICY CONCERNING GIFTS AND DISCARDS

Financial gifts are accepted on a restricted or unrestricted basis according to the donor's wishes.

Gifts of books and other materials are welcomed by the library, but with the understanding that they will not necessarily be added to the collection. The same standards of selection are applied to gifts as to materials purchased from library funds. Gifts which do not meet the library's standards will be placed in the Friends of the Library booksale. Unneeded duplicate copies may be placed in the booksale or given to another library.

Choice of Memorial books or recordings may be left to the library staff, or the donor may indicate a particular book or subject desired. Often the library selects a book which will reflect the special interests of the person being commemorated.

Memorial books are shelved with the regular collection, according to subject classification, so that they will be available and useful to persons seeking books on a particular subject. A memorial plate is affixed to each Memorial book.

Discards of CBA books will be decided upon by SALS and Crandall staff. Discarded books and their catalog records will be sent to the System.

Discards of Crandall books may be given to the Friends of the Library for its booksale, if in the judgment of the professional staff they would be of interest to the public.

Any offering to the library of nonlibrary materials, such as framed art, sculpture, etc., will be accepted or rejected by a committee of three. The committee will consist of a trustee or trustees, the Director and a staff member.

CONDITIONS AND LIMITATIONS

1. Crandall Library assumes and shall bear no responsibility whatever for personal injury to any member, affiliated person, guest, invitee or licensee of the using organization, or for loss of, or injury or damage to, any property of the using organization, its members, affiliated persons, guests, invitees or licensees.

CRANDALL LIBRARY
APPLICATION FOR USE OF
LIBRARY MEETING ROOMS

The Auditorium, the Brown Room and the Conference Room of the Crandall Library are available for meetings of area cultural, civic and educational organizations subject to approval of the librarian. The rooms are not available for social gatherings, religious services or commercial purposes. Library sponsored meetings will have priority in scheduling.

Permission to use a library meeting room, if granted, is strictly governed by the conditions and limitations which appear upon the second page of this application.

NAME OF ORGANIZATION: _____

_____

ROOM DESIRED:

_____ Auditorium (capacity *110 Seats*)

_____ Brown Room (capacity *25 Seats*)

_____ Conference Room (capacity *6 Seats*)

DATE(S) OF MEETING(S) _____

TIME MEETING WILL CONVENE: _____ WILL ADJOURN: _____

PURPOSE OF MEETING: _____

_____ _____

(See condition 7 on back)

PROBABLE NUMBER TO ATTEND: _____

NAME, ADDRESS AND TELEPHONE NUMBER OF PERSON WHOM LIBRARIAN SHOULD NOTIFY OF ACTION ON THIS APPLICATION:

Name _____

Address _____

Tel. _____

SIGNATURE AND TELEPHONE NUMBER OF PERSON MAKING APPLICATION ON BEHALF OF ABOVE-NAMED ORGANIZATION:

_____

Tel. _____

Please leave this application with the librarian.

2. The using organization and its individual members, jointly and severally, assume and shall bear full responsibility for loss of, or injury or damage to, any property of the Crandall Library as shall be caused or inflicted by the using organization, its members, affiliated persons, guests, invitees or licensees.
3. The using organization shall leave the meeting room and facilities in clean and orderly condition.
4. Light refreshments requiring no cooking may be served.
5. Smoking is *not* permitted.
6. No tacks, nails or cellophane tape are to be placed in or on doors, walls or furniture.
7. Meetings may extend beyond the 9:00 p.m. closing time of Crandall Library only if the using organization has so stated in its application for use of a meeting room, in which event approval will be conditioned upon payment to the library of a fee by the using organization.

St. Louis Public Library

COMMUNITY DESCRIPTION

St. Louis is a great and historical city caught in the quicksand of urban blight. In the mid-1970s it is a city in decline, losing its traditional position as economic and population center of the metropolitan region. Long a manufacturing, wholesale, and retail trade hub, these industries have suffered drastic setbacks as companies and the work force began the migration to open land beyond the city boundaries. In the face of this, however, the service industry is growing, major construction is in progress in the central business district, and there are signs that the City has started climbing out of its slump.

The pattern of the City is enriched by a number of discrete neighborhoods, remarkable for their diversity. Any overall, brief description of St. Louis such as this unfortunately cannot take into account the distinct and cohesive personalities of these communities.

St. Louis lost 17% of its population in the decade between 1960 and 1970 (compared to the suburban ring which saw an increase of 29%) and stands to lose steadily until 1990, according to projections. The greatest loss occurred and continues to occur in a series of concentric rings around the central business district. In-migration consists mainly of rural people coming to find work in the City and lately an important number of young middle and upper class couples who are buying and restoring older homes. Taken as a whole, the 622,236 persons still living in the City in 1970 were older, poorer and less well-educated than their counterparts living in the suburban ring. The proportion of elderly grows and the proportion of young diminishes as people of parental age leave the City and raise their children elsewhere. Almost two-thirds of St. Louis families make less than $10,000 a year, including a large number living below poverty level. Not quite 13% fall into the upper income range. As soon as families, both black and white, reach an income level and standard of living which enables them to trade urban problems for suburban living, they tend to do so.

In the area of education, the median number of school years completed by St. Louisans in 1970 was 9.6 compared to 12.3 for St. Louis County, 11.7

for the St. Louis metropolitan area, 11.8 for Missouri, and 11.2 for the nation. School enrollment is steadily decreasing. Black St. Louisans represented 41% of the total City population in 1970. That ratio is increasing, due not to an actual growth of the black population, for that growth peaked in 1969, but to the swelling out-migration of whites. While the central downtown area is being abandoned with alacrity by both races, blacks remaining in the City are generally migrating to the north and northwestern districts, while white St. Louisans are congregated in the south and southwest. The most important ethnic influence throughout is the German, followed by Italian, Irish, and Slavic. A large nonresident group for which there are no demographic characteristics available is the 181,850 people who work in the City but live elsewhere. From this group and other county residents, Main Library draws 3% of its registration and 30% of its in-building use of materials.

As the City becomes less residential, businesses become an increasingly important clientele for the Main Library, located as it is on the fringe of the central business district. Within the boundaries of the City are more than 16,000 businesses ranging from parking lots to major industries. Many large corporations located in other parts of the SMSA already depend heavily on the services of the library.

This, then, is a statistical overview of the patrons, both actual and potential, of the St. Louis Public Library system as they were in 1970. Many changes have taken place since then, changes which cannot be fully documented until the next census. The standard library dictum, "Know Your Community," has never been more important than now, at mid-decade, for only by first-hand observation can the librarian grasp the shifting patterns of the community and serve both the old patrons and the new accordingly.

GOALS OF THE ST. LOUIS PUBLIC LIBRARY

The fundamental role of the St. Louis Public Library is to help city residents in establishing and reaching their life goals and objectives, including the constructive use of leisure time. The ultimate objective is to encourage and maintain individual self-renewal, to support efforts of becoming free and dynamic individuals in a free society.

To pursue this course with limited resources forces the library to choose the nature of its role as an information agency, considering that current times offer the individual choice of a variety of media and modes of information. The distinctive advantage of what the library can offer over those sources of information contemporary people can provide for themselves is richness of resources and trained expertise in their use. It is the library's obligation to establish a priority of effort to satisfy information needs of the public and allocate resources in parallel proportion. To provide the most enduring benefits to city residents, this rank order of service objectives necessarily obtains:

1. Purposeful investigation or research;
2. Education—initial or supplemental;
3. Recreation and inspiration.

All these needs must be addressed in some measure by the library. Considering the ubiquity of commercial sources which can satisfy the majority of the individual's transient and entertainment informational needs, the library should place increased emphasis upon answering the first two priorities.

The primary library service objective at Main will be to maintain growth and development of the research and permanent literature collections which are to be used in purposeful investigation or research. The Main Library's rich collection and subject specialists will be used to support services given throughout the system, to answer supplemental information requests from the metropolitan area and state, and to serve as a natural link in any nationwide network of information resources. A parallel function of Main Library is to serve the informational and research needs of the growing commercial, industrial, governmental and professional clientele which constitute Main's growing daytime neighborhood patronage.

Through neighborhood branches, scattered over the city to reach the resident population, the library meets and expects to serve the majority of the public's reading and information needs. Each branch should provide a full range of materials and services for general popular consumption, reference service and the stimulation and guidance of children's, young adult and adult reading. These collections and programs should possess a specific focus to counter the public attitudes of ignorance, intolerance, indifference and prejudice which are antithetical to an educated and democratic society. The library program of materials and services touching the individual user at the branches should contribute to the growth of each individual as a free, conscious and creative human personality and as a responsible citizen in a democratic society.

Community Services' "Mission to St. Louis" program will be designed as constantly evolving to reflect the self-expressed interests and informational needs of the disadvantaged public of the inner city. These will be discovered and explored through special purpose outlets and materials centers located, as frequently as financing permits, within walking distance of user homes. Individual reading guidance will be used to develop their capacity to make increased use of the library system. Special materials will be sought to match the reading ability levels and to satisfy special educational or informational needs.

Extracted from "Mission of the St. Louis
Public Library in Contemporary
America" 1970

INTELLECTUAL FREEDOM POLICY

The public library is unique among institutions as an unbiased repository for the recorded expression of man's thought. It must, therefore, accept responsibility for providing free access by the public to all points of view contained therein. However, the addition of an item to the collection in no way represents an endorsement by the library of any theory, idea, or policy contained in it. In the collection of the St. Louis Public Library all sides of controversial issues will be represented as far as budget, space and availability of materials allow. Selection will be based upon the criteria given throughout this policy statement. The race, religion, nationality or political views of an author, the frankness or coarseness of language, the controversial content of an item, or the endorsement or disapproval of an individual or group in the community will not cause an item to be automatically included or excluded. The library subscribes to the provisions of the *Library Bill of Rights* and the *Intellectual Freedom Statement*.

Responsibility for the reading choices of children rests with their parents or legal guardians. Adult selection will not be inhibited by the possibility that materials may inadvertently fall into the hands of children, but circulation of adult materials dealing with mature subjects will be denied to children. No material will be sequestered except for the express purpose of protecting it from injury or theft.

The library will not indicate, through the use of labels or other devices, particular philosophies outlined in a book or other item.

BOOK SELECTION POLICY

Written and Adopted by Board of Directors
September 13, 1968
Re-adopted
April 11, 1975

In acquiring books and other materials, it shall be the policy of the St. Louis Public Library, within the limits of its budget:

1. To provide for all the people of St. Louis the most complete possible collection of materials of permanent and current interest to foster enlightened citizenship, to provide information, to encourage continuing education at all ages and enrich individual lives;
2. To include in its collection expressions of man's thought, no matter how controversial;
3. To conserve and increase, for the permanent enrichment of the people of St. Louis, and for the continuing use of scholars, comprehensive collections in the Library's fields of special strength: genealogy, architecture, costume, international relations, American folklore, education, chemistry, Western travel, Missouriana and others as may be designated by the Board of Directors on the recommendation of the librarian.

Selection procedures and specific acquisitions, consistent with the policy of the Board of Directors, shall be the responsibility of the librarian and staff.

MATERIALS SELECTION POLICY FOR MAIN LIBRARY

Objectives of Selection

The St. Louis Public Library collection may be defined as an in-depth general collection, current and retrospective, comprehensive in some areas, exhaustive in none. It is structured to:

1. Serve the practical information and purposeful investigation needs of the people of St. Louis;
2. Serve the educational needs of the independent learner;
3. Serve as a major resource collection from which the St. Louis Public Library Branch and Community Services agencies may draw;
4. Serve as a major resource collection from which other libraries in the state may draw;
5. Supply recreational reading materials.

Responsibility for Selection

Overall responsibility for collection development is delegated to the Coordinator of Book Selection, with specific areas of the collection assigned to the subject specialists. Other members of the staff as well as patrons may recommend titles for consideration. Ultimate responsibility rests with the librarian, who operates within this framework of policies determined by the Board of Directors.

Policies by Clientele Served

ADULT

Adults are the primary users of the Main Library and the collection will be geared for their informational and educational use. Materials for recreational use will be included but will be of third priority. Materials will be chosen according to the various interests, backgrounds, abilities and levels of education identifiable in the community. The young adult is considered a part of this primary user population and materials produced for this group will be considered proportionately in the overall selection process.

Specific criteria for selecting adult materials in all fields include:

1. Importance of the subject to the balance of the collection;
2. Potential use in the community;
3. Timeliness or permanence of the work;
4. Quality of writing and/or visual art;
5. Accuracy of information;
6. Reputation and significance of the author;
7. Scarcity of material on the subject;
8. Accessibility of material in other libraries;
9. Special features (plates, indexes, bibliographies, etc.);
10. Format and quality of technical production;
11. Appearance of title in special bibliographies or indexes;
12. Reputation and standing of the publisher;
13. Price.

An item need not meet all of these criteria in order to be acceptable. When judging the desirability of materials, any combination of standards may be used.

ADULT INDEPENDENT LEARNER

Accepting the role of learning center for the adult who chooses to study independently to reach his own educational goal, the library will provide learning opportunities, guidance and materials. The independent learner will be able to develop his interest in a subject from the basic level to the more advanced level within the resources of the library. As programs of study are developed by staff for the various subject areas, books and nonbook items of progressive difficulty and depth will be acquired as needed.

CHILDREN

Since the juvenile population of Main Library's immediate service area has almost disappeared in recent years, children have ceased to be a major clientele. Consistent with this change and with the reference and resource function of Main Library, the children's literature collection will now be built for the use of the adult working or studying in the field. While children will continue to have access to the collection, their reading needs will be better served by one of the branch collections.

STUDENTS

While the library is sympathetic to the needs of primary, secondary, and college students, it is not the responsibility of the library to provide specified curriculum-oriented materials for them, nor will it duplicate individual titles or subject materials as a result of class assignment demands. School and college libraries may be expected to meet the needs of the students formally enrolled in courses at their institutions.

BLIND AND PHYSICALLY HANDICAPPED

Anyone, juvenile or adult, who cannot read or handle conventional printed matter because of a physical disability is eligible for the services of the Wolfner Memorial Library. Under a contract with the Division of the Blind and Physically Handicapped of the Library of Congress, Wolfner serves the reading needs of patrons with these physical limitations throughout the State of Missouri.

General Policies for All Materials

The library will purchase, within budgetary limitations, the best materials of both permanent and current interest in all subjects which satisfy the objectives in this statement. It will be sensitive to the interests of the community, not only giving consideration to the demands of its steady patrons but also anticipating the needs of those who do not regularly use the library.

The library will handle neither the most ephemeral of popular materials nor the most esoteric of research documents. Exhaustive collections designed to serve the patron engaged in serious and extensive research are considered to be the province of the academic and special libraries in the area. Nonessential duplication of materials held by other libraries will be avoided. Nonprint media will be purchased if they represent the most suitable, useful and effective format in which to present the subject.

Three possible physical locations for material in the building represent three possible purposes for which material will be selected:

Popular Library. Materials selected for this service will be of popular interest. They will often be in high demand and/or of significant current interest, not always of enduring value.

Subject rooms.   Materials selected for these locations will be primarily those used in reference work.

Stacks.   Materials selected for this location will be of permanent value, giving strength and depth to the library's collection. These materials will be available for patron use but will not be high demand items.

Materials will be chosen on all these levels for all these purposes.

Policies by Type of Material

BOOKS

Hardbound.   A title will be purchased in the hardbound format if:
- It is important enough to be a permanent part of the collection;
- It will receive hard use for a short period of time.

Paperbound.   A title may be purchased in paperbound format if:
- It is available only in paperback;
- Only one copy is needed and its use will not be heavy;
- It is considered ephemeral material;
- It is in high demand and duplicate copies are needed to supplement one or more hardbound copies.

General selection policies and criteria will apply to the purchase of paperbound materials.

Books in large type   will be purchased for patrons with partial vision.

GOVERNMENT DOCUMENTS

United Nations.   The library will acquire selected monograph and periodical titles and extensive statistical series.

Federal documents.   As a large selective depository, the library will choose most classes of publications to be received automatically from the Government Printing Office. Items will be selected in conformity with the overall selection policy and in support of the nondocument collection. The following areas will be emphasized:

1. By type of material
   - Statistics of all types;
   - Agency regulations;
   - Directories;
   - Bibliographies and indexes;
   - Patents.
2. By subject of material
   - Ecology;
   - Climate;
   - Energy;
   - Transportation;
   - Interstate commerce;
   - Urban affairs, particularly St. Louis as available.

Other selection considerations:

1. Commercial (nondocument) reference books will be acquired as needed.
2. Technical research in medicine, agriculture, biology, oceanography and other sciences will be omitted, with the exception of selected papers.
3. Lectures or addresses will not be chosen since these are widely duplicated in other sources.
4. Duplicate copies of depository items will be purchased as needed to answer public demand or for distribution to branches.
5. Subjects of a general nature that are better covered in the nondocument collection will be omitted.
6. Nondepository documents will be purchased or obtained at no cost when they are:
   - Relevant to St. Louis, the St. Louis metropolitan area, or Missouri;
   - Of general reference value;
   - Popular enough to be acquired in multiple copies for the collection or for distribution to branches;
   - Publications of current awareness value only;
   - Locally initiated publications from federal agencies in St. Louis;
   - Technical reports needed by the subject specialists where subject content is the sole criterion.

Missouri.   Acquisition is sporadic and unregulated. Should a state depository law be passed, a selection statement can be written at that time.

Legislative reference.   This section of materials will be maintained primarily for the benefit of citizens interested in the actions of their state and federal governments. The library will not attempt to provide a complete collection of legal research materials, relying on the responsibility of the law libraries in the area. This section will contain:

1. Missouri bills, current and retrospective for 10 years;
2. Federal House and Senate journals;
3. Federal House and Senate calendars;
4. Any available indexes to the above material;
5. Congressional bills and slip laws, current only;
6. Congressional Record;
7. Federal hearing schedule;
8. Commercial legislative indexes and other reference tools.

Other states.   Current state manuals and statistical abstracts from all other states will be acquired as available. Other publications will be selected individually according to the criteria in this policy and will be treated as books, pamphlets, or serials rather than as a unique documents collection. Emphases will be engineering and geology including water surveys.

Local.   The library is a depository for St. Louis documents. This collection, housed in the Municipal Reference Branch, will include, but is not limited to, the following:

1. Ordinances and codes;
2. City Journal;

3. Board bills;
4. Sight sheets (abstracts of board bills);
5. Annual reports of all city agencies and departments;
6. Monographs, studies, surveys, reports published by any city or regional agency or department, or by any outside firm if they concern the St. Louis area;
7. Periodicals published by any city agency or department.

St. Louis County documents will be acquired as needed. Documents and codes of other local governmental units (in Missouri or other states) will be acquired on an exchange basis through the Documents Exchange Program among municipal libraries.

PERIODICALS

Periodicals will be purchased for the following reasons:

1. To supplement the book collection;
2. To keep the library's collection up-to-date with current thinking in various fields;
3. To provide information not yet available in books because of its currency;
4. To satisfy recreational reading needs;
5. To serve the staff as book selection aids and professional reading.

Selection of periodical titles will follow the monograph selection in terms of scope and depth of subject coverage, with the following special considerations:

1. Actual or potential use by the community;
2. Accuracy and objectivity of content;
3. Accessibility of content through library-owned indexes;
4. Contribution to the balance of the collection;
5. Availability of the title in other area libraries (complete listing available in *St. Louis Union List of Periodicals*);
7. Price.

Special types of periodicals:

1. At least one popular periodical in the French, Spanish, German, Italian and Russian languages, published in the country of origin, will be selected.
2. Titles in large print will be selected for readers with partial vision.

NEWSPAPERS

Newspapers will be purchased for the following purposes:

1. To provide current news coverage at all levels from local to international;
2. To satisfy reference needs;
3. To satisfy recreational reading needs;
4. To provide a unique source for local history information.

Newspapers will be purchased according to:

1. Geographical area
   - All St. Louis and St. Louis County newspapers of permanent news value;
   - Large Missouri cities and towns;
   - Large Illinois cities and towns;
   - Major U.S. cities, especially those in the Midwest;
   - Very closely selected representation for Canada, Western Europe and Latin America.
2. Special types
   - Newspapers of special groups, such as associations, religious denominations, political factions, etc., may be added sparingly. Public demand and balance of the collection will be prime factors in the selection.
   - One newspaper in the French, Spanish, German, Italian and Russian languages, published in the country of origin, will be selected.

PAMPHLETS

Pamphlets will be purchased for the following purposes:

1. To supplement the book collection in areas of heavy but short-term demand;
2. To supply current information not yet published in book form;
3. To make available material on subjects not easily found in books or other sources.

Pamphlets will be selected according to the objectives and criteria stated elsewhere in this policy with the following special consideration: Since many pamphlets are issued for propaganda or advertising purposes, it is important to maintain a balance of viewpoints and to avoid inflammatory treatment or distortion for commercial purposes. Pamphlet material, to be acceptable, should always have the issuing agency clearly identified.

TELEPHONE AND CITY DIRECTORIES

Telephone directories will be acquired for:

1. All Missouri towns and cities;
2. All Illinois towns and cities;
3. Capitals of all states;
4. Other U.S. cities of 20,000 population and over, except for sparsely populated states where directories from the 2 or 3 major population centers will be acquired, regardless of population;
5. Selected foreign capitals and other major foreign cities in the English language where available.

City directories will be acquired for:

1. St. Louis;
2. St. Louis County;
3. Other towns in the St. Louis metropolitan area, as available.

MAPS AND ATLASES

Maps and atlases will be acquired at a 4B level* to meet the identifiable interests of the community in the areas of travel, history, geography (both physical and economic), topography and science. Geographical emphasis will be as follows: St. Louis (4), U.S. (4), Foreign (3), Extraterrestrial (1).

Maps will be acquired as follows:

1. Topographic:
   - United States Geological Survey quadrangle maps covering the United States;
   - U.S. Army maps covering primarily foreign countries, secondarily the United States;
   - Current travel and road maps covering all states and most cities of the United States, all foreign countries and most major foreign cities.
2. Geologic, mineral, water for the United States;
3. Extraterrestrial;
4. Demographic;
5. St. Louis. An exhaustive coverage of the St. Louis area, both historical and current, will be maintained. All topographical, street, neighborhood, transportation, economic, political, especially ward divisions and plat books, racial and ethnic concentration and pictorial maps for the area will be acquired, (4-).

Atlases will be acquired as follows:

1. Important general and thematic atlases of the world, its continents, regions and nations, including a complete set of national atlases as available;
2. Important general and thematic atlases of the United States;
3. Selected important historical atlases.

The following points will be considered in selecting maps and atlases:

1. Need for coverage;
2. Date published;
3. Scale—large or medium scale will be preferred;
4. Type of projection;
5. Quality of color reproduction;
6. Readability of type;
7. Number and quality of insets;
8. Accuracy, comprehensiveness, and accessibility of indexes;
9. Authenticity, comprehensiveness, and currency of statistics.

RARE BOOKS AND MANUSCRIPTS

A collection of rare, valuable and/or unusual books and periodicals will be built in these areas:

1. St. Louis and St. Louis-related materials, especially:

*Collection levels and patron target groups have been assigned on the basis of the Subject Strength Scale and the Clientele Scale, pp. 102–103.

- Materials written or published by William Marion Reedy, exhaustive coverage;
- Materials published by William K. Bixby, exhaustive coverage;
- First and/or other important editions of St. Louis authors, except those already heavily collected elsewhere;
- Selected St. Louis imprints, especially those of a literary or historical nature.

2. First and/or other important editions of those authors who were close associates or proteges of Reedy, except those already heavily collected in other institutions;
3. St. Louis Public Library Archives;
4. Miscellaneous collection of rare, valuable and/or vulnerable materials of a literary or historical nature, already owned by the library, brought together because of their value as landmarks of man's achievements; highly selected.

Materials will be selected in accordance with the criteria given previously in this policy statement, with emphasis on the following:

1. Historical or literary merit;
2. Author's reputation and significance;
3. Publisher's reputation and significance;
4. Condition of materials;
5. Special features, e.g., autographs, annotations, outstanding or unusual binding, important edition;
6. Price.

Primary sources such as letters, manuscripts and diaries will not be acquired except as donations of local interest.

REFERENCE MATERIALS

In support of its role as a major resource center for the area, the library will actively build a strong and extensive collection of reference and bibliographic materials in all subject fields. Books in major foreign languages may be acquired according to need for the material or coverage. Areas of emphasis will be the same as for the collection as a whole.

The following types of materials will be included:

1. Encyclopedias, general and specialized;
2. Handbooks and dictionaries in all fields of knowledge;
3. Directories of people, institutions, firms, official bodies in all fields;
4. Atlases and gazetteers;
5. Statistical compendia;
6. Indexes covering both (a) material already owned or being acquired and (b) material not owned but available in other libraries, especially periodical indexes (selectively);
7. Bibliographies, national, trade and subject;
8. Biographical dictionaries of general, national or regional, professional or occupational types, with both retrospective and current coverage. "Vanity" works will be purchased selectively if they represent the only coverage in a desired field;

9. Abstract journals on a very selected basis, consistent with the subject levels stated in this policy.

These materials will be especially chosen for:

1. Usefulness to quality reference service;
2. Accuracy;
3. Authenticity;
4. Scope and depth of coverage;
5. Historical perspective as well as currency of data;
6. Ease of use;
7. Special locating features.

BRAILLE AND TALKING BOOKS

Books and magazines in Braille, Talking Book and tape formats will be handled by the Wolfner Memorial Library, a regional library of the Division of the Blind and Physically Handicapped of the Library of Congress. In effect, selection decisions for this collection will be made by the Division and materials sent to Wolfner automatically. Individual requests will be considered.

According to the selection policy of the Division, which therefore becomes the policy for the library, the book collection will contain a representative selection of fiction, nonfiction and classics, as well as popular materials, standard reference works when practical, pseudoscientific works expressing views which may not be generally accepted but for which there is reader demand, and standard works relating to the world's major religions (such as their holy books). The Division will not attempt to provide textbooks or other curriculum-oriented materials except as such materials also serve the general public, nor will it include local histories or other items of specific local interest. Novels will be selected to satisfy a large and diverse readership with vastly different tastes, interests, purposes, and reading levels.

The Division will provide periodicals in all media. Emphasis will be on, but will not be limited to, periodicals listed in the *Reader's Guide to Periodical Literature*. Other criteria are high interest and demand, balance of viewpoints, balance of recreational and informational reading, and reflection of current thinking in the various fields.

Special criteria for selection of adult materials:

1. Consideration of previous selections in the subject area and media previously used;
2. Target audience, including age and educational level;
3. Potential popularity;
4. Format of the book and the media to which it best lends itself.

The young adult collection, serving students in grades nine through twelve, is considered part of the adult collection and selection of materials will be governed by the same criteria.

The children's collection will be developed to meet the recreational reading needs of children from preschool through eighth grade. The criteria used and the collection's development are patterned after the adult policy.

SOUND RECORDINGS

The recorded sound collection will consist of phonodiscs and cassettes. Selection emphasis will be on classical music with semiclassical, jazz, and folk, especially Ozark, also represented. Popular, ephemeral music recordings of all types will be purchased, but sparingly. Other important sections will be nonmusical recordings, especially children's stories, language learning and other instructional recordings.

Sound recordings will be selected according to:

1. Need for material based on public requests and present holdings;
2. Quality of interpretation and technique;
3. Importance of the artist;
4. Technical quality of the recording;
5. Price.

MUSIC SCORES

Music scores (rating: 2+BC), both individual or collected as songbooks, will be purchased in the high-demand areas of new musicals, folk songs, especially Ozark, and popular instrumental works. Major works of all important contemporary composers will be chosen also. While replacements will be made to the older classics-oriented general collection as needed and as available, the library will not add retrospective depth and breadth to this part of the collection. Multiple copies for group use will not be acquired.

SLIDES AND FILMSTRIPS

Any item in these media will be purchased if it represents the most suitable, useful, and effective format in which to present the subject. All general selection criteria apply as to subject coverage. Additional technical considerations will be quality of photography or art work, color reproduction, and editing.

PICTURES

The purpose of the picture collection is to supplement illustrations in books and periodicals or to duplicate them for easy access. This collection will include:

1. Unframed art prints of good quality, representing the work of major artists;
2. Mounted and unmounted magazine and newspaper illustrations covering a broad range of subjects, including portraits, with emphasis on St. Louis, its history, buildings, and people.

Pictures will be selected according to:

1. Demand;
2. Authenticity of subject;
3. Quality and clarity of print or illustration, except that quality may be sacrificed if the picture is of local importance.

VIDEOTAPE

Based on this library's experience and the experience of other libraries throughout the country, videotape is an increasingly important tool for library service. As videotape facilities become more sophisticated and widespread, full selection criteria will be developed. At the present state of technology, it is possible for the library to produce or purchase taped programs in the following areas, in accordance with the selection objectives and public demand:

1. Training in selected subjects for the independent learner;
2. Reference services;
3. "Coping" information, such as insurance, tenants' rights, wills, tax returns, social agencies;
4. Instruction in library usage;
5. Audio-visual history;
6. Inservice training for the staff;
7. Library reports to the community;
8. Story hours and puppet shows.

MICROFORMS

Materials available in microform *only* may be selected as needed under the general objectives and criteria in this policy.

Microforms may be produced or acquired *in place of* printed materials to conserve space and to preserve material of permanent reference value and historical importance. When the original printed material has an intrinsic or historical value, it may be retained in addition to the microform copy.

Microforms will *not* be produced or acquired *in place of* printed materials in the following cases:

1. Periodical titles of which the St. Louis Public Library has unique holdings, as reported in the national *Union List of Serials–New Serial Titles* (duplication in microform will be allowed, however);
2. Materials in high demand for circulation or ready reference use;
3. Materials containing colored art work or graphics which must be preserved in the original state.

The following materials may be purchased in microform, using the accompanying guidelines:

1. Periodicals
   - If indexed in standard periodical indexes held by library;
   - If of significant and continuing reference value;
   - If of local interest.
2. Newspapers
   - If major sources of St. Louis news coverage;
   - If major sources of national news coverage and are indexed;
   - As they follow the collection's subject emphases generally.
3. Genealogical records, as available

4. Documents
   - Space-consuming series which do not receive heavy usage but which are basic depository series;
   - Currently received periodicals which are indexed;
   - Dead periodicals that occupy 12 feet or more of space, whether indexed or not;
   - Data sources for which usage is by chart, table or section rather than by complete volume, such as statistics, agency proceedings, regulations, standards, and directories:
   - Court and agency decisions when well-indexed;
   - Technical research reports for which there are abstracts and which do not get heavy use.

When there is a choice of forms, the following points will be considered:

1. Clearness of copy;
2. Ease of use;
3. The form in which related materials are already held;
4. Availability of adequate equipment for reading and printing.

Policies by Subject of Material

The following scales are used to give more precise definition to the various strengths in the library's collection. Level or depth of collection (1 to 5 on the Subject Strength Scale) and target group for whom the subject is being built (A to F on the Clientele Scale) have been assigned to specific subjects and materials, as applicable.

SUBJECT STRENGTH SCALE

1. Most basic important titles providing foundation for the subject. General subject treatment. Highly selected. One or two outstanding periodical titles. Mostly current. Considerable turnover. Basic reference tools.
2. Medium depth and scope of subject field, including most recognized standard books and periodicals plus judicious supplemental coverage as needed. Emphasis on current collection but also considerable retention. Retrospective materials sought only to fill significant historical gaps. Most important periodical titles giving general treatment of subject. Most important reference tools. State documents carefully selected on an individual basis. Introductory series of federal documents only. English language.
3. All principal materials covering all major and many minor aspects of the subject, heavily supplemented with additional materials of an increasingly specialized nature. Current and retrospective coverage. Important general and specialized periodical titles. Thorough reference tool coverage. State document series as needed. Wide range of federal documents, including some specialized series. Materials in major foreign languages and technical report literature as needed.
4. Entire scope of subject field covered, but degree of depth of coverage may vary. Strong retrospective coverage. Primary source material, extensive report literature and extensive document coverage (state, fed-

eral and other nations) included. Materials in foreign languages as needed. Scholarly treatment.

5. Exhaustive coverage, everything written, in all languages, both current and retrospective.

CLIENTELE SCALE

A. Casual user—One who uses materials for recreational purposes.
B. Independent investigator—One who seeks knowledge or information for a specific purpose or project.
C. Practicing professional—One who uses materials for a specific work-related purpose.
D. Undergraduate—One who uses materials in support of undergraduate course requirements.
E. Graduate—One who uses materials in support of graduate study.
F. Research specialist—One who uses materials in support of advanced and esoteric research.

ADDITIONAL SYMBOLS USED

−1 Only minimal coverage.
 + Higher level than the numerical rating assigned, but not high enough to justify moving to the next point on the scale.
4− The library will attempt to acquire everything currently available on the subject.

LIBRARY SCIENCE

Library science will be collected at a medium level (2) for the use of the practicing librarian (C), with special strength in public library-related materials (3). Materials will be chosen according to the general criteria given previously in this policy statement, with practicality and currency stressed.

PHILOSOPHY AND RELIGION

Philosophy

The collection will be of medium scope and depth (2), built for the independent investigator (B). Classic and standard works will be included as will treatments of modern philosophical concerns.

Religion

The collection will be of medium scope and depth (2), built primarily for the independent investigator (B). The professional clergy will be best served by the area's numerous theological libraries.

Materials shall include but not be limited to:

1. Sacred books of all major faiths, including all important versions of the Bible and the Bible in familiar foreign languages, as per demand;
2. Doctrines and histories of all religions and denominations, with emphasis on those found in the United States;
3. Commentaries and concordances;

4. Practical aspects of church administration, written for the layman;
5. Agnosticism and atheism;
6. New trends, ideas, and movements in religion;
7. Inspirational books and periodicals (also to serve clientele A).

Materials in both subjects will be chosen according to the general criteria given previously in this policy statement, with the following special considerations:

1. All religions and denominations will be represented as fairly as possible.
2. Strictly sectarian propaganda and tracts of an obviously proselytizing nature will be excluded. Those items written in an authoritative, informative and dispassionate manner will be preferred.
3. The very specialized and excessively theological or scholarly treatment will be avoided.

SOCIAL SCIENCES

The social sciences will be collected to medium depth and scope (2) with the independent investigator (B) as the target group. Urban affairs and government will be developed more extensively to serve the City and regional officials and employees (clientele C), a special target group. Psychology, Afro-American culture, feminism, and career advancement will also receive more emphasis; statistics of all types will be collected heavily. The adult independent learner will be served extensively by materials to further self-study.

Areas of selection in order by collection level:

- Statistics on all subjects, national, international, state, and local levels 4C, with emphasis on St. Louis statistics 4−, current.
- Careers and career development for the adult, current 3B.
- Afro-American history and culture 3B.
- Women, feminism 3B.
- Psychology 3B.
- Transportation 3C. This will be a practical collection of transportation materials aimed at the day-to-day needs of those involved with the transportation industry. Special areas of emphasis will be mass transit, river and rail transport, planning, technology and regulation.
- Government, coverage of all levels but emphasis on state and municipal government, 3BC.
- Urban affairs 2+C, St. Louis area 4C, including city and regional planning 2C, St. Louis 3C. The library is the designated depository for all City documents and publications and will acquire any other available material on St. Louis urban affairs from a non-city source.
- Public finance 2+B.
- Political science 2+BC.
- Sociology 2BC.
- Social problems 2B.
- Crime and criminology 2B.
- Education 2B. Parents are the primary target group.
- Adult Education (methodology) 2B.
- Adult Basic Education (methodology) 2B.

- Special education 2B.
- Vocational education (methodology) 1B.
- School Administration 1B.
- Teacher training 1B.
- International law and relations 2B.
- Labor 2B.
- Communications 2BC.
- Social work 1+C.
- Statistical methodology 1BC.
- Military science 1B.

Special types of materials acquired:

1. Test manuals, civil service and scholastic, with an emphasis on CLEP materials 4B;
2. College catalogs, from all institutions of higher education in Missouri and Illinois;
3. Programmed learning tools for the adult independent learner;
4. High interest—low level materials for the adult basic education student 3B;
5. Municipal codes, St. Louis and other municipalities in Missouri or other states.

Materials will be chosen in accordance with the general criteria given previously in this policy statement, avoiding the esoteric, the exceedingly specific, scholarly and technical, except for materials dealing with St. Louis which will be acquired as extensively as possible regardless of scholarly treatment or esoteric subject.

LAW

The law collection will be built for lay citizens and will provide enough scope and depth that their basic, legal information needs may be met (rating: 2). Lawyers, law school students and other legal researchers will be more adequately served by the area's law libraries. The collection will consist of the basic series, popular works, and some texts.

Areas of selection and types of materials acquired:

General

1. Popular books and standard texts (very selectively acquired) on court procedure, jury duty, wills, marriage and divorce, patents, copyrights, corporation law, criminal law and other works that pertain directly to the practical needs of the ordinary citizen, current only;
2. Reference tools, such as dictionaries, phrase books, directories, one-volume encyclopedias, guides to legal research, books of forms, current only.

Constitutions

1. United States, retrospective and current;
2. Missouri, retrospective and current;
3. Other states, current only;
4. Other nations, current only.

Statutory Law

1. United States:

   - Code, annotated, retrospective and current;
   - Statutes, retrospective and current;
   - Subject compilations of U.S. law, current only.

2. Missouri:

   - Revised Statutes, retrospective and current;
   - Session laws, retrospective and current.

3. Other states:

   - Illinois codes and statutes, current only;
   - Subject compilations of state laws, current only.

4. St. Louis:

   - Code, retrospective and current;
   - Ordinances, retrospective and current.

5. Other cities and counties:
   - Codes for St. Louis County, nearby municipalities such as East St. Louis, Kirkwood, etc., and selected other cities nationwide will be acquired, current only.

Case Law

1. United States:

   - Supreme Court decisions, retrospective and current;
   - Agency decisions (e.g., Patent Court, Customs Court, etc.) retrospective and current.

2. Missouri:

   - All Missouri court cases, retrospective and current (in commercial series, *Southwestern Reporter, Missouri Cases*);
   - Digest of the Opinions of the Missouri Attorney General.

3. St. Louis:

   - St. Louis Daily Record.

Materials Omitted

1. Commercial reporter series generally, except as noted above;
2. Statutory and case law from other counties, cities, states, and nations, except as noted above;
3. Legal encyclopedias;
4. Legal texts except see *General*, 1., p. 105.

Materials will be chosen according to the criteria given previously in this policy statement, with the emphasis on the practical and up-to-date rather than on the scholarly and historical. In all cases the most current material available will be acquired so that incorrect and misleading information is not dispensed.

LANGUAGES

Besides materials on the history and structure of languages generally, at least one grammar, dictionary, and reader (if available) will be acquired for any of the world's languages as needed. Additional materials geared to all levels of learning, including record and cassette kits, will be acquired in those languages which are emphasized: English, French, Spanish, German, Italian and Russian. Additional materials may also be acquired for other languages as needed.

Areas of selection in order by collection level:

- English 3B
- German language 1+B
- Romance languages 1+B
- American Indian languages 1+B
- Classical languages 1B
- Scandinavian languages 1B
- Slavic languages 1B
- African languages 1B
- Linguistics 1B
- Celtic languages −1B
- Oriental languages −1B

BUSINESS AND ECONOMICS

Business, economics, and related subjects (management, marketing, personnel, banking, finance, etc.) will be purchased at a 2 level, except for current business statistics (3). The business community, those persons actively and currently engaged in the field, (C) will be the target group. Investments as a subject, however, will be geared to the needs of the independent investigator (B).

Subjects related to specific St. Louis business interests will be collected most heavily, with business on the national level receiving the next highest emphasis, and foreign commerce being only selectively covered.

Special types of materials acquired:

1. Directories—product, geographic, business and organization; local (with emphasis on the St. Louis area 4−), state, national, international (2);
2. Looseleaf tax and investment services (2);
3. Annual reports of American companies, by decreasing emphasis: St. Louis area (4−), Missouri and Illinois, the rest of the country.

Materials will be chosen according to the general criteria previously mentioned in this policy statement, with the stress on relevance and currency.

SCIENCE AND TECHNOLOGY

The natural science collection will be built to medium scope and depth (2) for the use of the layman (B). Applied science and technology generally will receive greater emphasis (3). Materials in these areas will be acquired to serve the practical, daily needs of St. Louis' working engineers, chemists and manufacturers and the St. Louis business community as a whole (clientele C). Patent searchers, both lay and professional, are a special target group. Strengths will be built in the general subject areas of manufacturing, materials, mechanisms and machinery.

Areas of selection in order by collection level:

Science

- Ecology 3BC
- Energy 3C
- Climatology 2+B, strong statistical coverage local, state, national, world
- Chemistry 2C
- Applied Physics 2C
- Geology 2B
- Anthropology 2B
- Natural history 1B
- Biology 1B
- Botany 1B
- Zoology 1B
- Astronomy 1B
- Theoretical physics 1B
- Physiology 1B
- Oceanography 1B
- Mathematics 1B
- Cartography 1B
- Geodesy 1B
- Microbiology −1B

Technology

- Motor vehicle repair 4−C
- Small engine and appliance repair 4C
- Chemical technology 3C
- Mechanical engineering 3C
- Electrical engineering 3C
- Civil engineering 3C
- Manufacturing 3C
- Motor vehicles 3BC
- Computer programming languages 3C
- Electronic data processing 2C
- Petroleum technology 2C
- Food science and technology 2C
- Building construction 2C
- Nuclear engineering 2C
- Handicrafts, manual arts 2BC
- Aeronautics 2C
- Aeronautical engineering 2B
- Astronautics 2B
- Mining and metallurgy 2BC
- Agricultural engineering 2B
- Farming, farm management 2B
- Forestry 2B
- Animal culture 2B
- Gardening 2B
- Animal nutrition 1B
- Agronomy 1B

Special types of materials acquired:

1. Patents, U.S. complete, British abridged, Canadian abridged;
2. Industrial standards, retrospective and current, 4C;
3. Auto repair manuals, retrospective and current, 4−C; farm machinery manuals, 3C;
4. Schematics for radio and television repair, retrospective and current, 4BC;
5. House organs of some substance and technical value (not newsletters), with the emphasis on local companies.

Materials will be chosen according to the general criteria previously given in this policy statement, with the following special considerations:

1. Overall emphasis is on practical and applied science and technology, rather than on the theoretical.
2. Reputation of author and publisher, clarity of presentation and quality of illustrations are more important than literary quality.
3. Highly technical material on limited areas of scientific or technical development may be acquired only if they are of special importance to patrons and if their contents are readily accessible through indexes or other tools.

MEDICINE

Only nontechnical materials on medicine, dentistry, drugs, psychiatry, obstetrics, diet, disease, and related subjects will be chosen. This area of the collection will be geared to the lay reader rather than the health professional.

Areas of selection in order by collection level:

- Diseases and ailments 2B
- Public health 2C
- Nutrition 2B
- Medicine 1B
- Nursing 1B

Materials will be selected according to the general criteria previously given in this policy statement with special attention given to the reliability of authors and publishers.

HOME ECONOMICS

Home economics will be built to a level 2 for clientele B, with stress on the specific subjects of sewing, grooming, cooking and personal finance. Cookbooks, general and specific, basic and gourmet, representing all types of national cookery, quantity cooking and cooking for special diets will be collected (2). Child psychology, development and care will also be acquired at a medium level (2B). Special emphasis, however, will be placed on home improvement (4B), including planning, building, restoring, remodeling, repairing and decorating.

General selection criteria will apply.

ART, ARCHITECTURE, MUSIC

Architecture will be one of the library's strongest subjects, especially as it pertains to the St. Louis area. Art, particularly the practical and popular aspects, will also recieve heavy coverage.

Areas of selection in order by collection level:

- Architecture (especially St. Louis) 4CF
- St. Louis in art and photographs 4BC
- Antiques and collectibles 4BC
- Costume 4BC
- Arts and crafts 4B
- Decorative arts 3BC
- Individual artists, their lives and works, stress on Occidental artists, particularly western Europe and U.S. 3BC
- History of art 3B
- Commercial art 2C
- Music 2+B
- Music instruction and study 2B, especially "how to play" various instruments
- Drawing 2B
- Painting 2B
- Sculpture 2B
- Print media 2B
- Photography 2B
- Performing arts 2B
- Recreation 2B, the popular rather than educational treatment of sports, games and other recreational activities
- Drafting 1BC
- Art criticism 1BC
- Illumination 1BC
- Film study 1B
- Iconography −1B

Special types of materials acquired:

1. Catalogs of museum and private collections;
2. Guidebooks to collections or to cities, historical and current;
3. Exhibition catalogs, very selected;
4. Yearbooks of auction records;
5. Pictures, unframed (see p. 100 for selection criteria);
6. Art slides (see p. 100 for selection criteria);
7. Sound recordings (see p. 100 for selection criteria);
8. Music scores (see p. 100 for selection criteria).

Types of materials omitted:

1. Sales and dealers' catalogs;
2. Auction records.

Materials will be chosen according to the general criteria previously mentioned in this policy statement, with technical quality of reproductions and recordings stressed. Although English language works are preferred, important works in foreign languages will be acquired.

LITERATURE

Literature, as a broad subject, will be collected at a level 2+ for clientele B. The collection will consist equally of works of literature and works about literature, authors and playwrights.

Areas of selection in order by collection level:

- St. Louis and Missouri literature 4B
- American literature 3B
- English literature 3B
- Afro-American literature 3B
- Literary criticism 2B
- Poetry 2B
- Drama 2B
- Folklore, consisting primarily of the legends themselves rather than works about the legends 2B. Special emphases:
  fairy tales 4B
  American folklore 3B
  Ozark folklore 3B
  American Indian folklore 3B
- Literary history 2B
- German literature 2B
- Romance literatures 2B
- Journalism 1B

Special types of materials acquired:

1. Play scripts 3BC: Complete sets of works of major American and English playwrights, selected works of minor American and English playwrights, selected works of major European playwrights, very selected works of other foreign playwrights;
2. Literature and folklore on sound recordings.

Materials will be chosen in accordance with the general criteria previously given in this policy statement, with the following special considerations:

1. Complete works of individual authors will be collected only if the author is prominent and highly respected in the literary field or is a St. Louis

author, or if each title merits acquisition in its own right.
2. Highly learned treatises on esoteric literary topics will be excluded.

CHILDREN'S LITERATURE

The children's literature collection will consist of aids in the research and study of children's literature. It will contain two bodies of material in order of emphasis as follows:

1. Books and periodicals about children's literature for the use of adults working in the subject area (4BCD). This will include comprehensive studies, critical evaluations, guides, bibliographies, biographical material on children's authors and illustrators, and related subjects. Storytelling techniques will be another emphasis. Materials will be chosen according to the general criteria previously given in this policy statement.
2. Books and periodicals written for children from preschool to eighth grade, a current and historical collection of the best works available, emphasizing folklore, fairy tales and American award books. A small, representative collection of juvenile literature in foreign languages will be maintained.

Juvenile literature will be chosen according to:

- Suitability of content and vocabulary to age level;
- Importance to the balance of the collection;
- Quality of writing;
- Quality of visual art;
- Accuracy of information;
- Promotion of worthwhile ideals and values;
- Contribution to an appreciation of reading.

HISTORY, GEOGRAPHY, ARCHAEOLOGY, TRAVEL

Acquisitions in the area of history will be at the 2+B level. Most materials will be purchased for their comprehensive and general treatment of all countries, periods and peoples of the world. Primary emphasis will be on the United States, with secondary emphasis on the major countries of Western Europe and Africa. Specialized materials may be selected as needed in these areas.

Areas of selection in order of emphasis:

- St. Louis history 4B-F
- Missouri history 3+B-F
- U.S. history 3B
- American Indians 3B
- World War II 3B
- Civil War 3B
- World history and histories of other nations 2B
- Geography 2B
- Archaeology 2B, especially St. Louis area 3BF
- Travel 2AB

Materials will be chosen according to the general criteria previously given in this policy statement with the following special considerations:

1. Narrative travel accounts will be selected only if judged especially worthwhile.

2. Travel guidebooks for the U.S. and foreign countries, historical and current, will be purchased.
3. Extremely scholarly materials will be excluded.

Local History and Materials

One of the primary goals of the library will be to maintain a comprehensive collection of works about St. Louis and St. Louisans. Secondary but important coverage will be given to Missouri and the "Metro East" area. These emphases are mentioned throughout this policy as statements on specific formats and subjects require special mention of them.

Pertinent to the area of local history is a definition of a local author as one who (1) was born in St. Louis, (2) graduated from a St. Louis elementary or high school, (3) has lived here for at least one year, or (4) has gained local prominence.

Local interest materials will not be automatically added to the collection but will be considered according to the general objectives and criteria.

BIOGRAPHY

Biographies will be purchased in accordance with subject emphases and selection criteria stated generally throughout this policy.

Areas of selection in order of emphasis:

- St. Louisans and former St. Louisans—exhaustive as available (4−). Missourians (4);
- Individual biographies of well-known people in all fields—worldwide coverage but emphasis on Americans;
- Obscure persons whose lives are of general or representative interest;
- Collected biographies, including persons for whom there are no individual biographies or for whom additional coverage is desirable.

Special types of materials acquired:

1. Local, national, international and professional Who's Whos, acquired as extensively as available;
2. Biographical reference books and indexes with historical as well as current coverage (see also p. 98).

GENEALOGY AND HERALDRY

1. *Genealogy,* a unique collection for the St. Louis area, will be built to the research level (4BCF).

Areas of emphasis:

- Genealogical materials from St. Louis, Missouri and Illinois, heaviest emphasis;
- Genealogical material, especially county histories, from the East, Midwest and South, with particular emphasis on regional states which had the most influence on the population of Missouri: Virginia, North Carolina, South Carolina, Georgia, Kentucky, Pennsylvania, Ohio, Tennessee and Indiana. There will be general statewide coverage of other states as needed;

- German and German-American genealogical and historical source material;
- Genealogical material for the black race.

Special types of materials acquired:

- County gazetteers;
- Census records, territorial, state and federal and their indexes as available;
- Immigration and passenger lists;
- Military records;
- Landownership atlases.

2. *Heraldry,* insignia and flags, especially American and British, will receive medium scope and depth of coverage (2) and will be acquired to serve the needs of the layman (B). This collection also is unique to the area.

Materials will be selected in both subject areas in accordance with the criteria given previously in this policy statement, with the following special considerations:

1. Individual family histories generally will not be purchased. Exception: family histories of particular relevance to St. Louis, St. Louis County, Missouri and the Midwest will be acquired as available.
2. Highly technical works on heraldry, unless they contain large numbers of names, will be excluded.
3. Materials in familiar foreign languages may be acquired if they are of particular significance and value to the collection.

FICTION

Novels will be purchased for the following purposes:

1. To serve as educational tools and to enrich human understanding by dealing informatively with social, personal, racial, ethnic or religious situations;
2. To satisfy the need for recreational reading materials for patrons of differing tastes, interests, purposes and reading skills.

While it is not possible to set up a single standard of literary quality, the library will prefer fiction:

1. That is competently written;
2. That has constructive and plausible characterizations;
3. That gives an honest portrayal of the human experiences with which it deals;
4. That contributes to the balance of the collection in regard to (a) types and styles of literature, (b) subjects treated and (c) patron appeal.

However, a very limited selection of novels of lesser quality may be purchased to satisfy demand. If possible, such books will be purchased in the paperback format.

Other selection considerations:

1. A basic collection of standard and classic novels will be maintained.
2. Titles will be judged on their individual merit. No attempt will be made

to collect the complete works of an author except when she/he is prominent and highly respected in the literary world or is a St. Louis author.

3. Representative novels in French, Spanish, German, Italian and Russian may be added.
4. Experimental novels, while often controversial, will be considered for purchase as they reflect new trends and styles of expression.
5. Books written about St. Louis or with St. Louis as a setting will be especially considered for purchase.
6. Titles written obviously and exclusively for sensational or pornographic purposes will not be chosen, but the library will not exclude a title because of objectionable language or vivid description of sex or violence if the author is dealing honestly and realistically with her/his theme. The library recognizes that any given title may offend some patrons. However, selections will not be made on the basis of any anticipated approval or disapproval, but solely on the merits of the work in relation to the collection, the library's objectives, and the interests of the readers (see also *Intellectual Freedom Statement,* p. 386).

Gifts Policy

The library will accept gifts of books and other materials with the understanding that they become the property of the library and will be evaluated against the same criteria as purchased materials. The library will make the final decision on the use or other disposition of all donations and will decide the conditions of display, housing and access to the materials. If gifts of marginal value are offered, processing and handling costs and use of shelf space will be prime considerations. No special shelves or sections will be designated for gift collections but an appropriate book plate will be placed in each gift identifying the donor and purpose of donation. The library will not provide evaluations of gifts for tax relief or other purposes.

Funds for the purchase of materials will be accepted. The library encourages donors to place as few restrictions as possible on the funds in order to permit the most flexible use of the donation for the enrichment of the collection.

Maintaining the Collection

WEEDING AND DISCARDING

In order to maintain an active working collection of high standard, subject specialists will periodically examine the collection for the purpose of withdrawing unused items, unnecessary duplicates, outdated, worn or damaged materials, using the same criteria as are applied to acquisitions. In general last copies of important titles will be retained at Main.

DUPLICATION OF TITLES

Duplication of titles is not encouraged. Exceptions are the following:

1. Local materials. Two copies of books, documents, reports, surveys, on St. Louis, the St. Louis metropolitan area, important St. Louisans, or by

important area authors may be acquired. More copies may be acquired after careful consideration of need. Duplicates of important works on Missouri, on or by Missourians may be acquired.

2. Reference materials for which there is a need in more than one subject department may be acquired.
3. Books on any subject which are in heavy demand may be duplicated in the interest of providing good service both to individual patrons and to the System. Paperbound copies will be preferred as available.

In all cases, any request for duplication should be well justified.

REPLACEMENT OF MATERIALS

The library will not automatically replace all materials withdrawn because of loss, damage, or wear. Decisions will be based on the following considerations:

1. Demand for the specific title;
2. Importance and value of the specific title;
3. Number of copies held;
4. Existing coverage of the subject;
5. Availability of newer and better materials on the subject;
6. Availability of the item in another format.

Other considerations:

1. Materials chosen for replacement will be replaced by the most current edition available.
2. Reference materials will be replaced automatically as new editions become available.

MATERIALS SELECTION POLICY FOR BRANCHES AND COMMUNITY SERVICES

Objectives of Selection

The collections of the branch and community service units will be current, popular, flexible and general, molded very closely to the needs, interests and goals of the particular clienteles served. In each case, the aim is not necessarily a comprehensive collection, but rather a collection which responds to the individual community's informational, educational and recreational needs. Each unit must assess these needs objectively, weighing them in terms of System goals and patron demand, both real and potential. Collections should serve to counter ignorance, intolerance, indifference and prejudice in all their forms.

Responsibility for Selection

Responsibility for selection begins with the age-level coordinators assisted by the book evaluation committees who select and or compile recommended lists of materials. Age-level librarians in each unit then make the decision as to which of these preselected titles will be chosen for their units with the approval of the age-level coordinators. Age-level librarians, other staff members and patrons may suggest titles freely and these titles will be reviewed and given full consideration. Ultimate responsibility rests with the librarian, who operates within this framework of policies determined by the Board of Directors.

Policies for Selection by Clientele Served

ADULTS

Adults will be served by practical materials highly relevant to their day-to-day needs, interests and activities. All backgrounds, abilities and levels of education identifiable in the adult community served by the unit will be taken into consideration as materials are selected. The independent learner, bent upon an individual course of self-education, will be provided with introductory materials, with more advanced materials to be supplied by the Main Library.

Nonfiction

The units will provide the most useful and basic materials in all subjects of established or realistically anticipated demand in their particular communities. The emphasis in all cases will be on the current and popular treatment of subjects, with a view to maintaining a lively and active collection. General treatment will usually be preferred unless there is an identified need for specific treatment of the topic. The more advanced, sophisticated and technical materials of enduring reference value will be collected by Main Library. Heavy, permanent subject concentrations will not be built, but particular subjects may be emphasized as agency programs adapt to changing community interests.

Other criteria for the selection of nonfiction are:
1. Readability;
2. Accuracy of information;
3. Quality of writing and/or visual art;
4. Price;
5. Balance of viewpoints in the collection;
6. Reputation and significance of the author;
7. Format and quality of technical production;
8. Accessibility of materials in other libraries (without abdicating each unit's responsibility to cover its local patron demand from its own collection).

An item need not meet all of these criteria in order to be acceptable. When judging the desirability of materials, any combination of standards may be used.

Fiction

Fiction collections may be characterized as highly transient. Except for a few standard titles, no attempt will be made to maintain permanent collections. Novels will be purchased for the following purposes:

1. To satisfy the need for recreational reading materials for patrons of differing tastes, interests, purposes and reading skills;
2. To serve as educational tools and to enrich human understanding by dealing informatively with social, personal, racial, ethnic or religious situations.

Selection considerations:

1. Units will prefer fiction that is competently written, has constructive and plausible characterizations and gives an honest portrayal of the human experiences with which it deals. But novels which do not meet these criteria may be purchased to satisfy heavy reader interest. Whenever possible, such books will be purchased in paperback format.
2. Each title will be judged on its own merit. No attempt will be made to collect complete works of an author.
3. Experimental novels, while often controversial, may be considered for purchase as they reflect new trends and styles of expression.
4. Novels in foreign languages may be acquired according to demand.
5. Books written about St. Louis or with St. Louis as a setting will be especially considered for purchase.
6. Titles written obviously and exclusively for sensational or pornographic purposes will not be chosen, but the units will not exclude a title because of objectionable language or vivid description of sex or violence if the author is dealing honestly and realistically with the chosen theme. The units recognize that any given title may offend some patrons. However, selections will not be made on the basis of any anticipated approval or disapproval but solely on the merits of the work and the interests of the readers. (See also *Intellectual Freedom Statement*, p. 386).

YOUNG ADULTS

Young adults (roughly grades 7–12) will be served from the general collections but will also have access to materials specially selected to meet the particular recreational, emotional, and informational concerns of this age group.

Such collections will be fluid, flexible, current, and attractive, containing materials which are (1) in demand, (2) of special quality which will help young adults understand themselves and others, broaden their viewpoints and knowledge of the world, stimulate their curiosity, expand their reading ability and enjoyment, and guide them in the transition from children's stories to adult books and materials. Emphasis will be on popular, browsing materials, primarily paperbacks, records, and cassettes, rather than on reference tools and school-related materials which are available generally in the library. Any material, including that written for juvenile or adult audiences, may be selected if it meets these criteria and if it is appropriate in style, format and content to the young adult audience.

It is recognized that there is a great range of maturity between the ages of twelve and eighteen and that all books selected might not be equally suitable in subject and vocabulary for all ages. Discretion will be used, but selection for older teenagers will not be confined to levels appropriate for the younger ones.

CHILDREN

Branch and community service outlets are the primary public library service points for the children of St. Louis, preschool through the eighth grade. As such, most units will maintain broad juvenile collections, including materials ranging from standard titles to high-interest items. In all cases the children will be served by materials, book or nonbook, which most closely reflect their inspirational, recreational and educational needs, their interests, ages and levels of mental development.

Further goals of juvenile selection are:

1. To broaden the children's horizons;
2. To help them formulate their life goals;
3. To make them aware of the pleasures and knowledge to be derived from the use of books and other materials.

Juvenile materials will be selected according to:

1. Patron interest and need;
2. Literary quality and/or quality of visual art;
3. Fair and accurate treatment of the subject;
4. Suitability of content, vocabulary and style of presentation to age level.

Other selection considerations:

1. Each title of a series, whether fiction or nonfiction, must be evaluated individually, except for generally inferior series which will not be purchased.
2. Abridgements will be selected only when the story and concepts are considered suitable for children but the style of writing of the original is too involved for the average child. Generally, adaptations will not be acquired. Only the best retellings of folk tales will be considered.
3. Generally, comic books will not be acquired.

STUDENTS

Students' school-related needs will be served with supplementary reading and reference materials, but the units will not attempt to take over the curriculum-support function of the school library. It is expected that each school will meet its own curriculum demands with adequate books and other materials.

BLIND AND PHYSICALLY HANDICAPPED

Anyone, juvenile or adult, who cannot read or handle conventional printed matter because of a physical disability is eligible for the services of the Wolfner Memorial Library. Under a contract with the Division of the Blind and Physically Handicapped of the Library of Congress, Wolfner serves the special reading needs of patrons throughout the State of Missouri (for special criteria, see p. 99).

Policies by Type of Material

BOOKS

Hardbound.   Titles in hardcover will continue to be the mainstay of most unit collections and will be purchased for long-term use.

Paperbound. For reasons of economy, paperbacks will be increasingly considered in the selection process. Titles may be purchased in this format when:

1. The paperback edition of a title is available at the same time as the hardbound or very shortly thereafter;
2. Duplicates are needed to satisfy high demand;
3. The subject is anticipated to be of current interest only and a permanent copy of the title is not necessary in terms of the unit's goals;
4. The title is available only in paperback.

General selection policies and criteria will apply to the purchase of paperbound materials.

Special types of books.

1. Books in large type may be purchased for patrons with partial vision, according to local need. Main Library will be responsible for a large support collection of these books.
2. Textbooks will be purchased only when they provide the best coverage of a subject and are useful to the general public; they will not be duplicated to satisfy the demands of a specific school course. The library assumes its responsibility to be that of providing books which will broaden the student's interest in a particular subject that may stem from the use of a textbook, rather than in providing the textbook itself.

REFERENCE MATERIALS

Although almost any item in a library, whether book, magazine, newspaper, pamphlet, or nonprint source, can and will be used to provide reference service, traditional reference materials will be chosen to answer the specific information needs of the patrons served.

These reference books will be (1) the ready-reference sources, statistical, chronological and short narrative, including dictionaries and basic indexes, designed for providing short, quick answers, which will be available in all units and (2) the next level of somewhat more specialized but still basic reference tools which will be available only in branches. Units will select materials on the second level according to the individual community's needs. Main Library will be responsible for an in-depth, extensive, supporting collection of reference and bibliographic tools.

The following types of materials may be included:

1. General dictionaries and encyclopedias;
2. Selected specialized encyclopedias, as needed;
3. Handbooks and statistical compendia;
4. Directories, primarily local telephone and city directories;
5. Atlases and gazetteers, general;
6. Indexes covering material already owned;
7. General biographical dictionaries.

Reference books will be chosen for:

1. Accuracy and authenticity;
2. Community need;
3. Scope and depth of coverage;

4. Ease of use;
5. Special locating features.

PERIODICALS

Periodicals will be chosen for the following purposes:

1. To supplement the book collection as an additional source of information, especially current information;
2. To satisfy recreational reading needs;
3. To serve the staff as book selection aids and professional reading.

Selection of titles will follow general criteria in terms of scope and depth of subject coverage, with the following special considerations:

1. Community demand;
2. Accessibility of content through *Readers' Guide to Periodical Literature;*
3. Price.

Special types of periodicals:

1. Foreign language periodicals may be chosen according to demand, in areas which have significant concentrations of foreign speaking people.
2. Titles in large type may be acquired for patrons with partial vision.

NEWSPAPERS

Newspapers will be purchased for the following purposes:

1. To provide current news coverage;
2. To satisfy recreational reading needs;
3. To provide a unique source of local history information.

Both major St. Louis daily newspapers and the local neighborhood newspaper for the unit's service area may be acquired. In addition, the following may be acquired according to community interest and demand:

1. Racial or ethnic newspapers, in foreign languages, if necessary;
2. Major newspapers of national coverage.

PAMPHLETS

Pamphlets will be purchased for the following purposes:

1. To supplement the book collection in areas of heavy but short-term demand;
2. To supply current information not yet published in book form;
3. To make available material on subjects not easily found in books or other sources.

Pamphlets will be selected according to the objectives and criteria stated elsewhere in this policy with the following special consideration: Since many systems are issued for propaganda or advertising purposes, it is important to maintain a balance of viewpoints and to avoid inflammatory treatment or distortion for commercial purposes. Pamphlet material, to be acceptable, should always have the issuing agency clearly identified.

FILMS

16mm films. 16mm films will be considered an integral part of the System's collection. They will be purchased to provide (1) information, (2) education, (3) cultural enrichment and (4) entertainment in a unique medium to patrons of all ages. The collection will reflect current community interests and will be developed with a view to high turnover rather than historical permanence. Selections will be aimed at the general audience rather than special interest groups.

Selection criteria:

1. Patron interest;
2. Timeliness and usefulness of the message;
3. Effectiveness and originality of presentation;
4. Authenticity;
5. Fairness of viewpoint;
6. Power to evoke a response or to prompt discussion from the audience;
7. Technical quality including clear soundtrack, true color, sharp photography, concise and organized narrative. But there are occasions when flaws in technique are overshadowed by the importance or vitality of the subject matter. If a film has something to say and says it effectively, and there is a need for it, that film should be considered even if it is not technically perfect.

Special selection considerations:

1. Films on St. Louis will be bought as available and will be accorded a permanent place in the collection.
2. Representative films from various stages of development of film-making will be acquired.
3. Animated treatments of subjects may be acquired, but generally the popular children's cartoons will not be purchased.
4. Films will not be selected for classroom use or teacher training since this is the responsibility of the schools.
5. Sponsored films on loan or deposit will be added to the collection in accordance with general selection and gift policies. Sponsored films which are primarily advertisements of commercial products or propaganda for special interest groups will not be added.

8mm films. 8mm films will be chosen for recreational purposes but the collection will not be extensive. Demand will be the primary factor in selection.

SOUND RECORDINGS

Recorded sound collections will consist of phonodiscs, cassettes and 8-track cartridges. Selection emphasis will be on popular music. Readings, documentaries, children's stories, spoken word, language learning and other self-education recordings will be purchased according to demand.

Recordings will be selected with the following considerations in mind:

1. Demand;   3. Technical quality of the recording.
2. Price;

OTHER NONPRINT MEDIA

Other nonprint media will be purchased if they represent the most suitable, useful and effective format in which to present a subject to a particular clientele. All general selection criteria apply as to subject coverage and level. Additional technical considerations will be quality of photography or art work, color reproduction and editing.

GIFTS POLICY

The library will accept gifts of books and other materials with the understanding that they become the property of the library and will be evaluated against the same criteria as purchased materials. The library will make the final decision on the use or other disposition of all donations and will decide the conditions of display, housing and access to the materials. If gifts of marginal value are offered, processing and handling costs and use of shelf space will be prime considerations. No special shelves or sections will be designated for gift collections but an appropriate book plate will be placed in each gift identifying the donor and purpose of donation. The library will not provide evaluations of gifts for tax relief or other purposes.

Funds for the purchase of materials will be accepted. The library encourages donors to place as few restrictions as possible on the funds in order to permit the most flexible use of the donation for the enrichment of the collection.

Policies by Subject of Material

RELIGION

The following types of materials may be acquired:
1. Inspirational books by established authors;
2. Introductory treatments of comparative religion, theology and mythology;
3. Popular studies of new movements, trends and ideas;
4. Authoritative and informative histories and doctrines of major religions and denominations, fairly represented.

Strictly sectarian propaganda and tracts of an obviously proselytizing nature will be excluded.

MEDICINE

Only popular nontechnical materials on medicine, dentistry, drugs, psychiatry, obstetrics, diet, disease and related subjects will be chosen. General selection criteria will apply with special attention given to the reliability of the author and publisher of these materials.

LAW

Only popular treatments of practical legal subjects relevant to the lay citizen, such as legal and civil rights, jury duty, tenants' rights, court procedures, etc. will be purchased.

Compilations of laws of all states, condensed and nontechnical (such as the Legal Almanac series) may be included. Missouri and St. Louis codes, statutes and ordinances may be acquired as needed.

SEX EDUCATION

The units will openly provide books at all age levels which explain the processes of human physical development and reproduction in a factual, authoritative and up-to-date manner.

TEST MANUALS

Test manuals, scholastic, civil service and others, will be purchased freely as needed in the individual communities.

Maintaining the Collection

WEEDING

In order to maintain active, up-to-date, useful collections, age-level librarians in consultation with age-level coordinators will periodically examine all materials in terms of relevance to the collection, clientele and statements in this policy. Other specific factors to be considered in the decision to retire materials are:

1. Lack of usage;
2. Age of material and availability of more current material on the same subject;
3. Physical condition;
4. Accuracy;
5. Availability of the material in Main Library.

DUPLICATION OF TITLES

Although duplication of titles is not generally encouraged, multiple copies may be purchased in response to consistently heavy demand. Duplicates will be purchased in paperback if at all possible.

REPLACEMENT OF MATERIALS

The units will not automatically replace all materials withdrawn because of loss, damage, or wear. Decisions will be based on the following considerations:

1. Demand for the specific title;
2. Number of copies held;
3. Existing coverage of the subject within the unit or availability of materials at Main Library;
4. Availability of newer and better materials on the subject.

Materials chosen for replacement will be replaced by the most current edition available.

Knoxville-Knox County Public Library

DEFINITION OF RESPONSIBILITY

The public library is a unique democratic institution created to serve the informational, educational, cultural and recreational needs of the total community. Realizing its responsibility to provide the best library service possible to meet the varied needs of the residents of the metropolitan area, as well as to spend public monies wisely, the Board of Trustees of the Knoxville-Knox County Public Library has adopted the American Library Association's *Library Bill of Rights.*

USER-ORIENTED SERVICE

General Goal

The library aims to provide the highest quality user-oriented public library service which will effectively contribute to the development of our metropolitan area through the utilization of the broad range of contemporary media and technology.

Specific Objectives

1. Emphasize service to those library users whose needs are not the primary responsibility of other institutions in the metropolitan area.
2. Identify the informational and material needs the library can fulfill, and, when appropriate, provide referral service to other agencies.
3. Take the lead in planning cooperative endeavors with all institutional, organizational, industrial, and private libraries in the metropolitan area to assure the development, availability, and accessibility of resources in all subject areas in which all share proportionately the economic burdens and benefits.
4. In order to develop maximum, efficient, and economic library service, participate in cooperative informational services, networks, and systems on local, state, regional, national, and international bases.

Knoxville-Knox County Public Library, Knoxville, TN 37902

5. Determine methods and urge implementation of adequate remuneration for services rendered and services received between the Knoxville-Knox County Public Library and other governmental entities and private organizations.
6. Recognizing the public library as the logical center for independent and self learning, determine the public library's responsibility to students enrolled in educational institutions at all levels in our metropolitan area.
7. Develop a diversified public relations program which will generate increased library usage, support all facets of library service, and result in increased understanding and good will.
8. Develop the Lawson McGhee Library to provide in-depth resources and services to meet the identified specialized reference and bibliographic needs of the residents of Knoxville and Knox County, as well as those needs generated through cooperative networks such as the state-funded Regional Library system and the Area Resource Center program.
9. Continue to extend public library services into the community through a system of branch libraries, mobile units, and individual and group related services and programs.
10. To assure that each branch library, mobile unit, and special service will identify with its community, develop each unit with a uniqueness corresponding to the particular characteristics of its community.
11. Develop a program for improved communications with the staffs of community agencies in order to inform them about library services and materials useful to them and the people they serve.

MATERIALS COLLECTION AND SELECTION

General Goal

Develop collections of materials to meet the diverse library needs identified as the proper responsibility of the Knoxville-Knox County Public Library, including research and bibliographic requirements of residents with specialized research needs, as well as assuring that collections reflect the interests and cultural backgrounds of the communities served.

Specific Objectives

1. Continually revise the materials selection policy to assure that it reflects the changing interests and needs of this metropolitan area.
2. Recognizing the importance of the broad range of contemporary media as appropriate materials for, and approaches to, research, learning, and recreation, select materials without regard to format to best meet the needs of the community.
3. Communicate to the area's residents the responsibility of a free public library to make available information on all sides of all questions to all patrons.
4. To avoid unnecessary and expensive duplication of holdings and to insure that the residents of this metropolitan area have a total spectrum

of resources at their disposal, select materials cooperatively with all types of libraries in the area. The Knoxville-Knox County Public Library will assume responsibility for its share of specialized subject development.

5. Enhance the acquisitions program of the Lawson McGhee Library to insure greater scope of books and periodicals and other resources, both primary and secondary, for research, including national and subject bibliographies, foreign language publications, technical reports, documents, and significant ephemera.

6. Assure that the materials within each unit of the Knoxville-Knox County Public Library reflect the needs and interests of its community. However, an appropriate, balanced, basic collection will exist in each unit.

7. To meet the diverse needs of all levels of patronage from popular to specialized, utilize, in the selection of materials, the varying qualifications of library staff throughout the system.

8. In order to meet our responsibility for filling current informational needs, expedite the selection, acquisition, and processing of new materials.

9. Explore and utilize technological aids for more effective materials selection, assuring that efficient approaches to materials selection and acquisitions will support the philosophy of a user-oriented public library.

10. Continue to develop within the McClung Historical Collection an area resource and information center comprised of a comprehensive collection of materials pertaining to Knoxville, Knox County and East Tennessee.

THE LIBRARY'S COMMUNITY

The Knoxville-Knox County Public Library receives over 90% of its financial support from the governments of Knoxville and Knox County and in turn undertakes as its primary responsibility to provide the best possible public library service to meet the varied needs and interests of city and county residents. Currently the population to be served numbers nearly 300,000 and covers an area of 528 square miles. This includes the densely populated city which is separated into distinct communities by tradition, highways, ridges and rivers; the rapidly expanding suburbs; and the sparsely populated rural areas at the far reaches of the county, characterized by small, relatively isolated communities centered around agriculture or local industry.

Public library service to this developing area with its rising economic and educational levels is influenced by the existence of other libraries and information centers within the larger metropolitan area. These include the valuable resources of the main campus of the University of Tennessee, less than one mile from Lawson McGhee Library; the expanding library resources and services of the city and county public school systems; the specialized collections of the Tennessee Valley Authority, Knoxville College, and the Oak Ridge National Laboratories. Selection of public library materials will reflect cooperation with these and other institutions and complement rather than duplicate their collections and services.

In addition to local financing, the library also receives support from the state of Tennessee to serve as an Area Resource Center for three regions of the state-wide regional public library system, in order to provide specialized library materials, bibliographic information and interlibrary loan service. As long as this support continues and depending on the amount received, the library will select specialized materials and bibliographic research tools and services to respond to the broader community of users created by this program.

With these considerations in mind, and in keeping with the library's previously adopted statement of "Goals and Objectives," the Board of Trustees of the Knoxville-Knox County Public Library adopts this Materials Selection Policy.

DEFINITIONS

"Selection" refers to the decision that must be made either to add a specific item or types of material to the collection or to retain material already in the collection. It is a means of collection development to meet user needs and does not necessarily reflect the opinions or values of the individual selector or of the Library Board.

The words "book," "library materials" and other synonyms as they may appear in this policy have the widest possible meaning; all forms of recorded communication, from the traditional printed forms to the latest development in nonprint media, are therefore included in this definition.

The word "collection" refers to a group of books or other library material having a common characteristic or located in one place.

"The library" refers specifically to the Knoxville-Knox County Public Library.

RESPONSIBILITY FOR SELECTION OF LIBRARY MATERIALS

Ultimate responsibility for selection of materials rests with the library's director, who operates within the framework of policies, goals and objectives determined by the Library Board. The director will delegate to appropriate staff members authority to interpret and apply the policies in daily operations. It is the responsibility of each employee to record and communicate user requests and needs so that they may be considered in selection.

ORGANIZATION OF THE LIBRARY AS A FACTOR IN SELECTION

The library is composed of agencies and collections that are designed to make its total resources readily available and widely accessible to the community it serves. These agencies presently include:

- Lawson McGhee Library (the main library) with its departmental and special collections, extensive reference resources, and comprehensive circulating collection;

- Neighborhood branch libraries and the bookmobile, which have collections of general reading and reference materials planned to meet the particular needs of their communities;
- Deposit collections in a variety of locations.

Because the needs of the users of the individual units vary, so must the collections chosen for them, and it is in this respect that the organization of the library affects the selection of materials.

PURPOSE OF THE SELECTION POLICY

The purpose of this policy is to guide librarians in the selection of materials of contemporary significance and of permanent value and to inform the public about the principles upon which selections are made. Its primary objective is to ensure that public monies are spent wisely so that the library can provide the community with relevant materials in sufficient supply to make the library a dependable resource for most people most of the time.

GUIDELINES FOR SELECTION

Children's Collections

The library's collections for children will emphasize the development of reading and learning skills and reading for enjoyment by means of recreational literature and films. They also will emphasize the stimulation of a lifetime interest in continuous learning by means of accurate and interesting factual materials.

Adults' and Teenagers' Collections

The library's collections for adults and teenagers will emphasize their need to be accurately informed in order to make personal choices, to take responsible positions on current issues, and to keep up with changing developments in their vocational or avocational pursuits. Recognizing the different levels of interest and expertise based on age, experience, and educational or professional attainment, the library will select a wide range of materials in whatever media will best assist an individual or group to know and understand themselves and the world they live in.

All or some of the following general criteria will be considered when making selection decisions:

- Insight into human and social conditions;
- Suitability of subject, style and format for intended audience;
- Relevance to present and potential informational, educational and leisure-time needs;
- Importance as a document of the times;
- Reputation and/or significance of author;
- Attention of critics and reviewers;

- Relation to existing collection and other materials on the subject;
- Availability of material elsewhere in the community;
- Volume and nature of requests by the public.

Specific selection policies will be needed for particular subject areas, various formats, groups with special needs and the diverse community-centered units in the library system. These will be prepared as needed by staff appointed by the Director, who, after consultation with the Board of Trustees, will approve their implementation.

USE OF THE LIBRARY'S COLLECTION

The library recognizes that many books are controversial and that any given item may offend some patrons. Selections will not be made on the basis of any assumed approval or disapproval, but solely on the merit of the work as it relates to the library's objectives and serves the expressed or anticipated needs and interests of the community.

Library materials will not be marked or identified to show approval or disapproval of the contents, and nothing will be sequestered except for the express purpose of protecting it from injury or theft.

The use of rare and scholarly items of great value will be controlled to the extent required to preserve them from harm.

Responsibility for the reading of minors rests with their parents and legal guardians. Selection of adult materials will not be limited by the possibility that books may come into the possession of minors. Under ordinary circumstances children under the age of 14 will be expected to use the juvenile collections.

Patrons not finding desired material in the library's collection may request that it be borrowed on interlibrary loan or that it be purchased by using the "Request for Purchase" form. Patrons finding certain library material objectionable to the community at large may request that it be reconsidered by using the "Request for Reconsideration" form. Both forms will be available at all library units.

GIFTS

The library welcomes gifts of needed material or funds for the purchase of such material. The library reserves the right to evaluate and to dispose of gifts in accordance with the criteria applied to purchased material. The library discourages the attachment of conditions to gifts, and no conditions may be imposed relating to any gift after its acceptance by the library.

Gifts which do not comply with the library's objectives and policies will be declined and, when possible, referred to a more appropriate recipient. Gifts more suitable for a museum than for the library will not be accepted except in rare circumstances when the director decides that they meet a specific need of the collection.

COLLECTION DEVELOPMENT AND MAINTENANCE

The library will evaluate its collection on a continuing basis in response to the changing nature and needs of our community. The criteria used in the selection of material will be used in its withdrawal.

In order to maintain the collection in its most useful and attractive condition, the professional staff will consider for withdrawal material that is no longer in demand, that has been superseded by newer or more accurate resources, or that is in such poor physical condition it can no longer be used successfully. When appropriate, deteriorating items will be repaired or rebound. Replacement of a withdrawn item is not automatic; the decision to replace will be based on the selection policy.

REVIEW AND REVISION OF SELECTION POLICY

The materials selection policy will be reviewed continuously by the library staff to ensure that it meets community needs. It will be reviewed formally by the Board of Trustees every three years. It may be revised only with the formal approval of the Board of Trustees.

AREAS TO BE COVERED BY MATERIALS SELECTION POLICY

By Form of Material

GOVERNMENT PUBLICATIONS

The library has been a government depository library since 1973 and therefore receives selected depository items automatically. Documents are selected according to the principles applicable to books. To obtain items not received through the depository, the *Selected List of Government Publications* and the documents' *Shipping List* are checked for order monthly by the documents librarian. Selected documents are duplicated.

Most official publications of our state, city and county government are acquired, when possible. The *List of Tennessee State Publications* and the *Monthly Checklist of State Publications* are checked to select state documents.

Only the most important United Nations publications are acquired. Government publications of foreign countries are not acquired regularly, but are obtained as needed.

LARGE-PRINT AND SPECIAL MATERIALS FOR THE HANDICAPPED

Large-print and other special materials for the handicapped are purchased in sufficient quantity to meet the needs of each community. Special attention is given to large-print materials in small, light-weight editions. They are all judged by the same standards of content and format that apply to other material purchased by the library.

Talking books, tapes, and Braille material, which are readily available from other agencies such as the Tennessee Library for the Blind and

Handicapped and Tennessee Services for the Blind, are not purchased by the library.

The library takes care to provide adult books written especially for those with learning and reading disabilities.

MICROFORMS

Since space and availability are the major considerations for acquiring microforms, the library increases its holdings as needs arise. New sizes and forms of microform, microfiche, etc., are considered carefully before purchase, keeping in mind viewing and copying equipment and our need for the material. Each new addition is judged on its own merits, since we cannot predict what may come in this unstandardized, ever-changing field.

OUTLINES, SYNOPSES, STUDY GUIDES, ETC.

Selecting material of this type is based on the following factors: usefulness to staff and patrons, availability of material elsewhere and, within reason, demand for specific subjects and titles.

Study guides and outlines. Material of this kind, if prepared by a competent writer in the subject field, is added to the collection when there is a legitimate need and when it meets library standards.

Synopses. Collections of synopses, summaries and similar short-cut materials are purchased for reference use and in some cases for circulation.

Abridgments. Because abridgments and simplified versions of the classics lose in literary quality, they are seldom added.

Laboratory manuals and workbooks. Since this type of material is almost useless apart from the classroom, it is seldom purchased.

Examination manuals. Certain civil service and other examination manuals, e.g., GED manuals, real estate questions and answers, lineworkers' manuals, etc., are purchased in quantity.

PAMPHLETS

Pamphlets are selected for their content, low cost, timeliness, and local interest, and to supplement the book and periodical collection.

PAPERBACKS

Paperback material is purchased to provide multiple copies of books in demand. When a title is available in hardback and paperback the library usually chooses the hardback, unless its price is excessive. The standards that are applied in considering hardback books for purchase are also applied in the selection of paperback material.

PERIODICALS

Periodicals are a valuable resource for presenting current trends and ideologies and for providing material not available in books.

Criteria used in selection are: accuracy and objectivity, availability of content through indexes, usefulness in reference work to supplement book collection, and subject matter of local interest. Titles not indexed are considered for addition if there is a community interest or if the title is new and seems likely to be of importance.

Other factors in selection include: the periodical's reputation; adequacy of coverage in its subject area; public demand; format, and price. Various groups and their interests are considered and a balance of viewpoints on controversial issues is sought.

NEWSPAPERS

The main library maintains files of the *Knoxville News-Sentinel,* the *Knoxville Journal,* the *New York Times* and the *Wall Street Journal.* All these are preserved on microfilm. The library subscribes to other newspapers representing each major area of the country, with special emphasis on the state and region.

PICTURE FILE

The picture collection provides pictures on needed subjects to supplement illustrations in books and magazines, or to duplicate them in a form easy to locate and circulate. The files consist of prints, reproductions, and magazine illustrations on subjects often requested. Pictures are selected from a variety of sources, usually from free and inexpensive material.

TEXTBOOKS

No attempt is made to supply textbooks used in the schools and colleges of this area. Neither does the library try to provide books on supplementary reading lists designed for courses of study. A book is not excluded simply because it is a textbook: textbooks are purchased when they provide the best coverage of a subject, are the best sources of information available, and are of use to the general public. Authority, accuracy and up-to-dateness are all factors to be considered in the selection of these books.

By Subject (Using Dewey Decimal Classification as Outline)

000 GENERALITIES

Bibliographies

Bibliographies of particular subjects are purchased where there is a need for further references beyond our own resources. They are also selected specifically for use as buying guides.

Professional Literature

Material in the field of library science is selected primarily to assist in the professional development of the staff.

Encyclopedias

Encyclopedias are chosen on the basis of their accuracy, convenience of use, readability, price and demand. When possible, the collection is updated by revised editions, rather than by the purchase of yearbooks. On the other hand, it is felt that good library service is not dependent on owning the latest edition of every encyclopedia. Major works will be replaced every two or three years or as funds permit. Those in foreign languages or on specialized subjects will be purchased for the main library only.

Continuations

While many titles in this category need to be replaced every year (the *World Almanac* and *Statesman's Yearbook*), others can be used for two or three years without affecting quality library service.

Books in Series

Many series are desirable and are purchased in their entirety. When a whole series is not purchased, individual titles of outstanding merit or on a subject in demand may be selected.

100 PHILOSOPHY

In the fields of psychology and philosophy, the library tries to select material representing all the major areas of study. The library endeavors to purchase those works which are recommended by authoritative reviewers.

In the areas of the pseudosciences, public demand plays an important role in influencing the library's choices. Since many books of this nature (i.e., astrology, palmistry, ESP, ghostly phenomena, witchcraft, etc.) often are not reviewed in the usual book selection tools, we try to keep acquainted with new and popular titles through other media—television, popular magazines, etc.

200 RELIGION

The library attempts to maintain an impartial recognition of conflicting points of view in the field of religion. As an educational institution emphasizing goodwill and understanding among different races and religions, the library has a definite moral and social obligation to evaluate carefully sectarian propaganda materials which tend to foster hatred or intolerant attitudes toward racial groups, cults, or religious leaders. Such materials are added only if the title in question has convincing historical, research, or documentary values.

Inclusion or noninclusion in the library's collection of any book or other item in the field of religion is based on the considerations described in this policy statement and not on the personal religious conviction of any one staff member or group of staff members. The desire is to maintain a balanced collection which reflects all main points of view. Similarly, no book is removed from the collection solely because it is objected to by any religious or other group in the community, when it is in harmony with this policy statement.

Since users of the library vary widely in educational background and reading ability, an effort is made to choose material to fit differing needs avoiding the very specialized and abstruse, the immature, the oversimplified and the saccharine.

The library strives always to have copies of important editions of the Bible, and to include as many as possible of the other important sacred books of the world religions (such as the *Koran* and the *Talmud*).

The library adds gifts of religious material under the following conditions:

1. The library is not obligated to accept or add to its collection any unsolicited gift.
2. Gifts or subscriptions to periodicals are accepted if they meet one of the following provisions:

   • That the periodical is indexed in the Readers' Guide or other indexes in our collection;
   • That the periodical represents a denomination or faith which has organized groups in this community.

3. The library accepts as a gift only one periodical representing a religious faith, preferably a magazine which covers the broad aspects or program of a particular denomination.

300 SOCIAL SCIENCES

The social sciences include sociology, statistics, political science, economics, law, public administration, social pathology, education, commerce, and customs and folklore.

The library attempts to provide balance in each social science, representing as many viewpoints as possible on controversial and noncontroversial subjects. Basic subject materials of interest to the specialists, i.e., lengthy original scientific investigations, are included only where needed, or if they are famous as turning points in social history.

400 LANGUAGE

The 400s include general works on language and linguistics. Nonbook material, kept for the most part in the fine arts division, is not a concern in this section of the material selections policy. Language and language study is divided into the following areas:

1. English language.
   Books are included that provide a comprehensive coverage of the history, study and use of the English language in the following areas:

   • English language dictionaries. A selection of up-to-date dictionaries is provided for circulation to the public. Unabridged dictionaries are provided only as reference material.
   • Histories of the English language. Both popular and scholarly works on the history of English are included.
   • Regional English. Studies and dictionaries of regional English, especially of Southern Appalachian English, are a special interest of the library.
   • Adult education material and material for those learning English as a second language.

2. Foreign languages.
    The library has a limited collection of books in foreign languages. Because of the proximity to the University of Tennessee and the availability of material through interlibrary loan, materials in or concerning a foreign language are limited to the following areas:

    • "English to foreign language" and "foreign language to English" dictionaries in as many modern languages as possible;
    • Grammars for modern foreign languages including the introductory, review, and teach-yourself types;
    • Classics in major western languages.

500 PURE SCIENCES

The library recognizes the need to acquire current and authoritative materials in the area of the pure sciences. Selection aids which are regularly consulted include *AAAS Science Book List,* its quarterly supplement, *Science Books,* and *New Technical Books.* The levels of difficulty of selected materials and the types of patrons which the library hopes to serve are "secondary school students, college undergraduates and nonspecialists."

The library enjoys a unique position in its proximity to the TVA Oak Ridge National Laboratory and University of Tennessee science and technical libraries.

600 APPLIED SCIENCES

The applied sciences include the medical sciences, engineering, agriculture, home economics, business, chemical technology, manufacturing and building.

Materials useful to the lay citizen are sought on such subjects as drugs, diseases, diet, preventive medicine and sex. In this whole area, controversial and doubtful material is avoided, and an effort is made to have the most up-to-date material available.

Basic texts and handbooks are provided in each field of engineering. Books on electronics and automotive repair are purchased in large quantities to meet the demand.

The library selects numerous books on farming and gardening, home-making skills, animal husbandry and pet care.

The library recognizes its responsibility to provide the best and most up-to-date works on all business subjects, such as advertising and salesmanship.

The purchase of works dealing with chemical technology and manufacturing is limited to those recommended for public libraries.

The library purchases heavily in the field of building skills, which include remodeling, carpentry, house painting, cabinet making, and masonry. Do-it-yourself books are especially in demand.

700 THE ARTS

For material selection purposes, the arts include antiques, interior decoration, handicrafts, sports and other recreation as well as the fine arts.

An effort is made to acquire representative examples of major and minor artists in all fields, with special consideration of the arts and artists in the local area. The library feels a responsibility to select for the interests of the community and to introduce new and unfamiliar ideas in the arts.

Sheet music is not acquired by the library except that included in song-books and books of commentary.

800 LITERATURE

Essays, poetry, drama, short stories, and selected works of criticism on all these forms are included in the collection, but the library does not maintain an exhaustive or extensive fund of literary criticism on any author. Works on techniques of communication such as professional writing or public speaking are also included.

Precedence is given to British and American literatures; however, representative works of world literature are included as well. Writers who have been recipients of acclaimed awards—the Nobel Prize, the Pulitzer Prize, the National Book Award, and others—are accorded special attention. Only English translations of foreign languages are found in this section.

Due to the large quantities of modern drama and poetry published each year, the library purchases only titles considered the best, and those of local interest. Indexes such as Granger's Index to Poetry, Short Story Index and Play Index are checked regularly against the library's holdings.

900 HISTORY

This section embraces general works on geography and history, travel, genealogy, heraldry, biography and autobiography. It includes maps and atlases, travel guides and local history.

The library selects books covering all phases of human history from the beginnings of civilization to the present, with emphasis on American and local history.

Because of the great increase in world travel in recent years, the library acquires standard, up-to-date travel guides for all parts of the globe. Books by well-known travelers, personal reminiscences, and narratives by early explorers are included.

Biography includes autobiography, collective biography, journals, diaries, and letters. Special attention is given to biographies of local people and the pioneers of this area. When a substandard biography is the only one available, it is purchased as needed.

The library maintains a general collection in the areas of genealogy and heraldry. However, most of the books and publications in these areas are found in the McClung Historical Collection.

Books about local places and events are usually acquired by the library.

All types of maps and atlases are included in the library: political, geographical and historical.

FICTION

In selecting fiction the existence of a variety of types of novels and the need to satisfy readers of differing tastes, interests, purposes and reading abilities are recognized. The library's collection, therefore, includes representative novels of the past and present, notable for literary quality and cultural value; historical and regional novels; novels related to the fields of art, industry, science, social problems, and the professions; satire, fantasy and humor; mystery and suspense, science fiction, westerns and other adventure stories; romances; and short stories.

The library recognizes the importance of the novel in providing insight into the human situation, contributing to education, and affecting individual attitudes. A substantial number of novels of serious purpose are purchased. Attention is paid to maintaining a basic collection in attractive editions of standard novels, the classics, and the semiclassics of world literature.

Since each novel is ordinarily judged on its individual merits, there is as a rule no attempt at completeness in the library's holding of authors' works. Exceptions are made, however, of great novelists of the past, all of whose works are obtained if possible, and of outstanding contemporary novelists.

Novels widely advertised or in continuing demand because of the popularity of the author's other works, their conversion into film, appearance on television, or the timeliness of the theses are purchased if they are useful in answering the requests of readers, or if they will further efforts to serve a larger segment of the reading public. Although no rigid standard of literary quality is adhered to it may be said that the library's policy is to acquire fiction whether serious or amusing, realistic or imaginative, even though the writing may be sentimental, sensational or erotic. Serious works which present an honest aspect of life are not necessarily excluded for frankness of expression.

The library leases books to meet the demand for current titles.

Akron-Summit County Public Library

GOALS AND GUIDELINES

Broadly stated, the basic function of the public library is to serve people through print and nonprint resources, helping them, as individuals and in groups, to achieve informational, educational and recreational objectives.

In fulfillment of this common function the Akron-Summit County Public Library sets the following as its goals:

1. To select and organize reliable print and nonprint materials significant to the people of this area;
2. To serve as a multi-purpose organization, providing a principal resource and depository of a wide variety of library materials essential in cultural, inspirational, informational and recreational pursuits;
3. To fulfill its responsibility in a democratic society by providing each individual with easiest possible access to informational resources;
4. To provide the means for stimulation and encouragement for children, young people and adults in educating themselves continuously, and to promote self-development towards enrichment of their lives;
5. To give guidance in the use of library materials and resources toward meeting the needs of people individually and in groups and organizations;
6. To cooperate with groups and agencies in stimulating and supporting educational, cultural, and social awareness activities in the community, and to provide leadership in the search for solutions to community problems;
7. To actively seek out those individuals and groups which are not aware of the library system as a resource for achieving personal and group goals.

GUIDELINES

Services

To provide high quality service individualized to meet the specific needs of each client, the library will:

1. Identify the specific informational and recreational needs of clients and select and organize materials to meet these needs;
2. Afford access to materials and services of the library for all clients regardless of age, mental abilities, physical handicaps, social characteristics, economic status, neighborhood, ethnic origins, political beliefs or religion;
3. Increase availability of library services for each person in the county within his local environment;
4. Work with organizations, agencies and individuals to increase awareness of the library services available, and to promote methods of cooperation and opportunities to enlarge service;
5. Maintain and develop a diversified public relations and publicity program to inform clients and prospective clients of the availability and variety of library services.

Media: Print and Nonprint

To assure that clients will have access to the media that will most effectively stimulate and satisfy their needs, the library will:

1. Make available a wide variety of media for many different conceptual and age levels and provide expert guidance in their most effective use;
2. Establish, adopt, and frequently review media selection policies;
3. Utilize the talents and qualifications of a variety of staff and specialists in the community in the selection of media;
4. Encourage clients to aid in the selection of media by expressing their desires and needs;
5. Organize media for ease of use by the public;
6. Evaluate budget allotments, weighing print and nonprint expenditures in relation to service;
7. Be receptive to new media and hard/software necessary to utilize it;
8. Frequently review the library materials collection, eliminating and replacing those items considered to be inadequate, outmoded and ineffective.

Staff

To insure optimum effectiveness in anticipating and fulfilling goals of library service, the library will:

1. Employ professional staff who have, in addition to basic library school training, imagination, initiative, a desire to learn, an understanding of people and enthusiasm for working with them and a willingness to provide leadership in the process of public enlightenment;
2. Orient the supportive staff in the basic goals of the library and the organization of the library system, as well as train in the techniques and routines of special tasks;
3. Provide organized inservice training; update concepts of service; develop staff knowledge of varieties of service; stimulate among staff an open-minded attitude toward changing needs of clients and the materials they require.

Management

To insure the best possible library service, management efforts will:

1. Provide a framework for quality service at all levels and the atmosphere or incentives which will elicit the enthusiasm, commitment and creativity of each staff member;
2. Foster the concept of library service as a community investment. The setting of objectives and the planning of library services are community responsibilities and must involve other kinds of agencies concerned with the needs of people;
3. Implement interdepartmental planning and programming;
4. Provide for participation in management by staff members at various levels;
5. Encourage communication between library agencies and individuals;
6. Require systematic and frequent evaluation of services, measuring their use and effectiveness;
7. Identify and minimize barriers to use, often reviewing regulations and procedures which may seem arbitrarily restrictive from the users' viewpoint.

BASIC STANDARDS OF SELECTION

In developing the standards for selecting materials, the library follows those set by *Minimum Standards for Public Library Systems, 1966.**

"Within standards of purpose and quality, collections should be built to meet the needs and interests of people. Systems of libraries, both the community library and the headquarters unit, exist to serve their constituents. Materials are added because they serve agreed purposes, meet quality standards, and are of interest to readers and to organizations. Selection follows from conscious study of the needs of all groups: among others, industry, businessmen, gardeners, music lovers, labor, the handicapped, children.

"Sensitivity to interests, early recognition of needs before they are clearly expressed, and catholicity of contact and viewpoint mark the librarian who keeps the collection in tune with its public. Selection must be beyond the requests of particular groups who have come to use the library regularly, and must appeal (reach out) to segments in the population which do not as readily turn to it."

In order to build this kind of a collection, "continuous and periodic study of [the library's] community . . . to know people, groups, and institutions thoroughly, and to keep up with developments and changes" is very important in the job of selecting materials. Each agency of the library should participate in community activities in its area in order to keep in close and continuous touch with its needs. This gives vitality, purpose and relevancy to the selection of materials.

*American Library Association, 1967

CRITERIA FOR SELECTION OF
PRINT AND NONPRINT MATERIALS

1. Materials should meet high standards of quality in content, expression and format.
2. The content should be timely, timeless, authoritative and significant in subject matter.
3. Materials should be of immediate or anticipated interest to individuals or to the community.
4. Materials should include the widest possible coverage of subjects and viewpoints consistent with the needs and interests in the community, the budget available and the defined limits of the collection.
5. Materials should meet the standards of acceptability as to accuracy, technical excellence, effective expression, significance of subject, sincerity and responsibility of opinion.

ADULT MATERIALS SELECTION POLICY

Since the library's primary function is to contribute to the growth and maturity of people, the art of selection is designed to obtain books and other materials to further the library's program of providing inspiration, recreation, and information. The library provides fundamental, significant, and standard items in a wide variety of fields, including the sciences, the arts, and the humanities.

In carrying out these objectives, these factors are of importance:

1. Interests existing in the community;
2. Flexibility to meet new and changing community interests and needs;
3. Needs of special groups such as young people, the aged and minorities;
4. Widest possible coverage within the budget;
5. Availability of materials in other libraries in this and nearby communities;
6. Preservation of materials covering area history and by or about local people.

Books—General

Selection of books for general reading depends upon the ability and authority of the author, importance of the subject matter, need, format and availability of material in the region. The library considers readability, popular appeal, quality of writing and soundness of the author's attitude and approach. Division heads have a responsibility to buy titles in their subject areas which are suitable for branch use, as branches may select only those books approved for the Main Library collection.

Fiction

In selecting fiction, primary factors are honesty and sincerity of approach, literary quality, good taste and variety of reader and interest levels of those served. The book is judged by the author's purpose and its accomplishment. The library buys distinguished and important fiction titles and those which are competent, popular and experimental. The book is given special study when reviewers' opinions differ.

Subject Fields

In subject fields selection is based upon authority, accuracy, up-to-dateness and the honesty and integrity of the author. Selection is made at diverse levels of difficulty including elementary, scholarly and highly specialized materials.

Books on issues of current interest, which may be of temporary value, are purchased if timeliness gives them relevance and importance.

Books having potential future value for which immediate demand is small are often purchased.

The library buys courses of study and textbooks adopted in the community only if the material is not available in any other form. The library provides simple and introductory materials for adults who wish to pursue independent study or whose reading level is extremely low.

Student Use

In providing materials for student use, the library's function is to serve a wide variety of interests and a diversified clientele. It does not provide multiple copies of individual titles or duplicate subject materials extensively for student assignments.

Reference Materials

Subject value is stressed in technical and reference books. In special fields of local importance, such as rubber and plastics, almost all materials are purchased even if mediocre in quality of writing. In other subject fields the outstanding and significant contributions are purchased. Practical books, as well as scientific, are included in the collection. The interests and needs of the community, anticipated when possible, are the basis for much of the selection.

The purchase of expensive books, trade directories and financial services is determined by their relative importance in the collection and their availability in the area.

Books in Foreign Languages

The library's book collection includes over thirty languages with major emphasis on French, German and Spanish. Books selected for the foreign languages collection include:

1. Classics in the original language;
2. Works of significant authors, past and present;
3. Beginning reading books for those learning the language;
4. Standard and special books, such as cookbooks and the Bible;
5. American classics and translations of books about American culture, literature and history;
6. Books suited to the needs of the current immigrant.

Gift books in a foreign language are accepted after investigation of the source, authority, point of view and need.

Pamphlet Material

Selection of pamphlets follows the general policy outlined for other materials. Since this material is inexpensive and frequently free, useful pamphlets are duplicated. These serve as supplements to the book materials.

Pamphlets are selected with great care since many are issued for propaganda or advertising purposes. A balance of viewpoints on controversial subjects is the aim. Inflammatory and emotional treatment is avoided. Pamphlets which contain advertising that distorts facts, contain misleading statements, or intrude commercial messages unduly are not added to the collection. Acceptable pamphlet material should always have the issuing agency or publisher clearly identified and should be of current value.

Paperbacks

The same standards for selection are applied to paperbacks as to other materials. The original copy of a book is usually bought in hardcover, if available. Paperbacks, however, are purchased if:

1. There is great demand for a title;
2. It is a title which has only occasional or temporary interest;
3. No other edition is available;
4. The original title appeared only in this form.

Branch libraries buy paperbound titles that are in Main Library's collection. A paperback is examined carefully to insure that the text, translation, illustrations and format are of acceptable quality.

Periodicals

Periodicals are purchased to provide material on current issues, for research and for general reading. Principles governing selection are: community interests, accuracy, objectivity, accessibility of content through indexes, need in reference work and representation of a variety of viewpoints.

The library evaluates many new magazines, especially those indexed in *Readers' Guide,* with the purpose of adding to the periodical list. Files of current sample periodicals are kept in each subject division with evaluations attached. Selection of periodicals is reviewed annually.

At Main Library, a duplicate collection of magazines selected from the subject areas is available in the language literature history division for circulation. Selection is based upon balance of viewpoints and frequency of request.

Branches choose their periodicals from those titles approved at Main Library.

Newspapers

The library selects representative newspapers of leading cities and those which contain outstanding or significant contributions to national thinking. Cities are chosen according to size, breadth of coverage and geographical location. Microfilm editions of a few newspapers are maintained because of their importance as permanent reference material. All major newspapers published in Summit County are purchased as sources of local information.

Newspapers for branches are bought or accepted as gifts in accordance with the needs of the clients in the individual agency. Branches select newspapers from titles approved at Main Library.

Picture Files

The picture file, located in the fine arts division, has two major sections. The first includes illustrations and photographs of people, places and things chosen for their accuracy and importance. Diagrams and line drawings are selected for inclusion. The second section includes reproductions or illustrations of visual arts.

Selection of material is based on known present and projected future needs, significance of the subject, quality of reproduction and fidelity of color. Picture sources include postcards, magazines, books and any other printed matter available for clipping. Rarely are pictures purchased.

The scope of subjects is wide to cover a variety of uses.

A reference collection of historical pictures of the Summit County area is maintained with the local history books in the language literature history division. Pictures from the Summit County Historical Society calendar are added, and a special effort is made to acquire pictures of people and places related to Akron and Summit County history.

Phonograph Records

The purpose of the Record Section is to provide significant materials in recorded form for the use of individuals and groups in the community.

Music constitutes the bulk of the collection. Records are selected to cover a wide variety of music (classical, semiclassical, musical shows, jazz, folk, rock and ethnic) excluding the ephemeral.

Speeches, plays, poetry, short stories, sound effects, language instruction and records suitable for individual study in a variety of subjects are included. Records for children are purchased. These include classic and award-winning stories, poetry, nursery rhymes, songs, music appreciation and records which may be used in teaching children.

Certain works are selected because they are performed by a particular musical artist, conductor or literary personage. Different interpretations of a particular work may be purchased.

Records are selected with these points in mind:

1. Interpretation and technique;
2. Artist;
3. Technical quality;
4. Need based on public request and current holdings.

Tapes and Cassettes

Tapes are added to the library collection through donations of interviews, events and news broadcasts and from organizations.

Cassettes are acquired by Group Services as an accompaniment to filmstrips and for staff development. Children's Services acquires cassettes for specific purposes.

SELECTION OF YOUNG ADULT MATERIALS

Young adults in the Akron-Summit County Public Library are approximately 12 to 15 years old or in grades seven through ten.

The purposes of the young adult collection are to serve as a transition from children's literature to adult reading, to interest this age group in reading for pleasure and to encourage them to become lifelong readers. It is intended as a browsing collection to satisfy their recreational reading needs and interests.

The selection policy for young adults shares the major goals and objectives of the Akron-Summit County Public Library. The same criteria for selection of adult books should be followed when considering books for young adults. However, lack of literary style should not exclude books of high interest. Additional criteria to be considered are as follows:

1. Inclusion of a wide range of subjects to meet the recreational reading interests of young adults;
2. Recognition that 12- to 15-year-olds have many reading levels;
3. Selection of materials which encourage continued reading and which broaden the experiences of young adults;
4. Portrayal of people of all ages honestly;
5. Presentation of codes of conduct and morals without sentimentality or preaching;
6. Recognition of special characteristics of the teenage years: awareness of self, uncertainty and idealism often covered by aggression; need for a "hero" image and the close relationship with a peer group coupled with the need to conform to that group; breaking away from the family unit; uncertainty about the future while beginning to evaluate his or her own set of beliefs; sudden changes of interests, ideas, values and attitudes; and a desire to accept responsibility while striving for adult maturity.

MATERIALS SELECTION POLICY FOR CHILDREN'S SERVICES

Children are recognized as creative, inquiring individuals with unique capacities for intellectual and emotional growth. The resources of the entire library are accessible to them as the need arises.

Primary emphasis is placed on the selection of diverse print and non-print materials for all children (preschool through early teens) of the community which will:

1. Expand their knowledge of the universe and man's relationship to it;
2. Further their search for understanding of themselves and their environment;

3. Contribute to their aesthetic experiences;
4. Develop pride in their heritage and an understanding of other cultures;
5. Improve their ability to make critical judgments.

Secondary emphasis is placed on selection of children's materials useful to adults working with children and essential to the study of children's literature.

Examples:

1. Books of historical significance in children's literature;
2. Books of limited appeal to children but of importance because of author, illustrator, content or notability;
3. Books and bibliographies about children's literature;
4. Biographical and critical materials about authors and illustrators of children's books;
5. Professional literature on library services to children.

The library provides fundamental, significant and standard items of children's materials and tries to anticipate and provide for needs and interests of children. In carrying out these objectives the same factors apply as for the adult policy with these additional ones:

1. Books for children are selected by staff who are expert in children's literature and knowledgeable about children.
2. Nonbook materials for children, housed in other areas of the library, are selected in consultation with children's librarians.
3. Subject, vocabulary and format must be suitable to the age and understanding of the children for whom the material is intended.
4. A book may be approved even though it contains words and ideas not usually acceptable provided they are necessary to portray a period, environment, character or incident with sincerity and truth.
5. Titles which do not meet literary standards may be chosen to fulfill emotional needs, serve as stepping stones to better reading or serve some other special purpose.

All children's books are read or examined by the staff before being approved for the collection. Each title is considered for its individual merit. Where opinions of reviewers differ the book is given special study.

Books for General Reading

Selection of books for general reading depends upon popular appeal, authority of author, quality of writing, soundness of attitude and purpose, the importance of the subject matter and need.

Fiction

Consideration is given to plausibility of theme, well-developed plot, strong characterization, literary style, originality, sincerity of purpose, imagination, relevancy and lack of bias. The story should be for children, not merely about children.

Nonfiction

Consideration is given to author's purpose, qualifications, accuracy and literary style; to an adequate index and to an attractive format with illustrations, text, paper and binding well-integrated.

Picture Books

Generally designed for the preschool or primary grade child, picture books may be either fiction or nonfiction. They are distinguished by the art work which may be integrated with or take precedence over the text. The quality of illustration and format are of equal importance to the literary quality.

Easy Reading Books

Designed for the child beginning to read, easy reading books contain more text than picture books. They are distinguished by large well-spaced print, short sentences, wide margins and art work integrated with the text. They may or may not have "controlled vocabulary." A few primary school readers are classified as easy reading books. Easy reading in subject fields is usually classified.

Textbooks

Textbooks (and readers) adopted by local school systems are not knowingly purchased. Readers designed for upper elementary grades are not purchased.

Other textbooks are purchased if the information contained is not available elsewhere.

Books in Foreign Languages

A representative collection of the best children's literature of other countries in the original language is maintained in Main Children's Room.

Other books in foreign languages are purchased only if needed in the community.

Books for the purpose of learning a language are bought as needs arise. Translated children's books are included in the general collection based on the usual criteria for fiction and nonfiction.

Religion

The library provides Bible stories, lives of saints, biographies of religious characters and leaders, books on customs, beliefs and traditions of religions of the world.

Books that promote specific sectarian doctrines are not purchased or accepted for addition to the collection.

Reference Collection

Encyclopedias, dictionaries, atlases and reference materials in subject areas are selected by the same basic criteria as those for selection of nonfiction. A distinguishing characteristic of a reference book is ease of access to information; however, content is more important than format. Sometimes adult materials are duplicated for reference use.

Series Books

All types of books in series are evaluated on the individual merits of each title. Each is selected by the same criteria as other books.

Classics

Effort is made to maintain a representative collection of classics. These are periodically re-evaluated. When popularity or timeliness wanes, they are placed in the Early and Rare Collection as examples of children's books of historical significance.

Often several acceptable editions of a classic are purchased.

Adaptations and Abridgments

Adaptations and abridgments of classics and other books are compared carefully with the original and only those which retain the spirit of the originals are purchased.

Paperbacks

A title already in the system may be duplicated in a paperback edition if it is attractive and relatively sturdy.

The criteria for abridgment and adaptations are applied when necessary.

Original titles in paperback are given the same consideration as hardbacks.

Sex Education

The library provides books which explain the processes of human physical development and reproduction in a simple and scientific manner. Text and illustrations should be suited to age levels for which the book is intended.

Periodicals

Periodicals for children are selected on the basis of children's interests and reading ability, the literary quality of the contents and authoritative and accurate information, as well as popular appeal. Sometimes adult magazines are purchased because of subject interest. All titles are approved by Children's Services Office.

Picture Collections

Pictures on subjects of particular interest to children are selected from free and inexpensive materials. All material, especially advertising, is carefully examined for bias and inaccuracies. Frequent weeding is necessary to maintain usefulness of the collection.

Pamphlets

Pamphlets are purchased to supplement the book stock and to supply information otherwise not available.

Pamphlets are selected within the reading abilities of the children. For other criteria in selecting pamphlets, see Adult Materials Selection Policy, p. 143.

Local Authors

Books by local authors are accepted as gifts or purchased to preserve materials of local interest. Duplication of such materials depends upon the quality.

Maintenance of Collection

Duplication of titles is contingent upon the demands of the children, the balance of the collection and funds available.

No effort is made to provide multiple copies to fulfill the needs of mass assignments of local schools.

Some adult titles are approved for duplication in the juvenile collection because of their universal appeal, the overlapping interests of children and wide range of children's reading abilities.

Re-evaluation is an ongoing process based on the statement of Children's Services Division of the American Library Association.

Books of significance in the past that are no longer timely are placed in the Early and Rare Collection for research purposes only.

CONTROVERSIAL MATERIALS

The overall purpose of a work is the chief criterion of selection. Materials which have the dominant purpose of appealing to prurient interest are not considered for inclusion in the library collection. Materials which contain unorthodox language or frank treatment of certain situations which may be objectionable to some people are often included if, in the professional opinion of the librarians, the material provides accurate information and portrays realistic characters and situations.

Materials are selected on the basis of the content as a whole and without regard to the personal history of the author, composer or producer. Each work is considered on its own social and literary merit.

The library recognizes its responsibility to make available a representative selection of materials on subjects of interest to its users, including materials on various sides of controversial questions—religious, social, political or economic—to enable clients to make up their own minds about controversial subjects. Variety and balance of opinion are sought whenever available. The library does not label materials by such terms as "pro," "anti," "racist," "sexist," "rightist" or "leftist." (see page 154.)

Since the library has a responsibility to protect the rights of all clients, it does not limit the scope of its collection; neither are materials placed in restricted areas because some individual may object to their accessibility. Although librarians offer guidance in the selection, monitoring the reading of children is entirely the responsibility of their parents or legal guardians.

Materials which are extremely liable to theft or mutilation may be assigned to closed shelves. These materials are re-evaluated frequently to consider placement on open shelves.

POLICY STATEMENT REGARDING UNITED NATIONS

The Board of Trustees of the Library set the policy relative to the United Nations by the following statement adopted at a meeting on November 16, 1953:

"The public library is an educational institution whose major responsibility is to collect, organize and lend printed material on all subjects. Where different opinions occur on any topic, it is the duty of the library, within the limits of its resources, to represent all points of view. In controversial questions the staff in their official capacities should maintain an impartial position.

"There are certain questions, however, which are not controversial, such as the inalienable right to freedom and to the franchise, and the responsibility of loyal citizens to be informed on the problems of the day.

"The right of free citizens to strive for world peace through negotiation and association has likewise been widely accepted by our people. Since membership in the United Nations has been approved by an overwhelming majority in Congress and since, as a result, our own government has become a very important member of the United Nations, the library regards it as a duty to encourage its patrons to read, study and discuss all phases of its structure and activities."

SPECIAL PROBLEMS IN MATERIALS SELECTION

Sex Education

It is part of the function of the library to provide, in adequate quantity for lay readers, general books on sex which are well-balanced, authoritative, sound, up-to-date and scientific in treatment. Scientific and technical works written for specialists usually do not come within the scope of the library's collection. Materials are provided which are adapted to several levels of educational background and reading ability, as well as to differing social and religious beliefs.

Semi- and Pseudoscientific Material

Special care is taken in the selection of books in those borderline areas in which subject matter or treatment is not recognized by reputable scientific authority. Careful examination of such books rules out those which are misrepresented as scientifically accurate. In doubtful cases, it is necessary to wait for authoritative reviews or to consult experts in the field.

Books catering to morbid interests, the esoteric, the sensational, and the rabidly reformist rarely are added. Material on subjects as alcohol, tobacco, drugs and food fads are scrutinized for reliability and objective presentation.

Books by well-established authors and scientists who hold ideas which may be extreme in concept may be bought when the author's prominence makes the ideas presented of general intellectual interest. The author's reputation and method of handling the subject are deciding factors.

Microfilm

Microfilm editions of newspapers and periodicals are purchased to provide permanent reference materials. The quality of the paper, bulk of material when bound and frequency of use and cost are the considerations. Since it is necessary to subscribe to regular editions to be eligible to purchase microfilm editions, the choice is between binding and purchasing a microfilm edition. Valuable but infrequently used periodicals, bulky newspapers of permanent value (indexed or of local importance) and periodicals whose paper will disintegrate rapidly are purchased on microfilm as funds permit. Indexed periodicals of permanent value because of content and local-interest illustrations are bound. Occasionally important books or other materials not available in original form (such as old census reports) are purchased on microfilm or other microforms.

Maps

The library maintains a representative collection of maps of all countries in atlas form. Criteria for selection are accuracy, completeness, timeliness and cost. Free and inexpensive sheet maps, including street maps of major cities, are acquired to supplement those in books and atlases.

Historical maps and atlases of Ohio and Summit County are purchased, depending upon availability and cost.

If atlases of other areas of the United States become available at reasonable cost, purchases will be considered based on demand.

The library is a depository for the topographic maps of the U.S. Geological Survey.

Government Publications

The library is a selective depository for unclassified (not restricted) U.S. Government publications. Both original and new items offered to the library are evaluated by the division head in whose subject field they fall. Selections are reviewed at intervals of two years so that little-used items may be cancelled and those which are needed may be added. Nondepository material is selected on the same basis as books and pamphlets and is purchased or obtained gratis.

The library is a depository for all publications of the State of Ohio which are available for distribution. Publications of other states are purchased or requested as gifts on a very limited basis, usually as pamphlets and by the application of the usual standards for these publications. The same policy applies to Canadian, United Nations and foreign documents.

Every effort is made to acquire publications of all local government agencies. They are added to the permanent collection for their reference as well as historical value.

Media for Group Use

Group Services provides significant educational, recreational, cultural and aesthetic nonbook materials especially selected for effective use with groups in the community.

This collection of media consists of standard 8mm silent film, 16mm educational film, 35mm filmstrips (some accompanied by record and cassettes), library produced slide-tape programs and simulation games.

SELECTION POLICY

The selection policy for films follows the principles adhered to for other materials in the library. However, audio-visual presentation has such a strong emotional impact in imparting ideas and attitudes that it needs particularly careful evaluation. Most 8mm films are not previewed, but they are usually selected from the early silent film era and loaned for recreational use.

Nearly all 16mm films and filmstrips are previewed and evaluated by a committee before purchase or before acceptance as a permanent gift or temporary loan. Films are selected for use in informal adult education and for children's programs. Those especially designed for school curriculum purposes or for a highly specialized audience are not purchased. Films and filmstrips on philosophical, cultural, historical and comparative aspects of religion are added to the collection, but those that promote doctrine or denomination are excluded.

Factors important in the selection of 16mm films and filmstrips:

1. Content should have validity and significance, and be factually accurate and reliable in presentation.
2. Method of presentation should interpret and illuminate the material.
3. Overall desired impact should be reinforced by well-written text and imaginative photography, sound effects and music.

The same criteria are applied to children's films with additional emphasis on a strong story line told in a way to hold the interest of a child.

A film or filmstrip of a children's picture book will be purchased only if the book has been approved by Children's Services Office. Film adaptations from other children's books may be purchased if the film is approved by the reviewing committee.

Sponsored films are produced by or for an organization to promote directly or indirectly its activities or philosophy.

These additional points are considered when evaluating sponsored films:

1. Identification of sponsoring agency should be clear.
2. Content should be factual without distortion or simplification to prove a point.
3. Aims of sponsor should be in accord with the objectives of the library.

4. Special pleading or viewpoints through advertising should be fully evaluated.

Films are duplicated rarely because of their cost and their limited period of loan.

Simulation games are selected for their immediate applicability to local organizations and situations. Only those are added which are designed to increase self-awareness and sensitivity to others, to provide insight into solving social problems and to facilitate cohesion and unity in community planning.

GIFTS

The same principles of selection applied to purchases are applied to gifts. The library accepts gifts of books, pamphlets, periodicals, films, phonograph records, etc., with the understanding that they will be added to the library collections when needed or will be disposed of to the library's advantage.

Items sometimes are accepted as gifts although they ordinarily would not be purchased. These include replacements; denominational literature; expensive items of limited interest; local, privately printed and highly technical materials.

Gifts are cataloged for branch collections only if Main Library has a copy. Gifts of titles not already in the library system are placed in Main Library, so that all agencies have ready access to them. If requirement of the gift is that it be located in a specific agency, it may be borrowed from Main Library on indefinite loan.

Paperbacks and ephemeral books can be added unaccessioned and uncataloged to a branch collection, if they meet selection standards and have not been rejected at Main Library.

WEEDING

Except for materials of local interest, it is routine practice in this library to systematically remove materials which are outdated, worn out or mutilated, no longer in demand or of interest. Frequency of use, community interest and availability of newer and more valid materials are primary reasons for retaining or discarding materials.

Last copies of books to be retained are kept at Main Library. When the last copy of a title exists only in a branch collection, it will be transferred to Main Library or discarded. The subject division head and the head of Technical Processes will decide in consultation. The branch may borrow the title on long loan.

DUPLICATION

Duplication of titles is determined by popularity, importance of the book and budget. Materials of special local interest or reference value are dupli-

cated freely and immediately. Paperback editions of highly popular material
are bought. Pamphlets are duplicated if needed.

REPLACEMENT POLICY

Titles withdrawn because of loss, damage or general condition are
considered for replacement. Classics are replaced whenever possible in
better format.

The same considerations applied in original selection apply to replacements. In addition, other factors must be considered:

1. Availability of newer and better materials in the field;
2. The value of the individual title, whether for literary quality, subject
   appeal or authority and importance of the author;
3. Requests for the title or subject. Popular titles still in print should be
   replaced (see *Weeding*).

BINDING AND REBINDING

The library endeavors to bind periodicals which are of reference value.
Bound sets are available only at Main Library.

The choice of books for rebinding is made in accordance with the
established policies of original selection, discard and replacement. Factors
for special consideration are:

1. Value and use of the title and possibility of replacement;
2. Physical condition, including quality of paper, margins, illustrations;
3. Cost of rebinding versus cost of replacement;
4. Number of copies available.

PROCEDURE FOR RECONSIDERATION

Librarians are always willing to discuss with the public adding materials
which have been excluded or withdrawing materials which have been included on the basis of the principles stated in this selection policy.

Clients are encouraged to complete the form "Client's Request for
Reconsideration of Library Material" (Form #1064A).

SEXISM, RACISM AND OTHER "ISMS" IN LIBRARY
MATERIALS

Traditional aims of censorship efforts have been to suppress political,
sexual or religious expressions. The same three subjects have also been the
source of most complaints about materials in library collections. Another
basis for complaints, however, has become more and more frequent. Due,
perhaps, to increased awareness of the rights of minorities and increased
efforts to secure those rights, libraries are being asked to remove, restrict or

CLIENT'S REQUEST FOR RECONSIDERATION
OF LIBRARY MATERIAL

Author: _____ Hardcover ____ Paperback ____ Other ____

Title: _____

Publisher (if known): _____

Request initiated by: _____

Telephone: _____ Address: _____

City: _____ Zip Code: _____

Client Represents:

_____ Himself/Herself

_____ (Name organization) _____

_____ (Identify other group) _____

(If objection is to material other than a book, change wording of the following
questions so that they apply.)

1. Have you read the entire book? ____ If not, what parts? _____
   _____

2. Why do you disapprove of this book? (Please be specific: cite pages)
   _____

3. What do you suggest your library do about this book? _____
   _____

4. Can you suggest another book to take its place? _____
   _____

_____ Date: _____

Signature of Client

Form #1064A   Rec'd by Staff Member

reconsider some materials which are allegedly derogatory to specific minorities or which supposedly perpetuate stereotypes and false images of minorities. Among the several recurring "isms" used to describe the contents of the
materials objected to are "racism" and "sexism."

Complaints that library materials convey a derogatory or false image of a
minority strike the personal social consciousness and sense of responsibility
of some librarians who—accordingly—comply with the request to remove
such materials. While such efforts to counteract injustices are understandable, and perhaps commendable as reflections of deep personal commitments to the ideal of equality for all people, they are—nonetheless—in
conflict with the professional responsibility of librarians to guard against
encroachments upon intellectual freedom.

This responsibility has been espoused and reaffirmed by the American
Library Association in many of its basic documents on intellectual freedom
over the past thirty years. The most concise statement of the association's
position appears in Article II of the *Library Bill of Rights,* which states that
"libraries should provide books and materials presenting all points of view
concerning the problems and issues of our times; no library materials should
be proscribed or removed because of partisan or doctrinal disapproval."

While the application of this philosophy may seem simple when dealing
with political, religious or even sexual expressions, its full implications
become somewhat difficult when dealing with ideas, such as racism or
sexism, which many find abhorrent, repugnant and inhumane. But, as
stated in the *Freedom to Read* statement,

*It is inevitable in the give and take of the democratic process that the political, the
moral, or the aesthetic concepts of an individual or group will occasionally collide with
those of another individual or group. In a free society each individual is free to
determine for himself what he wishes to read, and each group is free to determine what
it will recommend to its freely associated members. But no group has the right to take the
law into its own hands, and to impose its own concept of politics or morality upon other
members of a democratic society. Freedom is no freedom if it is accorded only to the
accepted and the inoffensive. . . . We realize that application of these propositions may
mean the dissemination of ideas and manners of expression that are repugnant to many
persons. We do not state these propositions in the comfortable belief that what people
read is unimportant. We believe rather that what people read is deeply important; that
ideas can be dangerous; but that the suppression of ideas is fatal to a democratic society.
Freedom itself is a dangerous way of life, but it is ours.*

Some find this creed acceptable when dealing with materials for adults
but cannot extend its application to materials for children. Such reluctance is
generally based on the belief that children are more susceptible to being
permanently influenced—even damaged—by objectionable materials than
are adults. The *Library Bill of Rights,* however, makes no distinction between
materials and services for children and adults. Its principles of free access to
all available materials apply to every person, as stated in Article V: "The
rights of an individual to the use of a library should not be denied or
abridged because of his age, race, religion, national origins or social or
political views."

Some librarians deal with the problem of objectionable materials by labeling them or listing them as "racist" or "sexist." This kind of action, too, has long been opposed by the American Library Association in its *Statement on Labeling,* which says,

If materials are labeled to pacify one group, there is no excuse for refusing to label any item in the library's collection. Because authoritarians tend to suppress ideas and attempt to coerce individuals to conform to a specific ideology, the American Library Association opposes such efforts which aim at closing any path to knowledge.

Others deal with the problem of objectionable materials by instituting restrictive circulation or relegating materials to closed or restricted collections. This practice, too, is in violation of the *Library Bill of Rights* as explained in *Restricted Access to Library Materials* which says,

Too often only "controversial" materials are in the subject of such segregation, leading to the conclusion that factors other than theft and mutilation were the true considerations. The distinction is extremely difficult to make for both the librarian and the patron. Unrestrictive selection policies, developed with care for the principles of intellectual freedom and the Library Bill of Rights, *should not be vitiated by administrative practices such as restricted circulation.*

The American Library Association has made clear its position concerning the removal of library materials because of partisan or doctrinal disapproval, or because of pressures from interest groups. In yet another policy statement, the *Resolution on Challenged Materials:*

The American Library Association declares as a matter of firm principle that no challenged material should be removed from any library under any legal or extra-legal pressure, save after an independent determination by a judicial officer in a court of competent jurisdiction and only after an adversary hearing, in accordance with well-established principles of law.

Intellectual freedom, in its purest sense, promotes no causes, furthers no movements, and favors no viewpoints. It only provides for free access to all ideas through which any and all sides and causes and movements may be expressed, discussed and argued. The librarian cannot let personal preferences limit the degree of tolerance, for freedom is indivisible. Toleration is meaningless without toleration for the detestable.

PART

II

ACADEMIC LIBRARY POLICIES

Moorhead State University, Livingston Lord Library (MN)

Holy Names College Library (CA)

Northern Oklahoma College Learning Resource Center (OK)

Iowa State University Library (IA)

Gettysburg College Library (PA)

East Texas State University, James G. Gee Library (TX)

Montgomery County Community College Learning Resources Center (PA)

Portland State University Library (OR)

San Antonio College Library (TX)

University of North Carolina at Wilmington, William Madison Randall Library (NC)

Suffolk University College Library (MA)

Houston Community College Learning Resources Center (TX)

Dickinson College Library (PA)

Texas A&M University Library System (TX)

Livingston Lord Library
Moorhead State University**

The purpose of this policy is to serve as a guide in our attempt to achieve consistent excellence in the choice of materials and as a statement of our purposes and standards in building the collections of a college library.

THE LIBRARY—AN AGENCY OF THE COLLEGE

The policy for the selection of library materials for Moorhead State College shall be in accord with the responsibility, aims and policy of the college as stated in its constitution:

"Under the relevant provisions of the Minnesota Statutes, and at the direction of the State College Board, Moorhead State College is charged with the responsibility of providing programs in higher education involving teaching, research, and public service responsive to the needs of the State and the people of Minnesota."[1]

"Among the aims of the College are the transmission of knowledge, the pursuit of truth, and through these but less directly the improvement of society. Freedom, inquiry, and expression are indispensible to the attainment of these aims."[2]

"Academic freedom in research is essential to the advancement of knowledge; academic freedom in teaching is fundamental to the advancement of learning. It is the policy of the College to maintain, within the law, complete freedom of inquiry, discourse, teaching, research, and publication."[3]

RESPONSIBILITY FOR AND PARTICIPATION IN SELECTION

1. The head librarian has the final responsibility, as delegated by the college president, for the maintenance and development of library collections, facilities, and services.

**Name change to* Moorhead State University *was effective July, 1975. "College" as the third term in the title of the institution and the acronym "MSC" appear* passim *throughout this document.*

2. Participation in the selection process shall be a responsibility of the head librarian and the members of the library faculty.
3. The departmental faculty shall bear primary responsibility for recommending materials to support the courses they teach.
4. Student and staff recommendations for the purchase of materials shall be not only welcomed but solicited.

DEFINITION OF LIBRARY MATERIALS

Library materials are defined as print and nonprint instructional materials (e.g., books, periodicals, pamphlets, manuscripts, print and graphic microforms, maps, aural and visual recordings, etc.) organized and housed for retrieval and use by the members of the college community to fulfill the aims and functions of the college and its curriculum.

COLLEGE CATEGORIES

Materials in the following categories shall be considered for selection:
1. General and specialized reference materials;
2. Bibliographic indexes and catalogs for the identification of materials;
3. Materials useful in specific curricular fields;
4. Interdisciplinary and broadly cultural materials not specific to one curricular field;
5. In some instances, materials which relate to specific fields not currently included in the curriculum but which may reasonably be expected to be added in the near future.

COLLECTION PRIORITIES

General materials shall be selected for each field represented in the college curriculum in priority as follows:
1. The field as a whole;
2. Divisions of the field in which courses are offered;
3. Other divisions of the field in which courses are not currently offered but in which courses may reasonably be expected within the near future;
4. Specialized or advanced aspects of the field of interest to faculty members but not yet represented by course offerings.

Current Materials vs. Retrospective Materials

While both current and retrospective materials are essential to the needs of the academic community, current materials shall generally receive higher priority. Lesser-used retrospective materials shall be sought from existing external sources such as other Tri-College libraries, MINITEX, and other interlibrary loan services. Current materials are defined as those in print in the original editions; retrospective materials are defined as those which are out-of-print or available only in reprint (either as full size or microcopy).

Textbooks

Designation as a textbook shall not disqualify a publication for selection. (See, however, Multiple Copies, p. 164 below.)

Rare Books

Rare books shall be purchased as they are required to fulfill the aims and functions of the college and its curriculum. Such purchases shall not receive high priority when budgets are inadequate.

Popular Fiction and Nonfiction

While the library has a responsibility to encourage leisure reading, budget limitations will normally require that current, non-course-related popular fiction and nonfiction shall have low priority for purchase.

Research Materials

While the library has a responsibility to serve the research needs of the graduate program and the faculty, the major responsibility of the library lies with the teaching program on the undergraduate and graduate level, and this function shall receive top priority. After provision has been made for the top priority, research materials may be purchased in those curricular fields where graduate degrees are awarded. Only in rare instances may the materials required for the personal research of individual faculty members be considered for purchase. In most instances, specialized research needs of students and faculty alike can best be served by the use of MINITEX and other interlibrary loan procedures.

Foreign Language Materials

The college library shall purchase the foreign language material required to attain the curricular objectives of the college. However, most of our students do not read foreign languages easily, and a higher priority shall be given to material in the English language unless that material is to be used as an aid in the teaching and learning of foreign languages. In such cases difficulty and appropriateness of the material shall be a prime consideration before it is purchased.

Reviews

The use of critical, academic reviews is recommended and urged in making selections. Caution is urged in accepting publishers' statements at face value and in selecting titles on the basis of the author's or publisher's reputation. When priority decisions must be made, that priority shall be given to those requests accompanied by citations of favorable, critical, academic reviews.

SPECIAL PROBLEMS IN MSC BOOK SELECTION

New Serials and Subscriptions

Much care and thought shall be exercised in selecting and beginning new serials and subscriptions because the expense of such an undertaking is an annual expense. Requests for new serials and subscriptions shall be checked against the holdings of the Tri-College Libraries. If a longer run of a serial or a subscription is held by another member of the Tri-College University, the librarian in charge of serials or subscriptions shall consult with the appropriate faculty member for a recommendation regarding the serial or subscription in question. The availability of the material by MIN-ITEX shall be a consideration. The new serial or subscription shall not be started unless it is felt that it would receive substantial use at the MSC Library. Back runs of qualifying serials or subscriptions shall be purchased only as is deemed necessary and as budgets permit.

Multiple Copies

Generally only one copy of an item shall be purchased, and the use of the library book budget to supply course textbooks is discouraged. However, multiple copies of materials may be purchased when the need for such copies can be demonstrated by use.

Microform vs. Full-Size Reprint Materials

Microforms possess advantages for the storage and use of some materials such as newspapers and lesser-used periodicals; and microform may be the only practical form for some extensive collections (the ERIC collection is an example). However, because of the difficulty of using large bibliographic indexes and catalogs in microform, it shall be policy to purchase such materials in full size whenever possible.

Paperback vs. Hardbound Editions

In cases where materials will have long term value and receive heavy use for a long period of time, casebound editions shall be purchased. If materials are judged to be of transitory usefulness and the cost of rebinding added to the cost of the paperback edition is substantially less than the cost of the casebound edition, the paperback edition shall be purchased.

Gift Policy

Gifts to the college library shall be accepted with the understanding that they shall be added to the collection only after they have met the same evaluative requirements as materials which are to be purchased. Materials shall be accepted only with the understanding that the disposition of those not appropriate to the collections shall be decided by the library faculty.

Relationship of MSC to Tri-College University

While the primary responsibility of the college library shall be to serve the needs of its own students and faculty, all possible consideration shall be given to cooperative endeavors which shall serve the students and faculty of the other members of the Tri-College University. It shall be the policy of MSC Library to cooperate with the Tri-College Libraries in the selection and purchase of expensive and little-used materials, serials, and subscriptions. When feasible, active efforts shall be made to search for activities and functions which can be carried on cooperatively if they will enhance the services and collections that can be offered to our students and faculty.

Relationship of MSC Library to MINITEX

MSC Library shall use MINITEX for little used materials, keeping in mind that MINITEX is a supplement to our local resources and that it is not intended to take the place of the extensive collection of materials needed if we are to serve our students and faculty effectively within the framework of our curricular objectives.

Lost Items

Library materials which have been lost shall be replaced if they are available through the current book trade and if they are still considered to be appropriate for selection according to criteria stated above.

Out-of-Print Materials

Efforts to obtain materials on the out-of-print market shall be made if it is decided that the material is of enough importance to justify those efforts. Judgment of importance shall include probable frequency of use and shall involve the consensus of at least two members of the library faculty.

REFERENCES

[1]Moorhead State College, Moorhead, Minnesota. Constitution of Moorhead State College. Article I. Section 1.
[2]Ibid. Article III. Section 1.
[3]Ibid. Article IV. Section I. A. Academic Freedom.

Holy Names College Library

The purpose of this document is to serve as a guide in the selection of books and other library materials for Holy Names College Library. The policies stated herein shall not be considered unalterable regulations and may be amended when, in the judgment of the librarians, such amendment will permit the addition of valuable material to the general collection. Written amendments to this policy must be approved by the Library Committee and the College President before becoming a part of this policy.

The library is concerned with providing selected books and other materials which will aid the members of the college community in their pursuit of education, information, and the creative use of leisure time. The acquisitions program of Holy Names College Library is expected to faithfully reflect the educational objectives and support the approved programs of the College.

RESPONSIBILITY FOR SELECTION

Responsibility for the selection of library materials for the college lies with the entire college community.

Faculty members are largely responsible for recommending the acquisition of materials in their subject fields. Any member of the faculty may request that an item be added to the college collection by completing a book order form and submitting it, through the department chairman, to the librarian. Departments are expected to recommend library purchases which will develop the entire field of their discipline. Such purchases will be charged to that portion of the book budget allocated to that department.

Students, staff, and administrative officers may also submit recommendations for purchase to the librarian.

Because the librarians are in the best position to observe the quality and balance of all subject areas and because the librarian is ultimately responsible for the overall quality and balance of the entire collection, the professional library staff will select and purchase materials in all subject areas. Such purchases will be charged to the library's portion of the book budget. Final decisions regarding acquisitions are made by the librarian after consultation with appropriate members of the faculty and library staff.

INTELLECTUAL FREEDOM

Holy Names College Library asserts its duty to keep in its collection a representative selection of materials on all subjects of interest to its users (the college community) including materials on all aspects of controversial questions. No materials shall be excluded from the collection because of the race or nationality of the authors, or the political, moral, or religious views expressed therein. Holy Names College operates as a private college governed by its own Board of Trustees. Therefore, the library is not subject to criticism of library-owned materials or attempts at censorship which originate outside the corporate structure of the College. Criticism or attempts at censorship of library-owned materials submitted in writing by those related to the College will receive a written reply from the librarian quoting the above policy. Cases of continued criticism will be referred to the Library Committee for decision.

POLICIES BY CLIENTELE SERVED

The library's first priority is to serve the needs of the students; in not only the basic materials but specialized resources for the graduate and certification programs as well.

The library endeavors to serve the needs of the faculty either by purchasing (if they can be used by the student body) or securing through interlibrary loan those resources needed for their study and research.

The library serves the entire college community through the purchase of recreational, cultural, and general information materials.

POLICIES BY FORMAT OF MATERIAL

Hardback Books

In the acquisition of new titles, the major emphasis shall be on current publications and, among those, works which promise to fulfill future as well as current needs shall receive preference. Both in-print and out-of-print materials shall be purchased. Duplicate copies of titles may be purchased, as required, at the discretion of the librarian. When there is a choice, hardback books shall be selected over paperbacks because of their greater durability in the library.

Paperback Books

Paperbacks of primarily current value which support courses being given may be placed in the library's paperback collection by faculty request. Due to the "short-lived binding" and "current information" factors of these paperbacks they will be placed in this collection on a yearly basis.

Textbooks

Single copies of textbooks will be purchased only when that title represents the best source of information in that field. Library funds are not appropriated for the purpose of acquiring multiple copies in lieu of textbooks for specific courses. On the other hand, the library has a responsibility for having on hand sufficient copies of titles which are assigned reading in classes of average size. Therefore, the library will not purchase additional copies in excess of a total of two per title. Under special circumstances the library will place in the Reserve Section unaccessioned copies in any number, provided such copies (beyond the two) are purchased with nonlibrary funds.

Periodicals

Periodical subscriptions are recommended in the same manner as books. Purchase will be for a three-year subscription charged to the book allocation of the teaching department recommending the subscription. Thereafter the subscription fee will be carried by the library's periodicals fund and will automatically be renewed. In order to gain the widest possible periodical coverage on the funds available, second copy subscriptions will not be placed by the library. For economy in binding and storage, and for durability of content, microforms will be purchased for back files of periodicals. These microforms shall be selected over paper copies when both are available except in the cases of indexes and art periodicals when paper is preferred.

Microforms

The selection of microforms should, in general, be limited to books now out-of-print and likely to remain so, titles too costly for purchase in their original form, and back files of periodicals.

Pamphlets

Although much of this material reaches the library without expenditure of library funds, the purchase of any of these written and visual forms necessary to strengthen the vertical file and pamphlet collections should be allowed.

Government Documents

Holy Names College Library is a nondepository library and therefore selections must be made and orders placed for each publication desired. These publications are integrated into the general collection.

Records

Only those of the spoken word (plays, poetry readings, speeches, etc.) will be acquired by purchase. Music records are purchased from the music department's library budget allocation.

Newspapers and Maps

These may be acquired by purchase but are not bound.

Tapes and Other Materials

Tapes, cassettes, slides, films, filmstrips, pictures, manuscripts, rare books, lab manuals, synopses and outlines will not be acquired by purchase.

Scores

Music scores are purchased from the music department's library budget allocation.

POLICIES BY SUBJECT OF MATERIAL

General Collections (Fiction and Nonfiction)

Priority for books and other materials to be purchased for the library is given to those materials which meet the curricular needs of the students in the courses offered. After the primary needs have been met, consideration is given to other desirable materials which will give balance to the collection or meet special interests or needs of the college community.

Reference Collection

A reference book shall be defined as one used frequently to answer questions that do not involve extended study. This is a noncirculating collection of general and specialized books providing quick access to factual information on the entire range of human knowledge. Books will be selected, therefore, not only on matters of curricular interest but in all areas in which factual information may be desired.

Foreign Language Materials

Materials in foreign languages taught at the College are desirable purchases for the library. However, materials for nonlanguage courses which are published in languages other than English, with the exception of dictionaries, encyclopedias, and other reference tools, shall be bought only in those instances when there is evidence of their immediate usefulness to students and faculty.

Archival Materials

Printed, manuscript, and other archival materials pertaining to Holy Names College are collected and preserved.

Reserve Section

All library-owned materials with the exception of reference works and archival materials may be placed on reserve at the instructor's option. Materials taken off the library's shelves for the use of students in specific courses must be retained in the library's reserve section.

GIFTS POLICY

Gifts of either library materials or money to purchase them will be accepted provided they comply with the above policies and provided there are no restrictions attached to the gift. No commitment to accept gifts shall be made by anyone except the librarian. All such offers made indirectly shall be referred to the librarian. In respect to gift books, this policy shall be followed:

1. The librarian shall have the prerogative to refuse to accept gift books which do not contribute to the mission and purposes of the library. Where necessary, the librarian's decision will be subject to presidential review.
2. It shall be made clear to the donor that:
   - The library will determine the classification, housing, and circulation policies of all gifts just as with purchased items.
   - The library retains the right to dispose of duplicates and unneeded materials as it sees fit.
   - The librarian may provide a monetary listing for the donor but will not assume any legal responsibility if this statement is used for tax or other purposes.

DISCARDING AND REPLACEMENT OF LOST BOOKS

Lost books are replaced after 3 years (or immediately if needed) when a member of the faculty approves replacement; otherwise the lost books are decataloged and recorded in the withdrawn files. It is a responsibility of the librarian to notify the appropriate members of the faculty when losses are discovered. Weeding, or the removal of obsolete materials for purposes of discarding, shall be considered an integral part of the total organized effort to study and develop the collection. Excess duplicate copies of seldom-used titles and badly damaged copies shall be withdrawn from the collection. Similarly, items shall be weeded if they contain outdated or inaccurate information. Weeding shall be done with advisement by departmental representatives.

EVALUATION

Periodic evaluation of holdings by checking against bibliographies and check lists in the different subject areas is undertaken by the library staff and the Library Committee. Results of such surveys may be referred to appropriate faculty members for advice and attention.

Northern Oklahoma College Learning Resource Center

INTRODUCTION

The planned development of the collection of a library requires the application of a stated acquisitions policy. No policy statement can be definitive for all time, since a library is not a static institution. Ideas about its nature and content are constantly evolving. Therefore, a policy to guide the development of a library's collection must be responsive to change.

The following represents a statement of acquisitions policy which can be applied in the selection of the various types of materials which the Learning Resource Center (LRC) adds to and withdraws from its collection.

OBJECTIVES

The objectives of the Northern LRC are parallel to the objectives of the college. They are concerned with the intellectual, emotional, and social growth and development of the students. Consideration is also given to faculty and staff needs.

The major purpose of the LRC is to contribute to the educational program of Northern Oklahoma College by collecting, making readily available, and assisting in the use of books and other materials needed by students, faculty, and staff.

Although no library collection may be expected to meet all the demands which are placed upon it, students should not have to go to other libraries for materials used in their studies, except in the case of research for which rare, highly specialized, or very expensive items are required.

The library will not always be able to meet the needs of all faculty members for their published research, but no faculty member should have to depend upon another library for the preparation of lectures and teaching.

Northern Oklahoma College, Learning Resource Center, Tonkawa, OK 74653

The library should also provide those materials needed by the administration and staff in the conduct of college business.

Any material of sufficient importance to be mentioned in a course should be represented in the collection, in order that no student is prevented by the inadequacy of the library from following an initial lead given him in class. Likewise, no innovation in the curriculum which is thought to be educationally sound, such as independent study, should be handicapped or obstructed by library deficiencies.

It is of primary importance that in a systematic and comprehensive manner the library support the needs of the curriculum, including the long-range development of the college with reference to its programs. When a new course is to be added, the Library Director should be given time to provide adequate library materials to support the proposed course.

In the acquisition of new titles, the major emphasis is on current publications, and among those, works which promise to fulfill future as well as current needs receive preference. But both in-print and out-of-print materials should be purchased as required.

The number of students majoring in an area and their demand for library materials influence acquisitions. The strength of the collections lies in areas of evident faculty or student interest.

The right to select materials representing diverse positions on controversial issues is safeguarded by the college. The *Freedom to Read Statement* and the *Library Bill of Rights* adopted by the American Library Association are recognized as upholding the doctrine of freedom of speech and of the press. These are not official institutional policy, however. A form (see page 173) is provided for a request for reconsideration of material. It is to be considered and acted upon by a Review Committee of library, administration, faculty, and student representatives. A decision will be rendered by this committee. Until a final decision has been reached, no action shall be taken by the library. All decisions are subject to review and appeal to the college administration and ultimately by the board of regents if they desire to become involved.

When there is a choice, hardbound books are selected over paperbacks because of their greater durability in the library.

Multiple copies of titles are purchased, as required, at the discretion of the library.

For back files of serial publications, microforms are selected over paper copies when both are available, except in the cases of indexes and art periodicals, when paper is preferred.

It is the responsibility of students to buy their own copies of assigned textbooks. However, any copy of a book in the library which is being used as a textbook will be placed on reserve for limited use.

Gifts of library materials are accepted when they meet the same criteria as are applied to the purchase of new materials, and as long as the donor agrees that the final authority for the use and disposition of said materials rests with the library. A monetary valuation statement must be made by the donor for tax or other purposes, and NOC will assume no responsibility for such a statement. A book plate to identify the donor may be placed in gift books or books bought with gift funds. Gifts will be acknowledged immediately and donors will be notified of the books selected for purchase.

Weeding, or the removal of obsolete materials for the purpose of discarding, is considered an integral part of the total organized effort to study and develop the collection. The process of weeding is done with advisement by departmental representatives. Specific items withdrawn from circulation include materials with outdated or inaccurate information, worn-out or badly marked volumes, excess duplicate copies of seldom-used titles, and broken files of unindexed journals.

PERIODIC REVIEW

In order to maintain a set of library policies that is responsive to the changing needs and objectives of Northern Oklahoma College, a review of the Library Acquisitions Policy is conducted periodically. The Library Director, working with the Library and Learning Resources Committee and the administration, is responsible for major policy recommendations and the updating of policy decisions.

REQUEST FOR RECONSIDERATION OF A BOOK

Author

Title

Publisher, Date

Request initiated by

Telephone   Address

City   Zip

Complainant represents:

Himself

Organizations or Group

1. To what in the material do you object? (Please be specific; i.e. cite pages)

2. What do you feel might be the result of viewing/reading this material?

3. Is there anything good about this material?

4. Did you read/view the entire material?   What parts?

5. Are you aware of the judgment of this material by literary critics? (Or reviews by persons in the subject area?)

6. What do you believe is the theme of this material?

7. In its place, what material of equal literary quality would you recommend that would convey as valuable a picture and perspective of our civilization?

8. If this material is retained, what publication(s) would you recommend which presents a counterbalancing point of view?

   Signature of complainant _____ Date _____

Iowa State University Library

INTRODUCTION

The primary function of the library is to provide the staff and students of the university with those materials needed for current teaching, extension, and research programs. A corollary function is to provide for general informational needs as well as sufficient richness, depth, and completeness of materials to assist those many self-directed and independent studies which are not spelled out in the educational curricula and formal research and degree programs. The university community also has the right to expect the library to provide materials for recreational purposes and for pursuit of nonacademic interests. The library, further, must be informed of forthcoming research and degree programs as a certain lead time is necessary to acquire materials which will be needed. For this reason it is essential that the library administration be actively involved in the planning of any curriculum which requires library resources. Acquisitions policy must also take into consideration the fact that the library of Iowa State University is part of a national system of research libraries. The total publishing output of the world, past and present, has reached such proportions that it is beyond the reach of any library, including the largest national and research libraries, to obtain all materials needed. Consequently, libraries engage in cooperative acquisition programs and depend on interlibrary loan systems for borrowing infrequently used materials that are not available locally. A prime example of cooperative acquisition is the Center for Research Libraries in Chicago, which collects and makes available to its members rarely-used materials. A pamphlet describing materials available from the Center for Research Libraries is available upon request at the reference department.

NEED FOR AN ACQUISITION POLICY

The immensity of the materials available along with increased book prices and processing costs makes it mandatory that the library have a written acquisitions plan which stresses wise selection to strengthen the resources of the library. Such a document necessarily cannot be definitive for all time. The library is not a rigidly fixed entity but a constantly changing and evolving institution mirroring the needs of the university.

The policy, however, must reflect certain basic principles. One of these is that the collection must be built on existing strengths rather than on weaknesses. If this principle is not observed, there will be a rapid deterioriation of the holdings of present strengths. If the library should start to build exhaustively in areas previously neglected, it would become obvious that great research collections cannot be established rapidly without sacrificing strong collection areas. The objective of collection development must reflect the long-range goals of the university. Any collection building in weak areas must proceed at a gradual rate without neglecting the strengths of the collections. If large-scale building of these areas is indicated to meet the needs of new graduate programs, additional funding from the university is necessary.

SELECTION RESPONSIBILITY

Selection of library materials is a joint responsibility of the faculty and the library staff. While it is the prerogative of every library faculty member to participate in the book selection process in areas of their particular expertise, the primary responsibility for collection development lies with the Resources Development Unit, which currently consists of five subject bibliographers (biological sciences/agriculture, English and American literature, humanities, physical sciences/engineering, and social sciences) and the veterinary medical librarian. Each of the bibliographers, working closely with faculty, is responsible for specific areas. Their duties are to screen the books received on blanket plans, to evaluate collections with a view to locate lacunae, and to select retrospective titles and current titles not received automatically on blanket order arrangements, as well as to offer bibliographic assistance to faculty in terms of dealers' catalogs, lists, quotations, etc. While faculty recommendations are welcomed and their help solicited, the library staff must carry the responsibility for areas neglected by faculty in order to achieve a balanced collection and to coordinate the resources development of the library as a whole. The ultimate responsibility for the acquisitions directions and policy decisions, including adequacy and quality of selections, rests with the library administration in general and specifically with the Assistant Director for Resources and Technical Services.

OBLIGATIONS

While in general the obligations of the library have been spelled out in the introduction, they can be enumerated specifically. The library should plan to obtain within its financial capabilities miscellaneous library materials (books, periodicals, maps, pamphlets, newspapers, microforms, manuscripts, audio-visual materials, music scores, government documents, etc.) required in meeting these four obligations:

1. To procure and make available materials needed for all instruction and extension programs of the university;
2. To procure and make available materials required by students and faculty members in their research;
3. To procure and make available library materials of general information in subject areas not covered by instructional, research, and extension programs;
4. To preserve all important materials relating to the history and development of the university. This includes not only official records and publications of the university but also materials about the university published elsewhere.

LIMITATIONS

It will seldom be possible, for financial reasons, to meet the above-named objectives adequately. Therefore, the library will observe the following general guidelines:

1. When lack of funds limit acquisitions, current publications of lasting and scholarly value will be given priority over older and out-of-print materials.
2. Publications in English language will be given higher priority.
3. Cooperative acquisitions plans will be considered for infrequently used research materials; advantage will be taken particularly of the library's membership in the Center for Research Libraries.
4. Materials will be acquired in another suitable format if originals are not available or are too expensive (e.g. microforms).
5. If the library holds material in microform, hard copy will not be purchased unless sufficient cause is shown.
6. Duplicate copies will be purchased only by justification of heavy and continued use.
7. Specialized research materials will not be duplicated unless dictated by special circumstances.
8. Variant editions of a title held will be acquired only if they are "standard" editions or contain substantial changes and are needed for research purposes. This does not apply to updated editions of scientific publications.
9. The library will not purchase extensive in-depth materials for specific theses topics of graduate students or for short term research projects of staff members unless the library's acquisitions policy specifies intensive collection development in that area.
10. The library will make no special effort to collect materials in non-western languages, even in subject areas of comprehensive coverage, if there is no sizable number of researchers with facility in that language.

DUPLICATION

Insofar as the library's funds do not permit the purchase of all materials needed for teaching, extension and research, duplicate copies of books and subscriptions to journals will be acquired only in accordance with the following guidelines:

1. Multiple demand and heavy, continuous use of individual titles will be the primary consideration for duplication of these titles, i.e., patrons do not have reasonable access to a publication without acquiring another copy.
2. Duplicate copies of carefully selected books and periodical titles may be purchased for the undergraduate library and for the reading rooms in the several residence halls.
3. Duplicate copies of heavily-used materials will be purchased for authorized reading rooms if these reading rooms house academic working collections serving current awareness rather than research purposes. For outside research collections some materials may be unique enough not to need duplicating for the main library. Separate acquisitions policies will be developed for each reading room.
4. Additional copies will be purchased for the reserve collection if the instructor intends to make extensive assignments.
5. No duplicate publications will be acquired solely for the sake of preservation except for selected materials maintained for archival purposes in the special collections department.
6. Duplicate publications received as gifts or on exchange will be subject to the same consideration for addition as materials suggested for purchase.
7. Past policies and historical circumstances will not be considered as a justification for new and continued duplication.
8. The library will not purchase duplicate copies, or publications not held by the library, for the sole use of individuals, academic departments and administrative offices.
9. The cost of any given publication, together with the financial situation of the library, may be the overriding factor in applying these guidelines and in making ultimate duplication decisions. While a guideline for the percentage of the total acquisitions budget which could be allocated as a maximum expenditure for duplication has not been developed, only a relatively small portion of the budget should be expended for duplicate materials.

GIFTS

1. The library solicits and encourages gifts and donations of useful materials, or money to purchase them, provided they fit into the acquisitions policies and provided there are no restrictions attached. Gifts provide many valuable additions to the collection.
2. The library will not accept gifts with conditions as to their disposition or location except by express permission of the library director.
3. The library is free to dispose of any unneeded publications regardless of how they were acquired.
4. The library cannot legally appraise gifts for tax or inheritance purposes. The library may, however, assist the donor in obtaining, if available,

prices located in book auction records or in catalogs of secondhand
dealers. If a substantial collection is involved the library may help the
donor to procure a professional appraiser.

5. The gift/exchange section of the serials department is responsible for
   acceptance and processing of all gifts, except government documents.
   The subject bibliographers will determine the suitability of individual
   items for collections in accordance with the stated acquisitions policy.

EXCHANGE

The trading of publications among libraries is another means of
acquiring library materials. In all exchange agreements an attempt is made
to maintain an equitable balance in the value of materials sent and received.
The library will enter into exchange agreements with other institutions
whenever the desired publications are available only on exchange and whenever such exchange of publications is advantageous to the library, as determined by the head of the gift/exchange unit. Publications received on
exchange will be added to the collections in accordance with the acquisitions
policy. The suitability for inclusion of these in the library's collections will be
determined by the subject bibliographers.

The library will exchange the following categories of publications:

Current serials.   Current serial publications of the Iowa State University
which are available to the library free of charge or for minimal cost are made
available to exchange partners. The library receives in return similar publications of the exchanging institution. Most exchange institutions are located
in "soft" currency countries which do not have well-established book trade
and private publishing. Trade publications will be supplied to foreign exchange partners only if the needed publication cannot be obtained in any
other way.

Duplicates.   Duplicate copies of unneeded books and serial issues are sent
to the gift/exchange unit and can be used in exchange for needed materials
from other libraries.

LEVELS OF COLLECTION INTENSITY

It is recognized that the requirements for library materials vary in the
different subject areas. In many scientific and technological fields the primary needs are met by scientific serials. In the social sciences and humanities
books are still of main importance. Current and projected degree and
research programs have been used to indicate the degrees of acquisitions
intensity which the library will attempt to follow in meeting the needs of the
academic departments.

Minimal Level: A highly selected collection which would introduce and
define a variety of subject areas not necessarily represented in the university
curricula. It would include basic works of recognized writers, selection of
basic texts in all subject fields, reference and biographical works as well as
fundamental bibliographies in all subject areas and representative journals.
The level of coverage would include primarily English language materials.

Undergraduate Level: A collection of works to meet all instructional needs at the undergraduate level. It includes all basic works, complete sets of works by important writers and critical works about them, selections of works by secondary writers, a wide range of basic journals, reference works and bibliographies.

Instructional-Research Level: A collection of materials in English and in other Western European languages covering fundamental works of scholarship for use by upper level undergraduate students, graduate students, and faculty members. In addition to current materials, the library will attempt to obtain retrospective works on selected basis including serials, reference sets and bibliographies. This level would serve departments granting baccalaureate degrees and those beginning and projecting master level graduate programs.

Comprehensive Research Level: A comprehensive collection of materials for independent study of graduate students and faculty including all current and retrospective materials of scholarly value, an extensive assemblage of critical and biographical works, complete sets of serials as possible, reference sets, bibliographies, documents, and other pertinent materials. This collection level is intended to serve primarily those departments offering the Ph.D. degree or anticipating to do so in the near future.

List of Subjects

In the list of subjects appropriate numbers indicate how intensively the library will attempt to develop collections in a particular area. The letter assignments refer to subject bibliographers who are responsible for assessment of collections and selection of materials in specific areas as follows:

BS/A—Biological Sciences/Agriculture
EAL —English and American Literature
H   —Humanities
PS/E —Physical Sciences/Engineering
SS   —Social Sciences
VM   —Veterinary Medicine

Bibliographers may receive assistance from other library staff members who have expertise in certain subject fields.

Forms of Library Materials

While in general the collection intensity levels apply to all kinds of library materials, certain types of materials require special consideration. Acquisitions policies are spelled out for archives and manuscripts, audiovisual materials, government documents, maps, microforms, newspapers, serials, and miscellaneous other materials (dissertations, music scores, rare books, and textbooks) in separate sections following the list of subjects.

REVISION

This acquisitions policy will be subject to review at least once every year by the Acquisitions Council. Any portion of the policy statement is subject to change at any time by the Acquisitions Council. The members of the Council are invited to submit suggestions for revision to the Assistant Director for Resources and Technical Services. The policy as well as any changes must have a final approval by the library administration.

LIST OF SUBJECTS, LEVELS OF COVERAGE, AND BIBLIOGRAPHIC ASSIGNMENTS

Subject	Level of Coverage	Assignment
Aerospace Engineering	4	PS/E
Agricultural Education	3	SS
Agricultural Engineering	4	PS/E
Agriculture	4	BS/A
Agronomy	4	BS/A
Air Force-Aerospace	2	SS
Animal Science	4	BS/A
Anthropology		SS
Archaeological	2	
Cultural	2	
Physical	3	
Social	2	
Applied Art		H
Art education	2	
Arts in general	2	
Decorative arts	3	
Drawing, design, etc.	3	
Painting and paint media	2	
Sculpture	2	
Architecture	3	H
Astronomy—see Physics		
Bacteriology	4	BS/A
Biochemistry and Biophysics	4	BS/A-PS/E
Biomedical Engineering	4	PS/E-VM
Botany and Plant Pathology	4	BS/A
Ceramic Engineering	4	PS/E
Chemical Engineering	4	PS/E
Chemistry		PS/E
Analytical	4	
Inorganic	4	
Organic	4	
Physical	4	
Textile	3	

ARCHIVES AND MANUSCRIPTS: ACQUISITIONS POLICY

University Archives

The university's archives section of the special collections department is the depository of all university publications and records of historical and research importance.

UNIVERSITY PUBLICATIONS

The following publications will be included in the "C" or college collection:

1. Monographs by faculty while members of Iowa State University;
2. Monographs by staff while members of Iowa State University;
3. Publications of all departments, colleges, institutes, extension services, experiment stations, programs, administrative units, and associated organizations of the University;
4. Publications of all student organizations or groups;
5. Any other state-supported organization closely related to the university (e.g. State Board of Regents);
6. Publications about any of the above categories if authorship does not fit any of these categories.

The library will attempt to obtain two copies of most of the above publications to provide one copy for the general collections. If only one copy of a particular publication is available it shall be deposited in the special collections department and cataloged for the "C" collection rather than the general collection. No attempt will be made by special collections department to secure for its holdings publications of alumni or of academic personnel unless they fit into the above categories.

UNIVERSITY RECORDS

The university records shall include correspondence, documents, files, manuscripts, and photographs and other materials of historical and research value pertaining to the activities and functions of the university or its administrative officers and other staff members. Officers having custody of the records shall determine their administrative or legal need for them and, with the assistance of the university archivist, their historical value, and arrange the systematic transfer of those records deemed worthy of preservation to the university archives. University archives shall also include personal and professional papers and manuscripts of administrative and academic staff members as well as records of faculty and student organizations.

Manuscripts

Manuscript collections, business records, and other unpublished materials of individuals, companies and institutions not connected with the university will be sought and collected selectively in accordance with the general acquisitions policy. While primary emphasis will be given to archival materials dealing with agricultural, business, industrial, and political history of Iowa, collections of materials treating other areas may be accepted if deemed to be important to the programs of the Iowa State University.

AUDIO-VISUAL MATERIALS: ACQUISITIONS POLICY

Audio Cassettes

The library will purchase audio cassettes in the following categories:

1. Cassettes containing music selected by the music department staff for use by students enrolled in music courses;
2. Cassettes containing oral texts needed in instruction and research programs.

The cassettes will be fully cataloged and available in the Media and Microform Center.

Audio Tapes (Reels)

As part of the university's oral history the special collections department will record on tape interviews with outstanding staff members, visitors, and other individuals possessing information of historical importance.

Multi-Media Kits

The library will acquire such multi-media or mixed media kits for which the library has viewing and/or playback equipment and which are needed for specific course assignments.

Music Records

The library will purchase music records as requested by the music department staff and as funds permit, to meet the music appreciation and other instructional needs of that department. The music records are fully cataloged but currently housed in Music Hall as the library does not possess playback equipment and facilities.

Photographs

The special collections department of the library, as part of its archival and manuscript collections, will procure and maintain files of photographs of historical importance to the Iowa State University.

Slides

As part of its archival collections, the special collections department will procure slides of historical value to Iowa State University. Slides needed for course assignments will be purchased, fully cataloged, and located in the Media and Microform Center.

Video Cassettes

The library will purchase, on a selective basis, video cassettes which will be used in connection with course assignments.

GOVERNMENT DOCUMENTS: ACQUISITIONS POLICY

General

The government documents department, in consultation with the appropriate bibliographers and faculty, is responsible for the selection and acquisition of all United States federal government, United Nations and U.S. state government publications. The selection of foreign government and local government publications is the responsibility of the subject bibliographers according to guidelines provided by the general acquisitions policy.

In general, only one copy will be procured of each title with the following exceptions:

1. Titles needed for reserve;
2. Titles needed in authorized reading rooms as recommended by the appropriate librarian or bibliographer;
3. Titles for which there are intensive demands and continuous, heavy use.

All substantial monographs and serials will be fully cataloged and incorporated into the general collection. Ephemeral materials and publications which do not lend themselves easily to cataloging and those which can be serviced better by the documents librarians will be housed in the government documents department.

United States Government Documents

The library shall endeavor to secure comprehensively, depending on the collection intensity level of a given subject field, annual reports, bibliographies, congressional publications, directories, statistical compilations, and "laws, rules, regulations, and opinions" type of publications depending on the subject treatment. Speeches of government officials and career materials will not be collected comprehensively but will be retained selectively as received.

DEPOSITORY PUBLICATIONS

The library has been, since 1907, a partial depository of publications distributed by the Superintendent of Documents. Publications are selected on the basis of instructional and research needs of the university. Any depository publications not held by the library can be borrowed from University of Iowa Library which has been designated as a regional depository and receives all depository publications.

NONDEPOSITORY PUBLICATIONS

Government publications not available on depository from the Superintendent of Documents will be acquired selectively if needed for instruction and research. No attempts will be made to search and secure these publications exhaustively because all nondepository publications are available from the Center for Research Libraries in microprint.

OTHER DEPOSITORY OR BLANKET SUBSCRIPTION ARRANGEMENTS

The library receives the following United States government documents with beginning dates as indicated:

1. Arms Control and Disarmament Commission research reports, August, 1968–;
2. Atomic Energy Commission technical reports, 1946– (1963– microfiche);
3. ERIC (Educational Resouices Information Center) reports, 1967– (microfiche);
4. Housing and Urban Development Department—Area and regional planning reports, March 1969–;
5. Manpower Administration research reports, 1966–;
6. National Aeronautics and Space Administration technical reports, Fall 1969– (microfiche);
7. NTIS—SDM (National Technical Information Service—Selective Dissemination of Microfiche) class 11 (Materials—Metals), March 25, 1971– (microfiche);
8. Rand Corporation reports, 1957–.

TECHNICAL REPORTS

Technical reports to support instructional and research programs not received automatically will be purchased selectively from the National Technical Information Service in microfiche at the request of bibliographers and faculty members. Any report constituting a basic reference text, or intended to be used broadly and frequently, may be purchased in a hard copy, instead of microfiche, and fully cataloged.

United Nations Publications

The library has blanket subscription orders for all UN publication categories of relevance to the programs of the university. Retrospective files for 1954–1968 will not be acquired as they are available from the Center for Research Libraries. However, individual reference publications and titles in heavy demand will be purchased. The library will also acquire selected titles from FAO, UNESCO, WHO and other international agencies in accordance with the acquisitions policy.

State Publications

IOWA DOCUMENTS

The library shall attempt to acquire all State of Iowa documents of instructional and research value to the university. The University of Iowa Library is collecting all Iowa documents comprehensively and any publication can be obtained on loan from that library.

DOCUMENTS OF OTHER STATES

The library will acquire other state documents selectively for subject interest. The Center for Research Libraries has comprehensive files of all state documents since 1951.

Local Government Documents

Only the publications of Story County and City of Ames will be procured as comprehensively as possible.

Foreign Government Documents

Documents of foreign governments will be acquired selectively for their subject value in accordance with the acquisitions policy.

MAPS: ACQUISITIONS POLICY

General

The map librarian, in consultation with appropriate bibliographers and faculty members, is responsible for selection and acquisition of all maps. While the library will attempt to meet all instructional and research needs, it will not be possible to quickly develop large map collections comparable to those in other large university libraries. For this reason acquisition will be concentrated on a basic collection of the following to cover all aspects of cartography:

1. Agricultural maps;
2. Geographical maps (showing physical features and contours);
3. Geological maps (showing layers of the earth's crust);
4. Political maps (showing political boundaries and cultural features);
5. Street maps of the world's great cities, especially of American cities.

Topical and specialized maps will not be collected comprehensively. Maps issued by government agencies will be acquired on a higher priority basis because they are less costly and also because commercially produced maps are based on them. Materials will be acquired by purchase and as gifts. Gifts will be sought in accordance with the established gift policy of the library. Historically valuable maps will be handled by the special collections department.

Types of Materials

Basically the Map Room will acquire the following types of materials:

1. Sheet maps, individually and in sets;
2. Aerial photographs;
3. Bibliographic and reference tools to assist in using and servicing the collection;
4. Globes and relief maps, on a lower priority basis.

Geographical Areas

Maps will be acquired selectively for all geographical areas with emphasis on current materials according to the needs of the faculty.

MICROFORMS: ACQUISITIONS POLICY

General

Microforms (microcards, microfiche, microfilms, microprints) will be purchased in preference to printed copy, if available, in all cases involving bulky, expensive, and infrequently used research type materials. Microforms, in general, are less costly and also save considerable space.

Large Microproduction Projects

The library will subscribe selectively to large microform projects of relevance to research and instruction programs within the framework of the acquisitions policy. For example, the library has acquired or established standing orders for *Early American Imprints* (Evans, Shaw and Shoemaker) 1639–1819, *American Periodical Series* 1700–1850, *English Books* (Pollard and Redgrave, Wing) 1475–1700, *American Culture Series, Landmarks of Science, Wright American Fiction,* 1774–1875. The library will not purchase printed copies of books found in the large microform series which are received on subscription unless there are exceptional circumstances.

Monographs (Individual Titles)

Microform editions of single monographs will be purchased only if printed editions are not available or if the printed editions are very costly as in the case of rare books.

Newspapers

Newspapers will be retained permanently in microfilm only (see "Newspaper Acquisitions Policy"). The single exception will be the *Iowa State Daily,* which will be bound and retained for archival purposes in the special collections department.

Serials

Periodicals and other serials will be considered for purchase in microformat as follows:

1. Earlier back sets of serials, not held in printed copy, if to be used infrequently, or if the cost of hard copy is prohibitive;
2. Rarely used periodicals (printed copies of these will not be purchased, and if received, will be discarded upon receipt of microform copy);
3. Periodicals subject to heavy use, loss, and mutilation to supplement the printed sets.

Technical Reports

The library will purchase requested technical reports from the National Technical Information Service only on microfiche unless a specific report is intended to be used frequently and is worthy of cataloging and preserving it permanently. The library presently receives several technical report series in microform from a number of government agencies. For description of these series see "Government Documents: Acquisitions Policy."

NEWSPAPERS: ACQUISITIONS POLICY

The Iowa State University Library will acquire on a current basis newspapers for the purpose of meeting the teaching and research needs of the university by attaining the following coverage:

1. Foreign newspapers on a highly selective basis: only the important and influential newspapers from the major countries will be purchased;
2. Domestic newspapers on a relatively selective basis; i.e., newspapers of the major cities of the country;
3. Iowa newspapers on a selective basis: the library will obtain newspapers from major towns and cities and will retain them for a limited period of time.

The following factors will be considered in selecting new subscriptions:

1. Relevance to specific courses and research projects considered under these criteria:

   • Depth of study, e.g., faculty/graduate research, current awareness;
   • Continuity or extent of need;
   • Relatedness to several disciplines.

2. Current coverage of geographical area/language;
3. Subject/viewpoint representation, e.g., national political movements, etc.;
4. Coverage of specific historical events or periods, e.g., Civil War.

Retention Scope

Newspaper files are maintained at these retention levels:

1. Back file on microfilm and current subscription; all issues retained until microfilm is received;
2. Current subscription; retention period of two months; back files available from other sources, e.g., ARL Foreign Newspapers Microfilm Project;
3. Current subscription; short retention period not exceeding two weeks.

In making selections consideration will be given to the titles available through the library's memberships in the ARL Foreign Newspapers Microfilm Project and in the Center for Research Libraries as well as to the resources available within the state, particularly from the other two state universities.

Extensive back files on microfilm will be retained only of a highly selective group of significant newspapers which are needed on a frequently recurring basis. The original copies of these papers will be discarded after the receipt of the microfilm. Back files of those newspapers not retained will be readily available from the CRL and other research libraries through interlibrary loan service.

Special policies are applied to the following types of newspapers:

Church newspapers.   This library does not subscribe to church papers. Those published in Iowa and supplied free of charge will be retained for a limited time.

Labor newspapers.   Only the principal papers of the major national and state labor organizations will be considered for retention.

Political papers.   Only the principal papers of significant political movements will be considered for acquisition and retention.

Underground newspapers.

- Iowa papers will be collected comprehensively and retained permanently.
- For national coverage papers will be acquired on selected basis with the emphasis on the papers from the Midwest region. Back files on microfilm will be retained only of a few nationally prominent papers. The Center for Research Libraries has complete files.

Special interest newspapers.   Although special interest newspapers, including hometown papers, cannot be provided for the various segments of the university community, the library will consider housing current issues of papers received as gifts.

SERIALS: ACQUISITIONS POLICY

The acquisition of serials requires a higher degree of selectivity than that of monographic titles. Once a serial is selected an ongoing and costly commitment is made in terms of payments, binding, and storage for many years to come. Also, the large number of serials published makes it impossible to purchase all titles needed.

The library in general will attempt to acquire:

1. Complete holdings of the *leading* serials in all major subject fields;
2. Serials containing the results of professional scholarship;
3. Serials devoted to the informed discussion of public affairs;
4. Serials containing serious literature and criticism;
5. Serials presenting substantial factual information concerning economic, political and social events and scientific knowledge;
6. Selected American popular periodicals of research value;
7. Serials of research value published by government agencies as outlined in the government documents acquisitions policy;
8. Back files of serials in original format or microform, depending on research needs, frequency of use and availability of funds;
9. Complete files of serials published by the Iowa State University.

If a large number of titles is requested, the department concerned will be asked to assign priorities in order of importance. This will be observed particularly if the request involves extensive and expensive back files. The purchase of individual issues and scattered or incomplete files will be avoided. Depending on frequency of use, the library may elect to purchase a serial back set on microfilm rather than hard copy. This format not only saves space but is also much less costly.

As a general rule, the library will obtain only one copy of any given serial publication. Decisions on duplication will be made on a title by title basis. The main reason for duplication will be the frequency of use. As most reading rooms contain mainly working collections for current awareness in the subject fields, only high-use serials will be duplicated for them. Specific policies concerning duplication will be developed for each reading room. Whenever feasible the library shall establish standing orders for the selected serials to receive them on a continuing basis. Serials available on a gift or exchange basis will be subject to the same selection policies as serials obtainable by purchase.

Special policies will be observed for the following types of serials:

City directories. Only Ames and Des Moines directories are acquired.

College catalogs. The library will retain latest issues of selected university and college catalogs. Complete back files will be maintained only for catalogs of Iowa State University and University of Iowa. Catalogs will be obtained from all Iowa institutions offering post-high school education. The library will also procure catalogs from all major U.S. and Canadian institutions of higher learning including summer session catalogs as comprehensively as possible. For foreign university catalogs the coverage will be selective on the basis of need.

Corporation reports. The library will retain only reports of:

- Major Iowa firms;
- Selected large American industrial firms;
- Companies of historical significance to Iowa and Iowa State University.

The above applies also to annual reports of foundations. (Note: A file of current reports from selected American industrial firms is retained in the Engineering Reading Room.)

House organs. Only selected titles of subject interest will be obtained.

Newsletters of societies and associations. Only selected titles of subject interest will be retained. Limited files may be kept of newsletters not considered of permanent research value.

Religious periodicals. Selected official organs of major denominations will be retained. Limited files may be retained of other religious periodicals as received free of charge.

Telephone directories. The library will retain latest issues of directories for all major U.S. and Canadian cities (population of 500,000 and above), those of other cities in heavy demand, and any directories received from cities in Iowa. Foreign directories will be acquired only for the major cities of the Western Hemisphere. Back files will be retained only for Ames directories.

University reports. A five-year file is retained of annual reports from selected midwest state universities and other major universities of the country. Complete back files are kept only for the three state universities.

MISCELLANEOUS MATERIALS: ACQUISITIONS POLICY

Dissertations

Two copies of all Iowa State University dissertations will be retained permanently by the library. One copy will be bound, fully cataloged, and integrated in the collections. Another copy will be bound chronologically and retained as archival material in the special collections department.

Other dissertations will be purchased only in special cases on microfilm unless the anticipated frequency of use indicates the need for hard copy. As part of cooperation among the three state universities, the library will consider in all cases the availability of needed dissertations produced at any university in the country from the libraries of University of Iowa and University of Northern Iowa.

The library will not acquire dissertations for the individual's use. United States doctoral dissertations are retrievable through *International Dissertation Abstracts* and can be purchased by the individual from the University Microfilms, Inc. either on microfilm or in hard copy.

Music Scores

The library will attempt to acquire a working collection of music scores needed in current instruction and research programs as requested by the music department staff.

Rare Books

The present financial structure does not permit the library to engage in a building of a rare books collection in any subject area. Rare books *per se,* therefore, will not be purchased unless a strong research or instructional need is shown. In fact, the library has a good collection of rare books in the English language on microfilm received as part of *Early American Imprints, English Books,* and other large microform project series.

Textbooks

In general, the library will not acquire textbooks adopted as required texts for any given courses. Some textbooks, however, are valuable as reference and research works in their own right. They will be obtained in accordance with the acquisition policy.

PROCEDURES FOR ORDERING
VARIOUS TYPES OF LIBRARY MATERIALS

Since the library now acquires a great variety of materials in different formats, e.g., nonprint media, maps, government documents, etc., this document attempts to clarify the acquisition departments' responsibilities for these materials in order to provide clearer guidelines for bibliographers and other selectors. These guidelines are provisional and will be revised as necessary.

Monographs

All orders for monographs and monographic sets or series including microforms, with the exception of certain government documents (see "Government Documents," below), are to be submitted to the bibliographic search department. These materials include not only single volume monographs and multi-volume monographic sets, but also monographic series with projected completion and continuing monographic series in which individual volumes are cataloged and classified separately. Because of some comprehensive standing order arrangement the serials department still handles a number of "cat. sep." monographic series, e.g., National Academy of Sciences/National Research Council, etc.

Serials

Orders for all types of serials in all formats (hard copy, microform, etc.) are to be forwarded to the serials department according to the previously established policies and procedures ("Procedures for Acquisition of Serial Back Sets"—9/1/71, "Procedures for Serials Ordering"—12/6/72) with the following exceptions:

1. Certain government documents (see "Government Documents," below);
2. One or several single back volumes of a monographic serial which will be cataloged as monographs if there is no intent to acquire that title on an ongoing basis (see "Procedures for Acquisition of Back Sets"). Orders for such items are to be submitted to the bibliographic search department and to be ordered by the order department. These orders should clearly state that they are to be cataloged as separates. This happens rarely and applies mainly to selections made from second-hand dealers' catalogs;
3. Added copies of one or several issues of a monographic series, currently received on serials standing orders, to be cataloged as separates. Orders for such added copies are to be sent to the bibliographic search department indicating they are to be cataloged as separates. In most cases these added copies are for reading rooms or other separate collections.

Orders are to be sent to the serials department for verification for *only* certain years/volumes of an annual/irregular serial or other titles cataloged by Library of Congress as an open entry, if they are to be cataloged as "Library has" with no intent to acquire future issues on a regular or standing order basis. They will then be forwarded to the order department for appropriate funding and ordering.

Orders for single issues or volumes of a serial to be used on reserve are also to be submitted to the serials department. These materials will be forwarded without cataloging to the reserve desk.

Please note that serials often pose complex problems requiring ad hoc decisions in individual cases. This procedure guide could not cover the myriad of possibilities that could arise. If the bibliographic searching in any of the acquisition departments should reveal the need for reconsideration or further decision on any title, bibliographers and other selectors will be consulted for advice.[1]

Government Documents

Orders for the following government publications (monographs, serials, etc.) are to be submitted to the Government Documents Department.[2]

1. U.S. Government publications;
2. Technical reports (published or sponsored by the U.S. Government);
3. Publications of all fifty state governments;
4. United Nations publications (excluding its affiliated agencies—see #1 below);
5. Publications of the Organization of American States.

Most of these publications are received either on deposit, as gifts, or on standing orders, or are purchased from U.S. Government deposit funds. If they are not available by any of the above methods and need to be purchased separately, the government documents department will forward monograph orders to bibliographic search department and serials orders to serials department. Orders for the following government publications must be submitted either to bibliographic search department (monographs) or to serials department (serials):

1. Documents of United Nations affiliated agencies (FAO, UNESCO, WHO, etc.);[3]
2. Publications of European Communities (Common Market);[3]
3. Documents of other governmental international organizations (OECD, NATO, etc.);
4. Documents of foreign governments;
5. Documents of local governments (city, county, etc.).

Maps

All orders for sheet maps are to be submitted to the government documents department. If they are to be purchased that department will forward the orders directly to the order department, since they will not be cataloged by the catalog department. Orders for atlases and maps with accompanying texts are to be sent to bibliographic search department and processed as other monographs.

Nonprint Media

All orders for nonprint media materials should be submitted to the bibliographic search department unless they are identified as ongoing serials, in which case the orders should be sent to the serials department. The bibliographers and other selectors are asked to detach the yellow copy of the order card and forward it to the media room (Room 50) for their order file. For location of these materials *Media* should be indicated on order card in the appropriate space. At the present time the library has equipment to handle only the following media materials:

1. Audio cassettes;
2. Film strips;
3. Slides;
4. Video cassettes.

The library does not possess any playback equipment for phono records. Some records are, however, purchased for use of the music department and housed in Music Building. Orders for phono records are to be submitted to the bibliographic search department indicating *Music* as location. Anyone wishing to suggest purchases should consult the person responsible for selection in the area of music.

SELECTION OF SERIALS

The responsibility for the selection of new serials titles for the library's collections is as follows:

1. General collection (Main Library)—bibliographers;
2. Undergraduate Library—Undergraduate Serials Committee;
3. Reading rooms—appropriate subject bibliographer;
4. Veterinary Medicine Library—Veterinary Medicine librarian;
5. Reference collection—reference librarians.

Those responsible for serials selection should regularly monitor serials bibliographies and reviews in specialized scholarly journals.

All selections should be made in accordance with the library's acquisitions policy, e.g., only leading publications should be selected for collection intensity levels 1 and 2. Because of budgetary restrictions, new serial titles and back files are purchased on a very selected basis. Each year the serials acquisitions section will estimate the cumulative number of new titles that can be added along with an approximate dollar amount available for purchasing titles and back files. The serials department will report every three months to the selectors of serials on the status of new serial and back set purchasing.

As stated in the library's acquisitions policy, ordering of single issues/ volumes or scattered and incomplete sets is to be discouraged. Copies of single periodical issues, however, may be ordered for use in reserves without cataloging.

If reviews or other indicators of quality (publisher, sponsoring agency, etc.) are absent, it is advisable to procure a sample copy for inspection before an order is placed. The serials department will, upon request by the serials selectors (see above), obtain sample copies and forward them to the requestors for evaluation.

Publishers' advertisements and samples received automatically by the serials department are sorted by subject and routinely sent to the bibliographers for evaluation. If appropriate, such materials are also routed to the assistant directors, reference department, and the undergraduate library (serials of a wide and general scope or interest, serials of reference value, e.g., indexing and abstracting journals, etc.).

Reference staff is responsible for calling to the attention of serials selectors:

1. Journals frequently borrowed on interlibrary loan that are within the scope of our library's collection;
2. Volumes or issues of a title currently held missing from our collection.

Reference staff is responsible for calling to the attention of the serials department patron requests for serial issues and volumes that are mutilated or missing from our shelves.

All requests from faculty, staff and students for new serial titles for the general collection are forwarded by the serials department to the appropriate bibliographer for review and approval.

Titles costing more than $50 per year and back sets costing more than $500 require the approval of the Assistant Director for Resources and Technical Services.

Serials acquisitions may refer requests for doubtful or borderline serial titles including back sets to the appropriate bibliographer and assistant director for reconsideration.

Requests for reading rooms and branch libraries will be handled according to the separate documents on policy and procedures for processing reading room and branch library orders, dated October 14, 1971.

The responsibility for designating limited file holdings for a serial title rests with the librarians who are responsible for serials selection as defined above.

Serials acquisitions is responsible in consultation with selectors for buying microfilm backup for journals which are heavily used and frequently mutilated or lost.

The bibliographers are responsible for designating for display in the periodical room any new periodical titles ordered for the general collection.

Unsolicited serials received as gifts or on exchange will be referred to the appropriate serials selectors for evaluation. These publications will be subject to the same selection policies as serials obtained by purchase.

PROCEDURES FOR SERIALS ORDERING

All orders for serials, including those for back sets, are submitted to the serials department.

Orders Received from Bibliographers for General Collection

For new titles to be ordered the serials department receives from bibliographers serial order slips containing complete bibliographic information, including price, if available, and source of citation. The serials department also receives from bibliographers a marked copy of New Serial Titles classed list (check mark/initial indicates an order request; "sample"/initial indicates a request for a sample or a prospectus).

The serials department determines whether the title requested is in the library or on order.

If the title is in the library or on order, the order slip is returned to the requestor providing this information. This feedback will not be provided for titles checked in NST.

If the title is not in the library and not on order, the serials department places a standing order beginning with the current volume unless the request specifies back volumes. The serials department attempts to obtain back issues for serials up to three years old. Titles costing more than $50 per year require the approval of the Assistant Director for Resources and Technical Services.

If the purchase of a back set is requested, the serials department determines price and availability in hard copy and/or microform and consults the appropriate bibliographer concerning the cost and format before an order is placed. A back set costing more than $500 requires the approval of the Assistant Director for Resources and Technical Services.

If the publication cannot be identified or if there are any other difficulties with the request, the order will be returned to the appropriate bibliographer.

Orders Received from Faculty, Staff and Students for General Collection

The serials department determines whether the publication is in the library or on order and notifies the requestor accordingly.

If the serial is on order and the requestor asks to be notified, the serials department will add his/her name to the order card. The serials department will also indicate rush processing if this is desired by the requestor.

If the serial is not in the library and not on order, the request is forwarded to the appropriate bibliographer for review and approval. If the title costs more than $50 per year, it has to be approved also by the Assistant Director for Resources and Technical Services. Orders not approved are returned to requestors with explanation by the bibliographers.

The purchase of back sets is handled as described in the preceding section.

Orders for Reading Rooms and Branch Libraries

Requests for reading rooms and branch libraries will be handled according to the separate documents on policy and procedures for processing reading room and branch library orders.

PROCEDURES FOR ACQUISITION OF SERIAL BACK SETS

The purchase of serial back sets is often much more complex than the buying of books or the handling of current subscriptions. The high cost of many back sets dictates very judicious selection and careful decision-making. Often a number of alternatives are possible: a particular run of a journal might be available in microform, in reprint or an original second-hand copy.

For many years the purchase of back sets has been a responsibility shared by the order and the serials departments without a clearly defined assignment.

Beginning with fiscal year 1970/71, the major responsibility for back sets was delegated to the serials department in order to concentrate all serials work and attendant record keeping and serials data maintenance in one department. This, however, has not ended all complications and problems.

To clarify selection and acquisition of back sets the following procedures are to be implemented:

1. All orders for serials back volumes or single issues received by the bibliographic search department or the serials department are to be sent to the appropriate bibliographer after a preliminary search by the serials department has determined the correct entry and the possible holdings of the library.

2. The bibliographer must approve all back set purchases in accordance with predetermined priority lists, if such exist. The acquisition of future volumes should also be determined at this point. Extensive back sets costing more than $500 require the approval of the Assistant Director for Resources. It must be also determined whether hard copy is necessary or a microfilm copy is sufficient. The purchase of single isolated volumes or issues, unless they are intended to complete and enhance existing holdings, is to be discouraged. (This point is amplified under #5.)

3. At this point the orders are to be returned to the serials department for final check in the card catalog and the on-order file before ordering. It may be necessary for the serials department to procure information on availability, prices, etc., before orders are actually issued. The serials department requests LC copy from the bibliographic search department as required.

4. If a second-hand catalog has orders for books as well as for back sets of serials, the bibliographic search department, after searching, is to reserve the items using reserve letter procedures. After establishing that the title is available the bibliographic search department is to forward copies of the catalog pages containing the serial titles along with the address of the dealer to the appropriate bibliographer for action as described in #2 and #3.

   Needless to say, prompt handling in such instances is of great importance.

5. Decisions may be made occasionally to purchase one or several single volumes of a serial because of their exceptional value or specific need. Such volumes may be purchased by the order department and funded to the requesting department.

6. Decisions as to whether the title is to be cataloged as a serial and/or analyzed as a monograph will be made by the catalog department in conjunction with the serials department.

Definitions of back sets or volumes for funding purposes are:

1. A back set or volume is any serial volume or volumes except the latest volume which begins a standing order for future volumes.

2. If a serial has commenced only recently (for sake of argument, only four or five years ago), and if a single order is issued for these volumes as well as for future volumes, the amount involved is not to be funded to back sets.

3. As indicated in procedure number 5, occasionally single volumes may be funded to the requesting department.
4. Funding for exceptions will be determined by an agreement between the heads of order and serials departments.

REFERENCES

[1] A serial decision slip is being developed which will assist bibliographers and other selectors in transmitting their ordering decisions and cataloging suggestions.

[2] For more detailed explanation of government documents responsibilities see the government documents department's "Areas of Acquisition Responsibilities" as revised July 1972.

[3] The government documents department is planning to include the publications of these agencies within their scope of responsibility. Any changes will be reflected in the next revisions of this document.

Gettysburg College Library

GENERAL PRINCIPLES

The library exists to support the total program of the college. Therefore, the development of the library collection should parallel the development of the college itself. Library materials will be acquired in accordance with the following priorities, ranked in descending order of importance:

1. Materials to support the current teaching program of the college, noting that it is an undergraduate institution;
2. General reference works, and works in fields not currently directly related to college programs but which are of such importance that they belong in any respectable scholarly library;
3. Materials to support the research needs of the faculty and to assist administrative and service personnel in the effective performance of their duties (this may include works dealing with topics of current concern to members of the campus community);
4. Materials to support cooperative programs with other libraries or academic institutions; to maintain and develop a limited number of special collections; to form a foundation collection in support of anticipated future programs of the college; and to acquire appropriate varieties of recreational library material, as funds permit.

The library will not itself censor any subject or viewpoints, and will vigorously resist any censorship attempts from outside. The library endorses the *Library Bill of Rights* and the principles of that document are considered an integral part of this policy statement.

All materials purchased with funds allocated to the library become library property, available for the use of the entire campus community. It is highly inappropriate to use library funds to acquire materials for the exclusive use of any group or individual, and departmental or personal office collections should be bought with the funds of the department or person using such collections.

Priority will be given to materials in English, since that is the language of instruction at this college. Foreign language materials will normally be limited to those languages taught at the college, but material in other languages may be acquired to meet specific needs when it is unavailable in translation.

Since faculty members are most directly involved with the teaching and research programs of the college, it is important that they have the major role in selecting materials supporting these programs; to this end, a substantial portion of the materials budget will be allocated to the academic departments to be spent at faculty recommendation. The amount allocated will be determined annually by the librarian in consultation with the Faculty Library Committee, considering such factors as total funds available, number of faculty in the department, number of courses taught, number of students enrolled, and average prices of books and other materials in the subject area. The library staff will not normally overrule faculty requests for purchases as long as funds are available and the item requested falls within the guidelines of this statement, but the library staff has the responsibility for the development of a well-balanced collection. The library staff may initiate the purchase of material in a specific subject area and charge this purchase to appropriate library funds. The library staff has the principal responsibility for selecting materials needed to support service and administrative programs, and in categories two and four in the list of priorities.

Students seeking to have items added to the collection are encouraged to submit requests to library staff for referral to the acquisitions librarian. Requests from students will be given serious consideration whenever the material requested meets the guidelines of this statement.

Duplicate copies of heavily used materials will be acquired when genuinely needed, but duplication is not encouraged; every duplicate added means that some other title cannot be acquired at all. Duplicate copies of titles held in the main library will be acquired for the departmental libraries only if really needed physically in that location, but in general only very basic reference works should be so duplicated.

It is the responsibility of the students to provide their own textbooks, and the library will not undertake to maintain a textbook collection. At the discretion of the instructor, one or a small number of copies of selected texts may be purchased for the reserve collection, but this is not encouraged.

TYPES OF MATERIAL

Content, not format, will be the basic criterion for deciding whether to add any item to the collection. Since format does affect use and cost, however, it cannot be completely ignored.

Books

When a book is available in both hardcover and paperback editions it will usually be acquired in paperback if (1) the difference in price is significantly more than the added cost of having the paperback bound, and (2) if the anticipated use of the book will not be extremely heavy. When multiple copies are ordered, only the first copy will normally be bound. Paperbacks for which very limited use is anticipated may not be bound at all.

In the case of titles which have gone through several editions, the latest edition will automatically be acquired unless an earlier edition is specified because of historical value or because it contains material not in the later edition.

Out-of-Print Items

When a book requested is found to be out-of-print the order will be returned to the originator to determine if he wishes it searched. (Alternatively, a department may elect to specify that all out-of-print items shall be searched automatically.) The library will search any title when requested, but it must be borne in mind that it can never be anticipated that any out-of-print work will become available at a price judged to be reasonable by the acquisitions department. Reprint editions or microform will be acquired when available unless it is indicated that only the original is acceptable.

Use and space will primarily determine whether to buy any individual item in hard copy or in microform; at the present time space problems make microform preferable for items that will not be heavily used. If the library already owns a title in microform, hard copy will not also be acquired unless constant class use is anticipated.

Periodicals

Periodical subscriptions initiated by a department since July 1, 1975, will be permanently assessed to that department's allocation. Back issues will be charged to the department ordering them, without considering which fund is paying for the current subscription. As with out-of-print books, the availability of back issues cannot be anticipated. Backfiles will be acquired in microform if available or, failing that, in reprint unless the original edition is essential (e.g., microform would not be bought for art or biological journals in which colored illustrations are an integral part of the intellectual content).

Journal article reprints are not acquired for the permanent collection. If needed for reserve or individual use, uncataloged reprints may be acquired through the interlibrary loan office. A permanent cataloged file of reprints of articles published by faculty and staff is being assembled in the special collections room; all individuals publishing articles are asked to contribute to this file.

Government Publications

The library selects for purchase appropriate United States government documents, and is a depository for publications of the State of Pennsylvania. U.S. and Pennsylvania publications not received in this way may be ordered individually, but will be housed in the documents division rather than cataloged and added to the general collection.

Nonprint Media Materials

The audio-visual department of the library will select or respond to requests for records, tapes, cassettes, film strips, film loops, slides, motion pictures, media kits and similar multimedia instructional materials. Cost, budget, and potential use to the college will govern acquisitions decisions in this area, as audio-visual funds are not allocated for departments as are book funds.

Recordings, both musical and spoken, on disc, tape and cassette, will be acquired and cataloged, both for assigned use and recreational listening. Selections of popular material should be coordinated with other campus agencies such as the radio station.

Films will not be purchased, except under very unusual circumstances, because of both their high initial cost and maintenance (cleaning, storage and repair) thereafter. Only when cost of rental times fairly certain antici-pated number of uses equals or exceeds acquisition cost should serious consideration be given to purchase. Where purchase seems advisable, the department served should be prepared to offer some budgetary assistance.

Media kits and such multimedia instructional materials will be considered for acquisition with regard to whether they serve more as lab equipment in the facilities of a single department, or as instructional resources serviced and used in the library in a manner similar to records or reserve books. When acquired they will be cataloged.

Videotapes are not at this time acquired or housed by the library.

GIFTS

Materials received as gifts will be evaluated by the same criteria as materials purchased; nothing will be added simply because it is "free" (all items generate processing and storage costs) unless it enhances the in-tellectual value of the collection. Everything donated to the library becomes library property, to be used as the library staff deems appropriate; un-needed items will be disposed of by sale, exchange, donation or discard.

REPLACEMENTS

When titles in the collection are reported missing, those requested for teaching or research use will be replaced promptly, if they are still ob-tainable. Titles for which there is not an immediate need may not be re-placed for a period, since it has been the experience of the library that many titles reported lost are in fact only temporarily misplaced. When an in-ventory of the collection is taken, missing items will be replaced at once only if in demand. If missing in the following year replacement may be consid-ered or deferred, but at the end of four years a missing book will be removed from our records as permanently lost. At any time after a book is identified as missing, it may be replaced upon request by a user or staff member.

PROCEDURES

Orders should be submitted on the standard card which is provided by the library. The form should be filled out (preferably typewritten) as fully as possible, though it is not expected that full information will always be available to those initiating orders. Especially in the case of small non-commercial publishers, and publishers outside the English-speaking world, catalogs or brochures will be a helpful supplement to the order card itself; they will be returned to the person placing the order if he so requests.

When orders for out-of-print titles are submitted on the basis of a listing in a dealer's catalog, it is essential that the catalog accompany the order cards, and that the order reach the library as quickly as possible. The catalog will be returned if requested.

Departments are encouraged to spread their ordering evenly through the ordering period (July 1 to April 1 of each year), which will facilitate processing by the acquisitions department. Very large groups of order cards, especially late in the year, are subject to delays.

Orders are processed by the acquisitions department in the same sequence as received, to insure fair treatment to all departments. Priority handling can be given to genuine "Rush" orders, but this designation should be used sparingly, and only for titles which are genuinely needed by a specific date. If large numbers of "Rush" orders are received, it is obviously impossible to expedite their handling, and the designation will have to be disregarded. It must also be noted that publishers and wholesalers do not always honor "Rush" designations.

The normal cutoff date for ordering is the end of March, and all departments are expected to have enough orders submitted by that date to use up their allocation. To allow for discounts and cancellations, it is wise to submit orders with a total list price exceeding by ten to fifteen per cent the allocation. Funds are not carried over into the following fiscal year, and funds not spent are lost to the department. Orders received after the cutoff date will be held until the start of the next fiscal year, except that urgent orders can be placed if there are still funds in the departmental allocation to cover them.

The library will provide once a month except during the summer a financial statement on each department's allocation.

Departments which originate (as with oral history) or acquire material normally found in the library are invited to have it cataloged by the library whether it is added to the library collections or retained permanently in the departmental offices. This provision shall in no way be considered as a basis for establishing a departmental library, however.

East Texas State University
James G. Gee Library

INTRODUCTION

This is an official statement of university policy and procedure relating to the acquisitions of material by the James G. Gee Library.

When a new program is established, attempts should be made to consider initial library requirements in their totality with appropriate priorities established. A designated amount may be appropriated by the administration, library committee, or library staff to implement such priorities.

Major investments in materials primarily of sophisticated research value will be almost exclusively directed toward areas with substantial graduate programs.

Emphasis will be placed on materials in the English language with exceptions for literature and literary criticism.

Continual effort will be made to locate relevant subject and general bibliographies with which to check and improve holdings. Efforts should be made to complete purchase of titles in relevant sections of *Books for College Libraries* and *Opening Day Collection*.

Multiple copies should be purchased for use as part of the general collection when justified by the material or program enrollment. Duplication will be limited to five copies in education and three copies in all other colleges upon request of faculty.

In addition to consideration of the usual factors, decisions on the purchase of micromaterials will be based on the initial cost of equipment to service these materials, availability of catalog cards or other indexing, and expense of the equivalent hard copy.

Items costing more than $500 will be specially reviewed with the following considerations:

1. Importance of the item;
2. Specific relevance to a given course or courses;
3. Manner in which the item is to be used;
4. Reason for needing local availability if available through interlibrary loan.

A final decision rests with the director of the library, subject to administrative appeal.

East Texas State University, James G. Gee Library, Commerce, TX 75428

Collection building is a cooperative effort between the library and the teaching faculty; however, to insure uniform policy the final judgment regarding additions to the collection rests with the library staff and, ultimately, with the director of the library.

The *Library Bill of Rights* applies without exception to all purchases of library materials. The sole test of a controversial item will be its contribution to the academic program of the university and to the needs of the students and faculty.

THE INSTITUTION

East Texas State University is a multipurpose regional state university dedicated to serving the people of Texas as well as out-of-state and foreign students who qualify for admission.

Undergraduate, professional, and graduate courses of study are offered through a faculty organized officially into a College of Business Administration, a College of Education, a College of Liberal and Fine Arts, a College of Sciences and Technology, a Graduate School, and a Division of Continuing Education.

The following major elements have a strong bearing on the development of library collections:

1. East Texas State University has one-third of its head count enrollment within graduate programs. Over 68% of the graduate degrees awarded are within the teacher education program.
2. 55% of all degrees awarded are within the teacher education program.

THE LIBRARY

Teacher training and related disciplines constituted the primary interests of this institution from 1889 to 1967. The strengths and weaknesses of the library collection reflect this history and role of the university.

The transition from an essentially teacher-preparation institution to the broader role of a comprehensive university is far from complete in terms of the balance and adequacy of the library collection to support institutional programs now existing and those in prospect outside the area of teacher training.

Book deficiencies in collection development must also be related to the fact that information demands of education and living are expanding so rapidly in a sufficient number of directions that the traditional book library is rapidly becoming obsolete. Effort has begun to embrace nonprint media and online computerized services to facilitate access to information.

Interlibrary loan is not a panacea, but can provide deferred access to information when direct access is not possible. Unnecessary duplication of materials when deferred access is sufficient should be avoided.

Another resource available to our students is access to libraries within the Interuniversity Council and the Federation of the North Texas Area Universities. Here our students need not rely on interlibrary loan, but may use the libraries of member colleges on the same basis as students in those institutions.

The purpose of an acquisitions policy is to provide a statement of priorities for collection development, since it is obvious that personnel and financial resources will not permit purchasing all relevant literature for all subjects.

The goal of the library collection will be to provide materials for the academic programs of the university as well as to achieve the highest grade possible according to the "Standards for College Libraries." These standards are determined by a formula which takes into account the nature and extent of the academic program of the institution, its enrollment, and the size of the teaching faculty. Libraries which can promptly provide 100 percent of the volumes called for in this formula shall, in the matter of quantity, be graded A; from 80–99 percent shall be graded B; 65–79 percent C; and 50–64 percent D.

GENERAL PRINCIPLES

The *Library Bill of Rights* applies without exception to all purchases of library materials. The sole test of a controversial item will be its contribution, direct and indirect, to the academic program of the college and to the needs of the students. If the nature of the material makes theft probable, accessibility can be safeguarded through placing the item on permanent reserve or in the special collections area. Major investments in materials primarily of sophisticated research value will be almost exclusively directed toward areas with substantive graduate programs. This policy is necessary because of the extreme relative cost of such resources and, in many fields, general priorities favoring investments in other areas.

In considering major requests, virtually exclusive emphasis will be on the purchase of materials that will make a substantive long-range contribution to resource development. Thus, requests for expensive blocks of materials which may constitute fragments of a larger body of materials will be evaluated in terms of the extent to which they are viable entities in themselves.

Some criteria that will be used in evaluating requests for expensive research materials or a block of general material are the following:

1. Will the requested body of material continue to be useful as an entity over a period of at least ten years?
2. Will it continue to be useful, and used, after the faculty member initiating the request has left the university?
3. Does it make a contribution to objectives in collection development as defined in this statement?

Emphasis on purchasing materials should be on those in the English language, to be most useful to the majority of students and faculty. Obvious exceptions are literature and literary criticism. The purchase of expensive sets, both print and microform, should be avoided in the absence of a strong program to utilize them.

Multiple copies should be purchased for use as part of the general collection when justified by the significance of the material or program enrollment. The size of the enrollment and heavy concentration of students in some areas, e.g., most of the College of Education, will be given strong consideration. Multiple copies will not be purchased in lieu of textbooks for specific courses. Specifically, duplication will be limited to five copies in education and three copies in all other colleges upon request of faculty.

The purchase of out-of-print items will be considered on the basis of program relevance and cost. It is recognized that a growing collection will require substantial purchase of such materials.

In general, materials in paperback will be bound before being placed in the general collection. However, those of temporary usefulness or required quickly will not be rebound.

In addition to providing materials to meet instructional requirements the library will continue to purchase materials for recreational reading. Also, materials of local historical value will be acquired. Special emphasis will be placed upon those that also support an instructional program. Where possible and useful, significant series and continuations will be procured on a continuing order basis to insure completeness of holdings.

Continued effort should be made to locate relevant subject and general bibliographies with which to check and improve holdings. Efforts should be made to complete as rapidly as possible purchase of books in relevant sections of *Books for College Libraries* and *Opening Day Collection.* The practice of substantial current ordering from *Choice, Library Journal,* and other current book selection aids should continue. This should be considered a responsibility of the library staff with assistance from the faculty where appropriate.

When a new program is established, attempts should be made to consider initial library requirements in their totality with appropriate priorities established. A designated amount may be appropriated by the administration, library committee, or library staff to implement such priorities.

One of the most important principles in collection development is that this be a cooperative effort between library and teaching faculty. However, to insure uniform policy and unity of responsibility, the final judgment regarding the relevance of potential additions to the collection rests with the library staff and, ultimately, with the director of the library, subject to administrative appeal.

All requests for purchases that exceed $500.00 will automatically be reviewed. Procedures to be followed are outlined on page 207.

Micromaterials

Substantial difficulties in accessibility result from the present state of micromaterials use technology. For this reason, wholesale purchase of large sets must be considered in the light of potential use and direct program relevance.

1. Sets will be purchased only when they directly support curricular programs of the college.

2. Micromedia materials will be judged not only from the standpoint of initial cost, but also on the basis of the need for additional equipment to service these materials.
3. No major sets other than government documents will be purchased unless there are cards available or the possibility that the library can provide them within available staff time.
4. In general, microform is regarded as a less desirable substitute for hard copy and should only be purchased if the hard copy is excessively expensive or not available. Exceptions to this are newspaper back files, other material that deteriorates rapidly, and low-use material of great bulk.
5. Because of limited or nonexistent use of such material in the absence of specific assignment, its relevance to specific course offerings will have to be evaluated much more closely than that of material in other formats.

Procedures for the Purchase of Items Costing More Than $500.00

Requests will be reviewed by the library staff with the following items given consideration:

1. Importance of the item;
2. Specific relevance to a given course or courses;
3. Manner in which the item is to be used;
4. Reason for needing local availability if available through interlibrary loan.

At the option of the director of the library a meeting may be called if a request is considered to be of marginal value in the context of this policy. Such a meeting should include (a) the person initiating the request, (b) appropriate library staff and administration, (c) chairman or a representative of the library committee, and (d) other people whose presence may be helpful.

A final decision rests with the director of the library, subject to administrative appeal.

ACCEPTANCE OF GIFTS TO THE UNIVERSITY LIBRARY

Substantial gifts and loans of equipment made to the library are to be reported promptly. All gifts and loans of equipment made shall be reported through the Vice President for Academic Affairs, to the President by the Director as soon as information concerning the probability of making the gift or loan has been received.

The university cannot assume any responsibility or liability for loaned equipment, and all prospective lenders must be so informed.

The monetary appraisal of the gift is not the responsibility of the university.

The librarian may accept minor gifts without reporting such gifts to a superior, unless she or he wishes to do so as a matter of courtesy.

If the gift is direct from the donor, an oral "thank you" is sufficient; unless the librarian wishes to acknowledge its receipt in writing to the donor.

Donors should be informed of the fact that the library may keep or dispose of any gift as it so desires.

Gifts to the library as memorials to deceased relatives or friends are accepted with thanks. A special "In memory of" card is sent to the family of the person memorialized.

A special card is sent to persons who have signified orally or by mail that they wish to place a book or books in the library in honor of a friend.

The library prefers that a check or cash be sent to cover the purchase of a memorial, if the purchase is left to the library.

A running record of all memorials or honorariums shall be kept.

Montgomery County Community College Learning Resources Center

PURPOSE

The purpose of this statement is to bring together in one document the policies regarding the acquisition of books, microforms, journals, and audio-visual materials.

OBJECTIVES

The objectives of the policy are:

- To support the academic and curricular needs of the institution;
- To provide a balanced collection in all fields of knowledge;
- To offer items for leisure-time enjoyment and of general interest.

A conscious effort is made to present all points of view.

METHODS

The selection of materials is a cooperative procedure involving Learning Resources Center and classroom faculty.

Student and staff recommendations are given the same consideration as other requests.

Departmental allocations are avoided and purchases are made within the limitations of the budget.

Books and microforms are ordered by the acquisitions librarian from the appropriate Book Funds.

Audio-visual materials are ordered by the audio-visual librarian from the A/V Fund.

Journals and newspapers are ordered by the serials librarian from the Periodical Fund.

These individuals determine where materials are ordered, but the Director of Learning Resources is the final arbiter in determining what may or

Montgomery County Community College, Learning Resources Center, Blue Bell, PA 19422 may not be ordered, based on need, suitability, and/or economy. Censorship is not a factor in making this determination.

Flexibility in selecting materials is exercised so that personal biases are avoided.

Approval plans are not used.

Multiple copy purchases are generally discouraged so that funds and materials are not tied up where need does not exist.

A textbook collection is maintained so that students will have available to them a copy of every textbook in use during the semester; workbooks and manuals are not included.

Research or graduate materials are secured only when they directly serve a faculty member's teaching requirements.

In instances where the cost of an item is very high and demand is low, the holdings of nearby libraries are considered in determining whether we should or should not order.

Availability of certain materials through Interlibrary Loan might influence the decision to order.

GIFT POLICY

Mindful that well-meaning prospective donors sometimes offer materials to libraries that are not needed, not appropriate to the collection, or restricted in such a way as to make their usefulness questionable, the following policy on the acceptance of gifts to the Montgomery County Community College Library was approved by the Board of Trustees on September 1, 1966.*

1. Gifts that are not appropriate to the educational program that the Learning Resources Center supports cannot be accepted. For example, we would have no need of professional journals in the field of veterinary medicine. Old textbooks are not needed.
2. Materials cannot be accepted when a donor requires that they be kept together and not integrated into the whole Learning Resources Center collection, or that they must not be allowed to circulate.
3. Materials cannot be accepted on "indefinite loan." An exception would be the "indefinite loan" of some item of established value (listing in *American Book Prices Current* or *Bookman's Price Index*), left with the written statement that we are bound only to take the best care of the item possible under the physical and staff conditions prevailing in the Center, and that ownership would pass to us upon the death of the owner unless re-claimed by him in his lifetime.
4. We reserve the right to decide which materials to keep for the Center. Those that are inappropriate, or unwanted duplicates, will be handled in one of four ways, according to the will of the donor:
   - Returned to donor;
   - Disposed of by sale—either to a dealer, or by sale to students at a nominal price (Monmouth College in New Jersey was able to buy an

*Slight changes have been made to accommodate current terminology, December 5, 1975.

important library set of books recently through the proceeds of such sales);
- Sent to another library which may need and welcome the particular item or collection;
- Discarded.

5. Gifts of money to buy library materials are another matter, but, in general, the same limitations must apply. We could not accept money limited to buying materials that are inappropriate or not needed. We could not accept money for books to be kept together as a "collection within the Collection."

6. On the positive side, libraries depend heavily on gifts of money from generous benefactors. Large gifts invested so that the income only is used may have a special fund name with an appropriate fund bookplate. Such funds may be restricted or general as long as they support the college's program. Small gifts may go toward the purchase of needed materials and the materials so purchased will be given an appropriate plate, e.g., GIFT OF JOHN DOE.

7. In time we may be aided by an outside group such as the Friends of the Library or Library Associates. These groups usually provide funds for particularly expensive items, for worthwhile popular items, or for other purchases which the librarian may hesitate to charge to the appropriation monies.

Addendum dated August 30, 1966: Any appraisal for income tax purposes of a gift of books or other materials to the Center is the responsibility of the donor.

Portland State University Library

INTRODUCTION

There can be no question that any book selection policy is outdated before the ink has dried on the paper. A book collection beyond a certain size assumes a life of its own. Its growth may result from factors having little to do with a stated policy. Such factors include gifts, federally sponsored programs, interests of new, dynamic faculty members, current intellectual fads, new fields of scholarly endeavor, and financial constraints.

Portland State University, as an emerging institution searching for a unique and viable identity, has passed through many stages of growth and development in a relatively short period. The library, as a consequence, has had an enormous amount of difficulty in keeping up with the needs of new programs constantly being mounted while providing for a measured and continuing growth in materials to support ongoing commitments in basic programs. The result is a collection broad in its parameters, but shallow in almost all areas.

The library has undertaken in the last two years a systematic evaluation of its collections in every subject in which the university offers at least an undergraduate major or certificate. Since the work is still in progress, the results are, of necessity, inconclusive. However, there is no doubt that the results will cause a significant refinement of the selection policy and, hopefully, will form the basis of a strong statement, founded on facts, for greater financial and space commitments from the university.

Although the references to library materials in the following statement may be made principally to books and periodicals, the library collects extensively nonbook materials also. In addition to the various microforms we have adjacent to our regular books, our audio-visual collection, including films, video tapes, filmstrips, recordings and tapes, is quite extensive.

The following selection statement is purposely general and does not take into account the unique requirements for library materials of many programs.

Portland State University Library, Portland, OR 97207

SELECTION LEVELS

The library selects materials basically on four levels which conform to the levels of courses offered in the university's instructional programs. The higher levels of acquisition include all lower levels.

Level I provides support for courses offered at the lower division level. The materials purchased at this level are in support of the 100 and 200 courses. Introductory works, outlines, handbooks and general surveys comprise the major purchases. In addition, the library covers many subjects at this level in which no courses are offered, in response to general student interest and to provide general reference answers. The university has limited its course offerings to this level in only a few areas, such as beginning language courses in Czech or Polish.

Level II includes courses offered at the 300 and 400 level—the undergraduate major. Materials are acquired to support the specific courses, as well as to provide some coverage of every aspect of the particular discipline. Major subdivisions, periods, authors, etc., are covered in greater depth than auxiliary ones. Standard works, anthologies, compendia, etc., as well as the major commentators and the classics of the field are emphasized. A spectrum of the major periodicals, usually limited to the English language, is acquired. The principal selection tools are *Choice* and the various undergraduate catalogs—California, Michigan, Lamont and Street. Pertinent films, filmstrips, recordings and tapes strengthen the instructional program and provide supplementary materials.

Level III conforms roughly to courses added at the masters' degree level. However, in most disciplines the first level of graduate study means more courses offered in the 300 and 400 sequence with a few 500 level seminars and "graduate student only" courses. Consequently, preliminary material acquired overlaps with Level II. Courses are initiated to complete the general coverage of the discipline and its major subdivisions. In addition, major aspects, authors, periods, etc., will have courses devoted to them. The library acquires nearly all current material published on the subject by standard commercial publishers. At this level, the major source of significant materials becomes the university presses and the specialty publishers in the field, such as learned societies, national associations and the publications of federal, state and local governments. The importance of periodicals emerges and their acquisition is perhaps the most significant new endeavor for the library. Because of the emphasis, at this level, on the historical aspects of a discipline or on lesser studied areas, the library relies on the out-of-print market for a larger share of its materials. Out-of-print dealers' catalogs and reprint catalogs become a major source of selection. Standard published bibliographies in the field are important selection tools. Also, footnotes and bibliographies included in the major works, the classics and the encyclopedias are checked. Want lists are compiled and circulated to dealers specializing in materials in that particular discipline. Frequently, the library begins to acquire significant foreign monographs and periodicals for the first time. Outstanding series are identified and standing orders are set up for future publications. Classic documentary films and recordings are purchased as corollary materials.

Level IV conforms to programs at the advanced graduate level leading to the doctorate. The selection of materials at this level requires close coordination with the instructional faculty to determine selection priorities relating to their research interests and those of their students. No library beginning doctoral research programs can afford to specialize in every aspect of a discipline. Therefore, a clear selection policy is most required at this level.

The library will want virtually everything published on the subject in this country and England and a broad selection of foreign publications. The best way to acquire published materials at this level is through an automatic gathering plan. PSU Library is seriously considering the feasibility of joining one as soon as finances permit.

Again, the most important material for doctoral research frequently either is published by noncommercial organizations or is not published at all, i.e., primary source materials. At this level periodicals are more important than books. The selection and acquisition of primary source materials are both time consuming and expensive. PSU's doctoral programs are so new that areas of specialization at this level have yet to be determined.

Because of their expense and the relatively little use these materials receive, cooperative acquisitions and agreements have become an absolute necessity. The PSU Library is committed to making the best use of advanced research materials already in the area and is equally anxious that our little-used materials be available to other institutions.

In addition to PSU's regular degree granting programs, there are several interdisciplinary programs leading to a certificate: black studies, law enforcement and the four area studies programs—Middle East, Central European, Latin American and Pacific Rim. It is difficult to select materials in these areas because of their specialized nature, requiring a corpus of elementary materials benefiting relatively few students. The library works closely with the instructional faculty on the materials selection.

Also, the library acquires materials of a more or less general nature which do not benefit any one program particularly, but which are absolutely necessary for a well-rounded collection, including a selection of foreign and domestic newspapers, maps and atlases, and a large collection of federal, state and local documents. We are a full federal and state depository, and collect as many as possible of the area and municipal documents that we can obtain.

Certainly, the above criteria for selection are not absolute. They are goals toward which we strive and for which we plan when justifying budget requests for staff and books. However, they do represent a fairly accurate statement of the guidelines we employ in our selection practices.

San Antonio College Library

Director of Learning Resources and Acquisitions

The Director of Learning Resources is responsible for the selection of the books, audio-visual and other materials to be acquired for the library with the aid and advice of the faculty and within the limits set by the budget. She/he will examine the recommendations and requests made by the faculty, together with items located through standard lists, notices of new publications, out-of-print catalogs, and other sources and make the selection of those items to be acquired with the view of maintaining a balanced collection in all subject areas as well as meeting the curricular needs of the subjects taught.

Departmental Chairmen and Acquisitions

Departmental chairmen are urged to establish within their departments procedures for initiating recommendations for acquisitions which will develop the collection for the use of their students in areas of curricular interest under their jurisdiction.

Faculty Members and Acquisitions

Faculty members, particularly those who teach the only section or sections of a course and those who teach in programs offered only in the evening division, are urged to make their recommendations for purchase through their department chairmen.

Budget Distributions

Book budgets are not assigned specifically to each department. The procedures followed are sufficiently flexible to accommodate all reasonable instructional needs.

Priorities

Priority for books and other materials to be purchased for the library is given to those materials which meet direct curricular needs in the courses offered, including items needed for class assignments, collateral reading, references made in the textbooks, supplemental individual study or term

San Antonio College Library, San Antonio, TX 78284

papers and reports, including those reference and bibliographical tools which will facilitate finding and using these materials.

Secondary Considerations

After the primary needs have been met, consideration may be given to other desirable materials which will give balance to the collection or meet vocational, avocational, cultural or special interests or needs of the student body and the faculty.

Junior and Community College Materials

Because of the nature and mission of this institution a strong collection of materials pertaining to two-year colleges will be acquired.

Eighteenth-Century British Imprints

Acceptance of consortium responsibility and federal funds to obtain the Morrison Collection of eighteenth-century British books carries an obligation to continue to purchase a certain number of these rare and specialized volumes.

Texana and Mexicana

The library will continue to acquire research materials for both Texas and Mexican history and culture.

Materials Not Normally Purchased

With exceptions noted above the library does not purchase:

1. Rare books and first editions *per se;*
2. Extensive collections of materials in limited subject areas;
3. Research materials (except those for use in student papers);
4. Books in languages not taught at the college;
5. Current fiction;
6. Highly specialized technical books;
7. Textbooks for courses offered at the college;
8. Expensive materials easily available elsewhere in San Antonio.

Multiple Copies

Multiple copies will be acquired where the needs of the students and the continued demand make additional copies necessary.

Out-of-Print Materials

Out-of-print materials will meet the same criteria for purchase as other books. Where possible modern reprints will be preferred to out-of-print originals.

Gifts

Gift materials represent an outlay of far more library staff time and processing costs than new materials do. They will be accepted only if the library may dispose of them if their physical condition, obsolescence of the contents, or failure to be of sufficient use to the clientele of the library makes them undesirable. Should any large, unique, or significant collection in a limited subject area be offered as a gift, it might be judged in the value of the collection as a whole to the library and not on the value of the individual items in the collection.

Periodical Subscriptions

Periodical subscriptions will be entered after taking into consideration: (1) curricular needs, (2) interests of the students and faculty, (3) inclusion in periodical indexes, (4) availability in other libraries in San Antonio, (5) cost of subscription, and (6) near duplicate materials already received. Whenever possible periodical subscriptions will be entered to start at the beginning of the calendar year or volume.

Audio-Visual Materials Defined

Audio-visual materials which are included in the holdings of the library are: recordings (disc, audiotape, and videotape), motion pictures (8mm and 16mm), filmstrips (captioned and sound), transparencies (2×2 slides), and combined media kits. Other materials (such as overhead transparencies, games, etc.) are not considered as library materials.

College Policy on Audio-Visual Materials

All audio-visual materials (as defined above) acquired for any department of the college are to be cataloged and indexed in the library holdings regardless of the funds used to obtain them.

Selection of Audio-Visual Materials

Most audio-visual materials are purchased by the library on requisition from the departments and are paid for from department funds since instructional objectives constitute the basis for selection. Generally such funds as are included in the library budget for audio-visual materials will be used for interdisciplinary acquisitions or to meet needs not directly related to the curriculum, although inexpensive purchases (recordings or filmstrips, for example) may be considered. As a rule all audio-visual materials that cost over $50 should be previewed in advance, whether purchased from departmental or library funds.

University of North Carolina at Wilmington, William Madison Randall Library

INTRODUCTION

This statement of acquisitions and selection policies for the William Madison Randall Library has been drawn up by the library staff, under the authority of the university librarian and with the advice of the Faculty Library Committee, in order to clarify the general policies of the library with regard to principles upon which the library collection is built, both in general and with respect to specific types of material. The statement is subject to review at all times by the library staff and by the Faculty Library Committee. It should, in any case, be carefully reviewed at least every five years.

ACQUISITIONS POLICY

Definition

As used in this statement, acquisitions policy means the policy of the library with regard to the building of the collection as a whole.

Statement of Policy

The William Madison Randall Library is charged with the responsibility of serving the reading, reference, and research needs of the University of North Carolina at Wilmington, its faculty, and its students. Therefore, the acquisitions policy of the William Madison Randall Library is to build a collection containing those materials which best serve the objectives of that clientele, both now and in the future. With due regard to the availability of the resources of nearby libraries and with an eye toward the possibilities of cooperative acquisitions programs with other libraries in the area, it is the aim of the William Madison Randall Library to build, in all appropriate

University of North Carolina at Wilmington, William Madison Randall Library, Wilmington, NC 28401 fields, a collection of the highest degree of excellence, both qualitative and quantitative, that its monetary resources will possibly afford.

Implementation of Policy

Implementation of the acquisitions policy is the responsibility of the university librarian, who may delegate to others a portion of that responsibility. While the broad outline of the policy remains constant, the specifics of implementing the policy will change as the university changes and as its expectations change. Building a collection to meet the objectives expressed in the policy requires provisions for evaluating the collection and for expending funds designated for the development of the collection.

Evaluation

Evaluation of the collection, as the word implies, is exercised continually by judging it against qualitative standards, that is, through consultation of knowledgeable people and through comparison of the collection with standard general and specialized bibliographies. No quantitative goals are stated here, not only because these must inevitably fluctuate as the university grows, as the research needs of its faculty develop, and as the depth of instruction offered in various fields increases, but also because statistical assessment is useful only as a means of comparison with other collections or with standards suggested by expert opinion, both of which are subject to frequent change, and because such assessment gives no information concerning the content of the collection. Therefore, the size of the collection will be considered adequate only when it meets the increasing needs of the clientele of the library.

Allocation of Funds

The university librarian is responsible for the expenditure of all library funds. Those funds which are designated for the purchase of library materials and which are reserved neither for the maintenance of standing orders and subscriptions nor for meeting such fixed expenses as postage and taxes are divided annually among the academic departments by the university librarian and the Faculty Library Committee working in cooperation. A general fund is reserved for the purchase of replacements for materials lost or damaged beyond repair, materials of general interest cutting across subject fields, reference materials, and recreational reading books. The basic allocation takes into account the number of faculty members in each department, the number of units of instruction offered by the department (based upon the number of students taught), and the number of courses offered by the department (with upper-division courses weighted more heavily than lower-division courses). Adjustments are made annually in the resulting allocation to compensate for variations in cost of materials for the different subject areas, in rate of production of materials for the different fields, and in library use by the faculty members and students of the various departments. Special consideration is given each year to departments offering new courses, new programs, new majors, and new degrees.

SELECTION POLICY

Definition

Selection policy, as used in this statement, means the set of guidelines used in making decisions concerning the addition of specific materials to the collection.

Statement of Policy

The selection guidelines used by the William Madison Randall Library are an outgrowth of the acquisitions policy and may be summarized by saying that the materials selected for library purchase at any one time should be those among various possible purchases which promise to be, not merely of use, but of greatest use to the university, its faculty, and its students. Judgment as to whether specific materials meet this criterion is exercised most frequently by consulting the opinions of knowledgeable people, either on the campus or in such publications as standard bibliographies, dependable review journals, and lists of publications considered to be outstanding by authoritative boards of review.

Specific considerations applicable to almost all library purchases include:

1. The permanent or timely value of the material, for interest, information or enlightenment;
2. The accuracy of the material;
3. The authoritativeness of the material and/or its author;
4. The usefulness of the material with respect to other materials already in the collection or easily available from other collections, including:

   • The representation of all sides of controversial issues;
   • The avoidance of materials which merely duplicate, either outright or in substance, materials already held;
   • The avoidance of expensive materials of limited use when they are held by other local libraries or by other college and university libraries in the region.

5. The scarcity of material on the subject;
6. The cost of the material in comparison with other equally useful material;
7. The form of the material in comparison with other available forms of the same material.

At appropriate intervals, as determined by the university librarian, the collection or a selected portion of it is weeded by the application of the selection policy in reverse. Materials judged of no further use to the clientele of the library are then withdrawn.

Implementation of Policy

While a great part of the actual selection of library materials is in fact delegated to the various academic departments, primary responsibility for the building of the collection resides with the university librarian. Cooperation between faculty members and librarians in the selection of materials allows individual faculty members to bring their specialized knowledge to the task of selection and to assure the support within the collection of specific curricular needs. The responsibility of the librarians is to insure that no areas of development proper to the collection be ignored or slighted and that the collection as a whole be developed objectively, consistently and thoroughly.

Students and university staff members may request books for the library on a voluntary basis.

POLICIES CONCERNING SPECIAL TYPES OF MATERIALS

Periodicals

Back files of periodicals are selected on the basis of demonstrated student need and faculty requests. Preference is given to those back files of periodicals indexed in the major general indexes and in heavily-used subject indexes and bibliographies.

Current subscriptions are placed at the request of the faculty and on the basis of the needs and interests of the clientele.

Newspapers

The objective of the university library is to subscribe to representative major local, regional, national and foreign newspapers.

Back files of newspapers are purchased on the basis of need, cost and the availability of indexing.

Government Documents

The status of the library as a partial depository of United States government documents makes certain categories of government publications available free of charge from the Superintendent of Documents. Categories of documents to be received are selected by the documents librarian in consultation with faculty members and other members of the library staff. Generally speaking, items selected for this collection cover a broader spectrum than those of the general collection since the documents collection is meant to serve not only the needs of the university but also those people in this geographical area.

The library attempts to build a comprehensive collection of state and local documents.

Nondepository federal documents, United Nations documents, and documents of foreign countries are selected on the same basis as material in the general collection.

Foreign Language Materials

Except for materials to support the language curricula offered by the university, materials in foreign languages are purchased only when an adequate translation into English is not available or when a specific need is evident for a foreign language edition.

Little-Used Materials

Little-used materials and expensive sets are purchased for the collection only after consideration of the resources of other libraries in the area. Resources needed only for the research of an individual student or faculty member are obtained, whenever possible, through interlibrary loan rather than by purchase.

Out-of-Print Materials

Out-of-print materials needed in the library are sought through the catalogs of antiquarian dealers and/or through listing with such dealers, either individually or by advertisement.

Reprints

Expensive reprints are not ordered until the out-of-print market is checked for availability and comparison of price.

Paperbacks

A book is purchased in paperback only when it is unavailable in hard-back at a reasonable cost. In general, paperback books are bound before being added to the collection.

Textbooks

Because of the repetition of information frequently included in them and because they are often quickly outdated, books published solely as texts are not usually added to the collection unless their usefulness goes beyond that of the typical textbook. Except in extraordinary cases no textbook in current use on the campus is purchased for the collection.

Microforms

Materials are purchased in microform when available in no other form, when much less expensive in microform than in hard copy and yet easily usable, or when microform offers a considerable advantage in storage.

Audio-Visual Media

Many types of communication media such as film, slides, tapes, recordings, prints, radio, television, etc. are important in the transmission of information and as an adjunct to the learning process; however, no provision has yet been made for the establishment of an audio-visual center at the university.

The library acquires a limited number of phonodiscs and tapes. These are selected on the basis of curricular need and general interest to the library clientele, largely on the recommendation of the music, English, and drama faculties. As in adding other material to the collection, the general policy is to select the materials which will best serve the objectives of the university, its faculty and students.

The library will not attempt to duplicate the collections of audio-visual materials maintained by the various academic departments on the campus.

Duplicates

The library purchases duplicate copies only in cases of demonstrable need, such as when the number of students in a class or the concentrated use of material demands multiple copies.

Suffolk University College Library

OBJECTIVES OF SUFFOLK UNIVERSITY

1. To provide an environment which will encourage freedom of thought and expression in the pursuit of truth, scholarly excellence, and relevant and vital teaching;
2. To provide a strong liberal arts education in order to acquaint students with their cultural heritage and to develop a taste for the best, a sense of values, and an awareness of their roles and obligations as citizens of a democratic society;
3. To provide professional and pre-professional programs on both the undergraduate and graduate level in areas such as business administration, law, social work, education, medical technology, journalism and public service;
4. To provide educational opportunities for qualified men and women who might otherwise be deprived of them as a result of economic, social, or cultural handicaps;
5. To help Greater Boston and the Commonwealth of Massachusetts to solve their social, economic, and cultural problems.

OBJECTIVES OF THE COLLEGE LIBRARY IN COLLECTION DEVELOPMENT

The college library provides informational resources for the College of Liberal Arts and Sciences and the College of Business Administration which support the educational programs conducted by the colleges in accordance with the program priorities of the university. The collection is dedicated to the use, rather than to the preservation, of recorded knowledge and reflects an emphasis on current, rather than archival, needs for information.

Books and other forms of recorded knowledge will be provided which will encourage students to develop and extend their intellectual abilities beyond the specific requirements of the educational programs. The college library collection will be dedicated to supporting the intellectual activity of students and faculty as it is reflected in current inquiry into pressing social, economic, and cultural problems.

Suffolk University College Library, Boston, MA 02114

Comment: "The goal of college library collection development should be quality rather than quantity. A collection may be said to have quality for its purposes only to the degree that it possesses a portion of the bibliography of each discipline taught, appropriate in quantity both to the level at which each is taught and to the number of students and faculty members who use it." (*ALA Standards for College Libraries, 1975*)

POLICIES

Statements of policy are formulated which give guidelines to be used in developing and following the course of action to reach the stated objectives. They are designed to achieve it within the ordinary fiscal constraints of the university and the severe restrictions in building space. The policies stated in this document are not immutable: they should be expanded, modified or abandoned to reflect changes in objectives of the university and the programs of the colleges which the library supports.

General Collection Development Policy

Monographs, periodicals and reference materials should be selected and acquired which support the curricula of the College of Liberal Arts and Sciences and the College of Business Administration, and which encourage the intellectual growth of the students. To achieve the highest possible quality within the constraints of available space and resources, rigorous discrimination in the selection of materials to be added to the library's holdings must be maintained. Emphasis should be given to programs of acquisition which strengthen and improve the library's collection on given topics or fields.

The collection should be evaluated continuously against standard bibliographies and against records of its use for the purpose of identifying materials for prompt withdrawal once they have outlived their usefulness for the college programs. No book should be retained in a college library for which a clear purpose is not evident in terms of the institution's current or anticipated academic programs. When such a clear purpose is lacking, a book should be retired from the collection.

Library Materials Budget

The college librarian is responsible for the formulation of the budget, its allocation among the various collection requirements and disbursements from it. To facilitate the active cooperation of the faculty in the purchase of books and other recorded material, a substantial proportion of the budget is divided among the academic departments, on the basis of which each department makes recommendations for purchase. A sufficient portion is reserved also for the acquisition of general reference and noncurriculum materials, for unanticipated short-term program needs, and for binding.

Selection Tools

So as to ensure rigorous discrimination in the selection of materials, reliance should be placed upon the standard scholarly bibliographies reflecting the curricula of the colleges and supporting general fields of knowledge rather than specialized research requirements.

Among general bibliographies *Books for College Libraries* is useful for the purposes of identifying important retrospective titles. For current editions *Choice,* a periodical which reviews significant new titles for college libraries, is the best general selection tool. Supplementing these basic aids are the review journals of individual disciplines and specialized selective bibliographies. The use of publishers' announcements, commercial catalogs, and other nonselective sales-oriented lists is discouraged.

Subject Collections

In addition to the general collection development policy set forth, the library, in cooperation with the faculty, should maintain a set of guidelines for the selection of materials to be added and withdrawn from particular subject-areas in the collection. Holdings in each subject-area should be evaluated from the point of view of use, by comparison with established and up-to-date core collections (such as *Books for College Libraries* represents), and from the point of view of the overall collection development objectives. Experience teaches that such guidelines, if they are broad with respect to additions and narrow with respect to withdrawals, do not facilitate improving the quality of the overall collection.

Gifts

The rigorous standards which apply to the selection of purchased materials apply as well to those received as gifts. Gifts should be accepted only if they are offered without conditions as to their retention or organization in the library. Gift collections should be evaluated before a decision is made to accept them.

Duplicates

As a rule duplicate copies are not acquired. Exceptions are made for books required for course reserve, in which case sufficient copies are acquired to satisfy the demands of the students enrolled in a given course. Once a book is no longer in demand for a specific course, duplicate copies of it should be withdrawn.

Editions

The library always attempts to acquire the latest edition of textbooks. If an older edition held by the library is superseded by a newer one, the former should be withdrawn in most instances.

Nonbook Materials

Microforms. Microforms should be acquired selectively, yet systematically, to replace retrospective issues of periodicals. Monographs may also be obtained in microform if not available in hard copy. Easy access to information in microform should be ensured by the availability of sufficient readers and reader-printers. The acquisition of large, packaged book collections in microform is discouraged since these usually contain many titles and editions which either duplicate holdings or lie outside the scope of the collection.

Audio-visual materials.   Audio-visual materials are a component of the resources provided by the library in support of the curriculum. At this time, however, only selected phonograph records and listening equipment are provided in the library. No policy has been formulated for the acquisition and organization of other audio-visual materials.

Special Collections

General reference collection.   Particular attention is paid to the acquisition of reference materials and informational access tools. As well as encyclopedias, directories, dictionaries, statistical publications, etc., these include abstracting services, book catalogs and periodical indexes. Particular emphasis is placed upon the acquisition of bibliographical publications which enable the students to find abstracts and citations to materials held by other libraries in the metropolitan region.

Reserve book collection.   The library acquires at least one copy of every book which is assigned reading in a course and places it in the general reserve collection. When such a book is removed from reserve, it is reshelved in the general classified collection.

Afro-American literature collection.   The library endeavors to acquire the complete published works of all major Afro-American writers with particular emphasis on writers associated with New England. In addition, related historical, literary, critical, biographical and bibliographical works by writers of all races are acquired. Information in other media relating to the theme of the collection is also selectively acquired.

Irving Zieman poetry collection.   No collection policy. Since the death of its benefactor, no funds have been made available for additions to the collection. Volumes of poetry which relate to this collection continue to be acquired from the general book budget, however, upon recommendation of the English department.

OPERATING PROCEDURES

Allocation of Book Funds

Following approval of the book budget by the university administration allocations are assigned from it to the general purposes development fund, the reference fund, the nonprint materials fund, and the teaching departments. Expenditures are made from the allocations to acquire materials selected for the library by the librarians and the departments. The department allocations expire two months before the end of the budget year, and any unencumbered portions of them revert to the library's general purposes development fund.

Notification of Expenditures

Periodically during the academic year each teaching department is notified of the amount of money expended by the library from its allocation. The figure does not include encumbrances for outstanding orders.

Library Book Selection Aids

Reviews of new books for college libraries in the form of *Choice* "Reviews-on-Cards" are regularly sent to the departments; the requestor has only to initial and return the cards for the books desired. Reviews which are not selected should be returned to the library. In addition the library will assist departments in selecting books from standard bibliographic tools such as *Books for College Libraries,* Farber's *Classified List of Periodicals for College Libraries,* and other, more specialized bibliographical aids as they are acquired.

Order Requests

Specific guidelines for requesting materials to be ordered are listed on the attachment to the "Operating Procedures."

Periodical Order Requests

When a brand new periodical is requested, the library places a subscription to begin with the first number. If the periodical is not a new publication, a subscription is placed to begin with the current volume unless earlier numbers or volumes are specifically requested. Subscriptions are renewed automatically unless instructions are issued to the contrary.

If an annual publication or series is requested, a "standing order" should be indicated if future volumes are wanted as published; if not, only those volumes itemized on the order request will be acquired.

Reserve Books

Faculty who wish to place library books on course reserve should send copies of their syllabus to the library at the earliest possible date, at least six weeks prior to the beginning of the term. If material requested for reserve is not in the library, it is assumed that the library will order the material unless the faculty specifically requests prior consultation or the aggregate price of the material listed in the syllabus exceeds $200.00.

Acquisition of Out-of-Print Books

When books ordered are reported "out of print" by the vendor, a notice (usually a pink slip from the library order form) is sent to the requestor stating that the item is "out of print—cancelled." If the requestor believes that the book is essential to the collection, the notice should be returned to the library together with a request that the item should be obtained in the out-of-print market. All books selected from *Books for College Libraries* are added automatically to the library's out-of-print search file if they are no longer in print.

Replacement of Missing Books

Replacement copies of books missing from the collection are ordered upon demand. Departments are invited to select books for replacement from an inventory file maintained in the processing room of the library.

Faculty-Library Liaison

Regular contact is maintained between the college librarian and the department chairpersons or library representatives, who coordinate faculty selections and consult with the library on matters relating to the development of the collection.

Houston Community College Learning Resources Center

GENERAL POLICIES

Learning Resources materials are selected to provide information for education, personal development and recreation. It is the role of Learning Resources to support the curriculum of Houston Community College (HCC), to encourage the desire for vocational, social and cultural awareness, and to promote understanding in all areas of vital concern. We believe that books and other media in the Learning Resources collection have educational value if they contribute to the positive growth of a person, both individually and as a member of the community. To this end, materials are selected to provide essential information for classwork and for enrichment, selected to stimulate imagination and thought and to enlarge experiences. Materials about current issues and problems as well as materials of permanent importance are basic selections of the library.

Learning Resources seeks to provide standard works, classics, and popular titles in all curriculum areas. However, because of the number of research libraries in the immediate vicinity, it is not our intention to develop comprehensive collections in all areas. We will not attempt to duplicate collections or functions of academic, public, or special libraries in Houston. Only in subject areas not well-developed by other libraries will we try to develop extensive collections.

The staff regards as the first obligation service to Houston Community College students. Though consideration is given to personal informational needs of the faculty and to needs of the community at large, requirements of these groups are generally better met by other libraries or sources in the area. Learning Resources will serve the noninstructional needs of faculty and needs of the community as far as may be done without detriment to the service of HCC students, but the first obligation is to the students and to the support of the instructional program.

Freedom of speech and freedom of the press are rights of our heritage guaranteed by the Constitution and defended by our courts. Since the meaning of these doctrines is determined finally by the American people, it follows that Houston Community College must attempt to provide free access to all points of view on public questions. The student body of HCC represents many and varied groups of people. Therefore, selections are

Houston Community College Learning Resources Center, Houston, TX 77007 made by Learning Resources and represent as many points of view as possible.

On controversial subjects about which definite facts have not been established or which by their very nature are not susceptible of factual proof, Learning Resources will provide materials on varying points of view insofar as availability permits. An attempt is made to provide books which, although partisan, give evidence of a desire to establish and present facts. Books on controversial subjects or issues, though written in an extreme or sensational manner, may be acquired; but those that contain undocumented statements and accusations are added only rarely, when some special historic or scientific interest justifies their purchase. Decisions are made after reviewing and consultation among the staff, and questionable selections are referred to the director of Learning Resources for a final decision.

Learning Resources does not add or withdraw, at the request of any individual or group, books which have been chosen or excluded on the above principles. The director welcomes the opportunity to discuss the interpretation of these principles with individuals or with representatives of groups.

RESPONSIBILITY FOR SELECTION

Ultimate responsibility for the selection of books and other materials rests with the director of Learning Resources, who operates within the framework of policies determined by the Board of Trustees. The librarians are responsible for general guidance in the selection of materials in their curriculum liaison areas. Their duties include the selecting of materials, reviewing faculty selections, suggesting areas for special emphasis and ensuring that the collection in each area is appropriate to its function. Faculty selections are a very important basis for building the collection in each curriculum area and are given serious consideration. Student selection is also encouraged.

SELECTION CRITERIA

In the purchase of reference materials, Learning Resources considers:

1. Reputation of the author;
2. Timeliness or permanence of the materials;
3. Relevance of subject matter;
4. Availability of materials on the subject;
5. Inclusion of the title in recognized bibliographies and indexes;
6. Authoritativeness;
7. Quality of publisher;
8. Price.

Of main concern regarding supplemental materials are:

1. Reputation of author;
2. Prejudices of author;

3. Quality of writing;
4. Price;
5. Availability of materials on the subject.

The thoughtful and critical approach which guides the selection of books is also applied to the acquisition of periodicals, government documents, maps, pamphlets, pictures and audio-visuals. The cost, appropriateness for community college use and range of application are all considered before purchase of any item. Textbooks are purchased only when they provide the best coverage of a subject.

DUPLICATION

Every agency responsible for book selection has the problem of evaluating demands and needs for the purchase of multiple copies. With the establishment of mini-resource centers at several locations, it is necessary to supply some of the same basic materials at each center. However, due to financial constraints and accreditation guidelines, it is not feasible at this time to supply materials in duplicate at any one location.

The Learning Resources staff will maintain an awareness of other library resources in the Houston area to avoid duplication.

SELECTION POLICIES BY FORMAT

Fiction

The library's collection includes representative novels of the past and present, notable for literary quality and cultural value; historical and regional novels; character studies; and biographical and psychological novels. The library recognizes the importance of the novel in providing insight into the human situation, contributing to education and affecting individual attitudes. The presentation of significant social and personal problems or of racial and religious questions through novels of wide reader appeal may enhance human understanding. For this reason, novels of serious purpose are purchased, considering a public varying greatly in education, interests, taste and reading skill. Attention is paid to maintaining a basic collection in attractive editions of standard novels, the classics, the semiclassics of world literature, and novels having curriculum value.

Foreign Language Publications

In keeping with the basic objective of supporting the curriculum, purchases are made on the recommendation of the faculty members who teach foreign language courses. In selecting titles in all foreign languages, an attempt is made to buy representative fiction, biography, drama, etc., including the classics; standard and familiar authors of the past; the best of modern writers; and books describing cultural and religious traditions.

Paperbacks

Paperbacks are purchased if the paperback title is original, if the hardback edition is out of print, if the title is in heavy demand, or to provide popular reading materials at the mini-resource centers. They are usually treated as ephemeral and considered expendable. Some substantial paperbacks are purchased and treated as hardback editions if the hardback edition is expensive and the title would be limited in circulation.

Microforms

The Learning Resources acquires, in microform, materials not available in any other form, materials preferred in this form because of lower cost or reduced bulk, and duplicates of materials available in other forms but desirable also in microform for reasons of space.

Because of lack of standardization in the field of microforms, no one form is preferred. When there is a choice, selection is based on clearness of copy, availability of adequate machines, possibility of reproduction, ease of servicing and the format of microproduction of related materials which are already in the Learning Resources collection.

Audio-Visuals

Audio-visual materials can develop perceptions, present ideas, and relay other messages and information that are not readily transmitted through printed media. General policies and objectives outlined for book selection are applied to audio-visual resources, and additional considerations, such as quality of sound, photography, color reproduction, etc., are used as criteria where appropriate.

The audio-visual collection includes a wide range of formats, each of which is chosen for suitability in relation to content and purpose. It is the policy of Learning Resources to preview audio-visual materials before purchase of substantial items.

Periodicals

Periodicals are purchased to keep the collection up-to-date with current thinking in various fields; to provide material not available in books; to supplement the book collections; and to serve the staff as book selection aids, book reviewing media and professional reading. Titles which are needed for reference or research are duplicated in microform when available for long-term use.

Periodicals most in demand as a source of information are those which deal with current reporting, either generally or in a special field. In most fields of scholarship, technical research and creative writing, important new theories, discoveries, trends and viewpoints appear first in journals and are frequently dealt with in more detail than when they are later incorporated in books. Consequently, the building of periodical collections in the various subject areas must parallel the building of book collections.

An effort is made to provide periodicals in those fields in which books are not numerous, and in subject areas in which information goes out of date rapidly. As in book selection, choices are made which support the courses being taught in Houston Community College. Here also, faculty suggestions are welcomed. Those received by July 1 of each year will be given careful consideration for inclusion in the subscription list in preparation.

Dickinson College Library

INTRODUCTION

The planned development of a library's resources requires a definite acquisitions policy for all types of resources which a college library adds to its collections. This policy for the Dickinson College Library has been developed by the Department of Library Resources with the assistance of the Subcommittee for Academic Services to meet our general and specific needs for all library resources.

In this policy, the word "resources" shall be used to encompass all classes of materials which a library collects and makes available to its users.

RESPONSIBILITY FOR THE SELECTION OF RESOURCES

The Dickinson College Library will continue to be developed through the active support and interest of faculty members working with members of the Department of Library Resources to select resources pertinent to their teaching and research fields. The Academic Services Subcommittee allocates a share of the annual library budget to each department for library resources. The department chairman, or an appointed representative, is expected to make an equitable distribution of the departmental library allocation in such a way as best to provide library support for the work of the entire department.

The Department of Library Resources is responsible for the overall development of the collections of the library. A faculty member of the Department of Library Resources is assigned to each academic department and studies area of the college as a liaison person to assist in any way with library resources selection and use.

The Department of Library Resources will also select and purchase resources in all subject areas in order to develop a good general collection which will be of value to the programs of more than one academic department. Resources needed by the administration and staff of the college in the conduct of college business will be purchased by the Department of Library

Resources. In addition, some effort will be made to provide a limited amount of cultural and recreational library resources not covered by academic programs. All such purchases will be charged to the "general" portion of the book budget.

STATEMENT OF STANDARDS AND CRITERIA OF SELECTION OF RESOURCES

The following criteria should be observed in the selection of resources:

1. First priority will be given to resources that serve as either required or supplementary works for courses or to fulfill the general aims of a liberal education.
2. Only those resources will be acquired whose level of maturity is appropriate to the needs of the undergraduate student and the faculty.
3. The purchase of research materials solely for individual faculty use will be subordinated to the adequate fulfillment of the first priority of acquiring resources for the undergraduate, and should not normally exceed ten percent of department allocations. When possible, interlibrary loans or personal purchases should be used to fill specialized needs. The library will not always be able to meet the needs of all faculty members for their personal research; but no faculty member should have to depend upon another library for the preparation of lectures and teaching.
4. Resources selected should be in the English language except for basic and representative works in any languages taught at the college. Exceptions to this will be foreign language dictionaries and other materials determined to be necessary by the Department of Library Resources in consultation with academic departments.

CATEGORIES OF LIBRARY RESOURCES

Books

The book collection will consist of three main divisions: general, reference and special collections (see below).

1. Textbooks: Textbooks are not acquired unless they cover an area of interest and need for undergraduates for which there is no other general resource available.
2. Fiction: The library will purchase fiction when it is of literary merit and supplements the resources of the library in a way that nonfiction and scholarly works cannot do.

Documents

Dickinson College Library is a designated partial depository for federal documents. In addition, certain state and other federal documents are acquired to support teaching and research.

Microfilm, Microfiche, Audio-Visual and Other Nonbook Resources

Nonbook resources will be acquired to support the curricular needs of the college.

Morris Room—Special Collections

Acquisitions primarily come from gifts of the Friends of the Library. Purchases of manuscripts and rare and specialized books are generally limited to building current collections, to areas pertaining to the college's history, or occasionally to specific teaching needs of classes. The archives will be maintained in the Morris Room according to the policy promulgated by the President in 1974 with acquisitions determined by said policy and by the Archives Committee.

Newspapers

Newspapers will be purchased to give local, national and international news coverage. A limited number of titles available on microfilm is retained permanently.

Periodicals

Periodical subscriptions are recommended in the same manner as other resources. Initial purchase will be of the entire volume of the current year. The acquisition of back files will be selective and whenever possible such acquisitions will be made in microtext editions (microprint, microfilm, microcard, etc.). Subscription costs for periodicals that support academic departments' programs of instruction and research will be charged to the departmental library allocation. Periodicals of general interest will be purchased from library general funds.

Music Scores and Recordings

These resources are purchased from the music department library allocations.

Gifts

The selection of resources from the gifts offered to the library will be covered by the same criteria that govern the selection of resources for purchase by the library. Our general policy concerning the acceptance and recruiting of gifts is attached.

COOPERATION WITH OTHER LIBRARIES

Dickinson College Library is an active member of the Area College Library Cooperative Program of Central Pennsylvania and the Central Pennsylvania Consortium. These two groups reciprocate in lending and borrowing library resources. Agreements have also been made to share in the acquisition of library resources. Careful consideration will be given to requests for resources available on other campuses, and efforts will be made to share when possible. The library also recognizes its responsibility (1) to purchase, if possible, the works regularly consulted in other libraries or repeatedly requested on interlibrary loan, when these works are in print; and (2) to purchase a reasonable number of research materials to enhance total regional library holdings.

DUPLICATES OR MULTIPLE COPIES

Final decision on the number of copies of an item recommended for purchase will be made by the Department of Library Resources in consultation with the department making the request or recommendation.

REPLACEMENTS

Lost books are replaced after two years, or immediately, if requested.

WEEDING—WITHDRAWING AND DISCARDING

The Department of Library Resources will conduct a systematic program of weeding from the general library collection those items which are obsolete and no longer appropriate. Decisions to withdraw will be made in consultation with the faculty members of academic departments most directly concerned with possible future use of the resources. Two weeks before final action is taken on withdrawing any item, the library will announce such contemplated action in an official notice to all faculty members. Faculty members will thus be given time to request further consideration before any resources are actually withdrawn. All items weeded and withdrawn from the library's collections will be put in storage, exchanged, sold or recycled.

GIFTS AND BEQUESTS

After it is learned that a gift of library resources (books, periodicals, recordings, etc.) has been offered to the college, the following steps should be taken:

1. A list of the items offered should be submitted for review by the college library. The collections of a college library differ substantially from those of the library of general interest and circulation. Some books are of such nature that their use in our library would be limited, while they might be important additions to the collections of other libraries. The opportunity to review an advance list will enable the library to select those books and items that will represent significant and useful additions to the library where the donor's first interest is the Dickinson College Library, while at the same time giving the donor an opportunity to assist other libraries where the books would be more effectively used. This

procedure will also save the college library the cost of cataloging and storing those items which are not appropriate to its overall collection, or items which are duplicate copies.

2. After a list has been agreed upon, the donor should furnish an appraisal of the items selected when it is possible to do so. Under Internal Revenue Service regulations, this is the obligation of the donor and will probably be promptly recognized by an attorney or a trust officer. In some instances it might be appropriate for the college to submit a list of items selected for the library to a dealer for appraisal.

3. If there are "strings" tied to the bequest or gift, they should be ascertained and cleared with the library before the bequest or gift is accepted. This type of gift or bequest is probably less frequent today than it was in the past, but we should be alert to any restrictions placed upon what might otherwise be satisfactory bequests or gifts.

4. In addition to the gift of actual items, bequests of cash to be used for the purchase of library resources are welcomed.

GENERAL RULES AND PRIVILEGES

The college library is primarily for the use of the students and faculty of the college. High school students do not have borrowing privileges, except on interlibrary loan, and use by other members of the community is restricted to those with Town Borrowers' Cards. Students of the college are therefore required to show their ID cards when signing out books.

Students are urged to consult the library staff on any problems relating to the use of the library, and are invited to recommend titles for purchase. A part of the annual budget is regularly assigned to student requests.

Noncirculating Material

Books in the main collection, the Sharp Room, and the government documents collection may be signed out from the library. Materials in all other special collections do not circulate. Periodicals, both current and bound, do not circulate.

Loan and Renewal

Books available for circulation, except books on reserve and new books, may be borrowed for the regular loan period. If not wanted by anyone else, a book on loan may be renewed. New books may be borrowed for a two-week period only; one renewal only.

Recall and Hold Privileges

By application at the main desk, a person may reserve a book currently on loan to another individual. When the book is returned, it will be held at the desk and notice of its availability sent. All books loaned from the library are subject to recall. A recall notice demands immediate return to the library of the book or books cited.

Overdue Policy

The first and only overdue notice is sent one week after due date. A $2.00 service fee is charged for the notice. Charges (price of book plus $7.00 per book reordering costs) will be sent to the cashier's office 14 days after the overdue notice. If a book is returned after charges are sent to the cashier's office, they are removed, but an additional $2.00 service fee is charged.

Reserve Books

Loans.   Books may be borrowed from reserve for a period of one hour. A renewal for an additional hour will be granted if no one else has requested the book. Reserve books may be retained on loan during periods when the library is closed, but are due promptly at the time it next reopens. For example, a book signed from reserve at 11:45 p.m. for overnight use is due at the opening hour of 8:00 a.m. on the following morning.

Overnight fine.   A charge of 50¢ for each half hour is made on all reserve books kept beyond the next opening hour of the library, up to a maximum of $3.00 per day.

Lost or Damaged Books

Borrowers are expected to make good any loss or damage, and should report such incidents at once. A book recalled for another reader and not returned within a reasonable time may be considered a lost book and replaced at the borrower's expense. Ordering and processing costs are included in the charge for the lost books. These costs are $7.00 per book.

Exceptions to Rules

The library staff will make exceptions, in unusual cases, where they believe it may be to the best advantage of the borrowers. These exceptions must be made by the permanent staff—not the student assistants.

GUIDELINES FOR INDEPENDENT STUDY
IN SPECIAL LIBRARY TOPICS

Procedures to be Followed by Library Faculty

PURPOSE

1. To provide students opportunity to work in depth on library topics, with supervision to insure highest quality and integrity of work;
2. To provide for mutual communication and sharing of independent study experiences among library faculty.

GUIDELINES

1. Upon being approached by the student, the faculty member will clarify steps to be taken in submitting a proposal.
2. In cases where the student is unsure of basic topic area, the faculty library staff as a whole may discuss possibilities and make suggestions.

3. Upon receiving the student's formal proposal and list of preliminary sources, the faculty library staff will meet to discuss suitability of topic and availability of needed resources.
4. In cases where the subject of the independent study is related to a particular discipline, contact will be made with the pertinent department:
   • To establish approval for complete library handling of the independent study;
   • To set up an interdisciplinary independent study, with decisions made as to project responsibility and evaluative authority.
5. The faculty library staff will make a decision as to which member is to supervise the independent study, taking into consideration student and faculty preferences.
6. The individual faculty member will then confer with the student to make mutual arrangements as to meeting times, requirements and methods of evaluation.
7. At the conclusion of the semester, the faculty member will submit a brief summary of the independent study, including pertinent remarks as to success in topic approach, availability of needed materials, etc. This will be reviewed by the staff and kept in a permanent file along with the student's work and any final evaluation.
8. Each library faculty member will be limited to advising five independent studies per semester.

Texas A&M University Library System

INTRODUCTION

"Texas A&M University is a Land-Grant and a Sea-Grant institution dedicated to the attainment of excellence in teaching, research, extension and other public service functions." Thus reads the opening sentence of the "Statement of Purpose" prepared as part of Standard I of the Institutional Self-Study prepared in 1972 before the re-accreditation visit by representatives of the Southern Association of Colleges and Schools. The TAMU Library System bears the responsibility of providing access to the library materials necessary for TAMU students/faculty/staff. This information may be in such forms as magnetic tapes, although the library's primary collections consist of the traditional printed page and microphotographic reproductions of printed pages (microforms). The TAMU Library System attempts to meet some of the needs of other persons, but the essential goal remains to serve the teaching, research, extension and other public service functions of TAMU. The acquisitions policy statement should be in accord with the preceding statement.

The responsibility for the selection of library materials rests with the teaching and research faculty and TAMU professional staff and library faculty. Library departmental representatives play an important role in the total acquisitions process. Ultimate authority rests with the Assistant Director for Technical Services. Teaching and research faculty, because of their unique insights into special fields of study, bear particular responsibility for strengthening collections in specific areas of expertise. The library faculty recommends purchase of items for areas not covered by the teaching and research faculty, coordinates the collection as a whole, approves certain major selections and aids the teaching and research faculty with bibliographical assistance. Provisions shall continue for students to request either recreational reading titles or works useful in their studies.

The continuing escalation of costs of library materials necessitates a sound acquisitions policy and a regular review of the policy. No policy can suffice for all time, because a library is not static in that it reflects a university which is not static. Both the library's strengths and weaknesses must be taken into consideration as a policy is implemented. To discontinue purchases in a field where the institution is strong would abdicate a role of leadership, and to fail to strengthen a weak area might condemn that research topic to permanent inadequacy. It must be remembered, however, that no library can presume to expect eminence in all areas of inquiry. The TAMU Library System has been an active leader in the Texas Information Exchange, a cooperative network vital for providing excellent interlibrary loan services, and it should be remembered also that the library was the first in the Southwest to join the Center for Research Libraries, a national service enhancing the research collections of all member libraries. The TAMU libraries also are interested in other cooperative programs.

OBLIGATIONS

The TAMU Library System should acquire all library materials (books, pamphlets, periodicals, manuscripts, maps, photographs, microtext materials, audio-visual materials, etc.) needed to meet its obligations to support the programs of teaching, research and extension. These duties demand first priority for all library funds. Also, the library must own and make available those materials necessary for general information in subject areas not covered by the programs in the classroom and in research efforts. Finally, the library preserves through the university archives all materials relating to the history, development and character of TAMU. The acquisitions policy of the university archives shall be in accord with guidelines approved by the University Archives and Historical Committee.

LIMITATIONS

To insure the soundest use of available funds, the following priorities are to be implemented: (1) Current publications of lasting value will take precedence over out-of-print items. (2) When possible, considerations will be given to cooperative acquisition plans with other institutions. (3) The library will determine the format of a purchase when choice is available. Microforms will be acquired to the greatest possible extent. (4) Duplicate copies of monographs will be purchased only when necessary to serve instructional needs. Normally, the library will supply no more than one copy on reserve for each fifteen students, depending on the assigned work and the length of time available for these students to read the assigned volume. All multiple-copy requests must be specifically approved by the separates acquisitions librarian. Specialized research materials will not be duplicated. (5) Monographs costing $75 or more per volume or $200 or more per set will be purchased only with the approval of the separates acquisitions librarian.

EXTENT OF COVERAGE IN SPECIFIC SUBJECT AREAS

Each academic institution has differing library needs, relative to the various departments and their quality, level of programs, and faculty research in progress. In order to accommodate as well as possible these variables, it is necessary to attempt to define some general categories of acquisition intensity.

General Collection

A general, basic collection introduces and defines the subject and helps to serve the needs of beginning students. Such a collection may include textbooks, dictionaries, encyclopedias, major authors, surveys, biographies and some periodicals in the field.

Instructional Collection

This is a good working collection designed to meet instructional needs for an undergraduate program. A wide range of basic works, collections of the works of more important authors and critics, selections from secondary authors, yearbooks, handbooks, and a wide range of representative journals and basic bibliographies will be included in such a collection.

Comprehensive Research

This level of collection supports independent research, particularly for graduate students and faculty members. Such a collection is comprehensive in nature, including most current publications of research value and original editions of classics in the field, as well as current editions of these titles. There must be a wide variety of supporting works to complete such a collection: documents, pamphlets, journals, bibliographies, rare imprints, newspapers, and so forth.

Nonmonographic Library Materials

Library materials in other than monographic forms regularly present specific problems which require variations in processes. While being contained within the limitations outlined previously, the acquisition of nonmonographic library materials will additionally be controlled by the following policies.

SERIAL PUBLICATIONS

The multiplicity of new serial titles, the potential obligation to maintain a serial title in perpetuity, escalating costs of serials, cost of binding, and maintenance and storage costs make a high degree of selectivity mandatory.

Requests for serial titles may be initiated by faculty, students or TAMU professional staff and are reviewed by library subject specialists. After appropriate consultations are held, the titles are ordered on recommendation of the subject specialist. The final authority for ordering serial titles is a fiscal responsibility and lies with the serials acquisitions librarian.

The criteria to be considered in the selection of serial titles include the following points:

1. Titles which present substantial factual information related to the disciplines studied at TAMU;
2. Titles which are bibliographically accessible through indexes and abstracting services;

3. Popular titles suitable for recreational and avocational reading in the university community;
4. Other material as changing university needs dictate.

In general, the library will obtain and retain only one copy of a serial title. Any exceptions will be made on a title by title basis. Microforms will be the preferred format for retention except when it is unsatisfactory due to technical problems.

Gift subscriptions to serial titles will not be accepted without the specific approval of the serials librarian in consultation with the subject specialist. The acceptance of a gift subscription does not imply an obligation either to permanently retain or to bind the gift title.

BACK FILES

Back files of serial titles will be selected on the same criteria as current subscriptions, and will be purchased as research needs require and funds allow. Back files will be purchased in microform unless there are specific reasons the microformat limits utilization of the material. Copies duplicating back files held by the Center for Research Libraries will be purchased for the TAMU Library collection only on the strongest written justification of the requestor and the library selection officer for that subject category. Final decision rests with the library.

NEWSPAPERS

Domestic and foreign newspapers will be acquired on a current basis for the following purposes:

1. To meet teaching needs;
2. To meet research requirements by achieving:

- National coverage on a highly selective basis to give balanced geographical coverage;
- International coverage on a highly restricted basis to give balanced geographical coverage;
- Selective coverage of Texas which will include each of the major regions of the state.

In providing for the above needs, consideration will be given to titles available in the region and in the Center for Research Libraries. Newspaper back files will be retained exclusively in microform. Indexed newspapers will be given priority due to their increased utility.

OTHER

The acquisition of materials for the following areas includes the same processes used for the acquisition of materials for other areas of the library.

U.S. Documents

U.S. Government Printing Office (GPO) publications include both serials and separates publications. The TAMU Library System is a depository library and thus receives a significant amount of federally-published materials. The Readex Microprint series provides coverage of nondepository documents. Due to the great range of government publications and the great range of needs and interests in the university community, the goal is to maintain rather complete coverage of GPO materials appropriate for library use and retention.

Special Collections

Rare items, special collections of materials such as the Jeff Dykes Range Livestock and Science Fiction Research Collections, and other materials requiring special treatment are included in this area.

Maps

This collection is the principal depository for atlases, gazeteers and sheet maps.

Technical Reports

The Technical Reports Center includes corporation, academic and government reports.

Audio-Visual Materials

Audio-visual materials are acquired only on a limited basis by the library. When significantly large acquisitions are appropriate, a statement will be formulated. The library maintains a small, selective group of art reproductions, and additions to this collection will be purchased only with gift funds provided for this purpose.

Microforms

The library is interested in the greatest possible utilization of microreproductions. Both individual titles on microform and large sets or masses of materials on microforms will be considered. The library will subscribe to large microreproduction projects on a highly selective basis and will participate in microreproduction projects on a highly restrictive basis. Membership in the Center for Research Libraries makes available at shared cost the results of various large micropublishing projects. Desired materials will be secured in the most readily usable microformat unless the material is not suited to use in microformat.

GIFTS

In general, the TAMU Library welcomes gifts of books or funds with which to purchase books. Gifts of library materials, either monographs or serials, or of funds with which to effect their purchase will be accepted provided they are consistent with the goals of the library and provided that any restrictions are acceptable to the library. After the library has accepted a gift of library materials, it has the right to disperse the materials as it so determines. There is no assurance that the materials will be added to the

SERIAL SUBSCRIPTION REQUEST DATA

To assist the University Libraries in justifying new serial requests, please complete the following form for each title requested. All blanks on the form must be completed for the title to be considered. ATTACH THE COMPLETED FORM TO THE SERIAL SUBSCRIPTION REQUEST FORM.

1. Title _____

2. Priority Rating _____
   (see criteria on reverse side)

3. a. Courses this title will support:

   Department   Course No.   Course Title

   _____   _____   _____

   _____   _____   _____

   _____   _____   _____

   b. Faculty and/or research projects this title would benefit:

   _____

   _____

   _____

   c. Primary student user group:

   _____ Undergraduate _____ Masters _____ Doctoral

4. Title(s) of Serial(s) presently subscribed to in the same field which could be deleted, if necessary, in order to purchase the new title.

   _____

   _____

   _____

Your cooperation is appreciated. With your assistance, we shall be able to make the best use of the funds available for Serials purchases.

Criteria for rating new serial requests:

1. *Essential* for instruction and basic for research in broad areas of the discipline. Students and faculty consult this title regularly.

2. *Important* for the discipline though less closely related to existing instruction. May be of considerable importance for advanced research, but not as broadly applicable to the instruction and research program as item (1) above.

3. *Useful* but not basic or central to instruction and research programs of the university. May fill individual research needs, but these are likely to be highly specialized. (Interlibrary loan access, if prompt, would be satisfactory.)

4. *Marginal* to the department's instruction and research program and infrequently consulted. May serve occasional research needs; rarely used for instruction. (Interlibrary loan access would be satisfactory.)

TAMU Libraries collection. Only in unusual circumstances will a gift collection be accepted which has to be maintained as a separate entity. Any collections offered to the TAMU Library with such restrictions will be considered on an individual basis.

All gifts of library materials consisting of less than fifty items will be accepted without question unless there are restrictions attached to the gift (i.e., special circulation policy, housing as an individual collection, etc.). In such cases acceptance of the gift will be at the discretion of the Director of Libraries.

Any collections of library materials (over fifty items) will be evaluated by appropriate library or academic faculty. If the materials are determined to be of minimal use to the TAMU Library, the donor will be advised of this. Materials which do not enhance the total collection will not be accepted. Appropriate alternatives for the materials will be provided if the donor desires.

The library does not evaluate gifts or provide listings for tax purposes, but it will recommend persons who perform this service.

Monetary gifts are subject to the same general guidelines as are books. In the case of any restrictions, acceptance will be at the discretion of the Director of Libraries.

ANNUAL REVIEW OF STATEMENT

The Assistant Director for Technical Services will maintain a continuous monitoring of the Acquisitions Policy Statement. In January of each odd-numbered year the assistant director shall refer the statement to the Assistant Director for Public Services and the Assistant Director for Special Collections for appropriate review. Any resulting recommendations, together with any suggestions by the Assistant Director for Technical Services, will be reviewed by the technical services department heads, the Director's Council and the Library Administration for transmission to the University Library Council.

PART

PARTIAL LIBRARY POLICIES BY CATEGORY

Introductions
Philosophy and Goals
Objectives
Selection
Problem Areas
Special Formats
Gifts, Interlibrary Loan, Networks and Consortia
Intellectual Freedom, Censorship and Confidentiality
Weeding

Introductions

The Baltimore County Public Library

The purpose of the Baltimore County Public Library materials selection policy is to guide librarians and to inform the public about the principles upon which selections are made.

A policy cannot replace the judgment of librarians, but stating goals and indicating boundaries will assist them in choosing from a vast array of materials available.

The library sets as its major goal in materials selection: to secure for all residents of Baltimore County the informational, educational, cultural and recreational materials in all media, both published and unpublished, that fit their needs.

The word "materials" used for the specific forms of media has the widest possible meaning; it may include books (hardbound and paperbound), pamphlets, maps, magazines and journals, comic books, newspapers, broadsides, manuscripts, films, filmstrips, sound discs, sound tapes, slides, posters, videotapes, games, and art reproductions or original art work.

"Selection" refers to the decision that must be made either to add a given item to the collection or to retain one already in the collection. It does not refer to guidance in assisting a library user.

Wayne County Public Library

The materials selection policy of the Wayne County Public Library evolves from the goals and purposes of the public library itself: the free, informal, continuing education of the people; the dissemination and advancement of knowledge; and the provision of recreational and inspirational reading. Recognizing the wide diversity of tastes, interests, and cultural and educational background of the community, it is our aim to build a broad collection serving as many citizens as possible within the necessary limitations of space and budget. Keeping a balance between public demand (mysteries, light romances, popular fiction and nonfiction) and what the librarians know the library should hold is a major problem, especially for the extension services.

The Wayne County Public Library Board of Trustees endorses the statements of the American Library Association entitled the *Library Bill of Rights* and the *Freedom to Read.*

North Country Library System

The North Country Library System is a cooperative association of sixty-one chartered public libraries in Jefferson, Lewis, St. Lawrence and Oswego counties. Most of these libraries are small, staffed by dedicated local women, and directed by unpaid, public-spirited local trustees. Together, librarians, trustees and town boards sacrifice to give their communities year-round, on-the-spot library service. Serving these local community libraries is the mission of the Service Center of the North Country Library System; and an important factor in that mission is the Service Center's book selection policy.

A major twentieth-century problem, sociologists tell us, is lack of communication between people. This book selection policy statement is our endeavor to improve communication within the NCLS family. Your aims and ours are the same: to provide the best possible library service to the people of the North Country Community. Our patrons have a wide range of reading needs, and it takes individual dedication and mutual cooperation to meet all these needs in the time they should be met. We salute you for your efforts in the past, and we are confident that all of us, working together and understanding one another's problems, can do even better in the future.

Many years ago a man described the North Country as "a place where we have ten-and-a-half months of winter and six weeks of poor weather." This, of course, was poetic exaggeration and not strictly true. Most years we have eight weeks of poor weather.

Weather is one factor that shaped our history and still shapes our present. Another factor is the land—a scraped glacial plain lightly covered by scrub woods and conifers. This was not a land that invited mass immigration and it did not get it; yet émigrés from the Napoleonic era settled here and left a rich heritage including place names like Le Ray, Chaumont, Deferiet and LaFargeville. People came (and still come) to this region as individuals. Many paused briefly and then moved on. Others stayed, because there is something about this spare, hard, uncrowded land that they loved. It is hard to describe, but somehow winter or summer, even at its worst, the North Country is beautiful.

So today the North Country is a thinly populated, underdeveloped region. Although we are of many nationalities and occupations, we do not coalesce into blocs—social, economic, or otherwise. We have just two small cities, Watertown and Ogdensburg; otherwise we live in small, self-reliant towns and villages. Our major industry is dairy-farming, followed by paper products, aluminum, and tourists. We are beginning to attract new industries to the region. Nevertheless we are, at the moment, an economically depressed area, but somehow we are not socially depressed. We have a strong tradition of quality education, from elementary school through our excellent local colleges. And part of that tradition is our many local public libraries, and the Service Center of the North Country Library System.

The Public Library of Cincinnati and Hamilton County

The Public Library of Cincinnati and Hamilton County serves a large metropolitan community with many groups of varying economic, social and political backgrounds. The library provides these groups with material for education, information, recreation and research.

In a free society, information on all points of view in all fields should be readily available, so that individuals may decide which ideas are meaningful to them. In our society, the public library is the institution which provides free access to these ideas, even though they may be unacceptable to some. The library, consequently, has the responsibility for selecting materials which reflect divergent and unusual points of view.

Because of the volume of publishing, the limitations of budget and space, and the existence of the many highly specialized collections in the community, the library must have a selection policy with which to meet community interests and needs if it is to fulfill its objectives. This does not mean that all branch libraries will necessarily acquire all books acquired by the main library. Different criteria must be used in building both types of collections based on adequacy of funds and of space. This policy must be flexible and broad in scope, and have depth without excessive specialization. Books that are inaccurate or poorly written, or that contribute neither to a greater knowledge of a subject nor to a better understanding of life, have little place in a public library collection.

This statement of book selection policy is used by the library staff in the selection of material and acquaints the general public with the principles of selection.

Rolling Prairie Libraries

Every system and every library within the system should have a written statement of policy, covering the selection and maintenance of its collection. Since a library is always vulnerable to criticism from persons or groups who do not approve of material included in the library collection or who are unhappy because certain materials were excluded, a materials selection policy will put the library in a clearly defined position if its holdings or selection practices are challenged. A selection policy should also aid collection development in a library by establishing guidelines for selection. The more detailed the policy is, the more helpful it is likely to be, both in selection for the library collection and in explanation of the collection's contents.

Camden County Free Library

The purpose of the Camden County Free Library book selection policy is to guide librarians and to inform the public about the principals upon which selections are made.

A policy, however high its standards, cannot replace the judgment of librarians, but it can provide goals and guidelines that will assist librarians in choosing from the vast array of available materials.

The major goals of the Camden County Free Library in book selection are the advancement of knowledge, the education and enlightenment of the people of the community, and the provisions of recreational reading.

Seattle Public Library

The major factors in the community which have a bearing on the selection of library materials are the wants and needs of the people, individually and collectively, and the materials already available to them through other community agencies.

The people.   The Seattle Public Library serves over 500,000 persons within the Seattle city limits and many more persons in King County by contractual arrangement with the King County Library System. Like all large city libraries, Seattle Public Library serves people with a vast range of educational and cultural backgrounds and a wide variety of interests and needs. It is essential that all these people find in a public library materials for recreational reading, for improving job skills, for acquiring specific information and for educating themselves for life in today's world.

Because of its history and topography, Seattle is a city of distinctive neighborhoods. Each branch library includes a general collection and any special, cultural or vocational material appropriate for the neighborhood. Neighborhoods change constantly, and librarians must be aware of and anticipate the changing needs of the community. By providing a variety of materials throughout the system, the entire city is enriched. The Central Library also has a local clientele including, for instance, the downtown business community, but its main responsibility is to offer reference service and specialized materials to everyone in the library system.

University of California at Los Angeles Library

This document is the product of a project which dates back more than three years. At that time the then newly-formed Collection Development Committee first began to attempt to execute the directive which was contained in its charge, that the Committee "solicit the current guidelines used in developing the collections of the various units within the library system, including definitions of levels and limits and coverage."

Spelling out the collecting guidelines of a library system as large, heterogenous, and decentralized as this, and doing it in terms and in a form which would be useful to both library selection staff and library users, proved to be much more difficult than was first anticipated. It soon became apparent that two basic approaches to analysis were possible: by individual collection or by subject. The first would involve a series of statements about the various libraries or collecting units, indicating their purpose and subject scope, as well as their limitations in form, language, geographical areas, and chronological period. The second would involve a listing of all the subjects collected within the library system, with an indication after each subject of which library collects it, and in what depth.

Both approaches have rather severe limitations, however, for either a patron-oriented or internal document, and after abortive attempts in each of these directions it was decided to combine them.

The result is a series of narrative statements about each of the libraries in the UCLA system which state the general purpose and limitations of these libraries, but not the specific subjects collected. This is accompanied by a subject listing, by Library of Congress classification, with an indication after each subject of what library or libraries it is collected by, and in what depth. The level of coverage is indicated by a number, the lowest number indicating the greatest depth.

The format of the narrative statement was modeled after that developed for the Stanford Libraries policy statements, but without the "Subjects Covered" section.

A number of caveats are in order in connection with the use of this document, particularly the subject listing:

1. The subjects and levels of coverage listed for each library must be interpreted in the light of the scope and limitations of that library's collection policy, as it appears in the narrative statement.
2. The levels of coverage indicate the present collecting policy, which is not necessarily the same as the present collection strength. Subjects in which a library has just begun to collect in great depth may not now be represented by strong collections, although a 2 or 3 might appear in the subject listing. Conversely, a large, strong collection which for some reason is no longer being added to at the rate it formerly was might be represented by a 5 or 6.
3. The subject listing is not consistent. Selection officers in the various libraries have listed collecting strengths according to their own interpretations of how each particular collecting should be expressed, in terms of the Library of Congress classification system, and these interpretations differ, sometimes rather sharply. An attempt was made to review these listings and have them reflect a more consistent viewpoint, but the number of subjects and the number of viewpoints was simply too great.

A word or two about the University Research Library. Because of the broad range of subject matter covered by the University Research Library stack collection and the fact that there are twelve bibliographers, or selection officers, who are responsible for building various parts of it, it was not

practicable to have just one report on this collection. Instead, each of the
bibliographers has indicated the collecting levels for the subjects within the
collection for which he or she is responsible. In addition, the University
Research Library contains a number of collections other than that which is
housed in its main stacks. These include the public affairs service, reference,
special collections, and theater arts collections. While some of these are more
closely related to the stack collection than others, their narrative statements
and subject listings appear in the University Research Library section, after
the bibliographers' listings. (The Oriental Library is an exception. While it is
housed in the University Research Library, it appears with the other libraries, in regular alphabetical sequence.)

Any statement which describes collecting policy in as dynamic and multi-
faceted a library system as this will lose its usefulness very quickly if it is not
updated on a regular basis. To this end we hope to be able to record our
holdings, by Library of Congress classification, as they are gathered bien-
nially, and also to record use figures. A picture of how the collections are
actually growing and how they are being used should serve as an interesting
complement to what we were doing, or what we said we were doing, in April
1972.

This document represents the combined efforts of a number of people,
and I would like to express my appreciation to all of them, to the unit heads
and other selection officers who prepared statements about their collecting
policies, and then prepared others as the focus of the project changed, and
to the many members of the Collection Development Committee who la-
bored so hard to design and create a useful guide to the collecting policies of
the UCLA Library system. I sincerely hope that is what we have produced.

Kansas City Kansas Community Junior College Library

The planned development of a library collection requires the consistent
application of a stated selection policy. Because the community college is not
a static institution, the library, which operates within the framework of
institutional goals, must be responsive to change. The policy statement
which follows must, then, be interpreted as one which is currently in the best
interests of the college and as one which is responsive to institutional change.

Cattell Library, Malone College

The purpose of a materials selection policy is to assure the planned and
systematic provision of materials for the college:

1. To support the curriculum;
2. To offer materials in independent fields in addition to those related to
   the curriculum, thereby offering all views on an issue;

3. For student recreational and inspirational reading in addition to academic needs;
4. For the immediate community needs in areas less likely to be served by public and other private libraries yet supportive of academic stance;
5. Of a research and/or bibliographic nature to aid in research planning.

Roanoke-Chowan Technical Institute Library

The selection policy is designed to guide the faculty, staff and students and to inform patrons in the four counties serviced concerning the guidelines used for selecting and acquiring materials for the Learning Resource Center.

Media encompassing all types of printed and nonprinted materials will be selected in a manner consistent with the overall philosophy and purposes of the instructional program of the Roanoke-Chowan Technical Institute.

The selection policy adheres to the following:

Priority for media to be purchased by the center is given to those materials which meet the curricular needs of the students in the courses offered, including media needed for remedial assignments, class assignments, research, collateral readings and bibliographical tools which facilitate using and locating the media.

Blue Mountain Community College Library

This materials selection policy has been developed to insure acquisition of materials which will promote and strengthen the teaching program in all its aspects, arouse intellectual curiosity, and help to develop critical thinking.

Furthermore, such a policy will increase and maintain the confidence of the community in the colleges by the knowledge of the thorough and reasoned philosophies and procedures underlying the selection of materials for the college library.

This statement shall include all materials—both print and nonprint—which fall within the jurisdiction of the library.

Hoover Library, Western Maryland College

The acquisitions policy of the library should be consistent with the philosophy and objectives of the college, resulting in a solid collection of the most significant works of all ages. It should include those works necessary to acquire "a sound foundation" in the "areas or disciplines of knowledge" that make up the curriculum, and the materials needed to gain an awareness of current trends and differing approaches within those fields, as well as the interrelationships among them. Certainly the major reference works in these subject areas must be acquired and kept up to date, and the meaning of "significant work" interpreted to include not only books but also microforms, sound recordings, film and any other media in which appropriate materials may be available.

The library should meet the needs of students and faculty in preparation of their course work. It must be anticipated however that independent research associated with special studies and honors work will sometimes lead students into subject areas not covered in sufficient depth in the collection of Western Maryland College. In such cases it will be necessary to seek materials elsewhere. The library offers student and faculty as much assistance as it can to help locate and borrow materials from other libraries. To help attract and to keep an outstanding faculty the library should give as much support to faculty research as it can. In a relatively small liberal arts college library with limited funds, where collections are to be chosen primarily for undergraduate study, support for faculty research and student special studies is best accomplished through strong holdings in bibliography and in subscriptions to the most important indexing and abstracting services.

Philosophy and Goals

Learning Resources Center, Eastfield College

The Eastfield Learning Resources program has been planned to meet the curricular needs of the total college population. The primary function of the program is to facilitate and improve learning by providing resources and services—including instructional development assistance to faculty—for the implementation of the instructional program. The secondary function of the program is to provide resources and services relevant to the general informational needs, the intellectual and professional growth, the cultural development and the recreational activities of the total college population. Other objectives are to:

1. Provide instructional development services to assist faculty in the analysis, design, development, implementation and evaluation of learning systems and learning materials;
2. Acquire and prepare for use a collection of learning resources that truly reflects the needs of the college by involving students, faculty and staff in the selection process;
3. Organize and manage the learning resources program for minimum effort on the part of the user to access resources and acquire services;
4. Assist students, faculty and staff in the effective use of learning resources and communications technology;
5. Assist in the planning and development of college facilities for maximum use of communications technology and newer instructional techniques;
6. Provide materials, equipment, workspace and programs for the professional growth and development of the faculty and staff;
7. Produce audio, video and graphic materials needed for learning and teaching programs and public information activities;
8. Provide educational leadership to the local community through workshops, noncredit courses and consultant services in the areas of learning resources, communications technology and instructional techniques;
9. Provide opportunities for each learning resources staff member to grow personally and professionally;
10. Create an atmosphere in which persons in all areas of the learning resources center participate in the overall direction of the program;

11. Promote a strong liaison with local, state and national organizations for coordination and exchange of resources, services and ideas;
12. Evaluate on a continuing basis all learning resources program activities for outward effectiveness.

Library, Northeastern Illinois University

The primary goal of an acquisitions policy is to promote the development of a collection that supports and is compatible with the goals of the institution as well as the needs of the users. To determine a sound policy the institutional objectives must be clearly understood. In his position paper, dated October 7, 1971, Dr. Jerome M. Sachs, President of UNI from 1966 to 1973, stated the following goals for Northeastern Illinois University:

1. An increasingly excellent academic program;
2. The realization of urban potential in the composition of the student body and in the creation of diverse programs to meet the needs of different groups of students;
3. A realistic and appropriate program of involvement with the problems and promise of the local community and the larger urban complex;
4. A sound fiscal plan and a carefully drawn program of growth with priorities within dollar and space limitations;
5. A design for a spectrum of programs to enable each individual to realize his full potential.

Because of this commitment to the urban environment and community, Northeastern Illinois University must be an integral part of the community it serves. The library must accept its obligation in respect to this and must provide a collection which reflects this philosophy. At the same time collection development must be balanced, orderly, and steady, and it must also be coordinated in regard to student enrollment in the various departments and educational priorities. Consequently, financial support must always be provided to enable the library to develop in a manner supportive of the institution's educational goals.

It is essential that collection development receive high priority in all academic departments. The major portion of a university's book collection is the result of curriculum development and faculty needs. Therefore each area of concentration should be carefully reviewed at periodic intervals by both the classroom teaching and library faculties, and determinations and priorities should be set regarding the types of materials to be acquired. A selection policy must indicate clearly which materials are essential to the university's development and need to be bought as well as those which are not essential.

Northern Illinois University, dedicated to urban education priorities, must also develop a collection that will support the educational programs at both the undergraduate and graduate levels. In addition to preparing students in an area of concentration, a university should provide its community with reading matter that will enrich their lives personally and help them develop into mature adults, prepared to accept the responsibilities of intelligent citizens in an ever-changing, demanding society. Therefore, to provide such a well-balanced collection, materials should also be collected that are not solely geared to the curricular needs.

While an acquisitions policy must serve as a basis for collection development, it should not become a static entity. Universities change; faculties leave the campus, and departments become restructured. Objectives must therefore maintain a flexibility, and book acquisition must allow for this and make the necessary provisions for the changing needs of the community.

There is sound rationale in writing an acquisitions policy for NIU. It will provide the library faculty with a document that reflects the institutional goals together with the library faculty's interpretation of how to support this philosophy in the area of selection. There is also a practical need to define the full scope of acquisitions activity within the library. In order to keep this document viable and compatible with the university's direction, it is imperative that this policy be subjected to periodic review and revision.

Abbot Memorial Library, Emerson College

The Abbot is a specialized library serving the unique needs of Emerson's curriculum. The collection, which contains over 60,000 print and nonprint items, is focused on the communication arts and sciences, with major concentrations in mass communications, theater, speech and speech pathology. Media equipment and services are part of the library program.

The goals of the library are:

- To provide the teaching faculty with the media, services and systems that will enhance the effective communication of ideas in the presentation phase of learning;
- To provide the students with the media, services and systems that will enhance the effective communication of ideas in the self-programmed phase of learning.

The library staff is·here to help you. Please ask . . .!

Hoover Library, Western Maryland College

In order to stimulate and feed interests that transcend campus and classroom and continue after graduation, the library should go beyond providing materials needed to perform class assignments, not in trying to build research collections in any department, but rather in building a good general collection of standard works of the past and the best of current output, whether directly related to the curriculum or not, and including materials concerned with current issues and controversies.

Skyline College Library

Access to the widest possible variety of printed and media materials, the appropriate media equipment, and provision for preparation and production are basic to the most effective work of both students and faculty and provide a foundation for the implementation of innovative instruction. Formal instruction for groups, bibliographic support for utilization of all resources, attention to the individual interests and developmental needs of each student and instructor, special assistance for the handicapped and deprived, a program of displays, publications and exhibitions, cooperation in the development of regional networks and systems, and participation in the larger community generally, are all essential parts of a comprehensive program. Emphasis in the program is upon facilitating inquiry, exploring ideas and concepts, and developing the ability to use the resources in independent study. One necessity is a qualified staff, involved in serving the needs of students, faculty and community. Trained professional assistance is necessary in finding and interpreting the materials which are needed by the individual student and which are adapted to the student's skills and abilities. The library is thus an encouragement to learning and an agency for teaching, learning and innovation, with an internal validity of its own.

The college program requires an organized and readily accessible collection of material to meet instructional, individual and institutional needs of students and faculty. It is the role of the library to support and supplement the curriculum with a central collection of material, recognizing that the sources of information are unlimited, whether in the form of film, recording, videotape, newspaper, book or other resource. In the expanded library concept at Skyline, the Media Center is an essential and integral unit of the Learning Resource Center.

Roanoke-Chowan Technical Institute Library

We at Roanoke-Chowan Technical Institute believe that democracy is dependent upon an educational system capable of developing, to the fullest extent, the talents of its citizens. Therefore, the institute should be flexible in its offerings and adaptable to the changing needs and demands of the public and times.

As a member of the North Carolina Community College system, Roanoke-Chowan Technical Institute upholds the philosophy of total education and the "open door" policy as adopted by this system. Within its available resources, this institute will serve the people of its area, within the legal age limit, from the high school drop-out to the retired person, by providing:

- A core of general education courses and activities that will broaden and deepen students' cultural heritage and enhance awareness of the responsibilities citizens of their community, state, nation, and world face; and also provide paths of exploration and opportunity for part-time students who have already developed vocational, technical or professional competency;

- Training programs for students now employed or who are contemplating employment in vocational or technical areas upon completion of their work at Roanoke-Chowan Technical Institute;
- Continuing education programs based on regional interests and needs;
- Advisement, counseling, guidance and placement programs to better serve students.

It is the intent of Roanoke-Chowan Technical Institute to offer help to every student who seeks it, provided that the student can benefit from what is offered, and provided that the student is willing to try.

The Roanoke-Chowan Technical Institute Library Program is designed to help each student become prepared in this changing society for adequate living by providing a variety of materials to enrich each student's knowledge, by giving leadership and guidance in the use of the materials, and by challenging each student to use the library facilities to the maximum capacity.

Objectives

Virginia Beach Public Library Department

It is the function of the public library in America today to provide the means through which all people may have free access to the thinking on all sides of all ideas. The public library has become a practical demonstration of the belief in the universal education as a lifelong process. It is the responsibility of the library to supply books and nonbook materials for people of all ages and to give guidance in their use.

The Virginia Beach Public Library must offer opportunity and encouragement to individuals and groups:

1. To educate themselves continuously;
2. To keep abreast of progress in all fields of knowledge;
3. To maintain freedom of expression and a constructively critical attitude toward all public issues;
4. To be responsible members of the community, the country and the world;
5. To develop greater efficiency in the performance of their work;
6. To discover and develop their creative capacities for and powers of appreciation of arts and letters;
7. To use their leisure time in the enjoyment of reading.

Fresno County Public Library

The objective of the Fresno County Public Library is to select, organize, preserve and make freely and easily available to the people of the community printed and other materials, within the limitations of space and budget, which will aid them in the pursuit of education, information, research, recreation and culture, and in the creative use of leisure time.

The Public Library of Cincinnati and Hamilton County

The Public Library of Cincinnati and Hamilton County provides materials and services on a free and equal basis to all residents of Hamilton County in order to achieve its general objectives.

To keep its citizens informed in all fields of knowledge, the library acquires materials which are organized and housed in order to make them easily accessible to all members of the community so as:

- To assist students and those furthering their own self-education;
- To supply information for the individual and the entire community;
- To provide material for the creative use of leisure;
- To make available a broad and in-depth research collection;
- To cooperate with and support other educational, cultural, recreational and civic groups of the area.

The library, in addition to serving contemporary needs, has the responsibility of preserving materials for future use.

Hamilton Public Library

- To assemble, organize for use, and preserve such books and other printed materials as will be useful to the citizens of Hamilton in promoting their own or the community's welfare and enriching their personal lives; and to assist the public to make the best use of these resources;
- To serve the city as a general center of reliable information;
- To provide opportunity and encouragement for children and young people to discover the joy of reading and the many practical values to be found in books;
- To provide the best possible collection on local history.

North Country Library System

Keeping a balance between what is in immediate demand (and, to a great extent, of temporary interest) and what is of more lasting value is the greatest challenge in our book selection. Most of the libraries of the region are small and are supported at a minimum level; therefore the Service Center has assumed a large part of the responsibility for supplying even light materials. This means that ours is a dual policy: we try to meet the demand for at least some light reading matter; but at the same time we are striving for quality in our overall book selection.

Our principal objective is to select, from the flood of books currently published, those which are the best for our service program in the North Country; best as judged either by our staff or by professional book reviewers. In making our selection, we keep in mind all the people of the region, and attempt to acquire those materials which will enable them to inform themselves of the issues of the day, to further their education, and to enrich, entertain and amuse themselves.

Baltimore County Public Library

The primary objective of selection shall be to collect materials of contemporary significance and of permanent value. The library will always be guided by a sense of responsibility to both present and future in adding materials which will enrich the collections and maintain an overall balance. The library also recognizes an immediate duty to make available materials for enlightenment and recreation, even though such materials may not have enduring interest or value. The library will provide, too, a representative sampling of experimental and ephemeral materials.

Whitehall Public Library

The objectives of the Whitehall Public Library are to assist people to:
1. Educate themselves continuously;
2. Keep pace with progress in all fields of knowledge;
3. Become better members of home and community;
4. Discharge political and social obligations;
5. Be more capable in their daily occupations;
6. Develop their creative and spiritual capacities;
7. Appreciate and enjoy works of art;
8. Make such use of leisure time as will promote personal and social well-being.

Seattle Public Library

The Seattle Public Library acquires, makes available and encourages the use of materials in a variety of media which achieve at least one of the following objectives:
1. Meet the informational needs of the entire community;
2. Supplement formal study and encourage informal self-education;
3. Aid in learning and improving job-related skills;
4. Stimulate thoughtful participation in public affairs;
5. Give access to a variety of opinions on matters of current interest and encourage freedom of expression;
6. Assist the individual to grow intellectually and spiritually and to enjoy life more fully;
7. Support educational, civic and cultural activities within the community.

William S. Smith Library, South Georgia College

The basic objective of the William S. Smith Library of South Georgia College is to play its full part in support and stimulation of the purpose and philosophy of the college. In fulfilling this objective, the library serves as an instructional unit and as an aid to research, and makes provision for additional services to students, faculty, administration, staff and community. The foremost objectives are:

1. To provide a well-organized and readily accessible collection of materials and equipment needed to meet institutional, instructional, and individual needs of faculty, students and staff;
2. To provide leadership and assistance in the development of instructional systems which help meet both institutional and instructional objectives of South Georgia College;
3. To provide a qualified staff concerned about and involved in serving the needs of students, faculty and the wider community;
4. To encourage innovation, learning and community service by providing facilities and resources which make these things possible.

The library is primarily a teaching and research instrument. The professional library staff, administrative organization and building are so planned as to implement teaching, learning and research by the use of all types of library materials. The staff is composed, therefore, of educators who teach, not in the classrooms, but by mobilizing the resources of the library according to a well-defined program. South Georgia College recognizes this fact by giving faculty rank and status to professional librarians and media specialists.

Oregon State University Library

The library's overall objective is, in accordance with its acquisition policy, to develop one central collection of materials which will now and in the future best satisfy needs of the university community relating to study, instruction, research and administrative responsibility. This is a joint effort of faculty and library subject specialists.

Roanoke-Chowan Technical Institute Library

The goals of Roanoke-Chowan's materials selection policy are:

- To acquire and maintain a live, growing collection of books and materials in line with the demands of the curricula and the needs of the students;
- To make books, journals and other materials freely accessible in order to provide reference and bibliographical tools essential to independent study;
- To stimulate the student's curiosity in using the library as an investigating center for satisfying an aroused curiosity;
- To provide an instructional program on using the library effectively;

- To locate and make available less commonly used materials not in the institute library;
- To encourage lifelong education through the use of books and materials;
- To work cooperatively and constructively with the instructional and administrative staffs of the institute.

Library, College of the Desert

The library's collection of books, periodicals, and other materials should be so constituted as to support the full educational program of the college.

1. The collection should meet the full curricular needs of undergraduate students.
2. The collection should provide the resources necessary for keeping faculty members abreast of current developments in their fields and aid them in making such original contributions to their disciplines as are in keeping with the purposes of the college.
3. The collection should include standard works in attractive format and scholarly editions representing the heritage of world civilizations.
4. The collection should include a wide variety of the better books being currently published in all fields of knowledge to the end that students will have the opportunity to gain a well-rounded reading experience.
5. The collection should include the standard reference works and bibliographies in all major fields of knowledge.
6. The collection should include materials related to the historical development of the college and the area which it serves.
7. The collection should include special holdings dealing with selected facets of desert life in addition to other special collections.
8. Preference in selection should be given materials listed in authoritative bibliographies or indexes, or in scholarly journals in the several fields of knowledge.

Learning Resources Center, Eastfield College

All materials acquired by the Learning Resources Center should reflect resource needs of Eastfield College. This underlying principle will determine such basic matters as type, quantity and scope of resources to be acquired. In general, the resource needs of the college should reflect one or more of the following:

1. Curriculum support;
2. General information;
3. General or special professional growth;
4. Cultural enrichment;
5. Extracurricular interests.

Learning Resources Center,
Catonsville Community College

Many diverse elements contribute to the quality of instruction and to the development of students in the two-year college. No one of these is dominant or isolated from the others. Faculty, students, teaching methods, facilities, resources and educational philosophy each play a significant role in the educational achievement of the institution.

Education is more than exposure through lectures and rote learning to the knowledge, ideas and values current in society; education is a preparation for resolving the range of problems continuously encountered in living and in pursuing an occupation. The student must be able to explore fields of knowledge which will enhance his potential and be relevant to him. The means of exploration include active participation in the classroom, self-directed study and the use of individualized instructional resources. Trained professional assistance is necessary to help him find and interpret the print and nonprint materials which relate to his individual needs and which are adapted to his level of skills and abilities.

The instructor's success in guiding the student in exploration of knowledge depends heavily on access to materials. The widest possible variety of print and nonprint materials is necessary to meet our institutional objectives.

The role of the Learning Resources Center is fourfold:

1. To provide an organized and readily accessible collection of print and nonprint materials and supportive equipment needed to meet institutional, instructional and individual needs of students and faculty;
2. To provide a qualified, concerned staff involved in serving the needs of students, faculty and community;
3. To encourage innovation, learning and community service by providing facilities and resources which will make these possible;
4. To provide leadership and assistance in the development of instructional systems which employ effective and efficient means of accomplishing these objectives.

Selection

The Free Library of Philadelphia

RESPONSIBILITIES FOR SELECTION OF LIBRARY MATERIALS

The Board of Trustees in its bylaws has delegated responsibility for "the selection and purchase of all books, periodicals, newspapers, maps, manuscripts and other material for acquisition" to the director subject to the objectives and policies stated herein. In order to implement the selection policy, the director may establish such procedures for the examination and review of library materials as are necessary.

FACTORS INFLUENCING SELECTION

The chief factors considered in recommending library materials for purchase are:

1. Authoritativeness of publisher or producer;
2. Significance of subject matter;
3. Importance of author or filmmaker;
4. Accuracy of information and data;
5. Literary merit or artistic quality;
6. Potential or known use by patrons;
7. Importance to total collections;
8. Appearance of the title in important bibliographies, lists and recognized reviewing media;
9. Current and/or permanent values;
10. Scarcity of materials on the subject;
11. Availability of material elsewhere in the region;
12. Price;
13. Format.

THE IMPORTANCE OF THE BOOK REVIEW

Book reviews, both staff and commercial, play an important role in the book selection process at the Free Library of Philadelphia.

The Central Library can afford only a small proportion of the thousands of books published each year. Branches, in turn, can afford but a small proportion of the books acquired by the Central Library. It is therefore vital that the Free Library select those books which serve its needs to the maximum.

The key to good book selection is the review. All staff members who select books cannot possibly read all the books published every year, and, consequently, must rely on reviews. The quality of their selection is often only as good as the quality of the reviews they consult.

The Free Library uses three basic types of reviews: those written by Free Library staff members; those appearing in the published reviewing media; and those which the Office of Work with Adults and Young Adults book selection staff prepares by combining excerpts from published reviews with its own brief evaluations.

STAFF REVIEWS

Staff reviews are necessary for the following reasons:

1. Professional evaluation is essential to analyze the style and content of the book, and to relate the particular title to the Free Library's policies, the community, and other titles in the collection.
2. Commercial reviews are not always discerning. They may be slanted by the reviewer or editorial policy of the periodical in which they are published. They often appear too long after a book's publication date to be of practical value. Many books never receive reviews in the media at all.
3. Controversial materials require staff evaluation so that when a book selection decision is challenged by the public, it can be effectively defended. The fact that the Free Library takes sufficient care to have one or more staff members read and evaluate a book before it is purchased reassures many readers.
4. Staff reviewing is regarded as an important part of staff development. Both the quality and quantity of a staff member's reviews are considered when performance evaluations are prepared.

The staff review is used for:

1. Most fiction titles;
2. All new general trade books for which no adequate commercial reviews are available;
3. All new general trade books about which commercial reviews express opinions which are unclear or conflicting;
4. Most titles which are being considered for possible addition to young adult collections;
5. Controversial books. The object of the Free Library is not to withhold controversial books from the public, but the library must be prepared to defend its decisions in the face of community reaction. The reasoned and articulate staff review is one of the most effective defenses at its command.

COMMERCIAL REVIEWS

Commercial reviews are useful for the following reasons:

1. When commercial reviewers possess critical judgment as well as specialized knowledge not available on the staff their comments are invaluable. For example, a professor of physics can judge a book on nuclear energy

better than most librarians, and an experienced trial lawyer will usually be a better judge of books on criminal law.

2. Commercial reviews can often expedite the book selection process. There is insufficient time for the staff to review all books. Commercial reviews must be used if an unmanageable backlog is to be avoided.

Commercial reviews are used for:

1. Books of obvious quality for which there is a known demand and for which adequate commercial reviews are available, e.g., novels by popular authors of established reputation; biographies and autobiographies of personalities for whom there is strong public interest; instructional books, especially those in the fields of science and technology; and a variety of other kinds of books which have favorable commercial reviews and will be useful in branch collections;

2. Books which branches have already selected on the McNaughton Plan. Because McNaughton selections must be made quickly, the McNaughton Committee each month selects approximately 30 titles for branch consideration without benefit of staff review. Later when review copies of these titles arrive in the new book room to be considered for purchase, it is usually pointless to obtain staff reviews of books which are already circulating from agencies which subscribe to the McNaughton Plan. Therefore, in most instances, staff reviews are not obtained for these titles. They are offered with the same commercial reviews which were used when considering them for McNaughton selection and any other worthwhile reviews which have appeared subsequently. An exception is made in the case of titles of doubtful quality which are removed from consideration by the McNaughton Committee before offering the monthly McNaughton lists to agencies for selection. These receive staff reviews.

NEW BOOK ROOM REVIEWS

This category of review is midway between a staff and a commercial review. It usually consists of short extracts from one or more commercial reviews, frequently with some editorial comment added by the new book room staff. This type of review is used for books whose commercial reviews are so extensive that librarians visiting the new book room cannot be expected to scan them in the time they have available. It is also used to bring out the variety of critical opinion that often exists about the quality of a specific book.

Reviews are not required for:

1. Books which are offered "Central Only" because their content is too specialized for extension agencies;

2. New editions and reprints of books suitable for branches which have already been reviewed in a previous edition, unless the revision is extensive;

3. Books in well-known, reliable series, previous volumes of which have already been evaluated, e.g., *Time-Life World Library*, *Sports Illustrated* guides to sports, *Fielding Travel Guides*, etc.;

4. Books with very little text whose contents are almost instantly comprehensible, e.g., *Peanuts* and other hardbound comic books, pictorial guides to national parks and other places, collections of cartoons, etc.;
5. Books submitted by vanity presses which, upon examination by the new book room professional staff, are judged to be of obviously inferior quality, and should be rejected;
6. Contract fiction which is considered inferior and rejected without review by the head of the fiction department;
7. Books received on advance order. When, in the judgment of the book selection professional staff and the Central Public Department head concerned, a forthcoming book promises to be of high quality and enjoy a strong demand, it can be offered for purchase in advance of publication. The adoption of the McNaughton Plan has greatly reduced the necessity for the advance order but from time to time, special circumstances make it a device worth using. Usually, advance orders are offered with publishers' announcements only, because those are the only descriptions of the books available that far ahead of publication date.

Vigo County Public Library

The committee marking selection tools for initiating orders consists of the reference senior librarians, the public service librarians and the department coordinators. Each librarian has an assigned selection subject area.

All selection librarians can initiate an order for consideration by placing title, author, price, publisher and a review on a consideration card and sending it to the reference clerk who will place it in the consideration file.

THE SELECTION CRITERIA

Many factors must be taken into consideration by librarians in the choosing of materials. The librarian, unlike the machinist, does not have a "go-no-go" gauge against which items under consideration can be tested. Neither is it a question of "good-bad" or "right-wrong"; rather, selection is a complex, time-consuming process that brings into use all of the librarian's skill, experience, education and knowledge. Because of the multiplicity of factors which bear on each decision, the final judgment to purchase or not to purchase is determined through group deliberation.

The criteria for selection include accuracy, authoritativeness, objectivity, author or artist's reputation, publisher or producer's standing, price, format, degree of need for the material, suitability to local standards and relevancy to the life of the community.

Also taken into consideration are requests from patrons and the availability of material in other libraries in Vigo County. (A "Directory of Libraries and Information Resources in Vigo County" is published annually by the library.)

The priority of items selected for purchase is 1) those meeting known needs and interests, such as "best-sellers" in both fiction and nonfiction,

2) those providing reference and research information for patron and professional use, 3) those replacements which maintain the basic collection, 4) the nonbook materials, such as magazines, newspapers, pamphlets, paperbacks, films and recordings, and 5) those purchases which are made to fill anticipated needs and interests.

In addition, priority is also given to those materials on contemporary public affairs that will be of significant value to public officials and civic leaders in the resolving of local problems.

THE REVIEWING PROCESS

Obviously the librarians of the Vigo County Public Library cannot read all of the books and other printed materials that are published, any more than they can preview all of the audio-visual and other nonprint materials. Neither could they examine, skim, view or listen to excerpts of the outpouring of the information universe even if the means were available. Moreover, only a small percentage of the librarians' time can be allotted to reviewing and selection activities.

Librarians in Vigo County, as elsewhere, select materials for purchase on the basis of reviewing done by other librarians and critics. These reviews are published in reviewing services, professional journals and magazines.

THE SELECTION AIDS

The following are typical of the many selection aids used by the Vigo County Public Library:

American Record Guide
Billboard
Book-of-the-Month Club News
Booklist and Subscription Books
 Bulletin
Bulletin of Bibliography
Bulletin of the Center for
 Children's Books
Educational Screen and Audio-
 visual Guide
Film Library Quarterly
High Fidelity
Kirkus Reviews

Library Journal
Library Occurrent
Monthly Catalog of U.S.
 Government Publications
New York Public Library New
 Technical Books
New York Review of Books
New York Times Book Review
Publishers Weekly
Saturday Review
Vertical File Index
Washington Post Book World
Wilson Library Bulletin

In addition to the above, catalogs are published annually that list the best or most popular works of previous years. These are used to check the library's holdings, particularly in subject areas:

AAAS Science Book List for
 Children
Children's Catalog
Fiction Catalog
Junior High School Library
 Catalog

Juvenile Book Fare
Standard Catalog for High School
 Libraries
Standard Catalog for Public
 Libraries

Publishers Weekly should not be used for anything but needed purchases; however, if the selector desires, but does not have to have, a title in *PW,* he/she should write the word CONSIDERATION above the review. (This will place that card in the consideration file.)

The Reviewing Procedure for Publishers Weekly

Publishers Weekly is routed on a specific routing slip attached in technical services when the magazine is checked in. This sends it to the committee for marking for order. It ends with the coordinators of public, extension and reference services.

If any one of the coordinators questions immediate purchase of a title already marked by someone on the committee, she/he marks the review CONSIDERATION. The reference clerk makes a copy of all the marked pages, cuts the consideration reviews from them, pastes the consideration reviews on cards, and files them in the consideration file on the reference desk.

All other reviews marked for order are then sent, with the issue of *PW,* to the technical services, where the reviews are pasted on the backs of the order slips' tag cards (after the orders are typed) and sent to extension to be routed to the branches, which mark those they want.

These orders come back to extension and are returned by extension to technical services, which then searches them to be sure the library does not have the title.

The technical services coordinator then calls a meeting of the four department coordinators, who go through the orders, item by item, for a final decision to purchase. Titles which are rejected at this meeting are returned to the person who originated the order. Those remaining are now placed for order by technical services.

Other reviewing journals are also routed and treated in a similar manner to *Publishers Weekly.*

Fresno County Public Library

RESPONSIBILITY FOR BOOK SELECTION

Responsibility for initial selection of adult books rests with the Book Selection Committee, which is composed of a representative group of professional staff members. Children's and young adult books are selected by professional staff who are specialists in the field. Suggestions from readers are always welcome and are given serious consideration.

The final responsibility for book selection rests with the county librarian.

CRITERIA FOR SELECTION

Each acquisition, whether purchased or donated, is considered in terms of the following standards. Clearly, however, an item need not meet all of the criteria in order to be acceptable. In general, books which are written primarily in advocacy of a specific group are not added.

General Criteria

- Insight into human and social conditions;
- Suitability of subject and style for intended audiences;
- Present and potential relevance to community needs and interests;
- Contemporary significance or permanent value;
- Relation to existing collection;
- Attention of critics, reviewers and public;
- Scarcity of information in subject area;
- Availability of material elsewhere in community (holdings of specialized libraries within this community are considered in developing the library's collection);
- Price and format.

Specific Criteria for the Evaluation of
Works of Information and Opinion

- Authority;
- Comprehensiveness and depth of treatment;
- Clarity, accuracy and logic of presentation;
- Statement of challenging or original point of view.

Specific Criteria for the Evaluation of Works of Imagination

- Representation of significant literary or social trends;
- Vitality and originality;
- Artistic presentation and experimentation;
- Authenticity of historical, regional or social setting.

Virginia Beach Public Library Department

The privilege of and responsibility for selecting books and other library materials for purchase belongs to the librarian and staff at each branch. This is based on the assumption that no one person, nor few persons, can know enough about all subjects, nor the reading needs of all people, to be qualified to assume complete responsibility for book selection. Ultimate responsibility for book selection, as for all library activities, rests in the director, who operates with the advice of the Library Board.

In selecting books for the Virginia Beach Public Library the board considers the people it serves and the general aspects of the community as a whole. Virginia Beach reflects the fusion that is America; there are different races, creeds, nations represented; it contains contrasts of taste, opinion, education.

To serve a city of this variety in which the politician, scientist, industrialist, housewife, senior citizen, kindergartner and sportsperson meet each other at the library, there must be a collection of books broad in subject, comprehensive in viewpoint, with wide latitude in reading levels. There must be books for the reader's serious study and books which will satisfy personal needs for recreation and leisure.

St. Albans Free Library (Vermont Library Association)

The librarian utilizes professional judgment and expertise, based on understanding of community needs and knowledge of authors and publishers, in the process of selecting materials, and is aided by authoritative professional reviews, standard lists of basic works, recommendations of professional journals and bibliographic essays prepared by subject specialists.

Recommendations from the public are welcomed and will be given careful consideration in terms of overall objectives and the existing book collection.

All materials acquired should meet high standards of quality in content, expression and form. Factors to be considered in evaluating an item include: factual accuracy and authoritativeness, effective expression, significance of subject, sincerity and responsibility of opinion, current usefulness, interest, or permanent value. Relevance to the constituency and to the existing collection is of utmost importance.

Ontario Public Library

Initial responsibility for purchase suggestion lies with professional staff members. Each professional staff member is expected to read at least one standard book reviewing periodical from which recommendations for purchase are made. *Virginia Kirkus Book Review Service, Publishers Weekly, Library Journal* and *Paperbound Books in Print* are the primary book review periodicals used. Any other book review media may be used, such as *Time Magazine, New York Times,* etc.

RESPONSIBILITY FOR SELECTION

Final responsibility for book selection, as for all library activities, rests with the librarian who administers under the authority of the Board of Trustees. Most orders for materials are originated by heads of the main library departments. The selection of children's books and young adults' books is handled under the guidance of the supervisors of library service to those age groups. Many staff members participate in the selection of adult and juvenile books by reading and evaluating them. Suggestions for purchase are encouraged from the general public and the staff and are given serious consideration.

CRITERIA FOR SELECTION

Recognizing the many educational and recreational needs of the individual, as well as the needs of the community, the library staff considers the following criteria to be of importance in selecting books:

- Authority of the author;
- Timeliness and importance for contemporary society;

- Accuracy, presentation of subject, viewpoint of author;
- Readability, literary merit, organization of material;
- Reputation of the publisher;
- Suitable physical format—size, paper, print, binding;
- Price;
- Community needs and demands;
- Representation of various interests and viewpoints;
- Relationship to other material in collection;
- Availability in other local libraries;
- Permanent value to the collection.

The Public Library of Cincinnati and Hamilton County

ART

Material in the fine and applied arts is geared to the needs of the professional, the student and the amateur. While the aesthetic value of expensive, handsomely illustrated volumes is not overlooked for their visual value, serious consideration is given to obtaining the most authoritative and informative texts written by well-known art historians.

Cartoon drawings are purchased when they are of interest to the historian or have social significance reflecting the times.

CIVIL SERVICE

A large collection of study manuals for civil service examinations is maintained for those preparing for the tests; a reasonable attempt is made to meet demand for these manuals.

ECONOMICS

Besides books on economic theory and the various schools of economic thought, the library provides a broad range of materials dealing with labor problems, money and banking, investments, public finance and real estate. Writings of classic and contemporary economists are well-represented in the library's holdings. Our system of free enterprise is of prime importance, but other methods of economic production such as collective and cooperative systems are presented. The library has three primary aims in the field of economics:

1. To provide in-depth information for the business leaders of the community on financial institutions and investments, as well as for the small private investor;
2. To provide information for labor and management on mediation and arbitration, wages and hours, and fair employment practices;
3. To provide supplementary research materials for students of business administration.

EDUCATION

In the field of education the aim is to provide a well-selected collection of professional reading on topics of current and historical significance. The primary emphasis is upon American public education in its many aspects, including new educational trends and movements, developments in curriculum-making, experiments in teaching methods and discoveries in educational psychology.

The library emphasizes in its buying the literature meant for parents so that they may help their children in school and also better understand new teaching methods and educational trends such as the field of special education, i.e., work with the handicapped, retarded, gifted, etc.

FOREIGN LANGUAGE MATERIAL

Material in foreign languages is acquired so that students and others may read important works in the original language. The library also buys reference material, such as biographical dictionaries, trade directories and encyclopedias. The library provides books for the foreign-born and multilingual adult. Because of the many Germans who settled in Hamilton County, the library has an important collection of 19th-century German books and periodicals.

LAW

One major consideration in the library's policy in the selection of law materials is the availability of such materials in the Hamilton County Law Library.

The library purchases popular and standard books for the general reader and for those patrons active in state and municipal affairs. With emphasis on Ohio law, the library provides standard texts by recognized authorities on aspects of law such as corporation law and domestic relations. Legal dictionaries, encyclopedias and phrase books are purchased for general reference work.

In the area of statutory law, the library makes available the *United States Code,* the *United States Statutes at Large,* bills and slip laws of the current Congress, the *Code of Ordinances of the City of Cincinnati,* the statutes and codes of the three states in our metropolitan area and law digests of other states.

For case law, the *United States Reports* and *Ohio Reports* are made available. Few other reporting services are purchased. Case books which are generally used as texts by law students are not purchased.

The library occasionally purchases such encyclopedic sets as *American Law Reports, Ohio Jurisprudence* and *Corpus Juris Secundum.*

LOCAL HISTORY AND GENEALOGY

Since the beginning of the library, a strong collection of local history material has been a major objective. In fact, all published material on Cincinnati and vicinity is sought. Since the Cincinnati Historical Society collects manuscripts about Cincinnati, the library makes no effort to acquire this type of material.

This library has one of the larger collections of genealogy and heraldry in the country and acquires almost everything published in the field. The key to this collection lies in the library's own comprehensive genealogy index.

In both genealogy and local history the main emphasis is on the area east of the Mississippi River.

MEDICINE AND RELATED SUBJECTS

The library buys few books in the fields of medicine and dentistry. It is assumed that the needs of members and students of these professions will be served by the University of Cincinnati Medical Library or the General Hospital Library.

It is the library policy to buy for the general reader and high school and college student a representative number of basic texts in such sciences as anatomy, physiology, bacteriology and physiological chemistry. The library does not usually purchase clinical texts on diagnosis and treatment of disease, or textbooks on medicine, surgery or dentistry for students or members of the medical and dental professions. The library buys extensively in the fields of food and nutrition. Books on food and health fads are excluded unless authoritative reviews favor purchase. The needs of both registered and practical nurses are met by the purchase of texts, reviews and practice examination questions.

Standard drug and medical formularies, medical dictionaries and encyclopedias are obtained for reference use. Basic veterinary texts are acquired as well as authoritative books on the diseases of domestic and farm animals.

In the health alcove the library provides popular books and pamphlets recommended by health agencies of the city in such fields as personal hygiene, community health, mental retardation, heart disease and diabetes.

NARCOTICS AND OTHER DRUGS

The library provides accurate, up-to-date materials on the physiological and psychological effects of drugs and their use, as well as the dangers of drug abuse. It seeks to avoid sensational books which glorify the use of drugs.

MUSIC

The library serves the needs of music lovers, amateur performers, professional researchers, musicians, students and the general reader. Purchase is dictated by requests, knowledge of musical activities in the community and the requirements of a well-rounded collection, reflecting academic interests as well as general cultural trends.

Gifts of private music collections of representative classical works not in the cataloged collection make possible the buying of contemporary works by established composers and those works which are being currently performed in Cincinnati. Sheet music, both popular and classical, is ordered as well as study scores, chamber music works, operas, instrumental and vocal music. Books in all fields of music are bought for circulation and reference use.

POLITICAL SCIENCE

Broadly interpreted, political science is that science which deals with the institutions and processes of governmental regulation of men living in society. This includes types and forms of governments, suffrage, slavery and international relations. In addition to supplying standard works, the library purchases materials which show the foundation of our government and the ways of further developing it. The library does not acquire those books which contain undocumented accusations, which deliberately attempt to misrepresent and mislead, or which present biased attacks on the American way of life. However, in a library the size of the Public Library of Cincinnati and Hamilton County some examples of unsound and anti-social works are preserved for the use of scholars, who need to examine varying viewpoints if they are to appraise the confusing age in which we live.

PSYCHOLOGY AND PSYCHIATRY

In psychology and psychiatry it is necessary to keep a balance between the more advanced literature for the student and the professional person and general books for the lay citizen. Materials on child psychology and applied psychology have become increasingly important for readers of all educational backgrounds, and it seems important to duplicate heavily. Selection is based on reputation and authority of the author and publisher and authoritative reviews. Although the needs of professional workers are considered, it is felt that technical material for the doctor or advanced student will, in most cases, be supplied by a university or medical library.

PSEUDOSCIENTIFIC AND OCCULT MATERIALS

In the fields of pseudoscience and pseudopsychology, such as phrenology, graphology, astrology, telepathy, spiritualism and the occult, representative books to provide information for the general reader are purchased. Care is taken to avoid the sensational, poorly written and completely unsound. Serious works on parapsychology, psychic research and hypnotism which meet our general standards of selection are purchased.

RELIGION

In the literature of religion, perhaps more than in any other field, library selection must be broad, tolerant and without partisanship, yet consistently directed toward choosing the best books in regard to authority, timeliness and good literary quality. Careful selection is required because of the tremendous output of writing in this field, as well as the tensions often surrounding religious subjects.

The collection contains standard works of important world religions such as the *Talmud,* the Bible in many languages and versions, the *Summa Theologica,* the *Koran,* writings of the church fathers, Calvin, Luther and others. There is a reference collection of standard works such as encyclopedias, concordances, commentaries, dictionaries, histories and directories.

A wide selection of well-written and objective books on comparative religion, Biblical history and interpretation, church history, religious education, church administration, sermons and inspirational reading is provided for readers of various religious and educational backgrounds.

The library provides accurate and objective information on beliefs and practices of various religious denominations and sects through their official publications, directories, periodicals and histories. Denominational periodicals of many local groups are received as gifts. A particular effort is made to supply information on the larger local denominations and groups. However, there is no attempt to duplicate special collections such as those at Hebrew Union College or Xavier University.

SEX

The library strives to purchase only accurate, scientific and up-to-date books in this field for readers of all ages and varying backgrounds. Some of the areas covered are sex education for both parents and young adults, marriage manuals and family planning. Some books on sexual deviations are purchased for the use of social workers, teachers, ministers and persons in related fields.

Rensselaer Public Library

The Board of Trustees has adopted the following policies in regard to book selection. Ultimate responsibility for book selection, as for all library activities, rests with the librarian, who operates within the framework of these policies, established by the Board of Trustees.

Criteria for the selection of factual works are:

1. Authoritativeness;
2. Clarity and readability;
3. Importance of the subject matter to the collection;
4. Timelessness or permanence of the materials;
5. Accessability to the title through indexes and bibliographies;
6. Price;
7. Literary quality;
8. Physical format;
9. Potential usefulness;
10. Reputation and significance of the author;
11. Reputation and standards of the publisher;
12. Availability of materials elsewhere in the region.

In selecting fiction, the library has set up no arbitrary single standard of literary quality. The library does seek out fiction according to the following criteria:

1. Writing of acceptable literary quality;
2. Authentic portrayal of human experience;
3. Characterization and plot that are well-developed;
4. Characterization and language that are essential to the whole;
5. Cost;

6. Potential use;
7. Readability;
8. The durability of the author.

The ultimate aim of library work with young adults is to contribute to the development of well-rounded citizens with an understanding of themselves, of others and of the world around them. For this reason works of nonfiction for young adults are not separated from works of nonfiction for adults.

The objectives in the selection of books for children is to make available a collection that satisfies the informational, recreational and cultural needs and potentials of children through print and nonprint materials. The children's collection is designed for preschool age through twelve years of age.

Rolling Prairie Libraries

RESPONSIBILITY FOR BOOK SELECTION

The ultimate responsibility for selection of materials designed to build strong, usable and well-balanced collections, which are geared to the service objectives of the library system, rests with the director and assistant director of Rolling Prairie Libraries. Operating within the framework of policies and objectives determined by the Rolling Prairie Libraries Board, the selection of library materials, including books, periodicals, records, films, pictures, pamphlets, etc., shall be the primary task of the professional librarians assigned to the headquarters staff. The selection of library materials for the member libraries shall be the primary task of the person in charge of the administration of the member library.

POLICIES GUIDING THE SELECTION OF LIBRARY MATERIALS

General Statement

The selection of library material is based on several important factors that determine its value to the collection. These factors are:

Demand.   Any service institution must include demand among its criteria when considering acquisitions. This demand may be voided in any one of several ways by the member libraries' users, or it may flow from a special emphasis on subject areas and materials needed by libraries in the system.

Value.   Of equal importance in serving system users are various quality criteria: relevance, authority, reliability, literary excellence and other inherent qualities in the materials considered for acquisition.

Format.   The system shall collect and preserve material in any form, i.e., print, tape, microform, film, etc., as best meets the service obligations and operational facilities of member libraries. The same philosophy and standards of selection which apply to books apply to the selection of other materials.

Reviews.   Reviews in professional journals shall be used as an aid in the selection or decision process and shall be sought wherever possible, but the lack of a review or an unfavorable review shall not be the sole reason for not selecting a title that is in demand.

Specific Guidelines–Books

Criteria for selection of nonfiction:

1. Qualification of the author in subject field;
2. Scope and authority of subject matter;
3. Quality of writing (style, readability);
4. Date of publication;
5. Reputation of publisher;
6. Arrangement of materials (indexes, bibliographies);
7. Relationship to collection;
8. Physical qualities (binding, print, size, illustrations, margins);
9. Price.

Criteria for selection of fiction:

1. Style;
2. Appeal: popular, limited;
3. Characterization: constructive and true portrayal of character and life;
4. Literary merit;
5. Relationship to the collection, i.e., types: mystery, western, fantasy, science fiction, romance;
6. Publisher;
7. Price.

Techniques and Selection Aids

Standard selection aids for current fiction and nonfiction:

- *Library Journal;*
- *Booklist;*
- *The New York Times Book Review;*
- *Kirkus;*
- *Publishers Weekly;*
- *Choice;*
- *AAAS Science Books;*
- *Wilson Library Bulletin.*

Other sources are used. Bibliographies and lists prepared by various libraries and subject authorities are checked.

Techniques and Selection Aids for Materials Other Than Books

1. Pamphlets
   - *Vertical File Index;*
   - *Publications of the State of Illinois;*
   - *Booklist;*
   - *Selected U.S. Government Publications;*
   - List of government publications selected for high school and public libraries.

2. Periodicals
   - *Reader's Guide to Periodical Literature;*
   - *Library Literature.*

SELECTION

3. Audio-visual materials
- *Films.* Films supplied by reliable producers are previewed for addition to the collection. Professional reviewing sources such as *Previews* serve as a guide to films selected for previewing. Interested librarians in the area may be asked to participate in the selection process from time to time.
- *Recordings.* Reviewing sources are as follows:
  Library Journal
  Booklist
  Bro-Dart's Listening Post

Mansfield Public Library

Responsibility for selection of library materials rests with the director, who administers policies adopted by the Board of Trustees. Initial selection of materials may be delegated by the director to staff members qualified by training or experience.

Whitehall Public Library

The Whitehall Public Library has been established to provide library service for all residents of Whitehall Borough. The Library Board of Trustees will seek to make this service as comprehensive as possible within the framework of the funds available for library purposes.

The library will provide material for reference, for education and for recreation. The needs of the community will be the primary factor in the choice of books and other materials.

All subject areas will be considered in the selection of nonfiction. Quality always will be stressed. The best available books will be selected on the basis of reviews, criticisms and reputation of writers, personal examination by the librarian and reliable recommendations. To avoid duplication of material available in the schools, textbooks will not be purchased unless they are the best source of information.

Every effort will be made to present both sides of any controversial issue. The selection or rejection of any book will not be based on religious, political, racial or moral bias of a person or group, staff or public.

The selection of fiction will be based on at least two favorable reviews in reliable reviewing magazines, or listings in standard bibliographies such as *Wilson's Catalogue, The American Library Association* and others.

Emphasis will be placed on the continuous enlargement of the collection of classics, semiclassics and standard works. Sensationalism for its own sake will be rejected. Only exceptional mystery, detective or western stories will be purchased.

Any disputed book, unless an obvious and admitted error in selection was made, will not be removed from the shelves because of a complaint, except by a majority vote of the Board of Trustees. Such a vote for removal will be taken only after a full discussion of both sides of the matter has been heard by the Board.

Suggestions for improvement of the service and the book selection will be welcomed at all times.

Gifts of books will be accepted only with the explicit understanding that the library may dispose of them at its discretion.

The Baltimore County Public Library

CRITERIA OF SELECTION

No item in a library collection can be indisputably accepted or rejected by any established given guide or standard. However, certain basic principles can be applied as guidelines. Every item must meet such of the following criteria as are applicable to its inclusion in the collection:

1. The degree and accomplishment of purpose;
2. Authority and competency of the author, composer, filmmaker, etc.;
3. Comprehensiveness in breadth and scope;
4. Sincerity and fundamental objectivity;
5. Clarity and accuracy of presentation;
6. Appropriateness to the interests and skills of the intended users;
7. Relation to existing collections;
8. Relative importance in comparison with other materials on the subject;
9. Importance as a record of the times for present and future use.

CENTRAL SELECTION OF ADULT HARDBACK MATERIALS

There are three primary ways the selector will choose adult hardbacks: the subject area formula; the author list; and the popular category formula. Explanation of these follow.

Author List for Central Selection

The author list for centralized selection has been amended to represent those authors of fiction and nonfiction who are identifiably popular and are regularly purchased by a majority of branches.

The list is very large, as it must be, since it is unlikely that all of these authors will produce a book in one year. It can therefore make a large enough dent in book selection to save staff time and decrease the time between publishing date and order date.

Ordering will be done with professional reviews and/or an approval copy. Being listed does not mean that each and every author or title will be bought automatically. Obviously special or esoteric works would not be included. Much of the ordering will be done using the judgment of the selector. The list is intended to identify authors for the benefit of the selector so that branches will continue to receive the types of books they frequently order now.

Popular Category Formula

The Baltimore County Public Library also uses formulas for various categories of popular fiction and nonfiction. This is both a re-evaluation of past pre-pub formula and the inclusion of newly centralized purchasing. Branches of like circulation have been placed in five groups. For each category there is an average figure or a high and a low figure. Like the nonfiction subject area formula, these figures are guidelines for the selector and the number of copies ordered of a title will vary slightly with the quality of the book. The high and low figures are what the library would receive no more than or no less than. The actual order figures will range between them depending on whether the book is a best-seller candidate, an average title or somewhere in between.

This means that the terminology "pre-pub" is being replaced in BCPL by the phrase "central selection" since it includes so much more than previously. It is hoped that many more books than before will be ordered close to or before publication date to insure receiving them quickly. But not all titles will be ordered in this way since Greenaway and approval copies will also be utilized, and not all titles will be ordered in best-seller quantities. This concept is different from pre-pubs as we have known them and should be thought of in different terms.

Subject Area Selection and Formula

Another method to be used in the central selection of materials is the subject area formulas for 44 subject areas. Reproduced here is an example of one of the subject area formula cards to be used by the materials selector.

AUTHOR   Y (A) J

TITLE   Children — Care and Hygiene

| | | DATE | | PRICE |
PUB.   ED.   REC'D.

NO. OF COPIES

ORD.

Lib.	No.	Lib.	No.	Lib.	No.	Lib.	No.
BCR		Ga		Pi	2	Wo	
Ar	2	Ln	1	Ra	8	MM	
Ca	5	LR	3	Rn	3		
Cy	3	NP	3	Ros	3		
Du		Pa	4	To	8		
Es	4	PH	1	TS			

It is felt that the subject areas are broad enough to allow a large number of the titles purchased to fall into one of them. In each subject area the individual branch has the number of copies marked. This formula is to be used by the materials selector to allocate copies to each branch. The number is a guide, not an absolute, and the number of copies purchased may be higher or lower, depending on the merit of the particular title being purchased. In some cases individual branches may not receive any copies at all. If the number of copies a branch receives in a subject area is consistently too high or too low, the materials selection office should be informed so that a change can be made.

YOUNG ADULT SERVICE IN BALTIMORE COUNTY

Young adult work in the public library, as with other services, is essentially educational and recreational. The educational function is fulfilled through reference work and programming. The recreational function is fulfilled through the young adult collection which has a high percentage of leisure reading, and—again—through programming.

The young adult program should offer guidance through all the forms of communications which the library offers. The program should at all times be a part of total library service. It is planned for the average teenager who feels out of place in a children's room, and, on the other hand, is confused by the size of the adult collection. A young adult section is intended to bring the teenager to the adult reading world.

The program for teenage readers (age 13 up or 8th through 12th grades) is directed by the Coordinator of Adult Services who serves as chairman of a Young Adult Services Committee.

Staff Suggestions

A staff member in each agency interested in working with young people, getting to know them, their interests and disinterests is extremely important. It is true that all librarians work with patrons. However, having a staff member with a special empathy for young adults, who enjoys getting to know them as individuals and who enjoys talking to them about the media which interests them, books, films, records, etc., adds a special touch to library service as a whole and to the young adult library users.

In area branches the staff member who is doing young adult work should also be available to help community branches in booktalking and other outside programming for teenagers. This should not entail additional staff, but does entail understanding and careful scheduling and planning on the part of staff in each agency.

Staff doing young adult work should have scheduled time to investigate and visit agencies in the surrounding communities working with teenagers. This would make staff aware of what is being done for teenagers in the community, would eliminate duplication of programming effort, and would help staff see what the library can be doing with young adults. Cooperative programming between agencies might also be a result of this visiting.

Staff transfers should take into account the interest of the staff member doing young adult work. If the staff member wants to continue doing this work then sending the staff member to a branch with a young adult librarian already assigned would be self-defeating, if the branch from which the transfer is made is left without a young adult librarian.

Young adult services should be an integral part of the recruitment of adult services staff. With promotions of staff comes more responsibility; however, it is possible to continue to do young adult work.

The need to have understanding and encouragement from total adult staff and the administration to do young adult work as a part of the total library service is important. In-service training programs and attendance at workshops, conferences, etc., under the sponsorship of other libraries or associations would aid staff in developing readers advisory and programming skills which would benefit them as well as the patrons and the library system as a whole.

It is important for staff members working with young adults to have a varied experience in the branches as this contributes to individual growth and the efficiency of the branch. It is recommended that at least 25 percent of work time be spent in young adult work. This time may be used for reading reviews, evaluating books, collection maintenance, program planning and implementation, meetings or indirect readers service.

Programming Development

Young adults, like adults, have varied interests as well as "sudden" interests. Programming should be spontaneous and immediate as much as possible. The interests and involvement of young people contribute greatly to the success of any program. It should be the responsibility of both the Coordinator of Adult Services and the staff working with young adults to be aware of these interests and plan programs around them.

Ideas for the program may come from:

• Youth advisory groups or other discussion groups;
• Cooperative efforts with agencies in the community who work with young people;
• Other staff members.

Programming should take into account the use of the nonprint media other than just films. The possibilities of multimedia both in the branch and outside of it need further examination. Experimental programming aids in spontaneity.

Emphasis is needed on quality of programming, not quantity. Numbers in attendance should not always be expected to be in the hundreds. It should be understood by staff that branches serve large communities and that one program will not necessarily fulfill the needs or interests of the entire community. Library programming should not attempt to compete with outside agencies.

Cooperation with the Schools

Cooperation with schools should continue whenever possible in the form of fulfilling requests for class tours in library, preparing special bibliographies, or booktalks.

Book Collections and Selection

The book collections for young adult titles are set in a basic ratio of 80 percent of the collection from adult titles and 20 percent from teenage and children's titles.

Initial selection will be done by the Coordinator of Adult Services and the Young Adult Committee from the reviewing media and adult book selection. Staff in addition to the Young Adult Committee are also encouraged to make suggestions. Any book that is reviewed in the media as recommended for grades 7 through 9 and having earmarks of a juvenile book will be kept in the juvenile collection. Format, maturity of concepts and focus are factors in this decision. A few books will find a place both in the children's department and the young adult section. The ultimate decision is a joint one between the Children's Coordinator and the Adult Coordinator. Books reviewed for grades 8 through 12 will generally be found in the adult collection, unless little else is available on the subject at a lower level. Titles will be sent out for review to the staff and the young adult book selection will be in the book selection room for a month.

The book budget for the young adult section is a part of the adult book budget and will depend upon the size of the branch and of the young adult collection. It should be determined in consultation between the branch librarian and the young adult librarian. If necessary the Coordinator of Adult Services should participate in the decision on young adult budget.

The collection should be attractive and continually weeded for titles which are not circulating.

Camden County Free Library

GUIDELINES FOR SELECTION

The library takes cognizance of the purposes and resources of other libraries in the state, and shall not needlessly duplicate functions and materials. (The library shall, however, cooperate with other libraries in the exchange of materials according to the Interlibrary Loan Code of the American Library Association.)

The library does not attempt to acquire textbooks or other curriculum-related materials except as such materials also serve the general public.

Legal and medical works will be acquired only to the extent that they are useful to the lay citizen.

The library acknowledges a particular interest in local and state history. It will therefore take a broad view of works by and about New Jersey authors as well as general works relating to the state of New Jersey, whether or not such materials meet the standards of selection in other respects. However, the library is not under any obligation to add to its collection everything about New Jersey or produced by authors, printers or publishers with New Jersey connections, if it does not seem in the public interest to do so.

Because the library serves a public embracing a wide range of ages, educational backgrounds and reading skills, it will always seek to select materials of varying complexity.

In selecting books for the collections, the library will pay due regard to the special, commercial, industrial, cultural and civic enterprises of the community.

The County Library will continue to assist in building book collections in the public library which we now serve. Our relationship to the schools and school libraries will be to service them to the best of our abilities from our current stock.

Publishers Weekly, Kirkus and *Library Journal* are used for current acquisition. Staff members are urged to read journals in their own subject areas for additional material.

Reviews

The entire professional staff is involved in the book selection process. Each reviewer develops a particular area of knowledge using standard review sources and professional journals in her/his specific field.

1. *Publishers Weekly.* The fiction section is sent to the adult services librarian in reader's services and extension. The supervising librarian in extension and the library director does the nonfiction section and sends the periodical to the supervising librarian in reader's services. She/he checks the entire review section and sends it to processing for ordering.

2. *Kirkus.* The procedure used for *Publishers Weekly* is also utilized for this review source.

3. *Library Journal.* Using *Library Journal* reviews on cards, the cards are sent to professional staff members who have been assigned a subject area. Next, the reviews are sent to the supervising librarian in extension. Then, the supervising librarian in reader's services checks the reviews and submits them for ordering.

Lists

The Newark Public Library acquisition lists as well as the Free Public Library of Philadelphia lists are examined by staff members and submitted to the supervising librarian in reader's services, and appropriate titles are ordered.

Questions

Questions received from patrons by the reader's advisor and reference department often lead to further acquisition. Lists of topics from questions are sent to staff members on a monthly basis. Suggested additions to the collection are sent to the supervising librarian in reader's services for checking. Orders are sent to the processing department.

PROCEDURES FOR SELECTING CHILDREN'S MATERIALS

Requests

If the children's department does not have a book that has been requested, it is not automatically ordered. Reviews are checked whenever possible; the decision to purchase is made by the children's librarian.

Reviewing Sources and Lists

1. *Kirkus;*
2. *Bulletin of the Center for Children's Books*—reliable, highly selective;
3. *Horn Book;*
4. *New York Times;*
5. *School Library Journal*—reviews are not as selective as review media listed above so purchase books reviewed in *SLJ* with caution;
6. *Free Library of Philadelphia Book Review Lists*—monthly.

    Prepared by book review committee. Use these lists as a guideline for preparing the *Monthly Book Buying Guide for Member Libraries.* However, the reviews are not very selective so *Kirkus* is checked for all books considered for the *Book Buying Guide.* This gives us a good chance to reconsider books not originally purchased for purchase.

    Advantage—you get to see the actual book as the books are set up for reviewing in the Office of Work with Children. You must make appointments for visiting—usually made over a six month period, one visit per month;
7. Selective lists published by different educational and scientific organizations and libraries.

Seattle Public Library

Expanding areas of knowledge, changing social values, technological advances and cultural differences require flexibility, open-mindedness and responsiveness in the evaluation of all new and old library materials. Materials in a variety of media are acquired and made accessible as they are judged useful and relevant to the community.

Each type of material must be considered in terms of its own excellence and the audience for which it is intended. There is no single standard which can be applied in all cases. Some materials are judged primarily in terms of artistic merit, scholarship or documentation of the times; others are selected to satisfy the recreational and entertainment needs of the community.

Some materials are considered because of widespread or heavy local demand. Items having such demand may or may not meet the general and specific criteria contained in this policy. In either case the volume and nature of requests by members of the public will be given serious consideration. In addition, as the social and intellectual climate of the community changes, materials which originally were not selected for purchase may become of interest. Such materials will be re-evaluated on a continuing basis.

Librarians responsible for selecting purchased and donated materials will be guided by those of the following criteria which are applicable.

GENERAL CRITERIA

1. Present and potential relevance to community needs;
2. Insight into human and social conditions;
3. Importance as a document of the times;

4. Originality and creativity;
5. Usefulness to intended audience;
6. Skill, competence and purpose of author;
7. Reputation or significance of author;
8. Attention of critics, reviewers and public;
9. Relation to existing collections;
10. Appropriateness and effectiveness of medium to content;
11. Suitability of physical form for library use.

SPECIFIC CRITERIA FOR THE EVALUATION OF WORKS OF INFORMATION AND OPINION

1. Comprehensiveness and depth of treatment;
2. Objectivity;
3. Accuracy;
4. Clarity and logic of presentation;
5. Representation of challenging, though extreme or unorthodox, point of view.

SPECIFIC CRITERIA FOR THE EVALUATION OF WORKS OF IMAGINATION

1. Representation of an important movement, genre, trend or culture;
2. Authenticity of historical or social setting;
3. Vitality and inspiration;
4. Artistic presentation and experimentation;
5. Effective characterization;
6. Sustained interest and entertainment.

It should be emphasized that the above criteria are guidelines. The fundamental basis of book selection must be the professional judgment of the librarian given this responsibility. At the Seattle Public Library the head of each service unit, aided by the staff, selects pertinent materials. In all instances the director of the library, with the support of the library board, has the final responsibility for selection.

North Country Library System

CENTRAL LIBRARIES; CENTRAL BOOK AID (CBA)

Our book buying program is intimately connected also with the book selection policies of the Central Libraries. In addition to the books purchased from their local book budgets, our two Central Libraries (Watertown and Ogdensburg) have had thousands of books added to their collections through the Central Book Aid (CBA) program. The books, although owned by the Service Center, are housed in the two Central Libraries. This program is financed by the state, and its purpose originally was to bring the nonfiction collections (adult nonfiction, bound periodicals and books in foreign languages) of Central Libraries up to 100,000 volumes, which was considered the minimum level for a well-rounded reference and circulating collection. The library systems were given 10 years to reach that goal and, for several years after that, received 3,000 volumes each, per year. Legislation in 1973 changed the allotment from 3,000 volumes to $34,000 per year. This program is a great boon to the two Central Libraries and to the entire region as well, since it gives depth and richness to these collections.

CBA materials are selected to meet system-wide needs by a committee consisting of representatives from the two Central Libraries and the Service Center. They select substantial works, rather than the popular literature, in the arts, humanities and sciences. The objective is to provide the serious lay citizen and the student with the works necessary to pursue a subject in considerable depth. The intent is not to acquire materials for the professional or the scholar. Such works are available on interlibrary loan through the North Country Reference and Research Resources Council.

The directors of the three institutions have agreed to limit CBA acquisitions as follows: (1) books alone are to be purchased—microfilm, periodicals, phonograph records and other library materials will be excluded; (2) limited duplication will be permitted occasionally of essential reference works and, in rare instances, of circulating materials.

The book acquisition programs of the Central Libraries affect Service Center policy in two ways. First, we do not strive to build a balanced collection; this we leave to our Central Libraries at Watertown and Ogdensburg. Second, we do not add specialized reference works; we purchase only those standard works which will assist us in quick reference for the member libraries.

INDIVIDUAL MERITS OF THE BOOKS WE BUY

Each book in a public library collection should satisfy standards of literary quality and fill a need in the collection. Most book selection policies cite a long list of criteria such as authority of author, objectivity, style, good characterization, and so on. These guidelines are important, but their item-by-item listing is not. We judge a book by its totality: how well the author has accomplished the purpose he set himself, how useful the book will be to its intended readers, and how it meets the current needs of the collection. Book selection is an art, not a science; we must make decisions based on knowledge of the patrons' needs, wide reading backgrounds and the intuitive judgment that comes from experience. Unfortunately, we cannot have the book in hand when we make our selections. We must make a judgment on the basis of reviews in reputable reviewing journals, bibliographies and standard catalogs. With this limitation, however, we select as critically and impartially as possible.

CHILDREN'S BOOKS

Books for the Service Center's children's collection are selected to add depth, variety and scope to the collections of member libraries, and to provide a pool of basic titles for those member libraries with severely limited budgets.

Since children aged 2 to 13 have not yet developed the taste for what is good in reading matter and the ability to read critically, and since they are frequently exposed to mediocrity in their daily lives, the Service Center emphasizes quality in the selection of books for them. Books are selected to arouse their interest in reading enjoyment and to provide information in the fields of knowledge which are of interest to them. They are carefully chosen for children of all ages and abilities. The emphasis is upon books which attract and stimulate children, satisfy their curiosity at all stages of development, and develop in them an appreciation of good literature.

We search constantly for new titles of lasting value and add and replace standard works in great quantities. Standard bibliographies and current reviews are used as guides.

Since children's classics should be a permanent part of every library collection, member libraries are urged to purchase copies for their own collections. Therefore, the system buys classics only in limited quantities to help libraries with limited budgets and to help meet heavy demands. We do not purchase abridgments of classics; the only exception is when the original is incomprehensible to children and when an excellent adaptation is available.

Poorly written, repetitive, unimaginative series books, which follow the same stereotyped characters through one predictable situation after another, are not selected. Textbooks are purchased only when other acceptable titles are not available on a particular subject. Since the use of controlled vocabulary often results in inaccuracies and superficiality, we buy only the very best of the easy readers. Books on sex instruction are purchased when they present accurate information and wholesome attitudes.

YOUNG ADULT BOOKS

It is when young people are in the teenage years—roughly from 13 to 17 —that a lifelong reading habit is either developed or finally discouraged. We hope to assist our member libraries in awakening young adults to the intellectual excitement and satisfaction to be found in reading.

Too often, children who have delighted in books when young are frightened away by the necessary emphasis on reading-for-information which comes in the high school years . . . "Why should I read a book *now*? It's vacation time" . . . Therefore, in book selection for this age group, we stress first of all the sheer pleasure of reading.

The majority of books selected for young adults will be adult books in fields which especially interest young people; well-written and entertaining, mind-stretching but not so difficult as to be discouraging. We hope to leaven general nonfiction with current fiction of worth; books that challenge the mind with those that are just plain fun. There will also be included a smaller percentage of "transitional" fiction (romances, sport stories, etc.) and nonfiction relating to adolescent quandaries and questions (etiquette, study techniques, careers, sex, etc.).

On whatever level and in whatever field, we will look for liveliness of approach, literate style, honesty, realism and credibility; for books which

"give lasting pleasure and also contribute to the growth and understanding
of the young people who read them."

Hamilton Public Library

OBJECTIVES OF BOOK SELECTION

. . . we must select books, periodicals, etc., with one eye on quality and
the other on the known tastes and interests of our citizens.

In subject fields we ask:

1. Is this a subject in which a sufficient number of readers are interested to
   justify purchase?
2. Is the information sound and well-presented?
3. Will this be a useful addition to the books we already have on this
   subject?

In the field of literature our aim is to have in our collection the authors
mentioned in standard literary histories—i.e., a reader should be able to find
here the books referred to as of some importance in works of criticism—and
books which reputable reviewers recommend and discriminating readers
expect to find in their library.

We regard help in the business of earning a living as a basic requirement
and try to provide a wide selection of information relating to the industries,
businesses and vocations represented here.

We believe it is important to provide the books which help readers to
understand themselves and their personal relationship to others.

"For the enrichment of personal life," we provide the means to pursue
artistic, intellectual and spiritual interests.

In a democracy we must provide the citizen with information on public
questions, being careful to present both sides of controversial issues. No
book can be excluded solely because of the race, religion, nationality or
political affiliation of the writer, but we exclude from general circulation
books or periodicals which, in the judgment of the Books Committee, are
seditious by nature or intended or calculated to incite violence or provoke
disorder against any class of persons or against any person as a member of
any class in Canada or intended to arouse one group against another. Such
books are excluded only if the board is of the opinion that the library should
not be the vehicle for the distribution of such books, but such books may be
acquired by the library and kept in its collection for reference use only.

We heartily believe in the traditional role of the public library as the
agency par excellence of informal self-education.

We never forget the many people to whom reading is a great source of
pleasure, relaxation and recreation. Our libraries must always provide for
the person who just wants "a good book to read."

Books for children are carefully selected for popularity with children,
literary style, content, good format and quality of illustrations. We feel that
only the best is good enough for children.

The young moderns collections are intended as a bridge between children's and adult books. Only the best of the large output of so-called teenage books are purchased, together with such adult books as interest young people and will contribute to their growth towards maturity.

Sexism

The view of the male and female roles is one of the criteria for selection of new books. Older established titles and historical fiction written today are reordered on the basis of their literary merit, even though they reflect the values of the times which may be sexist.

Book Ordering Independent of the Book Committee

The members of the subject committee who work in the circulation department have a responsibility to read reviews on their assigned subjects within the century of Dewey which belongs to their committee. The basic review file is made up from reviews on cards which are copied from both *Library Journal*[4] and *Choice*[5]. In addition titles are circulated on route slips to the committee members:

Book List	*Publishers Weekly*
Books and Bookmen	*Quill and Quire*
Books in Canada	*Spectator*
Globe and Mail	*Times Literary Supplement*
Kirkus	*Wilson Library Journal*
New York Times	

CHILDREN'S BOOK SELECTION POLICY

Aims

1. To select materials that stimulate the enjoyment of books;
2. To maintain a collection of overall quality;
3. To represent all points of view;
4. To respond to changing trends and patterns in society;
5. To reflect the interests of the immediate community.

Scope of Collection

1. Age level: from preschool to end of grade 6 or age 12;
2. Reading level: for all abilities.

Selection Criteria

The collection contains books which express a wide variety of views and are suitable for all ages and abilities. The children's librarian's function is to choose this wide-ranging collection according to the criteria which follow, and to share her/his knowledge of this collection through advice and suggestions. Therefore, it is the responsibility of the parents to decide what their children may or may not read from this collection.

The following book selection criteria are applied.

Fiction.   When evaluating fiction, the following questions are asked.

1. Style: Is the book well-written, with a writing style that is appropriate to the subject matter and the intended audience?
2. Theme: If the book has a theme, is it developed as an integral part of the story, rather than as a forced, dogmatic message?
3. Characterization: In books where characterization is important, are the characters developed as real, believable people rather than as one-dimensional, cardboard figures?
4. Setting: Is the setting of the book such that it contributes to the overall worth of the book? Are the details given of the setting authentic and relevant to the overall book?

Nonfiction.   When evaluating nonfiction, the following questions are asked.

1. General criteria:
    *   Is the author qualified?
    *   What are the dates of publication?
    *   Are facts and theories clearly distinguished?
    *   Do the text and illustrations avoid stereotypes?
    *   Do illustrations contribute to meaningful concepts of size?
    *   Is anthropomorphism avoided?
    *   Is the book realistic?

2. Content and style:
    *   Are specific facts given?
    *   Does the author avoid "talking down"?
    *   Are new words explained in text and illustration?
    *   Is the author's style interesting?
    *   Does the book encourage further curiosity?

3. Illustrations:
    *   Do illustrations clarify and extend the text?
    *   Are the illustrations pleasingly spaced?
    *   Are diagrams clearly explained?

4. Organization:
    *   Does the book include table of contents and index?
    *   Does it have a pronunciation guide?
    *   Is information easily located?

5. Wide range of appeal:
    *   Will the book be of interest to several age levels?
    *   What is the reading level?
    *   Is this book of special information or generalized knowledge?

Format.   Qualities looked for are adequate size of print, attractive layout, strong binding and manageable size of book.

The book must be in all respects appropriate for the age level intended.

The book will be considered in view of its contribution to the balance of the collection to which it will be added.

The degree of child appeal possessed by the book will be another factor to be taken into consideration.

CANADIAN BOOKS

Reference Canadiana

This collection will include one copy of every children's book written by a Canadian author which falls into the category of "literature."

"Literature" is defined as:

- Fiction;
- Picture books;
- Folk and fairy tales;
- Poetry, collections of songs;
- Any book which does not fit into any of these categories, but is, in the judgment of the librarian, "literature."

All Canadian children's award-winning books will be included, whether or not they fall into the above categories.

A Canadian author is defined as one who has made his or her literary reputation while living in Canada.

A children's book is defined as a book which will be read mainly by those who are 12 years of age and younger.

University of Wyoming Library

Since the faculty has the most direct involvement with the teaching and research programs of the university, it is important that they have the major role in selecting materials supporting these programs; to this end, a substantial portion of the materials budget will be allocated to the academic departments to be spent at faculty recommendation. The amount allocated will be determined annually by the library director in consultation with the university library committee, considering such factors as total funds available, number of faculty in the department, number of courses taught (graduate and undergraduate), number of students enrolled, and average prices of books and other materials in the subject area. The library staff will not normally overrule faculty requests for purchases as long as funds are available and the item requested falls within the guidelines of this statement, but the library staff has the responsibility for the development of a well-balanced collection. The library staff may initiate the purchase of material in a specific subject area and charge this purchase to the suitable departmental allocation. The library staff has the principal responsibility for selecting materials needed to support service and administrative programs, and in categories three through six in the list of priorities.

The library exists not to serve itself, but to support the total program of the university. Therefore, the development of the library collection should parallel the development of the university itself. Library materials will be acquired in accordance with the following priorities, ranked in descending order of importance:

1. Materials to support the current teaching program of the university, both undergraduate and graduate;
2. Materials to support the research programs of the university, and to assist administrative and service personnel in the effective performance of their duties;
3. General reference works, and works dealing with topics of current concern to members of the campus community (including materials of primarily recreational value, as funds allow);
4. Materials to support cooperative programs with other libraries or academic institutions;
5. Materials to form a foundation collection in support of anticipated future programs of the university;
6. Works in fields not currently directly related to university programs which are of such importance that they belong in any respectable scholarly library.

Roanoke-Chowan Technical Institute Library

Because the librarians can best judge the quality and comprehensiveness of the total collection and because they have at hand current reviewing sources, the librarians assume responsibility for coordinating the collection and for providing bibliographic aid to faculty and staff. Faculty members are asked to recommend materials for purchase.

Materials for purchase are considered on the basis of:

1. Overall purpose;
2. Timeliness and factual accuracy of material;
3. Importance of the subject matter;
4. Quality of the writing/production;
5. Readability and popular appeal;
6. Authoritativeness;
7. Reputation of publishers or producer;
8. Price.

John Stewart Memorial Library, Wilson College

The John Stewart Memorial Library collection is developed primarily through faculty selection of resources which support the courses within the faculty member's particular area of specialty, and which maintain the strength of the discipline in the liberal arts curriculum.

Each discipline is allocated a share of the annual library budget. The allocation is designated to include costs of periodicals, standing orders, monographs and nonprint materials for the discipline.

The members of a discipline collectively plan an equitable distribution of that allocation among themselves so that the work of the entire discipline is supported.

The librarian and staff are responsible for the acquisition of reference tools and those resources which are general in nature, as well as for maintaining a balance among the disciplines within the collection.

Clermont General and Technical College Library

Selection is the responsibility of the library staff with the assistance of the faculty. Faculty are encouraged to submit suggestions for purchases in their respective disciplines. Selection is based on these general factors: relevance to the college's need, relevance to the existing collection, scholarly value and price.

Funds are not allocated for specific areas of the book collection, nor are funds allocated for specific use for nonprint materials, serials and periodicals, microforms, film rental, etc. It is the responsibility of the librarian to allocate funds to these areas within the total library materials budget. The librarian is responsible for seeing that funds are used for book purchase equitably in all subject areas. It is expected that library intensive subjects such as English, history and art history will require more funds than areas, such as typewriting or stenography, which are not library intensive. Areas in which the university library system does not purchase heavily, such as hotel and motel management, will also receive special attention even though the curriculum may not be library intensive. It is expected that research needs of the faculty will be met by the university library system.

St. Catherine Library

Selection is based largely on faculty recommendation and supplemented by student requests and library staff evaluation. Final authority for materials selection rests with the library director of St. Catherine Library who may delegate selection decisions to other library staff members but retains legal responsibility for all selections made.

Library, College of the Desert

The selection of library materials is the particular responsibility of the librarian, with the approval of the college president under authorization of the Board of Trustees. The librarian will be aided by the faculty in the development of the collection.

Grand View College Library

It is the librarian's responsibility, with the advice and counsel of the library committee, to see that an acquisition policy is set up and regularly carried out. Members of the faculty, administration and library staff are responsible for selecting materials in support of the curriculum. The librarian and library staff are responsible for selecting general reference books and bibliographic materials, noncurricular books, periodicals and other material intended to fulfill the general purposes of the library. The librarian has the final authority for the distribution of book funds in a systematic manner.

Based on the present collection and curriculum, the following general guidelines are recommended for the expenditure of book funds: humanities 20–25%; sciences 10–15%; social sciences 25–30%; general and reference 35–40%.

Snead State Junior College Library

The Virgil B. McCain, Jr. Learning Resource Center reference collection contains as its nucleus *Choice's Opening Day Collection* and is in continual revision as suggested by *Choice*.

In addition to the reference collection, the humanities, science and technology and social and behavioral sciences sections are being updated according to the *Opening Day Collection*. The *Collection* in these sections was completed in the 1974–75 school year. (This paragraph refers to the general shelves.)

The faculty participates in selection of books and other materials.* The library has available to faculty upon request several selection aids for colleges, including the following:

- ALA-*Books for College Libraries: A Core Collection;*
- *Book Review Digest;*
- *Library Journal;*
- *New York Times Book Review;*
- *Choice* (built specifically as a selection aid for community and junior college libraries).

The Learning Resource Center furnishes to faculty members order cards for requesting specific books and other materials, and urges faculty members to use them continuously to request materials as needed for support of classes.

Priority is given to teacher requests. Up to the present time, all requests from faculty have been honored, since these requests have been minimal in proportion to the budget. Thus, it has not been necessary to assign priorities to the various departments because of a tight budget.

When it does become necessary to allocate funds to the various departments, the basis for allocation will include the following factors:

---

*The process for selecting audio-visual materials and making allocations of the audio-visual budget is similar to the process of book selection and book budget allocations described on this page.

1. Departmental enrollment;
2. Extent of the need for books and materials by the different departments;
3. The cost per volume of books and materials in the departmental field;
4. The state of the collection in each field;
5. The needs of new programs;
6. The needs of new instructors.

Periodicals and newspapers are selected with assistance of faculty. Effort is made to keep the subscription list well-balanced in relation to the curriculum. Periodicals to promote reading for pleasure are also selected.

The library staff periodically solicits the aid of faculty to assist in weeding books located in their specific fields of teaching.

The Virgil B. McCain, Jr. Learning Resource Center gives preference to acquisitions of books and other materials requested by faculty members.

BOOKS ROUTINELY ACQUIRED

- Standard books of general reference;
- Standard reference books useful for specific fields covered by the curriculum;
- General books;
- Books for each curricular field;
- Books concerning important fields not covered by curriculum;
- Books for leisure reading;
- General and standard scholarly periodicals;
- Scholarly materials:

Research monographs	Cassettes
Serials	Recordings
Pamphlets	Music
Documents	Manuscripts
Microfilm	Archives
Prints	Reports
Maps	

Yavapai College Learning Resources Center

RESPONSIBILITY FOR SELECTION (LEGAL AND DELEGATED)

The ultimate responsibility for materials selection rests, by law, with the Board of Governors. The president, operating within the framework of board policies, delegates the responsibility to the librarians and the faculty.

Members of the faculty are responsible for the recommendation of titles in their subject fields. The librarians are responsible for building a comprehensive, well-rounded collection. They assume the responsibility for reviewing current and retrospective bibliographies and making selections in areas particularly neglected by the faculty. Librarians also select materials supplementary to the curricula as needed. Final decisions regarding materials to be acquired rest with the head librarian.

Cattell Library, Malone College

Faculty members of each academic division are responsible for materials to support their specific areas and curriculum.

The library staff is responsible for reference materials, completion of serials and any subject area needing strengthening.

Administration, staff, students and trustees are encouraged to submit recommendations.

The director, with the advice of Learning Resources Committee, is responsible for the balance of the collection and allocation of funds for purchase.

Generally recognized guides to selection are suggested in the following list of resources and organizations:

1. *Basic Music Library,* National Association of Schools of Music;
2. *Books for College Libraries,* ALA, 1975. 6v.;
3. *Granger's Index to Poetry,* Wilson;
4. Hoffman, H. R., *The Reader's Advisor and Bookman's Manual,* Bowker;
5. McNeff, P. J., *Catalogue of the Lamont Library,* Harvard College, 1953;
6. Winchell, C. M., *Guide to Reference Books,* ALA, 1951 Supplements 1952, 1958, 1962;
7. *American Reference Books Annual,* Libraries Unlimited, 1970–;
8. Serials and periodicals:
   - *Booklist;*
   - *Choice;*
   - *Education Index;*
   - *Essay and General Literature Index;*
   - *Humanities Index;*
   - *Index to Religious Periodical Literature;*
   - *International Index;*
   - *Library Journal;*
   - *Preview;*
   - *Social Science Index;*
   - *Resources in Education;*
   - *Wilson Library Bulletin* (reference books).

Muscatine Community College Library

The faculty has a three-part role to play in the development of the library collection. They have the opportunity to assist the library staff in the evaluation of new titles, the weeding of materials, and the filling of gaps in the collection.

The selection of library materials is based upon professionally trained librarians freely exercising their professional judgment, aided by these guidelines and the rules and regulations of the college.

Materials are selected by the library staff with the fullest possible assistance of the faculty. Selections in subject areas will be based upon evaluation of the faculty serving as subject area consultants.

The library attempts to encourage participation in the selection process by channeling appropriate information to the faculty for recommendations and by receiving suggestions initiated by the faculty. The library staff will select materials of a general nature and materials not covered by the curriculum or by faculty interest.

The final responsibility for selection rests with the library director, who is in the position to coordinate the development of the collection. It is the director's responsibility to work toward achieving a balanced collection which meets the objectives of the library.

Belk Library, Appalachian State University

The wise selection of library materials has become an increasingly difficult task. The quality and quantity of publications, the diversification of instructional programs and a limited budget require us to establish purposeful priorities for acquiring library materials.

In case of disagreements, the final decision on library acquisitions will be made by the library administration (dean of Learning Resources, university librarian and acquisitions librarian), after consultation with the concerned department chairman.

A librarian has been assigned to each academic department having a library budget, for the purpose of establishing a better means of communication between the departments and the library. The library representative from the department and the library liaison representative should work together to insure that request cards are prepared correctly.

ALLOCATION OF FUNDS

Each department receives an annual allocation of funds from the library for the purchase of library materials. Departmental allocations are based upon factors such as weighted student quarter hours generated, relative cost of books for each department, program offerings, number of faculty members, adequacy of present collection and past spending record of the department. The amount of these allocations is determined by the library administration and is limited by the total amount of the library budget appropriated by the state legislature.

Blue Mountain Community College Library

Selection of materials in each field is the primary responsibility of the department head serving the subject area, with assistance given by the head librarian and/or the audio-visual director through routing of selection materials pertinent to each area and through consultation between department heads and the head librarian and/or audio-visual director. Ultimate selection rests with the head librarian and/or audio-visual director who are directly responsible to the president of the college, who in turn is responsible to the board of Blue Mountain Community College. Final approval of the materials selection policy rests with this board.

Such well-established lists as the following shall be consulted for bibliographical information: *Publishers Weekly, Publishers Trade List Annual, Books in Print, Subject Guide to Books in Print, Cumulative Book Index, Ash-Subject Collections, American Library Association List for Junior College Libraries* (an updated list is soon to be released), and *Paperbound Books in Print.*

The following are representative of reputable reviewing media that shall regularly be consulted: Wilson's *Standard Catalog for Public Libraries*, Winchell's *Guide to Reference Materials, General Encyclopedias in Print, General Atlases in Print, Catalogs from U.S. Superintendent of Documents,* and lists in well-established periodicals, e.g., *Choice, Saturday Review, Harpers, Atlantic, New York Times Book Review* and those periodicals pertinent to special subject fields. Access to reviews and those periodicals is facilitated by use of *Book Review Index* and *Book Review Digest.*

Frazer Memorial Library, McNeese State University

RESPONSIBILITY FOR SELECTION

In order to build a sound book collection it is necessary to have a good working combination of administrators, faculty and library staff. Indeed, selection is the responsibility of all, as funds, in addition to a wise choice of faculty and library staff, must be provided by the university administration before intelligent selection can take place. After adequate funds and faculty and staff personnel are made available, it is the responsibility of faculty and librarians to select the materials needed by the university community. Faculty are urged to order books and other materials through departmental allocations to support their own curricula; librarians select with the goal of maintaining a well-balanced and superior core collection.

CRITERIA FOR SELECTION

Factors for determining whether a title meets the criteria will be based on reviews in professional literature, occurrence of the title in standard bibliographies and indexes, or the opinion of the faculty and professional staff. The availability of material in a particular subject area should also be taken into consideration in the selection process. Suggestions will be accepted from all members of the university community.

Library, Northern Illinois University

One of the most striking features of recent efforts in the library profession to meet the diverse needs of the community has been the assumption of greater responsibility by the librarians in book selection. Although faculty consultation remains a vital element in this area, this shift in responsibility has put book selection in the hands of those trained to do the job, while at the same time freeing faculty to concentrate on their own areas of expertise.

This has provided a more balanced collection. Since the library is not dependent upon faculty initiative the chances are minimized that certain areas may become overdeveloped in relation to overall needs, while other areas suffer, because some faculty may be less library-oriented.

Selection responsibility is the charge of several subject-area specialists, who act also as liaison with the faculty in their respective subject areas. At present, these areas are social sciences, literature and languages, fine arts, education, physical and natural sciences. Requests for major purchases are determined by bibliographers acting as a committee. The bibliographers also accept or reject gift and approval items. In liaison with the bibliographers the serials librarian is the coordinator of all requests, approvals, and gifts involving serials.

Library, Baker Junior College of Business

Materials are purchased on:
1. Recommendation of faculty and administrative staff;
2. Reviews and bibliographies in *Library Journal* and *Choice*, as well as other periodicals, general and specialized;
3. Bibliographies in texts used in courses.

Items over $25 are purchased only after approval of the managing director.

Knight-Capron Library, Lynchburg College

The library and the faculty cooperate in the materials selection process.
1. The library supplies the faculty with three-part multiple-copy request forms.
2. Each month the library sends to department heads the current appropriate book reviews and bibliographies clipped from *Choice*.

Learning Resources Center, Rockingham Community College

At the beginning of each fiscal year all money designated for the acquisition of LRC materials is budgeted in the following manner:
- 40% allocated to the librarians for purchase of items of general interest, replacements, continuation orders, indexes, etc.;
- 60% divided among departments.

The formula for departmental funds is based on the number of credit hours times the number of students enrolled; therefore, each department's allotment depends on its share of the teaching load of the college. There are provisions for new programs and a contingency fund. Slight adjustments are made to take care of the special cases such as extremely small departments.

No distinction is made between the purchase of print and nonprint materials. All requests originating from any faculty member are routed through the department chairman who approves or disapproves the request. Those approved are forwarded to the LRC. The card catalog and order file are checked to avoid duplication. Only in rare instances is a request turned down and then only after consultation with department chairmen, as long as money remains in that department line.

Kansas City Kansas Community Junior College Library

RESPONSIBILITY FOR SELECTION AND REMOVAL

Selection of Books

Faculty and student selection assistance is invaluable and should be encouraged by all members of the library staff. Any member of the faculty or student body may request that books be added by completing a request form and submitting it to a member of the library staff. Such requests of under $25.00 shall be automatically honored, assuming the availability of funds and the absence of similar materials. Final decisions regarding requests of material valued at more than $25.00 shall be made by the college librarians.

Because the librarians are ultimately responsible for the overall quality and balance of the total collection, they will select and purchase materials in all subject areas in an attempt to fill obvious gaps overlooked by instructors.

Specific Guidelines

1. Author's reputation and significance;
2. Importance of the subject matter to the collection;
3. Scarcity of material on the subject;
4. Timeliness or permanence of the title;
5. Appearance of the title in special bibliographies or indexes;
6. Authoritativeness;
7. Reputation of the publisher or producer;
8. Price;
9. Number of students enrolled in the subject area of the request.

Current Selection Aids Regularly Reviewed by the Staff

- *Booklist;*
- *Choice* cards and *Choice* special bibliographies;
- Essay and general literature titles selected for indexing;
- *Library Journal* cards;
- *Nation;*
- *New Republic;*
- *New York Review of Books;*

- *New York Times Book Review (Sunday Times);*
- Publishers' catalogs;
- *Publishers Weekly;*
- *Wilson Library Bulletin;*
- *Standing Order Checklists* from Doubleday and McGraw Hill (discussed below);
- "Sunday Arts" section—*KC Star;*
- *Virginia Quarterly;*
- *Yale Review.*

Review as necessary the following retrospective aids:

1. Retrospective bibliographies:

   - *Books for College Libraries;*
   - *Books for Junior College Libraries;*
   - *Books for Occupational Education Programs* (1971);
   - *The Junior College Library Collection;*
   - *Opening Day Collection (Choice);*
   - *Vocational-Technical Learning Materials* (1974).

2. Subject journals: particularly helpful for vocational-technical areas;
3. General interest periodicals, e.g., *Atlantic Monthly, Harpers,* etc.

Rules Governing Divisional Requests for Software

The library staff will accept only those software orders approved by the appropriate divisional chairman.

The library reserves the right to refuse to purchase materials which:

1. Have not been previewed by a member of the division or received at least one positive review;
2. Are of inferior quality;
3. May not serve future as well as present needs;
4. Could be produced better, cheaper or faster on-campus.

Audio-visual materials must be previewed during the loan period as established by the producer.

Audio-visual materials must be previewed by a faculty member prior to purchase.

Software Expenditures 1976–1977

Last year the library appropriated $2,600 for divisional purchases of commercially produced software. A $1,500 Title VI grant was similarly divided among the divisions.

This year the library will again allocate $2,600 for divisional purchases of software. Procedures for divisional encumbrances will remain the same, i.e.:

1. Faculty selections for preview must be approved by the appropriate chairman.
2. Audio-visual materials must be viewed before purchase.

3. A statement indicating unspent balance will be issued to chairmen in November and again in March.
4. No requests for software will be honored after April 1.

Tri-County Technical College Library

The responsibility of the selection of Learning Resources Center materials is delegated to the professionally trained personnel employed by the college. Selection of materials involves many people—teachers, supervisors, media specialists and students. The responsibility for coordinating the selection of materials rests with professionally trained Learning Resources specialists.

Skyline College Library

Within a framework of full participation by the total college community, responsibility for book selection rests with the library director, with final authority for the determination of policy vested in the Board of Trustees.

Learning Resources Center, Eastfield College

RESPONSIBILITY FOR SELECTION

The responsibility for selection is vested in the staff of the Learning Resources Center, which has the obligation of working closely with individual faculty and students and the Learning Resources Program Advisory Committee in coordinating the selection of materials and helping to build a collection that truly reflects resource needs of the college. Requests for purchase of materials may be submitted to the appropriate division chairmen for their recommendations, at the discretion of the Learning Resources staff; however, the final responsibility for approval of all resources recommended rests with the associate dean of instruction. When desirable, the Learning Resources staff may also require that materials be reviewed or examined by faculty, prior to a recommendation for purchase.

Oregon State University Library

Every library faculty member is encouraged to become a subject specialist involved in the processes of book selection and collection building.

The subject specialist is assumed to be familiar with both retrospective and current bibliographies and materials in her/his subject field and in related fields.

Subject specialists will accept requests from others and assign priorities.

Heads of public service departments will coordinate work of subject specialists assigned to areas under their jurisdiction, regardless of location on the staff.

Suomi College Library

Evaluation and selection should be expedited by consulting reviews, recommended lists, standard bibliographic guides and special releases, all the result of competent evaluation from qualified specialists. Needs of faculty and students as indicated above must be considered. Although generally all faculty requests will be honored, the final responsibility for selection must be vested in the professional librarian whose responsibility is materials selection.

Hoover Library, Western Maryland College

The job of building the collection is divided mainly between the library and the college departments of instruction. The library depends heavily upon the specialized knowledge of the faculty members for maintaining adequate collections in their subject fields. That is the reason for departmental allotments of the book budget; that is also the reason for asking each department head or representative to coordinate the selection of her/his colleagues and to serve as liaison officer to the library for them.

The librarians contribute their specialized knowledge to expedite the selection and acquisition of needed materials. Their selection activities should be concentrated on developing the general collection (i.e., books, periodicals, etc., which would not logically be selected by any one department or used by only one department) and the reference collection.

The responsibility for the whole collection rests with the librarian, who should try to strengthen weak spots and should challenge requests that seem inordinate. The library committee should serve as arbiter in case of disagreement over the appropriateness of any purchase.

Students and administrative staff also have a role in suggesting titles for purchase. Their participation should be welcomed and their requests considered in the light of the guidelines expressed below.

Individual departments will be allotted a portion, expressed as a percentage, of the total sum available to distribute to departments for purchasing monographic material. These funds will be apportioned by the librarian and submitted to the library committee for approval. Decisions shall be based primarily on the following criteria:

1. Annual statements solicited by the librarian from departmental chairmen;
2. Existing strength of materials in each department;

3. Size of department, as reflected by number of students, majors and faculty;
4. Rate of obsolescence of materials in the respective subject areas;
5. Cost of library materials in the respective subject areas;
6. The amount of use student and faculty make of library materials.

It should be recognized that criteria 3 through 6 are more likely than item 2 to be factors in the statements submitted by departmental chairmen.

Texas State Technical Institute Library

Selection by faculty will be encouraged. All titles submitted will be considered as suggestions subject to evaluation by the professional staff. The same selection criteria shall apply to faculty suggestions as would apply to other titles considered.

Priority of selection shall be assigned on the following bases:

1. Faculty requests—curriculum related;
2. Staff selections—curriculum related;
3. Faculty requests—general interest;
4. Staff selections—general interest.

Selection shall focus on titles published within the last five years, with preference given to the most current materials. Older titles will be selected only if nothing comparable has been published more recently. It is expected that selection of older materials will be made only upon an extremely favorable personal or published recommendation.

As far as possible, selection will be made from published reviews. Selection will be made from publishers' catalogs only when there is the objective of building a comprehensive collection in a certain area, when there is a need for material on subjects for which sufficient reviewed material cannot be located and when the author or publisher is unusually well-respected.

Regularly consulted selection aids include the following:

1. *Choice;*
2. *Library Journal;*
3. *New Technical Books;*
4. *AAAS Science Books and Films;*
5. *Booklist;*
6. *Technical Book Review Index;*
7. *Information News and Sources;*
8. *Directions* (science and technology only);
9. *New York Times Book Review.*

Materials costing over $50 will be selected with specific assurance that they will be used. Since cost is not a main consideration in restriction of circulation, expensive material will be justified not by the provision that it will remain in the building, but by the anticipated use it will receive.

Kalamazoo College Library

In order to build the best possible collection with the book budget available, careful selection must be made from the tremendous volume of material being published. Recommendations and requests for purchase are made by the faculty and the library staff with evaluations based on reviews in the literature and on personal, professional judgments.

One of the major sources for reviews of materials suitable for the college library is the periodical *Choice*. It is the practice of the library every month to send each department the appropriate section of this journal with the request that recommendations for purchase be made from it. We appreciate your cooperation in selecting from and promptly returning these lists to us.

Unfortunately, all books suitable for inclusion in the Upjohn Library collection are not selected for review by *Choice*. The library staff regularly checks other reviewing media. Many of the faculty also make selections based on reviews found in various scholarly journals.

Learning Resources Center, Catonsville Community College

RESPONSIBILITY FOR SELECTION AND PRODUCTION OF MATERIALS

The selection of materials is a responsibility shared by LRC and other faculty members, all of whom are expected to make recommendations. Specialists are urged to use their skills for development of the LRC collections. Recommendations from all college staff members and students are given full consideration.

Materials needed for the college program which are not available from commercial sources, or which must be geared to a specific need, will be produced jointly by the LRC and the requesting party as time and facilities permit.

Clatsop Community College Library

FACULTY PARTICIPATION IN SELECTION

Each department shall have a portion of the library funds assigned to it for purchase of books appropriate to its discipline. At least half of the library book budget shall be so allotted.

The library will endeavor to secure for the staff announcements and reviews of books in as wide a field as possible so the individual instructors will not be short on materials to select.

The librarian fills in obvious gaps overlooked by instructors and maintains an up-to-date reference collection.

Titles added to the collection shall be evaluated in terms of appropriateness for undergraduate use. Highly technical material is only to be acquired if a definite use is observable.

Recency of material is of major importance. No title published more than two years previously shall be added to the collection unless it satisfies a very definite and specific need.

Generally speaking, no effort is to be made to censor the collection. We feel the faculty and students deserve all sides of questions.

The collection shall not be developed to serve the interest of any special student.

The collection shall include titles for the serious adult readers and rely on the public library for materials of a lighter nature.

Format shall be considered when more than one edition of a title is available, and preference shall be given to attractive and readable editions.

Paperbacks shall be used when available to meet the need for multiple copies or books of limited use.

Books for faculty research will only be purchased if they can be used by the undergraduate student body. Interlibrary loans will be used to satisfy faculty needs for research materials. However, books and journals that will help the whole faculty understand junior college problems will be added as needed.

In selection of books priority will be given in the following order:

1. Continuations of material coming serially on standing orders, including all indexes;
2. Class need—a new class will be given extra consideration in meeting its most pressing needs;
3. Material requested by the instructors to supplement their field;
4. General reference material;
5. Outstanding books in fields not covered by the present curriculum;
6. General reading material (purchased with money from fines);
7. Fiction—purchased if a class has a need for it. Note (2) above; otherwise our fiction collection is, for the most part, the result of gifts to the library.

Hartwick College Library

All libraries have to be selective. The smaller the library, the more selective it must be. Selectivity means that those who bear the main responsibility for book selection—the faculty—must be very discriminating in not requesting books which are:

1. Not directly needed in the curriculum;
2. Not generally suitable for our undergraduates;
3. By their subject or degree of specialization not especially desirable for the cultural and general enrichment of the library;
4. Expensive, and whose value may be ephemeral (this category would include pamphlets whose price may be low but whose handling and preparation costs more than can be justified);

5. Not positively reviewed by reputable reviewers (occasionally an exception might be made in the case of an author or publisher known for uniformly high standards).

Brief written or verbal justifications must accompany all requests for expensive (over $20) or unusual books as well as requests for multiple copies.

William S. Smith Library, South Georgia College

With the exception of salaries, the materials budgets are the largest and most important items in the library budget.

The library has delegated authority to purchase materials, either outright or on approval. Orders do not have to go through the business office.

The library does not divide the materials budgets into allocations for each division. This practice was followed until 1970. Since then, the library budget has been too small to apportion. When it was apportioned the majority of the divisions did not use the allocation, although requests went to them twice each year. Some of those who did use the funds abused it by requesting books on the basis of titles only. Some requested twice the amount of their particular allocation. Such an apportionment plan prevents a systematic building of the library collection, and it tends to tie up funds which should be used for new programs.

Instead, the order cards distributed to the faculty provide a space for the requestor to indicate whether the item is essential to the collection. If so, every attempt is made to purchase it.

University of California at Los Angeles Library

DEFINITIONS OF LEVELS OF COVERAGE

Level:

1. *Exhaustive collection.* A collection in which the library strives for practical completeness. It includes almost everything written in the field, no matter in what form it is produced, in all languages, of all times, and in all editions. It may include translations and will certainly contain variant printings where the text is affected. An essential prerequisite is a carefully drawn definition of the subject itself.
2. *Research–exhaustive collection.*
3. *Research collection.* A collection covering the whole scope of a subject field or subdivision of that field with coverage sufficient to sustain extensive investigation and research. Insofar as possible, all source materials available in printed form will be included. All the important serial titles are included with a wide selection of minor titles. The definition of a research collection is dependent upon the nature of the subject itself.
4. *Teaching–research collection.*

5. *Teaching or support collection.* A collection on a subject which is taught by the university, but in which research work at the graduate level or above is not supported by the collecting library. Alternatively, a collection of materials in areas peripheral to the scope of the primary collection, but needed for interdisciplinary research, e.g., mathematics, spectroscopy, polymer chemistry in relation to biomedical research. Such collections would consist chiefly of reference works, a comprehensive collection of secondary works and important periodical titles.
6. *Minimal–teaching collection.*
7. *Minimal collection.* A collection sufficient to illustrate the extent and nature of a subject only. It may consist of basic reference works, a limited collection of representative secondary works and a limited number of the more outstanding periodical titles.

Abbot Memorial Library, Emerson College

The major consideration in acquisition of materials for the library collection is the curriculum of the college. In-depth development is done in the major subject areas of the performing arts, mass media and communication, communication disorders, and speech and communication studies.

Materials for supportive subject areas are acquired based on breadth of coverage, quality of coverage and interdisciplinary usefulness of materials. Specialized collection development plans are developed based on the strengths and weaknesses of the current collection, actual circulation of materials, theft factors and shifting emphases in the curriculum of the college.

Since it is unrealistic for the library to attempt to supply all materials for all possible needs, it is expected that reference service, interlibrary loan, and referral to other collections in the Boston area will supplement Emerson's specialized collection.

James E. Shepard Memorial Library, North Carolina Central University

POLICY ON APPORTIONMENT TO DEPARTMENTS

Formulae are more useful as general guides than as exclusive determinants in the distribution of book funds. Important problems relative to these formulae are the choice of factors; their weighting methods of combining factor data to produce a final index; and the methods of applying the index, in conjunction with factors not included, to the part of the book fund available for departmental apportionment.

At least 25% of the book budget is kept to be spent by the librarian to bridge the gap left after recommendations of the faculty have been purchased. This procedure assures a well-balanced book collection with adequate reference tools.

Factors considered in apportionment of the remaining 75% to departments are:

1. Book need factors (internal weighting):

   - Registration;
   - Courses offered;
   - Faculty (counted by rank);
   - Majors—graduate majors;
   - Student credit-hour load by departments.

2. Cost of materials factor—The cost of materials factor is a weighted mean cost per physical unit—volume or copy—in dollars and cents for each department. The number of units and their cost are determined and a mean secured for each department.

3. Nonquantitative factors:

   - Adequacy of departments' present library collection;
   - Teaching methods;
   - Recent additions to a department (new faculty or courses);
   - The permanent value of materials normally purchased;
   - The publication rate in each department's field;
   - The frequency with which faculty members publish books and articles.

4. Relative use of the library materials by departments:

   - Laboratory and textbook courses involving little or no use of the library by the students;
   - Laboratory and textbook courses involving occasional use of the library by the students;
   - Laboratory and textbook courses involving frequent use of the library by students;
   - Courses in which no textbook is used and in which the library becomes the primary source of reading materials.

Problem Areas

The Public Library of Cincinnati and Hamilton County

TEXTBOOKS

Textbooks are purchased only when no other material in a given field is available. In certain subject fields, such as psychology and history, textbooks often represent the best and only information. No attempt is made to supply student demands for textbooks in specific subjects.

PAPERBACKS

Paperbacks are used for the sake of economy and to fill ephemeral demands for hardcover titles. Four reasons for selection of paperbacks are:

1. To supplement and meet the demand for the title in hardcover;
2. To add only those books with suitable format and physical appearance;
3. To acquire original works that appear only in paperback (these are subject to the same selection standards as hardbacks);
4. To replace out-of-print material.

Hamilton Public Library

DUPLICATION

Multiple copies of books of a lasting nature will be purchased reflecting demand, budget and space. Any mass duplication of copies will be accomplished through paperbacks.

Camden County Free Library

NUMBER OF COPIES

Adult Fiction

2–5 copies (limited loan) plus number for extension and branches (note: 1st copy—Main only, 2nd or more—limited loan).

Translations—Usually purchase one copy. If foreign author is popular purchase more than one copy.

Replacement copies—Usually purchase one copy. For popular work purchase additional copies.

Best-sellers—3 to 5 for original order. For additional requests purchase 2 copies for every 6 requests.

Classics—Combination of hardcover and paperbacks (1–3 ratio).

Adult Nonfiction

2–5 copies (limited loan) plus copies needed for extension and branches (note: 1st copy—Main only, 2nd or more—limited loan).

One copy:

1. Title costing $15 or more;
2. Monographs, dissertations, scholarly works, series and multi-volume works;
3. Foreign language books;
4. Replacements.

Best-sellers—3 to 5 for original order. For additional requests purchase 2 copies for every 6 requests.

Juvenile and Young Adults

Number of copies depends on popularity of author and subject matter as well as budget.

1. Picture books (new) 3–5;
2. Juvenile fiction 1–3;
3. Juvenile nonfiction 1–3;
4. Young adults fiction 1–3;
5. Young adults nonfiction 1–3.

Replacements—to a total number 4 copies.

Historic children's books—1–2, and books about children's literature 1–2 (found in children's department, adult nonfiction and reference .028).

Extension Collection

1. Adult fiction 2;
2. Adult nonfiction 1–3;
3. Juvenile fiction 1–2;
4. Juvenile nonfiction 1–2;
5. Young adults fiction 1–2;
6. Young adults nonfiction 1–2;
7. Picture books 2–3 (additional copies may be purchased for classic material).

Paperbacks

Paperbacks are purchased for the regular circulating collection and for the paperback racks.

1. Adult fiction 2–4 copies;
2. Adult nonfiction 2–4 copies.

Wayne County Public Library

DUPLICATION

Duplicate titles are supplied within reasonable limits. Current books in great demand as well as multiple copies of some best-sellers may be furnished temporarily through a leased collection.

Assets of other libraries and institutions in the area and members of COIN are considered to avoid unnecessary duplication of expensive and seldom-used material.

Rensselaer Public Library

Duplication of materials, not a general practice, may however be necessary in the case of current problems, publications and items of great demand. Since the library accepts partial responsibility for the provision of supplementary materials for school and college students, some duplication in these areas may be necessary.

Ontario City Library

DUPLICATION

Every agency responsible for book selection is confronted with the problem of evaluating its needs for the duplication of materials. While the problem differs in the various departments, the library, in general, attempts to weigh the specific needs in relation to the library program and policies. Since titles are admitted only if they meet the approval standards of book selection, they will be duplicated if the patron requests—subject, of course, to budget limitations and to timely or permanent value of the material. It is the general policy of the library to consider duplicating titles for which there is an accumulation of five reserves. Initial number of copies to be ordered is a maximum of five and then only if the author is widely known and if there is a good probability the demand will necessitate duplicating.

Rolling Prairie Libraries

PAPERBACKS

The same standards apply to paperbacks as apply to other books. Paperbacks are bought for the following reasons:

1. Title is out of print or unobtainable in other format;
2. Title has not appeared in another edition;
3. Title is in heavy demand for temporary current interest or information;

4. Title is older and rarely used;
5. Price.

TEXTBOOKS

Textbooks should be purchased for the collection when they supply information in areas in which they may be the best, or the only, source of information on the subject. Customarily, textbooks used in the area schools and colleges are not purchased, but exceptions may be made if the text is considered useful to the general reader. Books (readers) used in primary grades to teach reading skills are not generally acquired.

Yavapai College Learning Resources Center

Multiple copies will be limited to three, if possible, and not to exceed five copies in any case.

The library will not purchase copies of a current used textbook unless that title is an important source of information in its field.

Paperbacks will be purchased only if bound volumes are not available because of the extra work procedures required in binding.

Lost books are replaced after one year unless immediately needed. If after a year the librarian decides that the items should not be replaced, they will be withdrawn from the current records.

Hartwick College Library

No texts for courses being taught should be requested.

Multiple copies should be requested only when (a) numerous students are (b) required to read within a limited time (c) substantial portions of a book which is (d) too expensive for the students to buy individually. Of course, a very high price also militates against the purchase of multiple copies; on the other hand assurance that the book will be used for many years counts in favor. As a rule we should start with the smallest possible number of copies and add others only as the demand, measured by circulation, justifies them.

Expensive books and series will usually be purchased only after we have established that they are not available in the main library, although in some cases heavy use will justify the availability of expensive items in both libraries.

William S. Smith Library, South Georgia College

Normally only one copy of each book will be purchased. However, timeliness and class-related assignments may require the purchase of an

additional copy of a given title. It is not expected that class-related assignments will ever require the purchase by the library of more than three copies
of a given title for student use. When the demand for more than three copies
of a given title for class-related assignments becomes evident, this title
should be considered as a textbook adoption.

TEXTBOOKS

Since it is the purpose of the library collection to supplement and
augment the curriculum, textbooks adopted for class use will not normally
be purchased for the library collection. Instead, the library will add books to
its collection which amplify the material found in the textbooks.

Grand View College Library

In the matter of duplicates, the library, as a part of an education institution, should first provide as many different sides to an issue as possible. The
library encourages the use of recommended reading lists. However, because
of the accepted use of "reserve" books in a college library and the large
number of students taking certain courses, duplicates are sometimes necessary. They will be purchased after consultation of the librarian with the
instructor.

The library does not attempt to purchase the textbooks for college
courses. They are purchased only for content, because they would be useful,
or because the information is not available in any other form, i.e., such as in
some math and science areas.

University of Wyoming Library

Duplicate copies of heavily-used materials will be acquired when genuinely needed, but duplication is not encouraged; every duplicate added
means that some other title cannot be acquired at all. Duplicate copies of
titles held on the Laramie campus will be acquired for the off-campus
centers in other locations as needed, but only very basic reference works will
be duplicated between the branch libraries on campus.

It is the responsibility of the students to provide their own textbooks,
and the library will not undertake to maintain a textbook collection. At the
discretion of the instructor, one or a small number of copies of selected texts
may be purchased for the reserve collection, but this is not encouraged.

DISSERTATIONS

An exception to the general principle that materials will not be pur-
chased for one individual's use must (because titles listed in *Dissertation
Abstracts* cannot be obtained on interlibrary loan, as a policy of University
Microfilms) be made in the case of dissertations. Photocopies or microfilm

will be purchased and charged to the appropriate departmental allocation. Such dissertations will be cataloged and become a part of the library's permanent collection, despite the fact that future use will almost certainly be slight.

When a book is available in both hardcover and paperback editions, the first copy will be bought in hardcover. Additional copies, when necessary, will be bought in the binding most suitable in terms of expected use. If a title is available only as a paperback, the first copy will be bound when feasible except when limited use is anticipated.

In the case of titles which have gone through several editions, the latest edition will automatically be acquired unless an earlier edition is specified because of historical value or because it contains material not in the later edition.

Library, College of the Desert

DUPLICATION

Purchase of duplicate copies is discouraged unless a faculty member or a librarian demonstrates a need for additional copies. Materials used for extensive required reading should ordinarily be duplicated at the rate of one copy for every fifteen students. This formula should be flexible, however, since consideration must be given to such factors as the length and difficulty of the reading.

Library, Baker Junior College of Business

Paperback books are purchased freely, with those judged of permanent value classified and intershelved with hardcovers. A separate paperback collection is maintained of general interest and recreational reading. These are unclassified, but indexed by author and title.

St. Catherine Library

Hardbacks are selected for works of permanent value and when the anticipated use will be heavy.

Paperbacks are selected for works of temporary value, when the anticipated use will be limited, when no other edition is available or when the price for a hardback edition becomes exorbitant.

Textbooks, laboratory manuals, synopses, outlines, etc., are not recommended unless no other similar material is available. If requested by faculty members these materials may be ordered and given to the department with or without being cataloged at the discretion of the library director. Printed materials exclusive of government publications, which are consistently needed by a given department but which would be awkward or difficult to incorporate into the library collection, should be ordered by the department using them from its own funds. Examples would be: games, recipe files, charts.

Texas State Technical Institute Library

The library will not automatically purchase books that are assigned as textbooks in the courses taught at TSTI, nor will it reject titles simply because of the likelihood that they may be used as such. The practice of placing titles on reserve because they are currently used as textbooks has been discontinued. At a faculty member's request, any title may be placed on reserve in order to support assigned work in a particular course. In no case will the library purchase multiple copies of a title in lieu of the students' purchase of their own copies.

Physical durability shall be stressed in selection. Hardbound editions will be preferred over paperbound. Because of extreme circulation difficulties, materials in looseleaf bindings will be selected only if the material is suitable for in-the-building use. The library will avoid the selection of looseleaf materials for which regular updating is not anticipated. Because of the expense usually involved, these materials will be selected in response only to specific need.

Multiple copies of titles will be purchased only in response to unusual demand. Use of the reserve system shall be suggested as a response to requests for multiple copies.

Special Formats

The Public Library of Cincinnati and Hamilton County

PERIODICALS

The library maintains an extensive collection of current periodicals, as well as a very fine collection of 19th-century magazines.

Periodicals are an important source of current information which has not yet appeared or may never appear in book form. A vast amount of information is made available through trade and professional journals in all fields such as science, business, industry, education, etc. Popular magazines for recreational reading are also provided in both the main library and branches.

An important consideration in the purchase of periodicals is whether or not their content is made available through standard indexes, abstracts and bibliographies. Other criteria are the reputation of the publication, qualifications of the contributors, the quality of the writing and suitability for binding and future use.

NEWSPAPERS

Newspapers are valuable for their up-to-date information on local, state, national and international events. Space severely limits the number of newspapers to which the library can subscribe. Local newspapers are available in bound volumes or on microfilm and are indexed for items of local importance. Out-of-town newspapers are subscribed to in an effort to cover the major geographical and urban areas of the United States. The *London Times,* and a few other representative foreign newspapers are also received.

PAMPHLETS

Pamphlets serve as an important supplement to the general collection. They are inexpensive, attractive, concise and up-to-date, and often present a quick overview of a subject. The selection of pamphlets follows the same criteria as those used for books. Special care in selection is to be taken since pamphlets are widely used for propaganda and advertising purposes.

MAPS

Library acquisitions are primarily depository items from the Federal Government and the United States Army. However, there are a number of sources checked for various types of new materials.

The decision to purchase is based on the type of map or atlas (e.g., topographic, hydrographic, geologic, political, etc.), scale, date of publication, area covered, price and the needs of the collection.

In the field of historical cartography, selections are determined by three factors: relevance to the collection, importance to the field of historical geography or cartography, and price.

Ontario City Library

PERIODICALS

Periodicals are selected and preserved for the following reasons:

1. To supplement the book collection with current material in various subject fields;
2. To preserve periodicals for reference use;
3. To aid the staff in book selections and professional reading.

No attempt is made to compete with the commercial market of current periodicals for recreational reading. Periodicals are considered for binding or microfilm.

Current periodicals are used for source material not found in books, and are needed both for reference work and for general reading. Criteria for selection is based on the following considerations:

1. Accuracy and objectivity;
2. Content available through indexing;
3. Need in reference work to supplement book collection;
4. Local interest in subject matter;
5. Availability in special libraries of the community;
6. Price.

Some scholarly types of periodicals may be purchased to supplement the library's book collection. Consideration in selection is given to:

1. Issuance of the journal by a well-known organization;
2. Inclusion in periodicals indices;
3. Authority of editors and contributors.

Gift subscriptions for denominational religious publications as well as trade and professional journals are accepted subject to the head librarian's approval.

All staff members of the library participate in periodical selection. Sample copies of new periodicals are requested and examined. Titles are added if they promise to be useful and if they meet this library's standards for inclusion.

Selection of pamphlets follows the general policies outlined for book selection. Initial responsibility for selection is placed with the reference librarian. All pamphlets to be ordered are subject to review. Principal sources checked for pamphlets are the *Verticle File Index, Publishers Weekly* and *U.S. Monthly Catalog.*

Useful pamphlets are frequently duplicated since they are an important source of attractive, short and simply-presented ephemeral material not available in book form.

The library does not exclude propaganda or advertising, but a proper balance of viewpoints is sought on controversial subjects. Therefore, propagandistic pamphlets which distort facts, intrude commercial messages unduly or contain misleading statements are not added.

An effort is made to avoid overloading the files to such an extent as to destroy the balance of viewpoint.

North Country Library System

AUDIO-VISUAL MATERIALS

While this policy statement is obviously related to books, we remind the reader that the North Country Library System has large collections of nonprint materials with which to serve the needs of the people of the region: 16mm films, phonograph records and framed art prints. We consider these forms equally important in providing information and recreation for library users. While there are special considerations in the selection and use of these nonbook materials, the same general philosophy expressed in regard to books applies to them.

Rolling Prairie Libraries

PERIODICALS

Periodicals of general interest and of a technical nature are acquired by the co-headquarters libraries and are borrowed through interlibrary loan by the system. Microfilm editions are purchased to provide permanent reference materials.

Periodicals are purchased by Rolling Prairie Libraries to furnish professional reading for its staff member librarians desiring to use and to aid the same in book selection.

FILMS

A sizeable collection of 16mm sound films is maintained by the multimedia services of the Corn Belt Library System and Rolling Prairie Libraries, from which all persons having a valid adult borrower's card are eligible to borrow films. Films are also available from the collections of two other library systems, Illinois Valley and Lincoln Trail. These intersystem requests should be made through Rolling Prairie Libraries. Criteria considered are content, treatment, authenticity and audio and picture quality.

RECORDINGS

Factors to be considered in the selection of musical recordings are composition, performer, quality of musical interpretation, quality of record materials, requests and use. Factors to be considered in the selection of nonmusical records are author, performer, requests, use and, in general, the same principles as those that apply to purchase of other library materials. No attempt will be made to acquire and maintain a collection of "best-sellers."

Types of Recordings Purchased

1. Classical, such as operas, symphonies and chamber music;
2. Semiclassical, such as show tunes and operettas;
3. Contemporary popular music, such as jazz, rock and dance music;
4. Folk music;
5. Literature, such as books, poetry and plays;
6. Documentary and historical records;
7. Foreign language study records;
8. Religious, such as masses, hymns and oratorios;
9. Miscellaneous, such as bird songs and instruction (selling, typing).

FRAMED ART REPRODUCTIONS AND SCULPTURE

The system maintains a circulating collection of framed art reproductions for educational and cultural enjoyment. An attempt is made to represent major artists and sculptors as well as various periods and schools.

Mansfield Public Library

The library feels a responsibility to serve as an archive for the works of local authors and for the collection of local history materials. These and other special collections, housed in the Sherman Room, are maintained for the use of the public. Because of their uniqueness or irreplaceable nature, access to them shall be controlled by rules and procedures approved by the Board. Selection of material for these collections shall be based on appropriateness to the purpose of the collection.

Because Kingwood Center has a special library for the subjects of horticulture, history of landscape gardening, flower arranging, botany and ornithology, this library may choose not to purchase specialized materials in these fields.

Hamilton Public Library

PERIODICALS

This library has from the beginning subscribed liberally to periodicals and now has valuable files which contribute very greatly to reference work.

We subscribe to most Canadian periodicals of merit, the best English and American literary, historical and general journals, and technical and specialized magazines in any field for which there is a real demand. The branches are supplied with magazines which appeal to their particular clientele.

Donated magazines are often of real value but because of limitations of space we cannot take all the ephemeral publications or those with limited appeal which are offered us. Therefore:

We will accept—

1. Periodicals of sufficient general interest or reference value to be:

   • Indexed in printed indexes to which we subscribe;
   • Kept on file and indexed by ourselves;
   • Clipped.

2. Periodicals and yearbooks of recognized Canadian churches organized on a national basis (or in the case of Baptists, in regional federations);
3. Trade magazines and house organs which contain scientific and technical articles of general interest;
4. Publications of nonprofit voluntary organizations of interest to our readers;
5. Local publications;
6. Publications which make a definite contribution to knowledge in fields not covered by the book collection and purchased magazines.

We will not accept—

1. Periodicals which don't meet the criteria given above;
2. Proselytizing organs of groups with something to sell;
3. In general, periodicals which, if presented in book form, would not meet our standards of book selection.

The Free Library of Philadelphia

PAMPHLETS

Definition

The Free Library has arbitrarily defined pamphlets, for selection and acquisition purposes, as material published in the United States or Canada and costing $2.00 or less, including free material.

Pamphlet Committee

The pamphlet committee is a permanent group composed of one representative each from Office of Work with Adults and Young Adults, Office of Work with Children, the Stations Department, regional libraries and branches.

The chairman of the committee reviews orders submitted by Central Public Departments and regional libraries, makes sure the information is complete, and sends the forms to the acquisitions department.

The committee meets every two weeks to review pamphlets that have been received as:

- Initial orders;
- Unsolicited gifts;
- Documents suggested by the government publications department for general purchase.

The committee selects titles to be placed in the OWA/YA new book room for branch and Central Public Services Departments selection.

The committee selects titles to be ordered by the committee for some or all agencies.

The OWC representative selects titles to be duplicated for the children's collections of agencies having a second floor children's room. Such titles appear in the new book room with both adult (salmon) and children's (green) order forms. If a pamphlet is selected for one of these agencies, at least one copy must be ordered for that agency's children's collection.

The committee can recommend that some titles be treated as books rather than pamphlets.

The chairman of the committee maintains the record of book budget expenditures as instructed by procedural policy.

Staff Members

Any staff member may recommend the purchase of a specific pamphlet by submitting to the chairman of the pamphlet committee a 3 × 5 card on which is written the suggested pamphlet's author, title, publisher, publisher's address, price and source of information. If the price is not known, the chairman of the pamphlet committee will obtain this information.

A staff member may request that pamphlets on specific subjects be offered for branch purchase by submitting a list of these subjects to the chairman of the pamphlet committee.

NONPRINT MATERIALS

The growing importance of nonprint materials and the increase in the quantity and variety of all materials available will undoubtedly result in a demand that will far outstrip the funds available to meet that demand. Consequently, an ordering of priorities according to well-defined goals is of the utmost importance if our collections, both print and nonprint, are to be significantly useful to present and future generations. It is expected that the guidelines suggested here will undergo many and frequent revisions as technical innovations affect the development of the newer media and as their convenience and usefulness are demonstrated in experience.

CRITERIA FOR PURCHASE, ORGANIZATION AND USE

Currently about 60 different kinds of media have been identified. We are attempting here to define only the most important examples from the library's point of view and to indicate some criteria for their puchase, organization and use. In projecting the future and establishing priorities, consideration should be given to the following:

1. The goals of The Free Library for the next decade;
2. The various media available and their potential use in The Free Library;
3. The cost of the media, considering initial purchase, replacement needs and growth of the collection;
4. The kind, cost (including maintenance) and quality of the equipment required to use the media;
5. The staff supervision required for the use of the media;
6. The specialized knowledge of both content and format required for sound judgment in selection and organization;
7. The practical problems associated with circulation control, space requirements and storage conditions.

It is the library's policy to organize and arrange collections on the basis of content rather than format whenever possible. In some agencies, such as regional libraries, "special services" departments may be the rule rather than the exception because of the equipment and special facilities required to handle nonprint materials.

It becomes increasingly evident that intershelving of the various nonprint formats in a departmental collection will not be a practical means of displaying a library's holdings in the future and browsing will only infrequently prove an aid to selection. The catalog or its successor may prove to be the principal means for revealing all the library's holdings on a given subject regardless of format.

LOANING OF NONPRINT MATERIAL

Circulation policies will vary with the kinds of materials acquired. Except as specified, the materials described herein will likely not be available on intra- or interlibrary loan because of the limited collections in The Free Library. Programming use may be an exception to this general rule, and as collections grow and funding patterns change, these policies may alter.

Instructional Materials

Some types of nonprint material are designed and are best suited for use in classroom instruction. These materials will usually not be purchased by The Free Library unless they will be useful for programs within the library. Materials suitable for formal, curriculum-oriented instruction are not our primary responsibility, but it is expected that we will serve those engaged in continuing education programs or in classes of a tutorial nature not associated with established institutions of learning.

Microforms

Microfilm, microfiche and other microforms are presently part of The Free Library's collections, and this category of nonbook materials will grow in the coming years. However, it is likely that the acquisition of microforms will be restricted to the collections in the central library and regionals and that they will be acquired primarily for the following reasons:

1. To preserve fragile material;
2. To reduce the shelf space required to house the material;

3. To make materials more readily accessible;
4. To supply a means for rapid scanning and/or print-out.

Audio-Visual Materials

Other nonbook materials, referred to under the general term of "audio-visual," have been accepted for decades as vitally important parts of a library's collection, e.g., prints, maps, films, phonorecords, etc. Today newer forms, such as cassettes and videorecordings, are being acquired by libraries. Every example of audio-visual material mentioned in these guidelines could conceivably fulfill a useful purpose in one or more of The Free Library's collections. As regards library use, these materials have one thing in common and possibly only one; rarely can they be selected, acquired, organized, housed or used by the methods developed for books.

Cassettes. From the point of view of content, as well as form, the cassette has wide popular appeal and must be considered a desirable and appropriate item for a public library's collection.

However, a decision to add this form of library material carries with it the obligation to consider copyright problems, devise new methods of circulation control, study new equipment requirements and, perhaps most critical of all, recognize the degree to which the use of this material requires the personal attention of individual staff members. Unlike most book collections, cassettes cannot be made available on a self-service basis; a staff member must service this material at all times. The space requirements resulting from the restrictions on such collections may preclude their inclusion in some branch collections. As of this date, many libraries, including The Free Library of Philadelphia, have had sufficient experience with cassette collections to learn first hand the practical problems inherent in the service and control of this material, but not sufficient experience as to make the solutions to these problems self-evident.

It is recommended that, for the immediate future, cassettes be considered supplementary to phonorecords in the development of FLP recordings collections. The general policy will be to purchase recordings in phonorecord rather than tape format if they are available in both forms. Cassettes may be purchased by those agencies which have regular budgets for the purchase of recordings. Generally, this will limit cassette holdings to new or remodeled capital agencies or to those branches which have access to private funds on a continuing basis. For the present, the original cassette will be circulated. When improved methods of copying and handling are developed, it may be feasible to expand FLP holdings of cassettes.

Cassettes purchased for the music department reference collection and for the literature department collection will be cataloged. It is recommended that cassettes in all other collections be selected, processed and circulated like phonorecords.

Film, 8mm and Super 8mm. Unencased, reel-to-reel 8mm and Super 8mm film will not be purchased by The Free Library. Few titles are being produced commercially in 8mm and Super 8mm, and whatever technical or price advantage these films had over loops and cartridges has seemingly disappeared.

Film loops, 8mm and Super 8mm. Loops are expensive and incompatibility of equipment is a problem, but as the subjects treated on loops become more suitable for public library use and equipment becomes standardized and improves in quality, 8mm film loops can make an important contribution to The Free Library's programs and collections. It is recommended that, at present, no portion of the library materials budget from state and city funds be allocated for the purchase of loops. It is recommended that private funds be sought to conduct a controlled experiment either in a single agency or on a regional basis. Such an experiment would be carried out under the direction of FLP's materials specialists in the coordinators' offices.

Film, 16mm. Since 1958, it has been the policy of The Free Library to provide a circulating collection of 16mm film. From 1966 to 1973, the films department was supported in whole or part by LSCA federal funding and operated as a regional film center for the public libraries of eastern Pennsylvania. The 16mm film collection which is housed in the films department of the central library consists of a wide variety of educational and feature films of interest to adults, young adults and children. Because of heavy demand, duplicate prints are acquired for popular titles.

Special rules cover the circulation of films from the films department. While Free Library regional libraries may serve as pick-up points for circulation of 16mm films, no collections are planned for regional or branch libraries.

An annotated book catalog is used to describe the holdings maintained by the films department. It is also recommended that, when funds permit, 16mm films be classified by subject and cataloged by *The Anglo-American Cataloging Rules*. They will appear in the appropriate central library departmental card catalogs as well as the main card catalog.

Filmstrips. Filmstrips are a useful and important component of a library's audio-visual collection because:

1. A variety of subjects and titles is available in this form.
2. They are relatively inexpensive compared with 8mm film loops.
3. They are widely accepted as teaching aids today so that children and young adults are familiar with their use.
4. They are appealing to those who are not book oriented.
5. They are suitable for both group and individual use.
6. The equipment required for their use is relatively inexpensive.

It is recommended that circulating collections of filmstrips be added to Free Library agencies. Because of fund limitations, development of such collections throughout the entire system will be slow. Circulating collections should be planned for central departments, regional libraries, new and renovated capital facilities and those agencies where private funds can cover cost of materials and equipment. In addition, collections should be continued in the Reader Development Program and the six branches that initially tested in-house use of filmstrips. Equipment which is compatible for use of phonorecords and cassettes should be available for viewing filmstrips in the library. Small hand viewers should also be provided for use in the library and for home circulation from new capital agencies when funds are available for their purchase.

Filmstrips will be classified by subject and cataloged by *The Anglo-American Cataloging Rules*. They will appear in the appropriate age-level Book Catalogs and Central Library Card Catalogs.

It is recognized that some in-service training in the use of filmstrips will be required as their use is extended throughout the library system.

Machine-readable data files. These are files of data or programs for manipulation by a computer or other equipment. The same file may exist in a variety of physical formats, e.g., punched cards, magnetic tape, disk or data cell. The content of the file need not change as the file is reformatted and transformed for reasons of local convenience.

Except for the Model Cities Community Information Center demonstration in the early 1970s, The Free Library has not participated in the creation of such a file, nor does it own any at present. The various computer applications in The Free Library, such as VICS, IRAS, New York Times Data Bank and OCLC, consist of on-line access to data files owned by and housed in other institutions. It is probable that this will continue to be the way in which The Free Library uses computers.

The machine-readable data file most likely to be prepared and owned by The Free Library is, of course, a catalog of either the central library or extension division collection or both. This could conceivably be used in an automated circulation system in addition to its primary function of bibliographic retrieval. It is far beyond our present financial resources, but should be studied carefully and planned for when appropriate or feasible.

Phonorecords. Phonorecords, both historic collections for reference use and circulating collections, are a legitimate and accepted component of a public library's collections. The Free Library of Philadelphia has had long experience with the former, very little experience with the latter.

In considering phonorecords vs. cassettes, each has advantages and disadvantages, e.g., technical problems limit fidelity and hence restrict selection of material in cassettes; phonograph records are cumbersome to shelve. Both are expensive to service and to circulate. Neither is self-servicing to the degree that print materials are. Both are popular and, in circulating collections, casualties are high and costly.

Since it is unlikely that money is going to be available on a continuing basis to support collections of phonorecords wherever desirable, it is recommended that circulating collections be planned for regional libraries and new capital facilities when a portion of the initial budget can be reserved for purchase of phonorecords. When private money underwrites the cost and maintenance of a circulating record collection, as at Roxborough, an exception to this policy can be made. Phonorecord collections in the central library will contain both reference and circulating materials.

It is recommended that phonorecords in central collections be classified by subject and be cataloged by *The Anglo-American Cataloging Rules*. For all other agencies, arrangement by broad categories determined by reader use is recommended.

Phonotapes. Phonotape or audiotape is defined in *The Anglo-American Cataloging Rules* as "magnetic tape on which audio signals are recorded."

Many phonotapes in The Free Library of Philadelphia's collections have been acquired as gifts and date back to the pre-cassette and pre-mylar era. It is recommended that FLP's present collections of phonotape not be augmented and that present holdings be phased out either through weeding or transfer to the cassette form. At this writing, the cassette enclosed in a cartridge seems likely to prove more suitable for public library use, although there are also many unresolved questions to be answered about cassettes.

The Library for the Blind and Physically Handicapped, with its special requirements, is not governed by the above statement. Also, a specific project requiring the use of phonotapes may be granted funds for their purchase.

Prints. Pictures and prints have long been accepted as important kinds of documentation and, hence, appropriate items for a library's collection. For at least 45 years The Free Library of Philadelphia has maintained a special collection of prints and pictures.

While it is acknowledged that branch and regional libraries could benefit from well-selected picture collections, the high cost of acquiring, maintaining and servicing such collections makes it imperative that we continue to concentrate our efforts and resources on the collection at the central library, where special expertise is available to handle this material efficiently and effectively. However, in order to extend the usefulness of this collection and to improve its accessibility to branch and regional libraries, it is recommended that consideration be given to liberalizing the circulation policy for mounted pictures to permit children to borrow this material and to allow mounted pictures to be circulated through interlibrary and intralibrary loans.

The fine print collection will continue, as in the past, to be a reference collection. Original prints and framed reproductions will not be circulated for home use.

Slides. The slides held in the various agencies of The Free Library today have frequently been prepared by individual staff members for their own use in connection with specific events or programs. Others have been received as gifts but have not been organized for use or even officially added (shelflisted).

It is recommended that the use of slides with book talks and programs be continued when appropriate but that no planned acquisition of slides be undertaken and that no money be allocated in the library materials budget for the purchase of this material. However, under exceptional circumstances special funds may be made available for a specific project or special collection.

Videorecordings. No other audio-visual material is currently undergoing as much change and technical development as videorecordings. Videorecordings are presently available in a variety of formats that include videocassettes, videodiscs and videotapes. Not only are there multiformats in videorecordings, but different sizes within a particular format such as videotape require different equipment to be viewed.

Many different technologies and competing incompatible systems are currently under development. When and if videorecordings become available at reasonable cost and can be used on hardware available in most homes, they will be a logical addition to reference and circulating collections in Free Library agencies. It is recommended that one staff member be charged with the responsibility for keeping informed on the developments in this phase of commercial videorecordings and for submitting reports as advances in the field dictate.

In the area of in-house production of videorecordings, long-range goals call for a multimedia center which will have capabilities for producing a wide range of video programs. Fiscal limitations prevent implementation of such an operation at the present time. For the immediate future, it is recommended that use of videorecordings be limited in application throughout the system. Video portapac equipment is available at The Free Library for a variety of in-house uses, including staff training, preparation of programs which can be presented on cable television, recording programming events and replaying videotapes produced by other sources. Equipment is also available to play videocassettes prepared by commercial sources or other agencies. General use of this equipment will be for specific programming activities.

Videorecordings produced as a result of the above activities will be retained in the coordinators' offices in archival files. These tapes may be copied or lent to other institutions at the discretion of the coordinators. Commercial videocassettes acquired for specific activities such as adult education tutoring projects will be maintained at agency sites or filed in the appropriate coordinators' offices.

Instructional Materials

Games.   The usefulness or appropriateness of games in a public library is open to question, and in the face of stringent budget limitations the acquiring of games has a low priority. No portion of the library materials budget will be allocated for the purchase of games. When educational games are purchased with special funds or received as gifts they may be retained for display (realia in this case) or, in a very limited number of agencies, used experimentally for the purpose of testing the usefulness of games as devices for reaching the nonreader. Such experimental use will not include circulation of this material. Games used for these purposes are not to be cataloged.

Multimedia kits.   The usefulness of the kit in a public library collection is acknowledged, but, for the foreseeable future, there will be no attempt to acquire this material in The Free Library. Kits acquired as gifts will be considered "specimens"; will be used for programming, when appropriate; will be housed in the coordinators' offices; and will not be cataloged. The single exception will be the Reader Development Program where kits will continue to be purchased for loan to teachers. It is recommended that a representative or representatives of The Free Library be selected to work with the staff of the Board of Education with the view to developing a wide acquaintance with the material available in this form and expertise in its critical evaluation.

Realia. There will be no allocation from the library materials budget for the purchase of realia and no program for their acquisition. If acquired through special funds or as gifts, realia may be retained for display. These will not circulate but may be loaned to other agencies of The Free Library system or the Philadelphia District and, under exceptional circumstances, to outside organizations and institutions.

Transparencies. The transparency is a useful classroom teaching device but inappropriate for public library collections and programs. This material will not be added to our collections.

Microforms: Microfilm and Microfiche

Among the various kinds of microreproductions available today, two, microfiche and microfilm, appear to be of the greatest importance for future collection building in The Free Library. It is generally conceded that microfiche will eventually supplant the microfilm roll as the most widely used microform because it is technically superior, is easier to use, requires simpler and cheaper equipment, can be copied satisfactorily and presents no insurmountable problems in bibliographic control. On the other hand, microfilm has a clear advantage over microfiche as regards the question of "file integrity." A file where pages and volumes are maintained in exact sequence without the need for filing and refiling is well-suited for servicing serial collections, for example.

In view of the above statements, it is recommended that, when microfiche or microfilm editions are available in satisfactory reproductions, second copies of serials in these forms be purchased in lieu of binding. When microfilm is purchased, 35mm is preferred over 16mm if both are available. Positive film is recommended over negative film when it is available.

It is recognized that the extent to which these recommendations can be implemented depends on the money available for library materials and the industry's resolution of such current problems as lack of standardization and the incompatibility of equipment. In addition, as monographs are issued in microfiche editions, their purchase should be considered in line with established book selection principles. For the foreseeable future, however, microfiche editions of this kind of material will probably be restricted to rare or out-of-print items or reference titles where the regular revision or addition of data is essential.

In the central library, microform editions will be selected and serviced by the departments that are selecting and servicing comparable material in printed form or macrotext. In regional libraries, the servicing of microforms may be centralized along with other special materials, depending upon the size of the microform collection, the nature of its use, the architectural plan of the building and other considerations.

Bibliographic control is essential for all microforms. Appropriate records, including analytics as required, will be prepared based on an examination of each item, as is done in the case of hard copies. The Free Library's present practices regarding the cataloging of this material, in force since 1968, will be continued.

Ultramicrofiche

The way in which ultramicrofiche material is selected, assembled and offered for sale suggests that it has little usefulness for FLP at the present time.

Microforms: Selection, Acquisition and Processing

Selection.   The general policy for acquisition of microforms is described in PS #74: Guidelines for the Acquisition of Nonprint Materials. Material in microform is selected, with the approval of the appropriate coordinator, by the department that is responsible for the subject area. Material that is new to the collection is selected according to the same criteria as are applied to the selection of ink print material.

The following additional considerations may influence selection of a microform in preference to, or sometimes in addition to, the ink print form of the same item:

1. Space conservation;
2. Preservation of rare, fragile, deteriorated or deteriorating material;
3. Filling gaps in a serial or other multi-volume file;
4. Material available only in microform;
5. By-product of a request for loan by an individual or another institution, or a micropublisher.

These considerations may overlap to a degree. Deteriorated material duplicated in microform may be discarded so that space is saved. A patron may request the loan of material that is too rare or fragile to risk in the mail, but which can be filmed satisfactorily. A volume lacking in a serial file may be easily available only in microform.

In priority order, the following guidelines are observed for selecting Free Library material to be duplicated in microform:

1. Significant material that cannot be bound because of deteriorating paper;
2. Significant material already bound, but deteriorating rapidly (N.B.: preference in these categories is given to items that are of local interest and importance, or are of value to a special collection);
3. Material needed to fill a gap in an existing file;
4. Less significant unbound material;
5. Bound volumes in good condition which are replaced to save space.

Method of acquisition.   Purchase from a commercial firm or another institution:

1. If the desired material is available, this is usually the most economical method of obtaining it. There is no risk of destruction to the ink print copy and the decision to retain or dispose of it can be made later.
2. An order like that for any other library material is placed and received by the acquisitions department or its serials section.

Microforms: Micro-Opaques

Micro-opaques (including microcards and microprints) were among the earliest microforms available, but today are no longer preferred by either industry or the library world. Consequently, in the future, only essential material that is unavailable in any other form will be purchased in micro-opaque editions. FLP collections in this form will be retained, and equipment necessary to service micro-opaques will be maintained.

Material not self-cataloged will be cataloged retrospectively but selectively, and this material will be shelved and serviced through the appropriate central subject department. Micro-opaques are not recommended for branch or regional purchase.

Maps

Unlike some other nonbook materials, The Free Library of Philadelphia does have an extensive collection of maps at the central library. This collection has grown without an acknowledged and agreed-upon plan regarding its purpose and scope. With a view to developing such a plan it is recommended that a report be prepared describing the holdings of the present map collection, the use this material receives and the effect of The Free Library's role as a depository library on both holdings and use. The present composition of the map collection may be inappropriate for our needs, duplicate other resources within the community or require an unreasonable commitment of staff and space.

It is not recommended that map collections as such be established in branches or regional libraries. In these agencies individual maps, when needed, will be filed in the vertical file or be displayed on the wall. Atlases will be purchased for reference and circulation.

Knight-Capron Library, Lynchburg College

PERIODICALS

Policy

The number of annual subscriptions shall not fall below the requirements of the Clapp Formula.

New titles will not be ordered if they are already held by libraries participating in the *Lynchburg Area Union List of Serials,* except when they are needed for very special purposes.

Back files may be ordered only when they are not available through the *Lynchburg Area Union List of Serials.*

Periodicals will be bound or secured in microform depending on use and the rate of volume growth.

Criteria

• Will it be used extensively?
• Is it indexed in the standard indexes?

- Does it have special significance for this library?
- Does it support a particular program?
- Does it have research value?
- Does it include material not found in other titles being received?
- Is it available through the *Lynchburg Area Union List of Serials*?
- Is it an isolated request which may be filled through interlibrary loan?

MULTIMEDIA MATERIALS

The head of acquisitions selects all materials, keeping in perspective the various curricula and departmental requests and needs.

Procedure follows that used for ordering books except that the following bibliographical tools are used for searching:

- *National Union Catalog:* music and phonorecords;
- *Library Journal/School Library Journal:* previews, news and reviews of nonprint media;
- National Information Center for Educational Media/NICEM: indexes.

Roanoke-Chowan Technical Institute Library

POLICY FOR PERIODICAL SELECTION

The general principles for periodical selection do not vary essentially from those governing the selection of books. Faculty members are asked to recommend periodicals for purchase. However, there are certain principles and procedures that are relied upon by the librarian in determining whether or not to add a new serial to the collection.

Periodicals and newspapers are purchased to upgrade and support the curriculum and programs offered the students. Furthermore, priority is given to titles that are analyzed in the standard indexing services to which the library subscribes, as *Readers' Guide, Education Index, Applied Science and Technology Index,* etc. Other factors governing selection are the financial resources of the library, the periodicals already subscribed to and the title's availability elsewhere. The librarian considers duplicate subscriptions on the basis of relative value and library budget. Which will further the library's program to the best advantage: extra copies or additional titles?

Every three years or so, the librarian should review each entry in the Kardex file and evaluate whether the title or extra copies are still worthwhile.

AUDIO-VISUAL MATERIALS

The Learning Resources Center has a large collection of filmstrips, transparencies, filmloops, tapes, records, art prints and 16mm films to support the instructional function of the institute. Materials which faculty request are ordered on a preview basis. These preview materials are reviewed by librarians and all interested faculty. Often classes are given an opportunity to preview the materials. This enables the faculty to observe the students' reactions and evaluate the material according to the various criteria for that particular need. If the instructor feels the material is appropriate for her/his teaching, the material is ordered for the Learning Resources Center.

The librarians use various tools such as library and media journals, publisher's catalogs, directories of audio-visual materials and brochures as sources from which to suggest new materials to the faculty.

PAMPHLET FILE

Any book with less than thirty-nine pages should be placed in the pamphlet file rather than cataloged and shelved on the regular shelves.

To place a booklet in the pamphlet file, follow these instructions:

1. Check *The Pamphlet File in School, College, and Public Libraries* by Norma Olin Ireland to see if the subject heading has been used before. Put a check next to each new subject heading used.
2. If the subject heading has not been used before (has not been checked), make and type the subject heading in all capitals on a blue-banded 4×6" index card.
3. If the subject heading has been used previously (has been checked in the book), type the exact title of the pamphlet on a plain 4×6" card.
4. If the subject heading has not been used before, you will need to type a label and prepare a folder for the pamphlet also.
5. Write in ink, in the upper right hand corner of the pamphlet, the subject heading under which it is to be filed and place "VF" in the corner.
6. File the folders alphabetically in the pamphlet file drawer; file the pamphlets alphabetically in their proper folder.
7. File the blue-banded index cards alphabetically in the pamphlet index. File the plain index cards alphabetically behind the proper subject heading in the pamphlet index.

Clermont General and Technical College Library

Funds for serials and periodicals are part of the library materials budget. The library maintains standing orders for new editions of a selected number of titles. Selection of periodical titles is based upon relevance to the curriculum of the college, indexing in periodical indexes subscribed to by the college, and price. The library maintains subscriptions to a small number of recreational general periodicals.

Microforms are a specialized form of nonprint materials used as a substitute for the same information in print form. The major form is microfilm, which is used in this library for keeping back issues of periodicals. The major criterion for selection of periodical microform is indexing in indexes received by the library. Other microform selection criteria are: relevance to the curriculum, space considerations, availability in hard copy and scholarly value.

The library materials budget is also used for rental of films and other materials for classroom instructional use. There is no allocation of funds specifically for this purpose, nor is there an allocation for specific subject areas. Films are ordered only at the request of the instructor with no limit on the number of films an instructor may order. As a general rule a film costing $50 or more will not be ordered unless it will be shown to enough students to make the cost equal to one dollar or less per student seeing the film (e.g., a $50 film shown to 50 or more students or a $75 film shown to 75 or more students). Films costing less than $50 may be ordered regardless of the size of the class.

St. Catherine Library

Periodicals.   The selection of periodicals is based on the same criteria as that for books. The balance is weighed in favor of rapidly developing technological fields. An attempt is made to select a wide variety of representative titles covering varying viewpoints. Whether or not the periodical is indexed or held by member libraries in the consortium is a major consideration.

Information file.   Pamphlets of topical interest that may not be contained in books are selected from the Government Printing Office lists, periodicals listing pamphlet material, *Vertical File Index,* and gratis material judged not valuable enough to be cataloged. Pamphlet material on women is acquired for the women's collection section of the information file.

Music scores/sheet music.   Selection is based on music curriculum needs and cataloged for the performing arts library collection.

Nonprint media or software.   The selection of this type of format is dictated by instructional or recreational use, facility of storage, and whether the item is solely available in this format and lower in cost. This type of material is ordered on an approval basis and returned if not sufficiently meeting selection criteria.

Audio-visual equipment or hardware.   Equipment selected supplements that owned by academic departments. Selection is based on standards proposed by the Association for Education Communications and Technology and the American Association of School Librarians, including usefulness, safety, sturdiness and cost. The collection should not duplicate hardware available elsewhere and is of specific limited application.

Kansas City Kansas Community Junior College Library

SELECTION OF PERIODICALS

Periodical subscriptions may be recommended in the same manner as books. Such recommendations shall be weighed against:

1. The availability of funds;
2. The amount currently expended for serial subscriptions in the subject area of the request;
3. The availability of indexing;
4. Reputation of the publisher;
5. Appearance of the title in special bibliographies or indexes;
6. Importance of the subject matter to the collection;
7. Scarcity of material on the subject;
8. Price;
9. Number of students enrolled in the subject area of the request.

Requests will generally be held until August of each year at which time a general evaluation of requests, holdings and current subscriptions will be made by the librarians.

Subscriptions regarding specific subject areas will not be added or dropped without consultation with the appropriate divisional chairman.

SELECTION OF AUDIO-VISUAL SOFTWARE

Current selection aids regularly reviewed by the staff include:

1. *Booklist;*
2. *Previews (Library Journal).*

Retrospective selection aids consulted as necessary are:

1. *Producers Catalogs;*
2. *NICEM Catalogs;*
3. *Media Review Digest;*
4. *AV Market Place.*

Selection

The responsibility for software selection rests with the faculty. Typically, the events leading to the acquisition of software occur in this order:

1. A faculty member contacts the library staff with a request for a specific software program or with a request for assistance in locating a program.
2. The divisional chairman approves the order.
3. If an official college purchase order is not required and if a company form is not supplied, materials are ordered on a special audio-visual order form. Because materials are ordered on a preview basis, no purchase order request is issued unless required by producer.
4. Materials are received and previewed by the faculty member who originated the request.
5. Materials are purchased or returned.
6. If purchased, materials are processed and cataloged.

SELECTION OF AUDIO-VISUAL MATERIALS

Auditory and visual nonprint materials will be acquired and processed by the library staff. A permanent record of audio-visual holdings will be maintained in the library's card catalog.

Assuming the availability of funds and materials, faculty requests for filmstrips, records, slides, transparencies, tapes and kits shall be honored. Because of their expense, films will normally be rented, not purchased.

Guidelines used in book selection shall apply to nonbook materials as well.

Acquisitions will be spread equally among the various teaching divisions assuming the availability of worthwhile materials.

Audio-visual orders will be reviewed by members of the production staff to determine whether or not requested materials can be produced more inexpensively on campus.

Hartwick College Library

Between them, the libraries at Hartwick and State University College at Oneonta make available a large number of periodicals. Because of high subscription, binding and shelving costs new subscriptions are added only after the most careful consideration of their present and future value. Any periodical that is available at SUCO or in the region, highly specialized, or not covered by one of the standard indexes stands a poor chance of being adopted.

Requests for subscriptions should be accompanied by a verbal or written explanation and should be addressed to the director.

Frazer Memorial Library, McNeese State University

PERIODICALS AND SERIALS

Periodicals and serials are included in the collection in accord with library and university objectives, with emphasis given to those titles included in indexing and abstracting services. Back volumes are purchased and gaps filled on the basis of recommendations from the faculty and professional staff when funds for these additions are available.

University of Wyoming Library

PERIODICALS

Periodical subscriptions initiated by a department since July 1, 1971, will be permanently assessed to that department's allocation. Back issues will be charged to the department ordering them, without considering which fund is paying for the current subscription. As with out-of-print books, the availability of back issues cannot be anticipated. Backfiles will be acquired in microform if available or, failing that, in reprint unless the original edition is essential (e.g., microform would not be bought for art or medical journals in which colored illustrations are an integral part of the intellectual content).

Journal article reprints are not acquired for the permanent collection. If needed for reserve or individual use, uncataloged reprints may be acquired through the interlibrary loan office. A permanent, but uncataloged, file of reprints of articles published by university faculty and staff is maintained in the reference department; all individuals publishing articles are asked to contribute to this file.

RECORDINGS

The main campus center for musical recordings is the music department collection housed in the fine arts building, which is independent of the library. Recordings other than musical and a small collection of musical recordings mainly for recreational use are part of the library's holdings. Orders for recordings will be evaluated by the library acquisitions department to determine where the particular title is appropriately kept, and only those recordings that are housed in the library will be purchased with library funds.

FILMS

The film library, though administratively part of the library, has a separate materials budget; therefore, orders for films will be referred to the film librarian and will not normally be charged to departmental allocations. Unless a film is going to be used repeatedly on campus or is suitable for loan to off-campus groups, rental should be considered as an alternative to purchase.

OTHER MEDIA

The Jayne Media Center has been created, independent of the library, to house the campus collection of the newer, more specialized instructional materials, such as multimedia kits. Therefore, such materials will not be acquired with library funds nor housed in the library. The acquisitions department of the library will determine which materials will be bought with library funds to be retained in the permanent collection.

Use and space will primarily determine whether to buy any individual item in hard copy or in microform; at the present time space problems make microform preferable for items that will not be heavily used. If the library already owns a title in microform, hard copy will not also be acquired unless constant class use is anticipated.

Grand View College Library

The library will subscribe to periodicals which best support the library's purposes. Periodicals indexed in the standard periodical indexes held by the library will be given first consideration for their reference value. Back files will be kept in a permanent form, either bound or on microfilm. Other titles not indexed will be considered on their individual merits and bound only when they have special use for local purposes. The titles not bound will be kept for varying periods, depending upon space and the joint judgment of the teacher and the librarian. As new titles are started a decision should be made as to the value of acquiring back files, either bound or on microfilm.

Newspapers of local and national importance are kept only until space runs out. One title, the *New York Times,* is available on microfilm since 1959 with ready access through an accompanying index.

The library recognizes the growing interest in nonprint materials. Attempts are made to follow audio-visual trends, i.e., stereo records rather than mono, tape cassettes rather than reel tapes. The library has built and is maintaining a good audio collection—both in music and the spoken word. Visual materials such as slides and filmstrips are purchased on the recommendation of faculty. The library's collection of framed reproductions for rent will be expanded in the future only if additional funds are available. All nonprint materials are cataloged and color coded for identification in the card catalog.

The library will be responsible for housing and cataloging college-produced audio-visual material unless of a very specific nature and used often in a particular department only.

Hoover Library, Western Maryland College

Since a periodical subscription request is often a significant financial investment (when taken together with its backfile), it is felt that the following policies should pertain:

1. New periodical subscriptions will be charged to general library funds, as they are available.
2. Each request for a new periodical title must be justified in writing to the library committee for decision whether to add, using the criteria noted in Section 3 below.

   - Cost and extent of backfile (including costs) should be included.
   - Consideration of backfiling will be considered together with the new title. (If the title is important enough to subscribe to, it is equally important to have backfiles.)

3. Criteria for adding new periodical titles should be:
   - Access through indexes and abstracts;
   - Priority of basic journals over specialized titles;
   - A realistic appraisal of anticipated use by students (i.e., curriculum or program need) and faculty within the framework of general policy for acquisition;
   - Listing in standard guides (i.e., recommended holding lists for college libraries—Farber, *Choice,* Katz, etc.).

4. Criteria for backfiling periodical titles already received should be the same as those for adding new titles.

Ricks College Learning Resources Center

FILM EVALUATION CRITERIA

1. Cost-effective formula of rental vs. purchase
   T = Number of times rented in 5 years to bring rental costs equal to owning costs
   P = Purchase price of film
   F = Rental fee

$$T = \frac{P}{F+2}$$

2. Film purchase cost per student estimated over a five year period
   C = Cost per student
   P = Purchase price of film
   S = Estimated number of students seeing film during one year

$$C = \frac{P}{5S}$$

3. Estimated times rented over 5 years
   t = Number of times film has been rented the past two years
   T = Estimated number of times film is rented in 5 years

$$T = \frac{5}{2}t$$

4. Cost of reordering a film not available on first order
   R = Cost of reordering
   N = Times film was not available the past two years

$$R = \$1.75 \times \frac{5}{2}N$$

5. Was film shipped other than parcel post?
   ____ yes ____ no.
   If yes the cost was ____

6. Is film available at
   (a) 5 or more libraries
   (b) 3 libraries
   (c) 1 library

7. Estimated number of times a film, if purchased, could be rented off campus on a pick-up and return basis only
   I = Annual income
   T = Estimated times film can be rented
   F = Rental fee

$$I = T\,F$$

7b. Estimated adjusted film purchase cost in 5 years
   A = Estimated adjusted purchase cost
   P = Purchase cost
   I = Estimated income

$$A = P - I$$

8. Is it possible to show the film to all sections with one regular rental?
   Yes ____ No ____ If no: (a) Is the film rented again?

   (b) Is there an extension on rental? _____
   (If yes, this is a 50% rental)
   (c) Do some sections miss seeing the film?
   _____

PERIODICALS

The Learning Resources Center periodicals collection will reflect the research and browsing needs of Ricks College and community.

Unbound current periodicals may be retained for five years as research material.

Periodicals will then be discarded and/or purchased on microfilm, and/or selected titles may be bound.

Gardner-Harvey Library, Miami University–Middletown (Ohio)

TYPES OF PERIODICALS SELECTED

1. Student collateral reading for course work with preference for those periodicals regularly assigned by the faculty;
2. Journals found in the standard indexes, to keep faculty members informed of current developments in their field;
3. Specialized journals not received by a faculty member whose need for them is justified in a consultation with the librarian;
4. General and recreational periodicals;
5. Periodicals that meet the research needs of the faculty and advanced students selected in consultation with the head librarian (considerations should be cost and availability through interlibrary loan).

Retention of periodicals is based on their continued appearance in standard indexing media and their general or popular value.

Yavapai College Learning Resources Center

PERIODICALS AND NEWSPAPERS

Selection of magazine titles may depend on their importance to the curriculum, the level of reading presented, the number of journals being received in the subject area, the availability of their contents in indexes, and the cost in proportion to anticipated use.

Backfiles of periodicals will be in microform except in the cases of periodicals already consisting of extensive runs or where the original is desirable because of color prints, art, etc.

Newspapers will be purchased to reflect local, state and national coverage. Prescott and surrounding areas served by the college will be emphasized.

NONBOOK MATERIALS

Nonprint items will be acquired according to the criteria for books whenever applicable.

Because of their high cost, nonbook items such as filmstrips, film loops, slide sets, etc., will be ordered on approval unless selected from a reviewing source considered reliable by the acquisitions librarian. Faculty members will be asked to preview such materials as soon as possible after they are notified of their arrival.

Films will not be acquired because of their excessive cost, limited use and proportionately short life span. Funds will be provided for film rental as the best alternative.

ARCHIVES

The archives of Yavapai College consist of the publications of the college, including catalogs, periodicals, handbooks, reports, yearbooks, brochures and the minutes of meetings of the Board of Governors, the division chairmen and the faculty association. They will also contain materials about the college.

Belk Library, Appalachian State University

REQUESTING PERIODICALS AND NEWSPAPERS

Request cards for periodicals and newspapers are submitted by the departmental representative to the library liaison person. In addition to the standard information on the book request card, the periodicals request card should include the desired beginning date of the subscription and whether back issues are needed. All requested back issues will be charged to the department. If available, the publisher's announcement should be attached to the request card.

The initial subscription to a periodical or newspaper will be charged to the departmental allocation. The cost of renewals will be paid from the general library budget. Whenever possible, back issues of periodicals and newspapers will be obtained in microform.

Periodical and newspaper subscriptions consume a large portion of the library book budget each year. Therefore, careful thought should precede requests for additional titles.

REQUESTING MICROFORMS

The term "microforms" includes microfilm, microfiche, ultrafiche, aperture cards, microcards, etc. These materials are obtained primarily to expand the library holdings in areas which place a heavy emphasis upon research. Generally, microforms enable the library to conserve storage space, save money and obtain materials no longer available in book form. Microforms will become even more important as man's recorded knowledge continues to grow.

Requests for microforms are processed in the same manner as requests for books. The request should include the publisher's identification number for the microform (usually found in the publisher's catalog), in addition to the standard information on the card.

The library administration occasionally will purchase selected microform publications with general library funds.

REQUESTING AUDIO-VISUAL MATERIALS

Audio-visual materials (films, filmstrips, tapes, recordings, etc.) may be requested by departments after careful evaluation of the materials. All audio-visual materials purchased with library funds will be housed in the library and supervised by library personnel.

Library, Northeastern Illinois University

Certainly the fastest increasing facets of the library's book buying are serials, periodicals and those books received on standing order. This includes continuing sets which are sent automatically to the library when published.

In a developing university library another sizeable area of expenditure must be the purchase of periodical backruns. The library tries to buy these items as they appear on the market. In addition, a large sum of money goes to the purchase of such backfiles in microtext format. The acquisition of antiquarian books also requires an increasing portion of the budget. The same is true for lost or worn out copies.

The purchase of an item in microtext should be guided by its availability in other formats, the degree and nature of its use, space considerations and the adequacy of microreading equipment in the library.

Ralph M. Paiewonsky Library, College of The Virgin Islands

In recognition of the changing methods of recording facts, ideas, concepts and experiences, the materials added to the library will include microfilm and other microprint, slides, motion picture films and sound recordings. To a considerable degree, acquisition of materials of this type will be made in the light of their value as supplements to the printed resources of the library.

Learning Resources Center, Catonsville Community College

MICROFORMS

Preference is usually given to the purchase of microforms rather than backfiles of the printed volumes because they cost less, are more easily available, require less storage space and are easier to control. Examples of exceptions are art, architecture and illustrated science periodicals. Monographs in microform are acceptable when originals cannot be obtained, but do not replace holdings of the printed volumes needed in the center.

Blue Mountain Community College Library

ACQUISITIONS—PAMPHLET FILE

Pamphlets are ordered from two basic sources: *Vertical File Index* and *Selected List of U.S. Government Publications*. These publications are rented to library staff and those items wanted are checked. Ordering is done by the library clerk who purchases $10 in stamps each month to use as payment for pamphlet orders. Each year $100 is allotted for pamphlet purchases and individual pamphlets are ordered only if their price is $1 or less.

Gifts, Interlibrary Loans, Networks and Consortia

Rolling Prairie Libraries

THE DEVELOPMENT OF SYSTEM COLLECTIONS

In accordance with an agreement worked out on January 31, 1974, the two co-headquarters libraries—Decatur Public Library and Lincoln Library of Springfield—and systems headquarters approved a cooperative acquisition program whereby the system would follow the initial pattern of building on strength, and, therefore, continue to financially support the development of subject collections at the Decatur Public Library and Lincoln Library rather than build a separate, centralized, in-depth subject collection at system headquarters. Subject to review, materials selected by professional staff members of Decatur Public Library and Lincoln Library are purchased by Rolling Prairie Libraries, and these system-owned materials are added to the appropriate subject areas in the co-headquarters on permanent loan.

Subject areas generally designated were as follows:

- Decatur Public Library: Dewey Classification 100s, 200s, 300s except political science, government and education, 500s, 600s and 700–749;
- Lincoln Library: 300s pertaining to political science, government and education, 400s, 750–799, 800s, 900s and fiction.

The "0" hundreds remain unassigned so that each library can acquire the bibliographies which might be most related to its specified acquisitions.

Rolling Prairie Libraries Administrative Headquarters: Library Science

The materials acquired under this plan are intended to be not the really popular items but rather the significant subject material that is called for less frequently in any one library but would be used with some regularity among the 40 member libraries. All such purchases should be based upon expressed requests of potential needs (demonstrated need for subject material presented) of many libraries in the system, not just one library. Specialized subject material should be made well-known throughout the system. Each of the three libraries is still held responsible for acquiring its basic collection to service everyday needs of its public.

GIFTS

The Rolling Prairie Libraries retain the right to make the most advantageous use of materials they accept. Gifts of books and other materials are accepted but without commitments as to final disposition and with the understanding that they are not necessarily to be added to the collection. The same criteria used for the selection of all other materials will be used in evaluating gift materials.

Gift materials will be shelved in the regular collection where they are most useful, rather than on separate shelves that take them out of the logical sequence.

As a general rule, Rolling Prairie Libraries will not accept for deposit materials which are not outright gifts. Certain objects which might be more appropriate for a museum are not accepted.

Virginia Beach Public Library Department

GIFT BOOK POLICY

Gift books are those unsolicited books a patron donates to a branch library. Gifts are accepted but the patron should be informed that the library, if unable to use them, will dispose of the books in an appropriate manner. Receipts for income tax purposes as to the number of books and date of donation may be given by the librarian when requested. The library system cannot assign a value to these books.

These donations should be restricted to paperbacks, fiction and popular nonfiction. It is best not to accept textbooks as donations as they are usually difficult to distribute and are rarely added to the collection due to old copyright dates.

Donations that the librarian wishes to save may be placed in either the honor collection or the cataloged collection. If the book has been previously cataloged within the system, the librarian need only call the cataloging librarian to receive a copy number and then prepare the book for placement in the collection. If the book has not been cataloged previously, it should be stamped with the branch locator stamp and sent to the cataloging librarian.

The Public Library of Cincinnati and Hamilton County

GIFTS

The library welcomes gifts but accepts them with the understanding that it has the right to handle or dispose of them in the best interest of the institution. Such material may be added to the collection provided that it meets the library's standards of selection; limitations of space and processing costs are other considerations in the decision to add gifts.

North Country Library System

NORTH COUNTRY REFERENCE AND RESEARCH RESOURCES COUNCIL

The service center played a major part in organizing the North Country Reference and Research Resources Council (NCRRRC), which was registered by the Board of Regents in 1966. North Country joined with the Clinton-Essex-Franklin Library System in securing a grant to pay for the survey, "Library Resources in the North Country Area of New York State," by Guy B. Garrison, which provided background information for the organization of the council. One of the principal services of the NCRRRC is a regional interlibrary loan service, which has been able to fill 47% of the requests referred to it. The benefits to the member libraries and their clients from being able to call upon the resources of the college libraries in the area have already been great. As the college collections grow in depth and quality, the serious students and professional people of the area will be increasingly benefited. They will have access to the advanced research materials of the area and the new organization will provide the machinery for making them quickly available.

Beyond the North Country, the NCRRRC is part of a network encompassing the major research libraries of the state and can call upon these to fill interlibrary loan requests which cannot be supplied from regional resources. These regional and statewide ties mean that the service center does not need to deplete its budget by purchasing scholarly works of interest to only a few people.

MEMBER LIBRARIES

The book buying programs of our member libraries influence greatly our service center policies. As we noted above, the limited budgets of many of the members have made it necessary for the service center to buy many copies of books of only temporary interest. But no matter how many copies of these books we buy, they are never enough. The fact is that many patrons have had to wait as long as two years for some of these books.

Clearly, this situation is not good. We can never meet the demand for best-sellers, highly advertised works, and other light reading matter from our limited income. Nor can we afford to supply in quantity those books which, because of lasting value and importance, should be in every member library. More and more, the service center must order selectively on a basis of supplementing rather than substituting for local library purchase; we must concentrate on rounding out and adding depth to the existing local collections. And it becomes increasingly imperative for member libraries, large and small, to have larger book budgets, and to assume more of the responsibility for purchasing best-sellers, other material in immediate demand, and books of lasting value.

St. Albans Free Library (Vermont Library Association)

The standards of selection that govern purchases are applied also to gifts. Gifts will be accepted on the condition that the librarian may select those items needed for the collection and dispose of unwanted items as is deemed best. Collections of materials offered to the library with restrictions which require special handling or which prevent integration of the item into the general library collection will not normally be accepted.

The library will attempt to borrow materials outside of and beyond the scope of the collection, through interlibrary loan.

Baltimore County Public Library

The library takes cognizance of the purposes and resources of other libraries in the metropolitan Baltimore area and shall not needlessly duplicate functions and materials. Through cooperative agreements with the Division of Library Development and Services, State Department of Education, and neighboring municipal, county or academic libraries, the resources of these libraries may be available to Baltimore County readers.

Whitehall Public Library

PUBLIC LIBRARY–SCHOOL LIBRARY RELATIONSHIP

The Whitehall Public Library assumes that the school libraries will provide curriculum-related materials. It therefore provides textbooks of general interest only, as well as the most useful materials in specific fields. It does not feel itself obligated to provide duplications of materials required for mass school assignments.

Teachers wishing to assure the availability of materials for mass student assignments on single topics are urged to contact the Whitehall Library in advance of the influx of students into the library. If materials are limited, the library may place a borrowing period limitation on these materials per student.

The Whitehall Public Library urges the students to make full use of the school library materials prior to using the public library.

Students will be encouraged to help themselves as much as possible; however, they will be referred to the card catalog, periodical indexes, encyclopedias and other reference tools and shown how to use them if necessary. Staff service to a student on time-consuming research may be interrupted to serve an adult patron.

Mansfield Public Library

The Mansfield Public Library in accord with the Ohio Library Development Plan cooperates with other libraries in multi-county library programs such as Central Ohio Interlibrary Network (COIN) and the Large Print

Book Cooperative Project. The library serves as a resource center for COIN in the fields of social science, education, business, science and technology. As a member of COIN, the library will coordinate its collection building with other COIN libraries to provide access to a broader range of materials.

The Free Library of Philadelphia

RELATIONSHIP WITH OTHER LIBRARIES AND INSTITUTIONS

Philadelphia and its environs have a number of university, private and special libraries. Since the Free Library is obligated to extend services to all residents, it cannot build research collections to the same extent as its more specialized neighboring institutions. It does have, as a large city library and by reason of the generosity of donors, valuable and important special collections of subject and form materials such as music, maps, prints, educational films and rare books, and it accepts the responsibility for keeping such collections active and growing.

The holding of specialized materials by other libraries does not necessarily release the Free Library from its obligation to acquire materials in these areas. Certain books, although duplicated in other libraries in the area, are purchased when the demands of the Free Library's patrons are great and when the hours of opening, location or terms of service of the other libraries are too restrictive for use by the general public. Certain expensive publications are purchased jointly with other libraries under specific terms of location and use.

Relationship to school, college and university libraries is one of cooperation based on the following premise:

The Free Library assumes responsibility for providing library materials for the personal reading and reference needs and interests of young adults and children, whether as individuals or groups. It supplements the school, college or university library but does not attempt to provide either circulating or reference materials in quantities to meet class assignments based on the prescribed curricula of these institutions. It purchases student-type materials if they are also of use to the general reader; or for informal self-educational programs, study and discussion groups; or for institutes and seminars which are not given for credit and are not the direct responsibility of a school or college. It also provides adult basic education materials for instructional programs.

Seattle Public Library

COMMUNITY RESOURCES

The library cooperates as fully as possible with other libraries and with community agencies, groups and organizations. Expanding techniques of interlibrary loan on a city, state and federal level should be utilized to improve service to Seattle Public Library patrons. To avoid unnecessary duplication of materials in the community, one factor in selection will be a consideration of the kinds of materials available to the public through other institutions. These include special libraries and educational institutions.

Special libraries.   Other libraries in the community where materials are available for public or professional use will affect the selection of materials in specialized subject areas. While materials suitable for the lay person's needs in all fields will be evaluated for purchase by the library, established special collections are considered the primary sources for professional needs. Purchase of expensive or specialized materials contained in collections like those of the King County Law Library and the King County Medical Society Library is generally avoided.

Educational institutions.   Cooperation with the entire educational community is a basic aspect of public library service. Responsibility for the provision of multiple copies of curriculum-related materials belongs properly to the schools, and extensive duplication by the public library to meet mass assignment demands is not feasible. However, the public library will provide materials which supplement and enrich the reference, research and recreational needs of student borrowers of all ages. Standards that apply to all selection will be used to evaluate curriculum-related materials.

Agencies and groups other than schools and universities are becoming increasingly involved in the educational process. These groups may or may not be aware of the Seattle Public Library and its resources. The library should be alert to new groups and responsive to programs in which it could participate. Although the library cannot provide special materials or multiple copies for specific programs, it will consider purchase of new materials to augment its collections.

Library, Northeastern Illinois University

POINTS FOR CONSIDERATION ON GIFT POLICY

1. Screening is to be done by bibliographers at least until an order librarian can make other arrangements.
2. Before accepting a gift from faculty or outsiders, it must be ascertained whether monetary appraisal for income tax purposes is required, since this cannot be done after books are dispersed. The library will supply only acknowledgement of items. Internal Revenue may accept neither the library's evaluation nor the donor's, but may require a disinterested, professional appraisal. Mr. Richard Seidel, former head of acquisitions at Chicago Circle, suggests that for a small number of ordinary books the donor may give an average value of $5.00 per book and it will probably not be questioned.
3. If appraisal is required, several conditions obtain:
   - The library may not pay for the appraisal.
   - The donor must pay, but may deduct the cost of appraisal, along with the amount at which gift is valued.

- The only appraiser we have been able to obtain, Mr. Alexander J. Isaacs, charges a minimum of $25.00, with the fee rising according to the value of the gift. He charged $100.00 for a gift valued at $3,480.00, and $35.00 for one valued at $471.40. He will make his appraisal from a descriptive list of materials (including condition), unless he feels it necessary to examine.
- There are probably other elements of this operation which should be investigated before a firm policy is set down.

4. The original stipulations under which this library has operated, and which should be explained to prospective donors, include the following:

- The library has the option to keep or dispose of gifts according to recognized library procedures.
- If kept, material will not be separate in any way but will be merged with the regular holdings, identified only with a bookplate (no permanent record or retrieval).
- If not needed for this library, the material may be disposed of by exchange or discard procedures.

Duplication of very costly items already available in the Chicago area may not be necessary in some cases. Programs for close cooperation with all Chicago-area libraries are to be encouraged. This includes more effective utilization of each other's collections and will help to reduce expensive duplicate purchasing.

Roanoke-Chowan Technical Institute Library

GIFTS OR LOANS

The acceptance of gifts will be governed by the criteria listed below, with the Learning Resource Center reserving the right to accept, catalog, display, discard or dispose of any gift item at the discretion of the librarian who will consult with the faculty most directly involved in the subject area.

1. Gifts should not be received without consulting one of the librarians for approval of the gift's usefulness, suitability and literary quality.
2. All gifts should be accepted with the understanding that the Learning Resource Center may use them in accordance with the decision of the librarian in consultation with the faculty.
3. All donors should be advised that keeping gifts intact does not serve the purpose of either students or faculty, and in lieu of this, a bookplate with the donor's name on it will be placed in each book.
4. Gifts in excess of 300 items should be visited at the place they are housed by a Learning Resource Center representative, who would select those items that would be a useful addition to the Learning Resource Center.
5. The librarians retain the authority to dispose of materials without recourse to the donor.
6. The Learning Resource Center will accept loan materials for exhibit or use. Responsibility for loss or damage will be limited.

7. Requests for appraisal of gifts to the Learning Resource Center by the
   owner for tax purposes will be handled individually at the discretion of
   the librarian.

New Hampshire Vocational Technical College Library

GIFTS AND DONATIONS

Gifts and donations to the library may be accepted by the director and/or
the librarian, with the understanding that any such gifts will have no restrictions placed on their use or on their disposal when their usefulness has
ended.

A thank-you letter should be sent.

No tax evaluation may be made. The librarian is rarely considered
qualified and such evaluation would not stand up in court. The donor
should be responsible for appraisals.

Texas State Technical Institute Library

Materials which are in general demand by our patrons and which the
library can afford to purchase will be acquired regardless of their presence
in other libraries. The use of neighboring libraries and the interlibrary loan
service, however, will be suggested as an alternative to the purchase of the
following types of materials:

1. Titles not meeting the selection criteria;
2. Expensive materials for which general use is not anticipated for patrons
   other than the requestor, e.g., materials supporting individual research
   projects;
3. Out-of-print materials;
4. Materials needed immediately by the patron.

Kansas City Kansas Community Junior College Library

GIFTS

Gifts of either library materials or cash donations to purchase library
materials will be accepted provided they conform to library guidelines and
provided there are no restrictions attached.

No commitment to accept gifts shall be made by anyone other than a
college librarian. Where necessary, the librarians' decision will be subject to
presidential review.

With regard to gifts accepted:

1. The library will determine the classification, housing and circulation
   policy of all gift items.

2. The library retains the right to dispose of gifts at any time and in any manner deemed appropriate.
3. The library will not be responsible for the monetary valuation statement of the donor for tax or other purposes.

Clermont General and Technical College Library

The Clermont College Library looks upon gifts as an important adjunct to the acquisitions program. Many significant items have been acquired through gifts. The library accepts gift books and periodicals of all kinds with the proviso that they may be disposed of as the library sees fit. Duplicates (unless needed as added copies) and unsuitable items are forwarded to the main library, where they may be added to their collection or sold at a semiannual book sale. The library does not appraise the value of gifts for tax purposes as the Internal Revenue Service considers this practice a conflict of interest.

Gardner-Harvey Library, Miami University–Middletown (Ohio)

The Middletown Campus library relies on interlibrary cooperation for use of materials of limited value to the campus and rare, highly specialized or very expensive materials. Exchanges take place through:

1. Oxford:
   - Books are for immediate use, if available.
   - Excellent service is provided through the cooperation of the circulation, reference and documents departments via the shuttle.
2. RAILS, Reference and Interlibrary Loan Service at Ohio State University Library;
3. Union catalog at the State Library;
4. Union *List of Serials in the Libraries in the Miami Valley.*

Suomi College Library

The library shall make its resources available to all members of the community. This includes students from Michigan Technological University, high school and grade school young people and people living in the area. The loan period will be the same allowed Suomi students. Borrowers shall be reminded that if a Suomi faculty member or student requires immediate use of the books or materials they can be called in. Community members shall be asked to adhere to library rules required of Suomi students.

Interlibrary loans through the Michigan State Library program are available to staff, faculty and students regardless of class. Interlibrary loan through other academic libraries must adhere to American Library Association standards, which limit this service to graduate students or faculty engaged in research.

Use of facilities can be made at MTU, Northern Michigan University, Houghton and Hancock Public Libraries.

- MTU—Will grant loans and photocopies (at a cost) to faculty—students must use facilities on campus;
- NMU—Same as MTU;
- Portage Lake District Library (Houghton)—A service fee is required if the student is not a resident of Portage Township or the city of Houghton. Books and periodicals and records are available on loan. Residents are asked to use this library for interloans from the state library rather than requesting through Suomi's library if they are not Suomi students;
- Hancock Public library—Loans are available as for townspeople.

Learning Resources Center, Catonsville Community College

GIFTS

Gifts are accepted only when they add strength to the collection and when the donor places no significant limitations on housing, handling or disposition of duplicate, damaged or unwanted items.

Gifts frequently require more time to screen, organize, catalog and process than new materials. Storage space and staff time requirements are considered in accepting gift materials.

In acknowledgment of gifts, attention may be called to government recognition of such contributions for tax purposes but a monetary appraisal is generally the responsibility of the donor. The LRC follows the policies and procedures in the "Statement on Appraisal of Gifts" adopted by the Association of College and Research Libraries in 1973.

St. Catherine Library

St. Catherine Library's first commitment is to its enrolled students and faculty currently serving on campus. Secondly, as a member of a consortium, it is obligated to meet the demands of other member libraries and will continue to serve any future network involvement as trends in higher education indicate. Thirdly, since the College of St. Catherine is operated by a religious community, the Sisters of St. Joseph of Carondelet, the library has a responsibility to its members. Finally, borrowing privileges are extended to alumnae of the college for materials exclusive of consortium materials (materials can be obtained from Minitex through a public library) and to other off-campus patrons upon payment of a deposit fee per book.

Intellectual Freedom, Censorship and Confidentiality

Vigo County Public Library

THE PROBLEM

Any woman who has selected food items in a supermarket for the family dinner knows that more often than not one or more members of the family will not agree with her selections. The severity of the disagreement depends upon the degree of tolerance and understanding existing within the family unit.

This commonplace incident is analogous to the Vigo County Public Library, whose dedicated and capable librarians strive continuously to select materials that will meet the needs, wants and interests of a diverse, unpredictable "family" of 108,000 persons, the citizens of Vigo County.

The Library Board affirmed its position on this insolvable problem in June, 1968:

The Library Board does not interpret its function nor that of its administrators to be the supervisor of public morals. We believe in the freedom of the individual and the right and obligation of the head of a household to develop, interpret and enforce his own code of acceptable conduct upon his own household.

The Library Board urges all patrons to discuss problems concerning the library with the professional staff at the library or branch involved and, if not resolved there, with the library director. The director is responsible for the total library operation within the framework of the law and the policies of the Board.

THE SOLUTION

Just as the supermarket will stock broccoli if its consumers want broccoli but will not stock eggplant if its consumers do not want it, so the library must respond to the wants of its "consumers." The library's degree of responsiveness to its consumers determines its role in the community: an irrelevant and passive storehouse for a nondescript collection of little-used books, or a dynamic community center utilizing all forms of information.

The group deliberation of librarians of the Vigo County Public Library in fulfilling their professional responsibility for the selection of library materials gives stability, direction and balance to the library's holdings. However, the requests and suggestions from the citizens of Vigo County are an important element in this selection process. Moreover, it is essential that the will of the community be discerned by all possible means—even through open public forum, if necessary. This was shown in Vigo County when a number of community residents joined together to protest the judgment of its librarians.* For in the final analysis, the community acting through its legal representatives, the Vigo County Public Library Board, does decide.

St. Albans Free Library (Vermont Library Association)

An attempt is made to acquire authoritative books representing all points of view and all sides of controversial issues. The library does not promote particular beliefs or views, but instead presents quality materials containing opposing views for examination by the public. The presence of an item in the library does not indicate endorsement of its content by the library.

The library will resist efforts to force inclusion of proselytizing works representing political, economic, moral, religious or other vested positions when these materials do not conform to the selection policies.

The Public Library of Cincinnati and Hamilton County

CONTROVERSIAL MATERIALS

In applying the above guidelines for book selection, it must be remembered that the library cannot satisfy the needs and desires of one group, at the expense of another. The library does not act as an agent for or against a particular issue but maintains its position as a free channel of communication and upholds its right to select books. The disapproval of a book by one group should not be the means of denying that book to all groups, if by library selection standards it belongs in the collection.

Virginia Beach Public Library Department

ACCESS TO LIBRARY MATERIALS

As stated previously, the Virginia Beach Public Library subscribes to the book selection principles contained in the *Library Bill of Rights.* In regards to the access of library materials to patrons, the system makes special note of Article V which states:

The rights of an individual to the use of a library should not be denied or abridged because of his age, race, religion, national origins or political views.

*Howard, Edward N., "Intellectual Freedom" column, *ALA Bulletin,* October, 1968, p. 1073–75.

It is the philosophy of the library system that the parent of a child, rather than the librarian, should be the one to determine what the child should read. Staff members may suggest alternative selections but the ultimate decision should rest with the parent.

PATRON'S RIGHT OF PRIVACY

The foremost relationship the library must foster is that between the library and the patron. The patron is our reason for being and we must continually be responsive to her/his needs.

This relationship is similar to that of a lawyer and client or a doctor and patient. Thus the feeling of trust and privacy must be maintained between the library and the patron. In response to this belief, the following resolution was adopted by the Virginia Beach Public Library Board. It is to be strictly adhered to.

"WHEREAS the Board of Trustees of the Virginia Beach Public Library appreciates the difficulty experienced by many law enforcement agencies in the pursuit of justice; and, WHEREAS, the Board recognizes and approves the goal of bringing arsonists and light criminals to justice but not at the sacrifice of basic personal liberties enjoyed by all the population; and, WHEREAS the library director believes that the releasing of any information concerning a patron would amount to an invasion of privacy which would result in a direct betrayal of trust between the library and its reading public and that a subpoena from an appropriate court should be required from any individual or organization wishing to examine said records; and, WHEREAS, the said Board endorses this position,

"NOW THEREFORE BE IT RESOLVED AS FOLLOWS:

1. That once a book is placed in the library, the reading and examination of said book becomes a private matter with each individual and is not subject to review by this Board or any other body;
2. That this Board's duty to protect the basic rights of readers takes priority over all requests of the above nature;
3. That the intent of this resolution is to clarify the Board's position, to reassure library users that no information of this nature has been revealed to date, and that the above policy will apply to all cases in future."

The right of privacy also includes the information contained in city directories. City directories are available in each branch for use by the public, but no information from a city directory may be given over the phone by any library staff member.

Fresno County Public Library

Because the library must serve as a resource for the individual to examine issues freely and make her/his own decisions, the collection must contain the various positions expressed on important, complicated or controversial questions, including unpopular or unorthodox positions.

Camden County Free Library

EXCLUSION OF MATERIALS

The Camden County Free Library recognizes that many books are controversial and that any given item may offend some patrons. Selections will not be made on the basis of anticipated approval or disapproval, but solely on the merits of the work in relation to the building of the collection for the purpose of serving the interests of readers in the entire community.

Library materials will not be marked or identified to show approval or disapproval of their contents, and no cataloged book or other item will be sequestered, except for the express purpose of protecting it from injury or theft.

Responsibility for the reading of children rests with their parents and legal guardians. Selection of library materials will not be inhibited by the possibility that books may inadvertently come into the possession of children.

The use of rare and scholarly items of great value may be controlled to the extent required to preserve them from harm, but no further.

The American Library Association's *Library Bill of Rights* and the *Freedom to Read Statement* of the American Library Association and the American Book Publishers' Council are integral parts of the policies of the Camden County Free Library.

Orillia Public Library

CONFIDENTIAL INFORMATION

Staff members are expected to hold in strictest confidence information about questions patrons ask, items consulted or borrowed by patrons, comments expressed or attitudes revealed by patrons.

Wayne County Public Library

OBJECTIONS

Serious objections to titles owned by the library should be in writing. The library provides a form for such objections, to be filled out and signed by the patron.

The Board recognizes that censorship is a purely individual matter. While individuals are free to reject for themselves books of which they do not approve, they do not have the right to restrict the freedom to read of others. Whenever the question of censorship is involved, no book or other library material shall be removed from the library except under court order.

Rolling Prairie Libraries

CONTROVERSIAL MATERIALS, CRITICISM AND CENSORSHIP

General Statement

The system stands for the freedom of communication, for the freedom of intellectual activity and for the freedom of thought. It strives to provide an opportunity for people to gain information and the various points of view on controversial issues.

Criteria for Selection of Controversial Materials

The major areas of controversial materials are race, sex, politics, religion, literature and economics. In selecting material on any of the above areas the following criteria are given consideration:

1. The materials on controversial issues should be representative of a particular point of view, and a sincere effort must be made to select equally representative materials covering contrasting points of view.
2. The material must not unfairly, inaccurately or viciously disparage a particular race or religion. A writer's expression of a certain viewpoint is not to be considered a disparagement when it represents the historical or contemporary views held by some persons or groups.
3. The materials on religion are chosen to explain rather than convince and are selected to represent the field as widely as necessary for the educational purposes.
4. The selection of materials on political theories and ideologies or public issues is directed toward maintaining a balanced collection representing various views.
5. In a literary work of established quality, the use of profanity or the treatment of sex is not an adequate reason for eliminating the material from the collection.
6. Materials on physiology, physical maturation or personal hygiene should be accurate and in good taste.
7. Materials should be selected for their strengths rather than rejected for their weaknesses.

Methods of Judging Criticisms and Censorship

Citizens of the community may register their criticism of library materials with the system and member library Board of Directors. The criticism presented to the Board of Directors must be in writing.

1. The statement must include specific information as to the author, title, publisher and page number of each item to which objection is being made.
2. The statement must be signed and identification given to permit a reply to be made after the criticism has been investigated.
3. The Board of Directors will appoint a committee to re-evaluate the materials being questioned and make recommendations concerning them.

4. The committee shall include the executive director and one professional staff member of Rolling Prairie Libraries, and one member librarian.
5. The committee may call in representative citizens from the community for consultation when desired.
6. The findings and recommendations of the committee will be submitted to the Board of Directors.

Clermont General and Technical College Library

The principles of intellectual freedom as outlined in the *Library Bill of Rights* of the American Library Association shall be adhered to in the acquisition of library materials. It is the responsibility of the librarian and all faculty selecting materials to insure that all points of view are represented in the collection and that materials are not removed from the collection because of partisan or doctrinal disapproval. Access to library materials shall not be restricted because of age, race, religion, national origins or social or political views.

Yavapai College Learning Resources Center

The book collection will reflect the widest possible variety of viewpoints regardless of their popularity or the popularity of their authors. Possession should not be interpreted as endorsement but rather as the fulfillment of a responsibility to present all sides of a question by the best spokesmen. Materials in a public community college should be selected without partisanship or prejudice in matters concerning religion, politics, sex, and all social, moral, economic or scientific issues. The maturity of the readers for whom they are intended is assumed.

QUESTIONED OR CHALLENGED MATERIAL

The librarian will reply verbally or in writing to any criticism by referring to the above policy. Persistant criticisms or attempts at censorship will be referred to the division chairmen, who will act as a review committee.

Criticisms will be registered and presented on a form completed and signed by the party challenging any given title. The recommendation of the committee will then be submitted to the president of the college and the Board of Governors for approval. The decision of the board will be relayed to the committee and to the person who requested the review.

Learning Resources Center, Catonsville Community College

Materials selection, while giving priority to those materials which meet direct curricular needs, includes representative works which might arouse intellectual curiosity, counteract parochialism, challenge current attitudes, help to develop critical thinking and cultural appreciation, or stimulate use of the resources for continuing education, personal development and recreation. One function of higher education is to develop adult citizens intellectually capable of taking their places in a changing society. Provision for materials beyond curricular needs is essential in order to fulfill this function.

Skyline College Library

Since investigation of circulation files by persons other than the library staff could be harmful to the process of free inquiry, such records are confidential in nature.

William S. Smith Library, South Georgia College

CONTROVERSIAL ISSUES

It is the college library's right and duty to keep on its shelves a representative selection of materials on all subjects of interest to its readers, including materials on all sides of controversial questions. Materials on any subject are properly admitted to the college library. The college library has no right to emphasize one subject at the expense of another, or one side of a subject without regard to the other side. It must carry the important materials on all sides and all subjects.

Labeling

The library will not indicate, through the use of labels or other devices, particular philosophies outlined in a book. To do so is to establish in the reader's mind a judgment before the reader has had the opportunity to examine the material personally.

Fiction

New fiction considered for purchase must satisfy the basic criteria of excellence and social significance. Best-sellers are considered on individual merits, as are the inferior works of a standard popular author.

Cattell Library, Malone College

Complaints concerning material from the collection must be submitted in written form with attention to the following points:

1. Name of person and group (if any);
2. Identification of material (title, author, publisher, date, etc.);

3. Statement on how much of book read;
4. Specific objections (pages);
5. Identification of author's intention to best of ability (textbook, research, etc.);
6. Suggestions for a better selection to achieve same goal;
7. Willingness to meet with committee for discussion of material.

Repeated and/or forceful written objections will be considered by the Learning Resources Committee. If further consideration is necessary, the following parties in stated order will be consulted:

1. Dean of Academic Affairs;
2. President of College;
3. Board of Trustees.

Roanoke-Chowan Technical Institute Library

CHALLENGED MATERIALS

Occasional objections to a selection will be made by the public, despite the care taken to select valuable materials for student, patron and teacher use and the qualifications of persons who select the materials. When this occurs, the principles of the freedom to read and of the professional responsibility of the staff must be defended rather than the materials.

If a complaint is made, the procedures are as follows:

1. The person receiving the complaint should be courteous to the patron but make no commitments regarding the challenged material.
2. The person filing the complaint should be asked to file the objections in writing so that a formal complaint may be submitted to the library committee.
3. The challenged material should be placed on reserve so that members of the library committee may read, reread or study it.
4. The librarian should inform the president and the dean of education of the procedures followed.
5. The library committee will:
   - Read and examine materials referred to it;
   - Check general acceptance of the materials by reading reviews;
   - Weigh values and faults against each other and form opinions based on the material as a whole, not merely on passages pulled out of context;
   - Meet to discuss the material and to prepare a report on it;
   - Send a copy of the report to the president and file a copy of the report in the library and in the administrative offices.
6. The president of the institute will announce the decision of the group regarding the challenged material. The patron will receive this announcement by means of an official letter.

Tri-County Technical College Library

CHALLENGED MATERIALS

Occasionally, objections to a selection will be made by the public, despite the care taken to select valuable materials for student and teacher use. The principles of the *Freedom to Read Statement* and the professional responsibility of the staff must be defended rather than the materials. This procedure is outlined below.

Policy concerning challenged materials should include the philosophy of the Learning Resources Center—which represents a wide range of political, moral, social and esthetic views, some of which may be strange, unorthodox or unpopular. While we do not endorse every idea contained in the materials which we make available, we do believe that such material should be made available to everyone who needs or desires them. Since tastes vary, we do not believe that one standard of taste or one opinion should be imposed on others; therefore, we will oppose and resist every encroachment on intellectual freedom by individuals or groups.

The procedure for challenged materials is as follows:

1. The person receiving the complaints should be polite to the patron, making no comment regarding the challenge of materials; the patron should be asked to file the complaint in writing to the chairman of the Learning Resources Committee, sending a copy to the director of the Learning Resources Center.

2. The director of Learning Resources will confer with the chairman of the Learning Resources Committee. They will:

   • Notify the committee members;
   • Place the challenged material on reserve so that members of the committee may read, reread or study it;
   • Check reviews on the challenged materials and get the general feelings of the reviewers;
   • Arrange a meeting with the patron and the LRC Committee. The chairman of the Learning Resources Committee will be in charge of the meeting. The director of the Learning Resources Center will not be in attendance.

   The values and faults of the challenged materials must be weighed very carefully; the group should then make a recommendation based on the material as a whole to the director of the Learning Resources Center.

3. Any party concerned that is not in agreement with the recommendation of the group should state this in writing to the president of the institution.

   The president of the institution should arrange a meeting with the complaining party, the LRC Committee and the director of Learning Resources. The president should be the presiding officer at this meeting.

4. If the decision of this meeting with the president is not satisfactory with all concerned, the unsatisfied party should inform the president in writing.

- The president shall arrange a meeting of the complainants, the LRC Committee and the Area Commission for the college.
- The chairman of the Area Commission shall be the presiding officer at this meeting.

5. All meetings called for the purpose of evaluating challenged materials shall be open to any interested party or group. During the process of evaluating challenged materials, the director of Learning Resources Center shall be responsible for placing the challenged material on close reserve so that anyone interested may read, reread or study.

Library, College of the Desert

CHALLENGE OF LIBRARY MATERIALS

If the selection of materials in the College of the Desert Library is questioned or challenged, the following procedure will be followed:

1. The citizen or organization initiating the objection will complete the form, "Citizen's Request for Reconsideration of a Book." This completed form will be presented to the Dean of Instruction of the college.
2. The librarian and the administrative staff of the college will serve as the committee to review the materials under consideration as soon as possible. This committee will meet with those persons or groups questioning college library materials in an attempt to resolve the problem or issue, keeping in mind the best interests of the students, the community, the school and the curriculum.
3. This committee will report its findings to the college president and the Board of Trustees.
4. The ultimate decision is the responsibility of the Board of Trustees.

Weeding

Virginia Beach Public Library Department

Due to the newness of the Virginia Beach Department of Public Libraries, large scale weeding of branch collections has been unnecessary. However, in an effort to keep collections up-to-date, from time to time older nonfiction materials which no longer contain current information or duplicate copies of once popular fiction are often removed from the collection. As a general rule any material taking up space which could be more profitably used for other materials is subject to re-evaluation and discard when warranted.

Techniques for weeding include:

1. Checking last date of circulation;
2. Checking the overall condition of the book;
3. Checking standard catalogs (i.e., *Fiction Catalog, Books for Public Libraries*, etc.).

Wayne County Public Library

Judicious and systematic discarding is recognized as important to keep resources alive and up-to-date. It is the policy of the library to re-evaluate its collection continuously in conjunction with the selection of new and replacement material. Titles withdrawn by reason of condition, loss or damage will be replaced if they meet selection criteria and are available.

Camden County Free Library

WEEDING PROCEDURES FOR ADULT CIRCULATING COLLECTION

Procedure. On a continuous basis obsolete and unused materials are eliminated from the collection. Weeding is done by the adult service librarians in headquarters. The extension department is notified; books of use to them are transferred to the extension collection.

Criteria.   Demand, use and last copy are all considered when weeding. Books can be eliminated if they have not circulated in three years. More than two copies of a book may be discarded if the circulation figure is low.

Last copies   of a book will be re-examined before discarding.

Discarding.   After extension has made its selection, the remaining books are sent to processing. They pull all records of the book and send the discards to the loan department for final discard from the building.

WEEDING PROCEDURES FOR THE REFERENCE COLLECTION

Weeding of the reference collection is done on a continuing basis by the professional members of the reference staff. Each member is responsible for a certain area of the collection. As new editions are received, old books are either stored or discarded unless they are useful for circulation. These are reviewed by the head of the circulation department (supervising librarian) before being put into the collection.

WEEDING PROCEDURES FOR THE EXTENSION COLLECTION

Since the extension collection is still in the building stage, weeding procedures have not been considered.

WEEDING PROCEDURES FOR THE CHILDREN'S COLLECTION

Nonfiction

There are several collections of recommended books in subject areas such as biography, American history, world history, etc. Three general books are: *Children's Catalog* (very conservative), Gaver's *Elementary School Library Collection* and Sutherland's *Best in Children's Books,* 1966–1972 (collection of reviews from *Bulletin of Center of Children's Books*). Check adult and children's reference for these books and use them as a guide for discarding and reordering decisions.

Science books and books on countries must be examined to determine if the material is out of date. If material is no longer meaningful the book should be discarded. The librarian can then purchase a revised edition or new book to replace the dated material.

Exceptions: "Land and People Series" and "Enchantment Series." These books, though often mediocre or poorly written, are updated because of the demand for this type of information. It is limited to two copies for the headquarters collection because of space problems.

Fiction

Check *Children's Catalog,* Gaver and Sutherland. If the book being considered for discarding is listed there, reconsider. However, if the book seldom circulates it may be discarded even if listed on one of the above lists.

Seattle Public Library

MAIN LIBRARY DISCARDING

Adult Books

Book discarding is a necessary adjunct of book selection. In fact, book selection and book discarding are the two sides of the coin representing a vital, useful, well-kept collection.

It takes time, skill, care and a thorough knowledge of the books and their possible future reference value to do a competent job of discarding.

In the Seattle Public Library a careful study is made of each book before it is discarded, taking into account many different factors: obsolescence, physical condition of the book, number of copies in the library, research value, adequate coverage in the field and the availability of similar material.

In general last copies and out-of-print books are retained. The decision to discard these books is the responsibility of the head of the department concerned. No definite period of time (such as five years, ten years, etc.) can be set for the withdrawal of a book; and no general rule can be applied to discarding a book which has been published in a newer edition. Only when the more recent edition contains all of the material of the previous book can it be discarded without question.

In some fields discarding is done sparingly, if at all. Examples of such fields are aeronautics, the dance, directories, encyclopedias, music, northwest education and northwest history.

Young Adult Books

The young adult collection is a live, circulating collection. Its purpose is to attract and stimulate readers. No books are in stacks and none are kept for historical or literary purposes. Books are discarded:

1. If they have not circulated for three years, after the librarians have re-evaluated them;
2. When they become unattractive in appearance or badly worn;
3. When the contents become outdated or inaccurate.

BRANCH DISCARDING

The book collection of a branch library emphasizes current and popular reading rather than scholarly works and extensive reference holdings. The whole book stock is usually upon open shelves for all patrons to see. This makes their physical appearance of paramount importance.

It is also true that each branch library has a maximum book collection beyond which it should not extend.

With these two factors in mind, it then follows that branch libraries discard more freely and transfer to the main library valuable items no longer in active use. Also, if one book is withdrawn for every one added, after the maximum count is reached, this action will result in a live working collection.

All branch library discarding is coordinated in the branch department, where last copies are held back for examination by a subject department head for the final decision to keep or discard.

DISPOSITION OF DISCARDED MATERIAL

The city librarian is authorized by the library board to dispose of discarded library material.

Library, College of the Desert

DISCARDING PROCEDURES

With the advice of the academic department concerned, the library staff pursues a systematic and continuous weeding process, resulting in the discarding of materials containing information which has become obsolete or misleading, superseded editions, surplus copies of standard works no longer in demand for supplementary use, worn out or extensively marked books, books which have an unattractive physical format and broken files of unindexed journals.

Careful evaluation is made of titles which were not used at least once during the previous five years. Such a book is retained if it is listed in at least one standard bibliography which covers the field represented by the book. Other unused titles may be retained if faculty members or other subject specialists indicate interest in their retention.

Roanoke-Chowan Technical Institute Library

The librarians have the responsibility for weeding the collection. The following criteria should be considered when discarding a book:

1. *Obsolescence.* Is there a later edition of this item? Even if there is not, the material may be worthless or even harmful.
2. *Physical condition.* Is the material in such poor shape that the use does not warrant the cost of rebinding or whatever is deemed necessary?
3. *Insufficient use or basic value.* This may be more of a subjective judgment, but the authority of the author and publishers should be considered. Also, the usefulness with regard to the needs of the curriculum and students and faculty should be considered.

Materials which are not needed by the Learning Resource Center will be discarded, subject to the approval of the librarians, and may be given away, sold or destroyed.

INVENTORY

Since inventory work is done most efficiently when practically all the books are in their places on the shelves and when demand for library service is at a minimum, inventory will be taken annually during the last week in the month of August.

The taking of inventory involves using the shelf list to check the book collection and records which account for the whereabouts of books not located on the shelves. Its chief purpose is to discover what books are missing from the library and unaccounted for so that those which are not found may be either replaced or withdrawn from the catalog records. The detection of discrepancies in library records and the discovery of books in need of repair are incidental but useful byproducts of the process.

The following procedure should be followed:

1. Arrange the books in correct order on the shelves.
2. Compare the shelf list cards in their order with the corresponding books on the shelves. Make a note of any books not found there.
3. Check the record of books not located with the circulation records and other records which might account for the missing books.
4. Make a periodic search for missing books.
5. Withdraw catalog records of books not found.

Muscatine Community College Library

The removal of materials of limited usefulness is essential to maintaining the quality of the collection. The process of weeding requires the same participation by the faculty as does the selection of materials. The library will direct to the faculty those materials which should be considered for withdrawal. As in the selection process, the recommendations of faculty are essential and will be given full consideration. The final decision will rest with the library director.

Several factors may be involved in the decision to withdraw a book. Some of these are:

1. Value to the collection;
2. Physical condition;
3. Number of copies in the collection;
4. Coverage of the subject by other materials;
5. Age or obsolescence;
6. Use.

Discarded materials will be disposed of by being offered to:

1. The departments and faculty of the college;
2. The other campus libraries of the college district;
3. Other libraries in the Muscatine area.

William S. Smith Library, South Georgia College

Weeding is part of the public service to the library users, because it helps maintain the best possible library collection. The librarians are responsible for deciding which materials should be discarded. Faculty members should be consulted on major weeding projects.

Three categories of materials should be discarded:

1. Those of poor content which are outdated or badly written;
2. Those which no longer serve the purposes of the library—duplicates, "shelf sitters";
3. Those in poor physical condition—dirty, worn, and badly bound or badly printed volumes.

Only standard works should be replaced with the same or with a newer edition. Only books requiring minor mends (5–15 minutes) should be repaired. Otherwise, they should be withdrawn and a decision on whether to replace or not must be made.

The weeding process is a continuous one. However, a major weeding of the entire collection will be done every five (5) years.

GUIDELINES FOR WEEDING NONFICTION

Encyclopedias.   Add new edition every 5 years. Maintain one set from each decade, for historical use.

Philosophy.   Retain philosophical systems. Retain historical and explanatory works. Update psychology collection annually and discard outdated texts.

Religion.   Retain information on different religions. Discard old encyclopedias when a new edition is added. Weed sermons, prayers and meditations ruthlessly.

Social sciences.   Discard old texts in sociology, marriage and family, economics and political science every two years. Retain standard works on costumes, folklore and customs. Retain all works dealing with Georgia history.

History.   Accuracy and viewpoint should be the main criteria for judging.

Law.   Discard all outdated law codes and texts yearly.

Languages.   Retain large dictionaries. Discard old grammars.

Sciences.   Currency is very important. Discard after five years, except for botany and natural history.

APPENDICES

APPENDICES

Library Bill of Rights

Adopted June 18, 1948
Amended February 2, 1961, and June 27, 1967,
by the ALA Council

The Council of the American Library Association reaffirms its belief in the following basic policies which should govern the services of all libraries.

1. As a responsibility of library service, books and other library materials selected should be chosen for values of interests, information and enlightenment of all the people of the community. In no case should library materials be excluded because of the race or nationality or the social, political, or religious views of the authors.
2. Libraries should provide books and other materials presenting all points of view concerning the problems and issues of our times: no library materials should be proscribed or removed from libraries because of partisan or doctrinal disapproval.
3. Censorship should be challenged by libraries in the maintenance of their responsibility to provide public information and enlightment.
4. Libraries should cooperate with all persons and groups concerned with resisting abridgment of free expression and free access to ideas.
5. The rights of an individual to the use of a library should not be denied or abridged because of his age, race, religion, national origins or social or political views.
6. As an institution of education for democratic living, the library should welcome the use of its meeting rooms for socially useful and cultural activities and discussion of current public questions. Such meeting places should be available on equal terms to all groups in the community regardless of the beliefs and affiliations of their members, provided that the meetings be open to the public.

Freedom to Read Statement

*Adopted June 25, 1953
by the ALA Council
Revised January 28, 1972*

The freedom to read is essential to our democracy. It is continuously under attack. Private groups and public authorities in various parts of the country are working to remove books from sale, to censor textbooks, to label "controversial" books, to distribute lists of "objectionable" books or authors, and to purge libraries. These actions apparently rise from a view that our national tradition of free expression is no longer valid; that censorship and suppression are needed to avoid the subversion of politics and the corruption of morals. We, as citizens devoted to the use of books and as librarians and publishers responsible for disseminating them, wish to assert the public interest in the preservation of the freedom to read.

We are deeply concerned about these attempts at suppression. Most such attempts rest on a denial of the fundamental premise of democracy: that the ordinary citizen, by exercising his critical judgment, will accept the good and reject the bad. The censors, public and private, assume that they should determine what is good and what is bad for their fellow-citizens.

We trust Americans to recognize propaganda, and to reject it. We do not believe they need the help of censors to assist them in this task. We do not believe they are prepared to sacrifice their heritage of a free press in order to be "protected" against what others think may be bad for them. We believe they still favor free enterprise in ideas and expression.

We are aware, of course, that books are not alone in being subjected to efforts of suppression. We are aware that these efforts are related to a larger pattern of pressures being brought against education, the press, films, radio and television. The problem is not only one of actual censorship. The shadow of fear cast by these pressures leads, we suspect, to an even larger voluntary curtailment of expression by those who seek to avoid controversy.

Such pressure toward conformity is perhaps natural to a time of uneasy change and pervading fear. Especially when so many of our apprehensions are directed against an ideology, the expression of a dissident idea becomes a thing feared in itself, and we tend to move against it as against a hostile deed, with suppression.

And yet suppression is never more dangerous than in such a time of social tension. Freedom has given the United States the elasticity to endure strain. Freedom keeps open the path of novel and creative solutions, and enables change to come by choice. Every silencing of a heresy, every enforcement of an orthodoxy, diminishes the toughness and resilience of our society and leaves it the less able to deal with stress.

Now as always in our history, books are among our greatest instruments of freedom. They are almost the only means for making generally available ideas or manners of expression that can initially command only a small audience. They are the natural medium for the new idea and the untried voice from which come the original contributions to social growth. They are essential to the extended discussion which serious thought requires, and to the accumulation of knowledge and ideas into organized collections.

We believe that free communication is essential to the preservation of a free society and a creative culture. We believe that these pressures towards conformity present the danger of limiting the range and variety of inquiry and expression on which our democracy and our culture depend. We believe that every American community must jealously guard the freedom to publish and to circulate, in order to preserve its own freedom to read. We believe that publishers and librarians have a profound responsibility to give validity to that freedom to read by making it possible for the readers to choose freely from a variety of offerings.

The freedom to read is guaranteed by the Constitution. Those with faith in free men will stand firm on these constitutional guarantees of essential rights and will exercise the responsibilities that accompany these rights.

We therefore affirm these propositions:

1. It is in the public interest for publishers and librarians to make available the widest diversity of views and expressions, including those which are unorthodox or unpopular with the majority.

Creative thought is by definition new, and what is new is different. The bearer of every new thought is a rebel until his idea is refined and tested. Totalitarian systems attempt to maintain themselves in power by the ruthless suppression of any concept which challenges the established orthodoxy. The power of a democratic system to adapt to change is vastly strengthened by the freedom of its citizens to choose widely from among conflicting opinions offered freely to them. To stifle every nonconformist idea at birth would mark the end of the democratic process. Furthermore, only through the constant activity of weighing and selecting can the democratic mind attain the strength demanded by times like these. We need to know not only what we believe but why we believe it.

2. Publishers, librarians and booksellers do not need to endorse every idea or presentation contained in the books they make available. It would conflict with the public interest for them to establish their own political, moral or aesthetic views as a standard for determining what books should be published or circulated.

Publishers and librarians serve the educational process by helping to make available knowledge and ideas required for the growth of the mind and the increase of learning. They do not foster education by imposing as mentors the patterns of their own thought. The people should have the freedom to read and consider a broader range of ideas than those that may be held by any single librarian or publisher or government or church. It is wrong that what one man can read should be confined to what another thinks proper.

3. It is contrary to the public interest for publishers or librarians to determine the acceptability of a book on the basis of the personal history or political affiliations of the author.

A book should be judged as a book. No art or literature can flourish if it is to be measured by the political views or private lives of its creators. No society of free men can flourish which draws up lists of writers to whom it will not listen, whatever they may have to say.

4. There is no place in our society for efforts to coerce the tastes of others, to confine adults to the reading matter deemed suitable for adolescents, or to inhibit the efforts of writers to achieve artistic expression.

To some, much of modern literature is shocking. But is not much of life itself shocking? We cut off literature at the source if we prevent serious artists from dealing with the stuff of life. Parents and teachers have a responsibility to prepare the young to meet the diversity of experiences in life to which they will be exposed, as they have a responsibility to help them learn to think critically for themselves. These are affirmative responsibilities, not to be discharged simply by preventing them from reading works for which they are not yet prepared. In these matters taste differs, and taste cannot be legislated; nor can machinery be devised which will suit the demands of one group without limiting the freedom of others.

5. It is not in the public interest to force a reader to accept with any book the prejudgment of a label characterizing the book or author as subversive or dangerous.

The ideal of labeling presupposes the existence of individuals or groups with wisdom to determine by authority what is good or bad for the citizen. It presupposes that each individual must be directed in making up his mind about the ideas he examines. But Americans do not need others to do their thinking for them.

6. It is the responsibility of publishers and librarians, as guardians of the people's freedom to read, to contest encroachments upon that freedom by individuals or groups seeking to impose their own standards or tastes upon the community at large.

It is inevitable in the give and take of the democratic process that the political, the moral, or the aesthetic concepts of an individual or group will occasionally collide with those of another individual or group. In a free society each individual is free to determine for himself what he wishes to read, and each group is free to determine what it will recommend to its freely associated members. But no group has the right to take the law into its own hands, and to impose its own concept of politics or morality upon other members of a democratic society. Freedom is no freedom if it is accorded only to the accepted and the inoffensive.

7. It is the responsibility of publishers and librarians to give full meaning to the freedom to read by providing books that enrich the quality and diversity of thought and expression. By the exercise of this affirmative responsibility, bookmen can demonstrate that the answer to a bad book is a good one, the answer to a bad idea is a good one.

The freedom to read is of little consequence when expended on the trivial; it is frustrated when the reader cannot obtain matter fit for his purpose. What is needed is not only the absence of restraint, but the positive provision of opportunity for the people to read the best that has been thought and said. Books are the major channel by which the intellectual inheritance is handed down, and the principal means of its testing and growth. The defense of their freedom and integrity, and the enlargement of their service to society, requires of all bookmen the utmost of their faculties, and deserves of all citizens the fullest of their support.

We state these propositions neither lightly nor as easy generalizations. We here stake out a lofty claim for the value of books. We do so because we believe that they are good, possessed of enormous variety and usefulness, worthy of cherishing and keeping free. We realize that the application of these propositions may mean the dissemination of ideas and manners of expression that are repugnant to many people. We do not state these propositions in the comfortable belief that what people read is unimportant. We believe rather that what people read is deeply important; that ideas can be dangerous; but that the suppression of ideas is fatal to a democratic society. Freedom itself is a dangerous way of life, but it is ours.

Endorsed by:

AMERICAN LIBRARY ASSOCIATION
  Council, June 25, 1953

AMERICAN BOOK PUBLISHERS COUNCIL
  Board of Directors, June 18, 1953

Subsequently endorsed by:

AMERICAN BOOKSELLERS ASSOCIATION
  Board of Directors

BOOK MANUFACTURERS' INSTITUTE
  Board of Directors

NATIONAL EDUCATION ASSOCIATION
  Commission for the Defense of Democracy through Education

Intellectual Freedom Statement

An Interpretation of the Library Bill of Rights

Adopted by the ALA Council, June 25, 1971
Endorsed by the Freedom to Read Foundation,
Board of Trustees, June 18, 1971

The heritage of free men is ours. In the Bill of Rights to the United States Constitution, the founders of our nation proclaimed certain fundamental freedoms to be essential to our form of government. Primary among these is the freedom of expression, specifically the right to publish diverse opinions and the right to unrestricted access to those opinions. As citizens committed to full and free use of all communications media and as professional persons responsible for making the content of those media accessible to all without prejudice, we, the undersigned, wish to assert the public interest in the preservation of freedom of expression.

Through continuing judicial interpretations of the First Amendment to the United States Constitution, full freedom of expression has been guaranteed. Every American who aspires to the success of our experiment in democracy—who has faith in the political and social integrity of free men— must stand firm on those Constitutional guarantees of essential rights. Such Americans can be expected to fulfill the responsibilities implicit in those rights.

We, therefore, affirm these propositions:

1. We will make available to everyone who needs or desires them the widest possible diversity of views and modes of expression, including those which are strange, unorthodox, or unpopular.

Creative thought is, by its nature, new. New ideas are always different and, to some people, distressing and even threatening. The creator of every new idea is likely to be regarded as unconventional—occasionally heretical— until his idea is first examined, then refined, then tested in its political, social, or moral applications. The characteristic ability of our governmental system to adapt to necessary change is vastly strengthened by the option of the people to choose freely from among conflicting opinions. To stifle non-conformist ideas at their inception would be to end the democratic process. Only through continuous weighing and selection from among opposing views can free individuals obtain the strength needed for intelligent, constructive decisions and actions. In short, we need to understand not only what we believe, but why we believe as we do.

2. We need not endorse every idea contained in the materials we produce
    and make available.

We serve the educational process by disseminating the knowledge and
wisdom required for the growth of the mind and the expansion of learning.
For us to employ our own political, moral, or esthetic views as standards for
determining what materials are published or circulated conflicts with the
public interest. We cannot foster true education by imposing on others the
structure and content of our own opinions. We must preserve and enhance
the people's right to a broader range of ideas than those held by any librarian
or publisher or church or government. We hold that it is wrong to limit any
person to those ideas and that information another believes to be true, good,
and proper.

3. We regard as irrelevant to the acceptance and distribution of any crea-
    tive work the personal history or political affiliations of the author or
    others responsible for it or its publication.

A work of art must be judged solely on its own merits. Creativity cannot
flourish if its appraisal and acceptance by the community is influenced by the
political views or private lives of the artists or the creators. A society that
allows blacklists to be compiled and used to silence writers and artists cannot
exist as a free society.

4. With every available legal means, we will challenge laws or governmental
    action restricting or prohibiting the publication of certain materials or
    limiting free access to such materials.

Our society has no place for legislative efforts to coerce the taste of its
members, to restrict adults to reading matter deemed suitable only for
children, or to inhibit the efforts of creative persons in their attempts to
achieve artistic perfection. When we prevent serious artists from dealing
with truth as they see it, we stifle creative endeavor at its source. Those who
direct and control the intellectual development of our children—parents,
teachers, religious leaders, scientists, philosophers, statesmen—must assume the responsibility for preparing young people to cope with life as it is
and to face the diversity of experience to which they will be exposed as they
mature. This is an affirmative responsibility that cannot be discharged easily,
certainly not with the added burden of curtailing one's access to art, literature, and opinion. Tastes differ. Taste, like morality, cannot be controlled by
government, for governmental action, devised to suit the demands of one
group, thereby limits the freedom of all others.

5. We oppose labeling any work of literature or art, or any persons respon-
    sible for its creation, as subversive, dangerous, or otherwise undesirable.

Labeling attempts to predispose users of the various media of communication, and to ultimately close off a path to knowledge. Labeling rests on
the assumption that persons exist who have a special wisdom, and who,
therefore, can be permitted to determine what will have good and bad
effects on other people. But freedom of expression rests on the premise of
ideas vying in the open marketplace for acceptance, change, or rejection by
individuals. Free men choose this path.

6. We, as guardians of intellectual freedom, oppose and will resist, every encroachment upon that freedom by individuals or groups, private or official.

It is inevitable in the give-and-take of the democratic process that the political, moral and esthetic preferences of a person or group will conflict occasionally with those of others. A fundamental premise of our free society is that each citizen is privileged to decide those opinions to which he will adhere or which he will recommend to the members of a privately organized group or association. But no private group may usurp the law and impose its own political or moral concepts upon the general public. Freedom cannot be accorded only to selected groups for it is then transmuted into privilege and unwarranted license.

7. Both as citizens and professionals, we will strive by all legitimate means open to us to be relieved of the threat of personal, economic, and legal reprisals resulting from our support and defense of the principles of intellectual freedom.

Those who refuse to compromise their ideals in support of intellectual freedom have often suffered dismissals from employment, forced resignations, boycotts of products and establishments, and other invidious forms of punishment. We perceive the admirable, often lonely, refusal to succumb to threats of punitive action as the highest form of true professionalism: dedication to the cause of intellectual freedom and the preservation of vital human and civil liberties.

In our various capacities, we will actively resist incursions against the full exercise of our professional responsibility for creating and maintaining an intellectual environment which fosters unrestrained creative endeavor and true freedom of choice and access for all members of the community.

We state these propositions with conviction, not as easy generalizations. We advance a noble claim for the value of ideas, freely expressed, as embodied in books and other kinds of communications. We do this in our belief that a free intellectual climate fosters creative endeavors capable of enormous variety, beauty, and usefulness, and thus worthy of support and preservation. We recognize that application of these propositions may encourage the dissemination of ideas and forms of expression that will be frightening or abhorrent to some. We believe that what people read, view, and hear is a critically important issue. We recognize, too, that ideas can be dangerous. It may be, however, that they are effectually dangerous only when opposing ideas are suppressed. Freedom, in its many facets, is a precarious course. We espouse it heartily.

As we looked more deeply into the problem of labeling, we found that it is not an uncommon proposal. In addition to the Sons of the American Revolution, we discovered that other groups have tried to use it as a technique of limiting freedom to read. Religious groups sometimes ask libraries to label, if not to ban, publications they find objectionable. There are also indications that so-called "patriotic" organizations other than the SAR are moving dangerously close to similar proposals.

In April, President Graham received a letter direct from the Montclair Chapter of the Sons of the American Revolution requesting this Association to adopt the SAR policy. This letter urged, as did the original resolution, that so-called communistic and subversive materials not only should be labeled but also should be segregated in libraries and given out only upon written and signed application.

By this time, members of the Committee on Intellectual Freedom had had an opportunity to study more fully the background of the problem and to submit their recommendations. When the issue was put to them formally, nine out of 11 members voted, and all nine were united against the idea of labeling as proposed by the Sons of the American Revolution. It was recognized by some of us that the committee's unanimity might stem from the fact that we were unusually sensitive to the subject of intellectual freedom. There was also some concern over the fact that, for the most part, we represented large public or institutional libraries; whereas the practical problems of labeling seem likely to develop in smaller libraries. It was therefore considered advisable to seek a slightly broader basis for judgment, and we proceeded at once to obtain the counsel of 24 other practicing librarians in libraries located geographically from Texas to Minnesota and from North Carolina to the state of Washington, the selection emphasizing but not being restricted to small and medium-size public libraries as well as college, university and state libraries.

Twenty out of the 24 to whom we wrote replied to our inquiry and without exception opposed labeling. Despite the smallness of our sample the unanimity among the replies seems impressive.

Although our request suggested possible pros and cons, plenty of leeway was left for individual points of view and the manner in which our colleagues took advantage of their right of free expression indicates that intellectual freedom is not yet dead. Without naming names, I would like to quote some of their remarks because they put the case more eloquently than I possibly could:

I

"Libraries must oppose the practice of labeling if they wish to maintain their positions as *impartial* agencies providing information on all aspects of any question."

II

"I am opposed to the idea of labeling books as pro or anti anything, because there can be no reasonable end to such an attempt once it is begun."

III

"Personally, I . . . think labeling is as dangerous as the evils it may attempt to correct—and I am aware that some real evils do exist. . . . Recognizing this time as a period of danger, and also realizing that the Soviet Communists do not play under the same set of rules as does a democracy, I still vote strongly against any labeling program such as the SAR requests."

IV

"I am opposed to such a procedure. . . . Those who read should be able to discriminate—to think for themselves."

V

"You may put me down as opposed to labeling any literature in American Public Libraries, regardless of the 'slant' or the subject. . . . Once labeling is started on behalf of one group or organization, libraries would have to label other material for its slant, political, religious, economic or whatever. (Imagine the book *You Must Eat Meat* being labeled: 'This book is considered objectionable by the Vegetarians of America.')"

VI

"Labeling is not merely an 'attempt to prejudice the reader.' It is surely in the minds of some of its proponents an attempt to control or frighten him."

VII

"How soon after we start labeling books will we begin to burn them?"

VIII

"The suggested action if undertaken would seem to me (1) to invade the privacy of the individual and (2) to deny a democratic principle that people are able to weigh the evidence and to make sound conclusions. The outcome (of labeling) will be that public libraries will purchase only books which will not be challenged, with the inevitable result that the original and experimental will be driven out. . . . The idea of requiring readers to make written application for the use of materials labeled as Communist slanted seems in some ways more frightening than labeling."

IX

"If we wish to live in a free country, we must develop our minds to recognize propaganda and to *think*. A label is merely the thinking of one person or a group of persons."

X

"There is room in America for all people to read and form their own opinions. . . . In a democracy people must have the right to know facts about *everything*. (This) does not necessarily mean they advocate everything about which they know. Maybe quite the contrary. . . . I oppose all efforts to predispose readers for or against any materials. . . ."

XI

"To require labeling of material with any particular slant—such as communism—is to sacrifice the *principle* of free thought and opinion. American citizens of the future are going to be free to consider *all* points of view— or they are not going to have that freedom. Many of us—not only the

Index

Compiled by Carolynn Weiner

professional anticommunist—have blind spots. But librarians must not agree to putting blinders of any kind on their readers. The principle of free inquiry, which is fundamental to American librarianship and American democracy, must be maintained against labelers as against all other censors."

XII

"Every group in the country with an axe to grind must be happy in the thought that if one of them can make an opening wedge to wreck the 'Library Bill of Rights,' the rest of them can all come in, and the Free Public Library will be a thing of the past. . . . Everyone working here is against labeling. Where would the Sons of the American Revolution be today if their great grandpas had been as 'scairt' of different viewpoints as they are?

"I spent an afternoon asking borrowers what they thought of labeling books (particularly subversive books) so they would not fall into the hands of the easily persuaded. Their answers were obvious, but the *shock* registered in their faces at such an idea was something to see. Here are some of their comments:

"A well-educated old lady: 'Hitler began by burning the books. Isn't this another form of the same thing?'

"A college girl: 'It's an idea of old men. We young people are able to make decisions that are good. Give us credit and the chance to do it.'

"Another college student: 'They talk about the wonderful education we get in America. How are we going to make use of it, and really know that democracy is right, if we are only allowed to read what they want us to believe?'

"Housewife: 'Stalin tells only one side of the question. I thought Americans didn't believe in his methods.'

"Man: 'I'm an adult. Sound mind. Good education. Who the hell has the right to tell me what to read or warn me what not to read?'

"Teacher: 'What are you trying to do? Take away freedom of thought and freedom of conscience? The Constitution gives me the right to read and think as I please, regardless of what anyone else thinks. I pay taxes to support the library and expect to find a good selection of books on the shelves. I'll be my own censor.'

"Housewife: 'It violates all principles of freedom of thought. It is treason to the principles on which the country was built.'

"High school senior: 'How can we tell that our way is right if we can't make comparisons? Are they afraid of comparisons? Then Democracy is sure on the skids.' "

RECOMMENDATIONS UNANIMOUSLY ADOPTED BY THE ALA COUNCIL JULY 13, 1951

In view of our own convictions and those of other practicing librarians whose counsel we sought, the Committee on Intellectual Freedom recommends to the ALA Council the following policy with respect to labeling library materials.

Librarians should not use the technique of labeling as a means of predisposing readers against library materials for the following reasons:

1. Although totalitarian states find it easy and even proper, according to their ethics, to establish criteria for judging publications as "subversive," injustice and ignorance rather than justice and enlightenment result from such practices, and the American Library Association has a responsibility to take a stand against the establishment of such criteria in a democratic state.
2. Libraries do not advocate the ideas found in their collections. The presence of a magazine or book in a library does not indicate an endorsement of its contents by the library.
3. No one person should take the responsibility of labeling publications. No sizeable group of persons would be likely to agree either on the types of material which should be labeled or the sources of information which should be regarded with suspicion. As a practical consideration, a librarian who labeled a book or magazine pro-communist might be sued for libel.
4. Labeling is an attempt to prejudice the reader and, as such, it is a censor's tool.
5. Labeling violates the spirit of the *Library Bill of Rights.*
6. Although we are all agreed that communism is a threat to the free world, if materials are labeled to pacify one group, there is no excuse for refusing to label any item in the library's collection. Because communism, fascism, or other authoritarianisms tend to suppress ideas and attempt to coerce individuals to conform to a specific ideology, American librarians must be opposed to such "isms." We are, then, anti-communist, but we are also opposed to any other group which aims at closing any path to knowledge.

Statement on Re-evaluation of Library Materials for Children's Collections

Adopted by the Board of Directors,
Children's Services Division,
American Library Association
January 29, 1973

Librarians must espouse critical standards in selection and re-evaluation of library materials. It is incumbent on the librarian working with children to be aware that the child lacks the breadth of experience of the adult and that librarians have a two-fold obligation in service to the child:

1. To build and maintain collections of materials which provide information on the entire spectrum of human knowledge, experience and opinion;
2. To introduce to the child those titles which will enable him to develop with a free spirit, an inquiring mind, and an ever-widening knowledge of the world in which he lives.

Because most materials reflect the social climate of the era in which they are produced, it is often difficult to evaluate some aspects of a work at the time of purchase. But social climate and man's state of knowledge are constantly changing and librarians should therefore continuously re-evaluate their old materials in the light of growing knowledge and broadening perspectives. In the process of re-evaluation it may be found that an old title is still fresh and pertinent, or even that it was produced ahead of its time and now has a new relevance. It may, on the other hand, no longer serve a useful role in the collection. It may have been superseded by better books.

In making his decision, the librarian has a professional obligation to set aside personal likes and dislikes, to avoid labeling materials, to consider the strengths and weaknesses of each title, and to consider the material as a whole with objectivity and respect for all opinions. Only after such consideration can he reach a decision as to whether the title is superseded in coverage and quality, and should be discarded, or should be kept in the collection.

The Board of Directors of the Children's Services Division, American Library Association, supports the *Library Bill of Rights* and *Free Access to Libraries for Minors.* Re-evaluation is a positive approach to sound collection building and should not be equated with censorship.

Statement on Appraisal of Gifts

Developed by the Committee on Manuscripts Collections of the Rare Books and Manuscripts Section. Approved by the ACRL Board of Directors on February 1, 1973, in Washington, D.C. This statement replaces the 1960 policy on appraisal (Antiquarian Bookman, v.26, December 19, 1960, p. 2205).

1. The appraisal of a gift to a library for tax purposes generally is the responsibility of the donor since it is the donor who benefits from the tax deduction. Generally, the cost of the appraisal should be borne by the donor.

2. The library should at all times protect the interests of its donors as best it can and should suggest the desirability of appraisals whenever such a suggestion would be in order.

3. To protect both its donors and itself, the library, as an interested party, ordinarily should not appraise gifts made to it. It is recognized, however, that on occasion the library may wish to appraise small gifts, since many of them are not worth the time and expense an outside appraisal requires. Generally, however, the library will limit its assistance to the donor to: (a) providing him with information such as auction records and dealers' catalogs; (b) suggestions of appropriate professional appraisers who might be consulted; (c) administrative and processing services which would assist the appraiser in making an accurate evaluation.

4. The acceptance of a gift which has been appraised by a third, and disinterested party, does not in any way imply an endorsement of the appraisal by the library.

5. An archivist, curator, or librarian, if he is conscious that as an expert he may have to prove his competence in court, may properly act as an independent appraiser of library materials. He should not in any way suggest that his appraisal is endorsed by his library (such as by the use of the library's letterhead), nor should he ordinarily act in this fashion (except when handling small gifts) if his institution is to receive the donation.

Nonremoval of Challenged Library Materials

An Interpretation of the Library Bill of Rights

Adopted by the ALA Council on June 25, 1971

WHEREAS, The Library Bill of Rights states that no library materials should be proscribed or removed because of partisan or doctrinal disapproval, and

WHEREAS, Constitutionally protected expression is often separated from unprotected expression only by a dim and uncertain line, and

WHEREAS, Any attempt, be it legal or extra-legal, to regulate or suppress material must be closely scrutinized to the end that protected expression is not abridged in the process, and

WHEREAS, The Constitution requires a procedure designed to focus searchingly on the question before speech can be suppressed, and

WHEREAS, The dissemination of a particular work which is alleged to be unprotected should be completely undisturbed until an independent determination has been made by a judicial officer, including an adversary hearing,

THEREFORE, THE PREMISES CONSIDERED, BE IT RESOLVED, That the American Library Association declares as a matter of firm principle that no challenged library material should be removed from any library under any legal or extra-legal pressure, save after an independent determination by a judicial officer in a court of competent jurisdiction and only after an adversary hearing, in accordance with well-established principles of law.

Labeling

A Report of the ALA Committee on Intellectual Freedom

Presented to the ALA Council on July 13, 1951,
by Rutherford D. Rogers, Chairman,
ALA Committee on Intellectual Freedom

At the Midwinter Meeting, the report of the Committee on Intellectual Freedom dealt briefly with five or six cases. This morning, I ask your consideration of only one problem, but it is one which has manifold implications of a rather serious nature. This is the problem of labeling.

What is labeling and how has it become a matter of urgency? Approximately eight months ago, we received a report that the Montclair (N.J.) Chapter of the Sons of the American Revolution was exerting pressure on libraries in New Jersey to put a prominent label or inscription on "publications which advocate or favor Communism, or which are issued or distributed by any Communist organization or any other organization formally designated by any authorized government official or agency as Communistic or subversive . . ."; furthermore, such publications ". . . should not be freely available in libraries to readers or in schools to pupils, but should be obtainable only by signing suitable applications."

The committee noted that the SAR resolution did not make clear who would do the labeling, who would decide what is communistic or "subversive" or by what criteria such decisions would be made. It would appear that labeling, if done in the local library, would require a member or members of the staff to examine carefully into the contents of, and attitudes in, every item acquired by the library in order to ascertain whether or not there was any communist or subversive slant, espousal or authorship therein. It is fair to assume that a variety of labels or statements would have to be fashioned to apply to the great diversity of shades of opinion or guilt in the light of whatever criteria might be established. It is conceivable that such a project could be handled centrally by the ALA or the government, but the implications of this sort of politburo arrangement are repulsive to people reared in the democratic tradition.

The committee felt that the practicability and financial problems of such a project were not necessarily relevant to its decision, which should be made on the basis of the principle involved.